Praise for *The Tan*

REVIEWS OF CZECH, GERMAN, AND HEBREW EDITIONS

"You will be amused, and often laugh out loud, because Tenenbom is funny." — *Neues Deutschland* (Germany)

"Without prejudice, and employing subtle humor, Tenenbom listens to his interviewees as they are desperately justifying themselves." — *Mitteldeutsche Zeitung* (Germany)

"Knowing how to deal with the everyday comic moments of life, while integrating the bizarre parts of the same life, is a craft and Tenenbom has it." — *taz, die tageszeitung* (Germany)

"Tenenbom's writing is laced with great entertainment, while at the same time providing much knowledge." — *Hamburger Abendblatt* (Germany)

"Tenenbom is the Egon Erwin Kirsch of our time." — **Henryk M. Broder** (Germany)

"Razor sharp, sarcastic, occasionally even shocking, and very entertaining." — *MF DNES* (Czech Republic)

"What differentiates this book from other books: This book is *very* funny." — **Channel 11 TV** (Israel)

"An excellent book!" — **Channel 13 TV** (Israel)

International Praise for Tuvia Tenenbom's Previous Work

"Highly engaging and emotional, eminently readable, brutally honest." — **Publishers Weekly**

"Irresistibly fascinating … seductive and engaging." — **New York Times**

"Illuminating and alarming." — **Wall Street Journal**

"Tenenbom's insights are sharp and clear.… Tenenbom loves, likes, mocks, confronts, debates, embraces, scorns and handles contradictions well.… Read what Tenenbom has to tell us, without bias. We don't have the privilege not to know." — **Haaretz** (Israel)

"Hugely entertaining, terribly funny, sarcastic, engaging, powerful, accusatory, judgmental, good!" — **National Review**

"Tenenbom's laughter touches our soul in places where mere intellect could never reach." — **Die Zeit** (Germany)

"Tuvia is curious as a cat, sly as a fox, friendly as a Labrador, and is also a man with seismographic sensitivities." — **Mida** (Israel)

"One of the most iconoclastic and innovative of contemporary dramatists." — **Corriere Della Sera** (Italy)

"A daring and hilariously written account." — **Commentary**

"A piercing storyteller whose writing is full of humor and irony." — **Frankfurter Allgemeine Zeitung** (Germany)

"A mystical provocateur." — **Le Monde** (France)

"Tuvia Tenenbom is Michael Moore and Borat in one." — **Die Welt** (Germany)

"A free artist who fights for truth and tolerance." — **Le Vif/L'Express** (Belgium)

"Brilliant." — **Deutschlandradio** (Germany)

"*The Lies They Tell* ranks Tenenbom among the best social anthropologists, like Comte Alexis de Tocqueville and Mark Twain."

‑ American Thinker

"Tenenbom rides the razor's edge… and goes all the way off."

‑ Amsterdam News

"If Kafka had written non-fiction, he could not have bested Tenenbom's latest book.… This is one of the finest pieces of reporting I have seen in quite some time."

‑ Asia Times

"Relentlessly honest."   ‑ Mitteldeutsche Zeitung (Germany)

"Amazingly original."   – Jewish Currents

"Here is a man, a writer, who does not follow patterns of thought dictated by others, nor does he abide by a code of language that others have imposed. And yet, he keeps his sense of humor throughout the pages."

‑ Spiegel Online (Germany)

"A force of nature… provocative, satirical, intellectual."

‑ La Repubblica (Italy)

"Tenenbom dares."   ‑ La Razon (Spain)

"He sees and he hears. Exactly as it is."

‑ Frankfurter Rundschau (Germany)

"Tenenbom's hodgepodge of politics, zealotry and literary genres is fresh and audacious."   ‑ Village Voice

"A New Jew."   ‑ Maariv (Israel)

"An anarchist."   ‑ Stern (Germany)

The Taming of the Jew

A Journey through the United Kingdom

Tuvia Tenenbom

gefen
publishing house בית הוצאה לאור
JERUSALEM ◆ NEW YORK Est. 1981

Cover drawing: Shay Charka
Cover design: Leah Ben Avraham/Noonim Graphics
Typesetting: Optume Technologies
Editor: Kezia Raffel Pride
Organization, advice, and photos: Isi Tenenbom

ISBN: 978-965-7023-43-3

1 3 5 7 9 8 6 4 2

Gefen Publishing House Ltd.
6 Hatzvi Street
Jerusalem 9438614,
Israel
972-2-538-0247
orders@gefenpublishing.com

Gefen Books
c/o Baker & Taylor Publisher Services
30 Amberwood Parkway
Ashland, Ohio 44805
516-593-1234
orders@gefenpublishing.com

www.gefenpublishing.com

Printed in Israel
Library of Congress Control Number: 2020923904

To Isi

For being my sounding board every step of the way,
For capturing every image with her camera lens,
For gracing every day with her presence,

For being the loveliest spouse that she is,
This book is dedicated.

Contents

The Cat and the Rat

Once upon a time, in the oldest church in Dublin, a cat chased a rat, something cats have been known to do long before there were churches. The rat, an Olympic runner from birth, ran for its life into the church's organ, right inside one magnificent pipe. The cat, a creature never to be outfoxed by a rat, valiantly followed the rat inside the same pipe. The rest, as the believers say, is history. For years and years and years, maybe a thousand years and maybe less, the dead cat and the dead rat lay side by side, their bodies fully preserved by the holy air flowing inside the pipe and by the sacred hymns lovingly sung by lovely saints. Until, that is, a few bored humans, perhaps even unbelievers, made up their minds to clean the organ's pipes, for reasons unbeknownst to any of us to this very day.

It was then, once the music had paused, that the cat and the rat slipped out of the sacred organ, looking the same as they did a thousand – maybe more – years ago.

Rumor has it that since that very day, if you come to pray to Jesus or his mother, you might meet neither mother nor son, for they are in heaven, but you will surely see the cat and the rat.

On my way to the UK, I say to myself: I must see this miracle with my own two eyes. I board a plane, fall asleep, and when I wake up, I'm in Ireland.

That's the fastest way to get to Ireland, if you ever want to get there: Board a plane, wherever, fall asleep, and before you can say Jack Robinson, you'll be in Ireland.

Moments after the plane touches ground, I go outside the airport and light up next to a smoking lady.

What does it mean to be Irish? I ask her.

"We are friendly people."

How about the Brits – are they also friendly?

"British people are heavy, too serious. We, the Irish, we are relaxed, not like the British people."

Do Irish people like the Brits?

"Half of us like them, the other half don't."

I am Austrian. Do you like the Austrians?

"I don't know them."

According to the *New York Times*, citing a World Health Organization survey, "Ireland is second only to Austria in rates of binge drinking." So, I think, why not introduce myself as an Austrian, a fellow drinker?

Often, when interviewing people I don't know, I tell them I'm a German journalist by the name of Tobias. In my experience, people respond more honestly to me when they think that I'm German. Sometimes, if circumstance so designs, other nationalities come out of my mouth.

In any case, I take a taxi to my hotel, the Brooks Hotel in Dublin's center, where I meet another hotel guest. He tells me that I should go to the nearby Fade Street, where, he says, the famous drunks of Dublin congregate.

I rush to Fade Street, but I can't find a single drunk creature. Where are the drunk Irish?

"Come back on Friday night," a young man tells me. "Come late, late, and you'll see them all."

Okay, will do.

It's a sunny day, most comfortable weather, and I go to Christ Church Cathedral, where the beloved cat and the rat rest.

No one is praying in the church, not now. Now it's the time for the tourists, and they must pay an entrance fee.

God, if I understand correctly, is undergoing some financial difficulties lately. Okay.

Downstairs, a sign says, is the crypt.

I go down. The cat and the rat, known to some as Tom and Jerry, stare at me in all their glorified, mummified selves.

Oh, Holy Ghost, this is the ultimate eyesore!

Why did I think that I would enjoy being in the presence of a dead rat? Stupid me.

I run out.

Once outside, I slowly walk the streets of Dublin. Everywhere I look, I see signs in dual languages, Gaelic and English. How many of you speak Gaelic? I ask some Irish people passing by. Personally, most of them answer, they don't speak Gaelic, but they think that somewhere between 3.9 and 10 percent of Irish people do.

The clock moves, one hour replaces the other, and when my stomach demands food, I go to have lunch. Next to me sits a well-dressed man by the name of Michael Fitzgerald, aka Mike, an Irishman who used to be Catholic, like so many other Irishmen, but no more.

I ask Mike to introduce his country to me. Is there one issue that unites all the Irish people? I want to know.

Yes, there is.

"Ireland," Mike tells me, "is the most anti-Israel, anti-Jewish country in Europe – though we will say that we are just anti-Zionist."

Say what?

I shouldn't be surprised, he says. "In World War II, we allowed sixty-five Jews, in total, to enter Ireland. The taoiseach [prime minister] at the time, Éamon de Valera, even expressed his condolences to the German people on the death of Adolf Hitler."

Aren't the English people, not the Jews, the ones who have wronged you?

Well, yes. For hundreds of years, so Mike says, England murdered the Irish left and right, forced Irish culture almost out of existence, and made Gaelic a language spoken primarily by the dead. Not only that. Centuries ago, he tells me, Queen Elizabeth I "brought in Scottish Protestants to the north of Ireland, gave them land, at the expense of the Catholic population – who were kicked off the land, and this created a rift between the north and the south of Ireland, which exists to this day."

Let me see if I got it: The English kill the Irish, and that's why the Irish hate the Israelis-slash-Jews?

"Yes. In Ireland, we don't care much about reality; we love mythology."

What are you talking about?

"We believe that the leprechauns lived here at the beginning of time. And then, suddenly, we were here."

I love it! Other countries were established by people who came in, killed everybody around, irrigated the earth with the natives' blood, and took over the land. Not the Irish. They killed nobody and took nobody else's land.

Genius.

I go to a pub, to fully digest what I've just heard. Today, I think, I'll have Guinness.

The waitress here is a lovely girl, with a totally non-Irish accent. Where you from? I ask her.

"Romania."

What a coincidence! My mother is also Romanian.

"Do you speak Romanian?"

Sadly not; my mom never taught me.

"It doesn't matter," she comforts me; "the blood is still there." That's bloody nice.

Full disclosure: I'm not a beer drinker. The only beer I like is the Belgian Chimay, especially Chimay Blue, and that's it. Outside looking in, Guinness might look like a Chimay, but it is not. Not the same blood, as the Romanian waitress might define it. Still, I'm doing my best. A sip, another sip, another sip, and then one more. Maybe by the end of the process, I'll become Irish and declare St. Patrick as my patron saint. Why not? If leprechauns can turn into Irish, can't Austrians like me as well?

On the next day, I go out to mingle with Irish folks, as many as will take their time to chat with me. And I hear stories, fascinating stories.

Approximately two months ago, one sweet-looking Irish lad tells me, an Irish senator who goes by the name of Frances Black introduced a bill in the country's Senate "to make it an offence for a person to import or sell goods or services originating in an occupied territory," punishable by "(a) on summary conviction to a class A fine or to imprisonment for a term not exceeding 12 months or to both, and (b) on conviction on indictment to a fine not exceeding €250,000 or imprisonment for a term not exceeding 5 years or to both."

This proposed bill, to be clear, is not about Russia, which occupies parts of Ukraine and habitually slaughters Muslims in Chechnya. Nor is it about China, a country in love with occupying wherever it feels like occupying and forcibly reeducating its Muslim population out of their faith. It's also not about Syria, Yemen, Turkey, or a host of other law-abiding countries on our planet.

What country, then, is this proposed law about?

Senator Black, when introducing the bill, explained it in detail. "Israeli settlements in the West Bank are war crimes," adding, "I believe it's time we stood clearly against this injustice."

In her speech to the assembly, I find out, she also said the following: "I'm a little bit nervous because I'm told that the whole of Palestine is watching us today, so the members can imagine that I'm anxious. I just want to ensure that I say everything I need to."

Whole of Palestine?

The whole of Ireland, not including Northern Ireland, which is part of the UK, has fewer than five million people. Why would the whole of Palestine bother to watch an Irish senator?

In order to understand this logic, and since I'm already in Dublin, I write to Senator Black, requesting an interview with a German journalist, me.

In response, her office notifies me that Senator Black is willing to meet me. On Wednesday, her secretary says, she'll be waiting for me in her office at 3:30 p.m. sharp.

When Wednesday comes, I rush to meet Senator Black, and at 3:30 sharp I am at the Parliament building, the Leinster House, where I am asked to present my press card. My press card, of course, states my name: Tuvia Tenenbom – not a classic German name, to say the least.

I pass security, but steps before the senator's office door, her secretary, Ms. Emma, greets me. "Sorry, but we have to cancel. Senator Black cannot meet you today."

In all the years that I've been in journalism, I've never experienced such a late cancellation. Why didn't you call me ahead of time, and save me the time of schlepping myself here? I ask Ms. Emma.

Sorry, says Emma. Call me tomorrow, and I'll try to reschedule.

I call.

Nothing happens. Was Mike right?

I do a little research. Earlier this year, I read in the *Irish Examiner*, the "Dublin City Council has voted in support of a boycott and economic sanctions against Israel." The current lord mayor, or Ardmhéara, is a man by the name of Nial Ring. At the time of the BDS vote, Nial was just a member of the city council, and he voted in favor of the BDS against Israel and also in favor of flying a Palestinian flag over Dublin's city hall for one month, in solidarity with the Palestinians.

It's not just Senator Black.

I chat with an Irishman from Cork, a city way south in Ireland, and he shares a little anecdote with me. For his last vacation, he chose to spend a few days in Israel. After he came back, with a nice tan, his neighbor asked him where he had been. When he told him he was in Israel, the neighbor called him "skunk."

There are rats in Ireland, it seems, who are alive and well, and they have no plans to meet their deaths inside any organ pipe.

Let me turn into a cat, a Jewish cat, and join the historic enemies of the Irish, the famed Brits. Yes, I am a Jew. Full disclosure.

It is time, this Jew says to himself, to make his acquaintance with a bunch of naked British men, "full Monty," on the stage.

The Full Monty, a British comedy, will be performed this evening at the Gaiety Theatre in Dublin. *The Full Monty* is based on the twenty-two-year old British smash hit movie by the same name. Set in Sheffield, England, where the steel industry had just gone belly-up, it tells the story of a bunch of unemployed, moneyless former British steel workers who try to make a buck any way possible. Their idea for a quick buck is quite simple: perform a male-only striptease show for one evening, get the badly needed cash, and start life again.

But be warned: these Brit males, with minor exceptions, are no hunks. They include the fat, old, and handicapped.

Most of the people at the Gaiety this evening – actually almost all of them – are women. In this day and age of political correctness, the women here have come to see naked men of all ages and diseases.

The Irish might not love the Jews, but they love the Brits.

The actors on the stage speak in heavy British accents, half of which I can't comprehend. People around me, Irish from birth, tell me that they can't understand the actors either. But they, I, and almost everybody around just can't stop laughing. We laugh and laugh and laugh and laugh, all evening long.

This is the power of British theater, which I remember from years past.

When I was young – I mean younger than I am now – I would fly to London for a couple of days, whenever the mood so struck me, and run from one theater to the other. What a joy! No other actors on our planet, let me assure you, can play like the Brits. No one. They know the shtick. They created it. They are the masters of theater. No one else can go on the stage and lie, which is what the acting profession is all about, better than the Brits. They go on the stage and they say, "I am King Lear," and you believe them!

Yeah.

I enjoy this production very much and hope to see many more like it once I am in the UK, where I plan to travel for a few months.

Hopefully, once I arrive in England, whenever that'll be, I'll get to visit Sheffield. This production makes me want to see its people.

If you wonder: the "Full Monty," meaning full nudity, never really happens. But who cares? By the time the show ends, you can't laugh any more, and no unexposed penis will get in the way of your pleasure.

Brilliant.

One by one, the happy members of the audience leave the theater, each a big smile on her face, dreaming awake of the wild Monty, the one that was not exposed. Not yet.

And once the Irish ladies have left, the Brits leave as well. Their kind have been fooling the Irish since long before they were born, and they will most likely continue to do so.

When all are out of the Gaiety, the lights go off, and the theater shuts its doors for the night.

Outside, the weather gets colder and chillier, night becomes darker and deeper, and some unfortunate Irish, the homeless of the tribe, come by. They lie down by the locked theater doors, their faces touching the pavement, until they fall asleep.

These poor are no Palestinians – they don't even know where Palestine is – and no Irish man or woman stops by to say hello, to offer a slice of bread, to give a single penny.

Where is the cultural elite of Ireland, its singers and writers, when the nights of Dublin chill the human bones, and the homeless are in danger of freezing?

Back at the Brooks, under a warm blanket, I read about the elite of the Irish art world. Here's what the *TheJournal.ie*, among many others, writes:

"RTÉ will not sanction any member of staff who doesn't wish to travel to Israel for next year's Eurovision Song Contest. Director General Dee Forbes and others from RTÉ on Wednesday met with representatives of an Irish campaign group which is calling for the contest to be boycotted."

RTÉ is Ireland's national television and radio broadcaster.

The Irish campaign group, whoever they are, wants to boycott the next Eurovision contest because it is scheduled to take place in Israel, the Jewish state.

Come morning, I contact the office of RTÉ's director general, Ms. Dee Forbes, requesting a meeting with Her Honor.

The response from Dee Forbes's office comes within minutes.

"We will not be making anybody available to [you] for interview regarding the issues referred to," writes Neil O'Gorman, Corporate Communications Manager, RTÉ.

This response is straight, direct, and impolite.

This kind of response you won't get from any communications person who knows what he or she is doing, unless they think you're way out of line. For instance, if you ask why Israel would be boycotted.

Mike seems to be right. Isn't he? Let me check a bit more.

I walk over to Trinity College, to chat with the young of Dublin and find out what they think about the Jews living thousands of miles away from them.

I spot a group of students, sitting at a table in the open air and smoking cigarettes right under a No Smoking sign, in dual languages, and I sit down with them.

I light up my cigarette and ask the group about RTÉ's stand regarding the Tel Aviv Eurovision boycott.

"Tel Aviv," a young business major tells me in a totally nonchalant manner, is an "inhumane society."

His friends nod in agreement.

How do you know that?

"Why do you ask? Are you Israeli?"

No. I'm from the Netherlands.

I have no idea how the word *Netherlands* came to my mouth.

"What part?" he asks.

Amsterdam, I say.

"Nice."

So, you don't like the Israelis? Why?

"Don't you read the papers?"

Not really.

"What do *you* think about the Israelis?"

What do I know? All I can tell you, being Dutch, is that we've never liked the Jews.

"What do you mean?"

We, I mean Europeans, have been killing Jews for two thousand years. We didn't like them then, and we don't like them now. That's all I think.

The young Irishman never met a Dutchman talking like this. He is struggling to find words to utter for the occasion, until the word "Yes," finally comes out of his lips. "It's tough. Tough. I think I have to go," he adds, then gets up and leaves.

His friends join him.

A few years ago, while traveling in Germany, I had some German students saying practically the same things to me. With one difference: the Germans were arguing their case, with passion, but these students don't. They make a statement, and when I ask questions, they disappear. Like Senator Black.

I stick around. I want to learn more about Irish students.

Shane De Rís is the president of Trinity's Student Union. And I start chatting with him. The "student body," he tells me, had run a referendum on the BDS issue, and they decided to call for BDS against Israel, with two thirds of them voting in favor. There should be no trade with Israel, period. The people of Gaza, he tells me, have been abused by the Israelis, and the students here don't want to be part of it.

BDS, for the uninitiated, stands for Boycott, Divestment, Sanctions.

Is this also your personal opinion? I ask Shane.

"Yes."

Have you ever been to Israel?

No, he says, but "I've been acquainted" with the issue of the Arab-Israeli conflict.

How so?

Well, some Palestinians told him about it.

Are you familiar with the Sunni-Shia conflict? I ask him, referring to the age-old conflict between two sects within the Muslim world that has produced an untold number of deaths and suffering along the centuries, and still today produces hundreds of thousands of victims in a number of Muslim countries.

Not very much, he says.

Do you know what kind of conflict that is?

"There is a different, I don't know what words to use – "

This Shane, whose mother tongue is English, can't find the English words to use while talking. And so, he stops talking.

Can you say anything more about it?

"No, I can't," he says, shaking his head.

Do you know anything about Hamas?

"Hamas represents the people of Palestine," he replies, happy to show his immense knowledge on this issue.

He's wrong. Hamas, a fundamentalist Islamic organization founded over thirty years ago by Sheikh Ahmad Yassin, took over control of the Gaza Strip after a bloody battle with the Palestinian government.

I tell this to Shane, a fact that he could have easily found on his own, but his brain cannot process what he hears. There are cells inside his head that stop operating at certain times, such as this.

But he knows much about the issue, of course. What does he know?

Israel, he tells me, denies Gazans access to medical care.

Let's say that's true. Do you have any idea why the Israelis are doing this?

"They want to force the Palestinians off their land."

For what reason?

"The Israelis want to build settlements there [in Gaza]."

I don't really know why we're discussing this issue in Dublin but, for the record: Israel evicted all its citizens from the Gaza Strip and withdrew its army from it, in 2005. This Shane, I see, knows as much about the Middle East conflict as I know about the sexual habits of elephants.

How often does the student body deal with this issue?

"This is an ongoing campaign."

Well, that's why we're discussing Gaza and BDS in Dublin, because this is what the young in Dublin think and talk about.

Is there any BDS movement at Trinity College against China, for occupying Tibet, or Russia, for occupying parts of Ukraine?

"Not to my knowledge."

There's also no BDS campaigns against Syria, Libya, Yemen, North Korea – or whatever. Just Israel. Why so? Well, quite simple. "The Israeli government," says Shane, "shoots Palestinian children."

And Hamas fires rockets at Israeli civilians, doesn't it?

No, says Shane.

Who does?

"Organizations."

Which organizations?

"I don't know. I'm not involved with them!"

An "ongoing campaign." Yeah.

One day, hopefully, I'll understand the young of Dublin. We're in Ireland, but we talk Israel.

We, the young Irish and yours truly, should be discussing Brexit, sex, gender, soccer, weed, Irish Catholic trans people who want to be nuns, polygamy, Guinness; not BDS. It would even make more sense, I think, to discuss plumbing with them. Plumbing, at least, has the potential to affect our lives.

But they don't care about plumbing if the toilet is not Palestinian.

I stick around a bit more, chatting with more and more students. All of them, so far, tell me that the one characteristic defining the Irish is friendliness. Another thing they all agree on is Palestine. They all think about Palestine, and they all love Palestine.

If I were Irish, I would be thinking of Brexit now. Have they not heard of Brexit?

In June 2016, the people of the UK were offered the chance to participate in the "United Kingdom European Union membership referendum," where they had to choose "Remain," to stay in the EU, or "Leave," to leave the EU, and close to 52 percent of those who participated in the referendum voted Leave. As a result, and in fulfillment of Article 50 of the Treaty on European Union, Britain is set to leave the EU on March 29, 2019 – and I'm planning to be in the UK at least until that day.

This process, known as Brexit (British Exit), could potentially have huge implications for Ireland, as nobody yet knows how the border between the UK and the EU will take shape on March 29, Brexit Day. Where will it be, if at all? Will the border between the EU and the UK be in the Irish Sea? Will it be at the same place it was decades ago, between the Republic of Ireland and Northern Ireland? Will it be an invisible border? Will it be a hard border, with

police, army, and customs posts? Will the UK parliament reject Brexit at the last moment?

Brexit could adversely affect the Irish economy and politics, many pundits argue, especially if a hard border takes shape inside the island of Ireland. But I have yet to meet one Irish person more passionate about Brexit than about Palestine.

Why is it so?

Let me chat with the lord mayor of Dublin, His Honor Nial Ring, for perhaps he can direct me to the very soul of the Irish people.

Kill Every Jew

His Honor greets me graciously at the Mansion House, a very lovely place, with fresh coffee, soda, and plenty of sweet cookies.

That's Irish hospitality, and I'm flattered.

We smile to each other, we are nice to each other, and we chat between bites and sips.

First off, I ask His Honor about the homeless situation. This is, let me share with you, the most absurd topic to chat about while my tongue delights in the sweet taste of the Irish cookies and my belly blooms with the calories they produce. But forget that. The lord mayor, believe it or not, doesn't even know what I'm talking about. What homeless? Where? The "homeless" people sleeping on the street, he says, are there because they want to be there. The authorities provide shelter, sometimes in hotels, even in five-star hotels, for every person who has no roof over his or her head.

This is not Gaza, this is Dublin, and here the poor live in five-star hotels.

Full stop.

I sip my coffee from a really nice cup, for a moment there thinking that I'm one of the homeless of Dublin. So many riches in this mansion, all for me – what else could I be if not a homeless Irishman?

I ask His Honor if I could hang around for a few days in his mansion, but he doesn't think so. After all, I'm not a homeless Irishman; all I am is just a German journalist.

Yeah, I told him that. I told him everything about myself.

One day I'm Austrian, the next day Dutch, today German, and soon, if I feel like it, I'll be Ethiopian.

I am, in case you didn't know by now, the whole of the UN in one person. Why not?

In any case, let's stay on topic here: the Irish people.

Irish people, as everybody in Ireland knows, are good people. Very good.

"Irish people," the lord delights in telling me, "would have a lot of sympathy with the Palestinian people. Like, for example, we flew the Palestinian flag over City Hall as a solidarity."

Was it your decision?

"This was the decision of the Council." Did you vote in favor?

"Yes. And I would vote for it again."

Did you also vote for BDS against Israel? "Oh, yes, absolutely."

If I wondered why there was this Irish sympathy toward the Palestinians, he is glad to explain it to me. "We know what it's like to be oppressed, we know what it's like to be discriminated against, because of your religion, because of your whatever."

Have you been to Israel?

"No."

Do you know the issues there?

Not exactly, he admits, but he still has a "reasonable idea" about it. Israel, as he knows it, is illegitimate: "To some people it is still an illegal state. It is the US supporting it unequivocally."

The right honorable lord mayor supports Hamas. "People need representation," he tells me, and Hamas is the party to offer it.

According to Hamas, I tell him, it's the religious obligation of every Muslim to kill every Jew alive.

"Right."

Doesn't this bother you?

"Well, it can be your obligation, but is it something necessary to do?"

According to them, yes.

"But they don't do it."

They do, but the lord mayor doesn't care. Nor does he want to know anything more about Hamas or Israel. He was never in Israel, and he doesn't plan to be there in the future, he tells me. All he and his brethren want is to help needy people. Not the homeless of Ireland, of course, because they don't exist, but the suffering Palestinians.

Why is Dublin's City Council, I ask him, not calling for BDS against Russia, China, Turkey, Syria, etcetera, etcetera? Are you aware of the atrocities going on around the world, let's say in Chechnya, to this very day?

Yes, he says. He's fully aware of that, "but we can't be consumed with every" misery out there. Palestine is enough.

It seems to me that no journalist has ever challenged him on this issue, and he's wondering why this German, yours truly, does.

He wonders not for long.

"As a German speaking about Jews," he tells me, sharing his impression of me, "it must be quite difficult."

Oh, Lordy Lord, if he only knew what kind of German I am.

Personally, I was born in Israel, but currently I live in both Germany and the United States. So I can call myself "German" or "American." But my English doesn't sound very American, and certainly it's very different from the English of the most-talked-about American, the current American president Donald J. Trump, so "German" seems a better identity for me.

Should I assume the identity of "Christian" as well? Well, let me try.

Do you believe in Santa Claus? I ask His Honor.

"Absolutely!"

Do you believe in Jesus Christ?

"Of course."

Do you pray on a daily basis?

"Yes."

To the Holy Mother?

"I used to have a great devotion to Our Lady," but then, upon reading the Bible, he understood that one should pray only to God.

To Jesus?

"Yeah."

Do most people of Ireland believe in Jesus?

"Of course."

I have a question, and I would like to get an answer no longer than ten words. Here goes: What does it mean to be Irish?

"Oh, less than ten words… Christian. Caring. Empathetic. Community."

What's unique about the Irish character, as opposed to any other people?

"Friendliness. I think Irish people are very friendly. They reach out to people. They are caring. And more caring than a lot of others, I'd say, very much caring and friendly."

He has toned down his hate of the British along the years, he reflects, but they are not his favorite people. "There are, what, two hundred countries in the world? It's only twenty-seven countries that the British didn't either invade or cause a conflict or interfere in. Twenty-seven out of two hundred."

How would you characterize the Brits? Are they as friendly as the Irish?

"Oh, no, they are not! We are the most friendly in the world!"

The Brits, as he sees them, are "standoffish, more conservative, less relaxed, less outgoing, and more uptight" than the Irish.

And so, I leave His Honor and go out to meet the friendliest people in the world, who are strolling somewhere outside His Honor's residence.

I am on Grafton Street, and here I see a couple of Amnesty International ladies, dressed in yellow tops, trying to collect money for refugees, and other great causes.

How many refugees has Ireland taken so far? I ask them.

In the last two years, the yellow ladies say, about one thousand were welcomed to Ireland.

Nothing to brag about, given that the Germans took in close to two million in the past few years, but I must admit that a thousand is better than sixty-five.

I keep on walking, slowly making my way to the Irish parliament, where I befriend a few MPs or, as they call them here, TDs (Teachta Dála). I tell one of them, a charming parliamentarian, that Senator Black stood me up. She is now downstairs, he says to me, and if I so wish, he will go to her and ask her to meet me.

I so wish, and he goes downstairs to fulfill my wish.

And fast enough he rushes back. "I know who you are," he says, in quite a hateful tone.

Who am I?

"You are a TV presenter who tricks people!" He walks away.

She found out, it seems, just before we were to meet that I'm Jewish, which makes me a trickster.

Another TD, who's even more charming, tells me that the Israelis behave badly.

What have they done?

"Why do they put up Israeli flags in Jerusalem?" he asks me.

What's the problem with that?

"It bothers the Palestinians!"

Bizarre.

I walk to the Brooks.

On Drury Street, I see three young men, in their early twenties or so, and they are walking the other way, meaning toward me. Each of them seems to have just had a great lunch, happily chatting and cheerfully smiling to one another.

Excuse me, guys. Do you know of a great restaurant around here?

Each offers his favorite eatery.

Thank you, guys. By the way: Do you love the Palestinians?

Yes, they all do, they say.

At exactly what age did you first feel this love for the Palestinians? Is it from birth? Were you born like that? Did it start on the day you started to talk? Is it from the day you started walking? I mean, when did you first discover this immense love for the brown people of Palestine? Did you just wake up one day and suddenly feel this enormous urge to free Palestine?

"I started identifying with the Palestinian people in my teenage years," the one with the longest blondish hair says.

The others agree, more or less. One started feeling this love at the tender age of fourteen, and the other at around fifteen.

It's the first time in my life that I've asked such a stupid question, and I can't believe that they took it seriously and actually answered it.

There is a reason for it, must be. For them, as well as the others to whom I spoke, Palestine does not seem to be something they argue about; it's just part of their reality. At night it's dark, Guinness is a beer, and Palestine is something you love. That's it. No more, no less. And then there is the Jewish state, called Israel, where evil animals reside.

I've been around in the world and have seen many Israeli- or Jew-haters on our globe. But never before have I encountered this kind of hatred – so simplistic, so potent.

In Irish lore, St. Patrick extracted a promise from God that he would be the judge of the Irish on Judgment Day. The Irish would be doing even better if they got Sheikh Ahmad Yassin to be their judge, for he would certainly pardon them all their misdeeds – if they've ever committed any, of course.

It's Friday night, five minutes to midnight.

I'm going to Fade Street. Gotta get drunk with the Irish.

Fade Street is full of people, some tourists and many Irish. All drink, drink, and drink. But nothing much more to report. No one is vomiting, not one loudmouth; just people drinking, many young, and that's it.

I look at them. They are very well dressed tonight, and they look just great. They are beautiful, they are lovely. I like them, but they hate me.

Let the organ play. I need a Chimay. Goodbye, Ireland. I am crossing over.

The Red Devil

Belfast.

Have you ever been to Belfast? I've never been to Belfast.

Until today.

The train from Dublin to Belfast takes a little over two hours and, at first, Belfast seems to be the abode of a totally different people. I try to communicate with them in English, and they understand every word I'm saying, but I have no clue what they are saying back to me.

For the first couple of hours, it feels quite funny, but after a while I'm totally lost. Do you know English? I finally dare to ask a number of them.

It is at this point that they stare at me, wondering if I'm deaf, mentally challenged, or both. Luckily, this bizarre situation endears me to the Northern Irish people.

Yes.

Today, believe it or not, is World Mental Health Day, and everybody is extremely nice to the mentally challenged. At a local bank, for example, three different people invite me to eat a cookie, free of charge.

It happens at the Danske Bank, one of the bigger banks here, which today is offering free cookies, coffee, and tea, to everybody and anybody in honor of the mentally disabled folks – like me.

Life couldn't be better.

The only problem is, as you might guess, that World Mental Health Day lasts for only one day. No bank is going to give the mentally challenged free cookies after today.

To solve this problem, I walk the streets of Belfast, mostly at the city's center, and listen very carefully to people talking to each other, in order to get used to their tongue.

Little by little, never giving up, I start connecting with the various accents of Belfast.

In due time and course, feeling more confident, I make up my mind to start chatting with the locals. The question is: About what should I talk to them? I want to endear myself to them, since I love to be loved, and I decide to talk to them about Palestine. They are Irish, too, I say to myself.

I don't know if it will work, but let's give it a try.

I approach a young woman with a gorgeous shopping bag and ask her: What do you feel about Palestine?

Picture it for yourself. Imagine it. What would you do if some-body you don't know from Adam approached you with this question? You would think that the man is a nutcase, right? Well, you're not Irish.

The young Irishwoman thinks this is a most reasonable question for a stranger to ask. And she takes the time to answer it.

"I feel so bad for the Palestinian people! Their land has been sto-len, they live under occupation. Very similar to the Irish experience. I feel very close to them."

I, the famous German, say thank you and move on.

Good to be German in Belfast; we both have some issues with Jews.

Belfast used to be in the news often, almost always in the darkest of contexts: explosions, bombs, dead, injured, bullets flying all over, neighbors shooting each other, and rivers of blood flowing on the streets.

But then, miracle of miracles, it all ended.

Today, shoppers in Belfast's Victoria Square, where I am at the moment, are not worried that a crazy Catholic or a raging Protestant will shoot them in the head before they get to enjoy their new purchases.

How did all the mayhem end? I ask people.

First, the friendly Irish tell me, the fight was never between Catholics and Protestants, but between Unionists and Republicans. The Unionists, also known as Loyalists, are the ones who want Northern Ireland to be part of the United Kingdom; the Republicans, on the other hand, want Northern Ireland to be part of the Republic of Ireland – they want a united Ireland. Yes, the friendly Irish tell me, historically speaking, almost all of the Unionists also happened to be Protestant, and almost all of the Catholics also happened to be Republicans, but it's not necessarily so today.

What's today?

Today, they say, it's more complex. How complex?

It's so complex, they answer, that no words could explain it. Okay. How did the fight between the two camps end?

It ended, they tell me, with the Good Friday Agreement of 1998, an agreement that was approved in a referendum.

What was the agreement about?

It is at this point that the Irish folks get confused. "I was born after 1998" is what an attractive young girl tells me, to cite but one of the responses.

A middle-aged man, who believes that he understands complex Irish issues better than anybody, tells me that the 1998 Agreement was about sharing power. Before the agreement, he says, the Unionists were the only ones in the government of Northern Ireland, but now there's a representative government, which means that all big parties join in governing.

Very nice that the government now has all kinds of people drawing salaries, not just the Unionists. But how much power does your government have, I ask him, compared to the movers and shakers in Westminster, the UK government?

In reply, he goes on and on and on, talking about queens and kings, wars and battles, Vikings and Celtics, Anglo-Saxons and Scandinavians, and a long history of the region since the days before God.

Let me rephrase, I say to him, trying to make it a bit less confusing: Who had the real power before Good Friday?

"England."

Who has the real power today?

"England."

So, what did change?

Well, everything else, which means nothing.

Of course, there are people who can explain it all much better, in case you're interested. David Ford is one of them.

David Ford, a former justice minister in the Northern Ireland government, puts it to me in these words: "There are those who say that on Good Friday 1998, Republicans lost and conceded their demand for a united Ireland, but they were too smart to let on that they had lost. The Unionists won, but they were too stupid to realize."

The Irish people, be it in Dublin or in Belfast, supply no firm arguments as to why they were killing one another, and they are equally in the dark as to why they stopped the killing.

This is not the only issue that the Northern Irelanders don't know how to handle. For well over a year now, for example, they have failed to form a government in Northern Ireland.

The seat of the first minister, which would have been taken by the Democratic Unionist Party, DUP, and the seat of deputy first minister, which would have been taken by the Republican Party, Sinn Féin, remain empty because these two parties cannot agree on a coalition agreement. One of the main sticking points is Sinn Féin's demand for an Irish Language Act, which the DUP strongly opposes.

"The street signs in Northern Ireland are in English only," a charming twenty-year-old by the name of Gemma tells me, because "some people consider themselves British, but I'm Irish. I speak Gaelic."

Had the act taken effect, road signs in Northern Ireland would be in dual languages, one language that everybody speaks, and the other language understood by fewer than 4 percent of the population.

I light up a cigarette, which I bought last night at a Tesco store. There are atrocious photos on cigarette boxes sold here, of dead people or those about to die, in combination with various dire warnings. In the old days, the Church used to warn the people with severe punishments if they didn't behave, but today it is human rights preachers and the state doing it.

Nothing much has changed. It's always one European who tells everybody else what to do.

I don't even know what brand of cigarette it is, since all brands sold here look the same, but I feel good despite it all because I'm neither Catholic nor Protestant. It's a great feeling; don't ask me to explain.

"You should take the 'Belfast taxi tour,'" a local journalist tells me, "if you want to understand the conflict." She is talking about the Irish conflict, and she obviously thinks that a taxi driver could explain the issue better than a former minister.

Being that I'm in Northern Ireland, a place with its own mind, I'm going to heed her advice.

When morning arrives, I take time to read the news. The *Guardian*, I think, would be a nice place to start.

Yes.

I read.

Here is an opinion piece by a South African writer.

"We South Africans know apartheid when we see it. In fact, many recognise that, in some respects, Israel's regime of oppression is even worse."

I leave my hotel room.

Outside I meet Billy, the nicest-looking taxi driver in Belfast, and he'd love to drive me around in his romantic "black taxi," the coolest thing the Brits have invented since Queen Elizabeth I.

Does the word *Belfast* have any meaning? I ask him. "Yes, it does. Belfast means city of the beautiful guys." Funny man, my Billy.

Billy, by the way, is very proud of his country's many historical achievements. "We gave America seventeen of its presidents. Most recently, Bill Clinton and Barack Obama."

Americans think that Obama is black, but they are of course wrong, because Obama is Irish. "And we gave Israel Chaim Herzog, who was born in Belfast."

Who is Chaim Herzog?

"He was a Catholic Jew, and the president of Israel."

"Catholic Jew."

I, a Sunni Protestant, love this Billy.

Upon more reflection, Billy tells me that Ireland has given the world much more than just presidents. Ireland, he says, gave America the hillbillies, who originated in Ulster, and Ireland also gave the world some of the best writers ever, like Oscar Wilde, and the best footballer of all time, George Best. "George Best spent his money on women and drinks, and the rest he wasted," is how he puts it.

That's Irish humor for you.

Billy, a Belfast man with a heavy accent, loves to talk, but he enjoys driving even more. He is driving me through a wide variety of sights: imposing churches, picturesque pubs, pinkish gay clubs, expensive restaurants, and murals that pop in and out every few houses.

Murals.

Billy picked me up in Belfast's city center, but now we are in West Belfast, a place of many murals, some with extremely romantic titles. For example: "The death of the dove of peace, killed by the arrows of Christianity."

Ain't this lovely?

Some murals touch me, such as the one containing this text: "Those We Love Don't Go Away, They Walk Beside Us Every Day."

West Belfast, historically a Catholic stronghold, deeply identifies with suffering people around the globe, meaning Palestinians.

Look up the road. Can you see the big painting of a Palestinian flag on the wall? The line "Resistance Is Not Terrorism" is printed over it. Do you see?

To make sure that we, mortal people, never forget the Palestinians, Palestinian flags are flying above houses, and sometimes more than one flag per house.

The Brits have slaughtered the Irish decade after decade after decade, but the Irish are busy with the Palestinians.

I'm not touched by the murals anymore.

I tell Billy that I'd like to get a Diet Coke, and he stops next to a mini market somewhere in West Belfast. Opposite the mini market, I see two flags flying high and proud, an Irish and a Palestinian.

What flags are they? I ask the salesgirl.

"The Irish flag."

And the one next to it? "A World Cup flag." Yeah.

She reminds me of an Irish saying: "If you're going to say anything, say nothing."

Driving through working-class neighborhoods, which means poor neighborhoods, I notice many black flags flying all over.

What's with the black flags? I ask a local, once Billy stops the car for a few minutes.

"The hunger strikers."

Who's on a hunger strike today?

"Not now."

When?

"Forty years ago."

Forty years ago. And that's why you fly black flags today?

The man looks at me as if I were the devil incarnate and walks away.

I guess, though I'm not sure, that he refers to a point in time during the era known here as "the Troubles," the nearly thirty-year bloody conflict that ended on Good Friday, 1998. It was in 1981 that a number of Irish prisoners began a hunger strike that ended only after ten of them had died of starvation. To this day, these strikers are heroes in the eye of many an Irishman, and poems are still composed in their memory.

But Billy says that the black flags are in memory of the eleven civilians shot dead in 1971 by British soldiers in Ballymurphy, West Belfast, in what is known as the Ballymurphy Massacre.

The Ballymurphy Massacre, Billy says to me, is not the only time when British soldiers murdered Irish civilians. A year later, he says, the Brits killed fourteen civilians in Derry, in what would later become known as Bloody Sunday.

Needless to say, the Irish didn't take lightly being shot at, and they responded in kind, killing and maiming Brits at every opportunity they had.

The task of killing Brits was undertaken by the Irish Republican Army, IRA, whose political wing is the Sinn Féin Party.

The IRA, at least as a paramilitary group, is supposedly no more, but the Sinn Féin is alive and well, and doing fine.

The Sinn Féin Party, blessed be Our Lady, has a bookstore in West Belfast, and Billy drops me off next to it.

This Sinn Féin bookstore is not your average bookstore, to be sure. First, the entrance door is locked. If you want to acquire knowledge, you have to ring a bell, pray, and wish to Our Lady that you'll be buzzed in. Secondly, this is a small bookstore, and its clients are not necessarily book readers, but they love memorabilia, especially if it is directly related to Irish history and folklore. For example, colorful "Free Gaza" T-shirts, or a nice selection of big Palestinian flags. If you insist on buying a book, *My Walk with Palestine* could be your cup of tea. If you happen to have no money, but still want to remember your visit to the Sinn Féin bookstore, the people of Sinn Féin offer great postcards, free of charge. "Since 2000," reads one of the postcards, "over 1,800 Palestinian children have been killed in Palestine by Israeli occupation forces and illegal settlers."

Palestine, I see, is more important than the Troubles.

I'm starving, and my stomach demands that I eat right now. But where should I eat?

An older man recommends that I go to a place he calls Cultúrlann, a community center nearby. They have excellent traditional food, and you'll enjoy great Gaelic music, he says.

I abide by his advice.

Two middle-aged men play Gaelic music by the entrance doors, and people are filling up the place, slowly but surely. Some are old, some are young, and there are infants as well.

The Cultúrlann, I slowly realize, offers Gaelic language studies and excellent merchandise for sale. Here I can buy, lucky me, Palestinian soaps made out of olive oil that were manufactured in Nablus, Palestine, in support of the suffering Palestinian people.

Aidan, a potential shopper, explains to me why the Irish care so much about the Palestinians, while practically ignoring all other suffering people the world over. It is so, he says, because "the Palestinian issue is much more romantic."

The food at this establishment is so-so, the music is not very inspiring, and soon I walk out – still starving.

Up the road is a sweet-looking house, painted red, which goes by the name of the Red Devil. Now, that's what I would call "romantic."

I walk over there.

When I get closer, I notice three Palestinian flags flying above. Is this a Palestinian embassy?

Not exactly. It's a bar. Football fans, young and old, all locals and all male, sit around and drink beer.

Why do you fly Palestinian flags on top of your pub and not Celtic football flags? I ask the bar's manager.

"Last week the Jews played against Northern Ireland, that's why we put the Palestinian flags," he answers, totally sober.

The football match, Northern Ireland versus Israel, took place in this country, and the Palestinian flags flying above are for the purpose of sticking it to "the Jews."

I need to get out of West Belfast. Let me try East Belfast.

A well-dressed man explains to me everything I need to know about the area. "This is East Belfast," he says. "I live here. Almost everybody in East Belfast is Protestant, but we have a small Catholic enclave, right there, behind the fence. I'm sixty-one years old, and I never went there."

Not even today?

"I'll never go there."

Let me ask you something, if you don't know the people personally, can you still tell who's Catholic and who's Protestant?

"One way of knowing is the name. My name is Samuel, and many of us have Old Testament names. Catholics have New Testament names, like Peter."

Tell me, Samuel, do you know a good restaurant around here?

"How much do you want to spend?"

Not much.

"Why, are you Jewish?"

No, I'm Austrian. We are stingier than the Jews!

"I hope I didn't offend you."

No, not at all.

This obsession with Jews is too much for this Jew to handle, and I need a reprieve from it all. The food can wait.

I take a taxi to the Grand Opera House, where the American musical *Shrek* is playing. I'm enjoying every second of it!

Yes, true, *Shrek* is extremely simplistic, lacks any real meaning, and when it's over after two and a half hours, you forget everything you've just seen. But for me, watching *Shrek* was the most refreshing experience I had while in Ireland, simply because for two and a half hours, nobody accused the Jews of anything, nobody stuck any flag in my face, and nobody tried to boycott anybody.

The famed Europa Hotel is right next to the Grand Opera House.

The Europa was bombed thirty-six times during the Troubles, locals have told me, but today, I hope, the hotel has a good restaurant or two.

Two guards stand next to the entrance door, one Catholic and the other Protestant, and both deny that the hotel was ever bombed. There were explosions outside the hotel, they say, but never in it.

How are the two of you getting along?

Fine, the Catholic and the Protestant reply.

Will your children marry each other?

Never, they both respond. Nobody's bombing anybody at the moment, they say, but underneath, it's boiling hot.

"There will never be peace between us," says the Catholic, and the Protestant agrees. Perhaps I should find a more cheerful place to eat.

How about a kosher restaurant? Let me eat with the Jews and see how they feel living here.

If a kosher restaurant exists in Belfast, I say to myself, it would probably be located near where the Jews live, in case they live together.

I ask around.

Nobody I ask knows where the Jews of Northern Ireland are. Lots of Jew haters around, but nobody has seen even one Jew yet. As far as the people here know, all Jews are in Palestine, killing little Palestinian children. Eighteen hundred and counting.

There might not be many Jews around here, I dream I hear a huge, gorgeous eagle flying high in the sky saying to itself, but there are ghosts not far from here, beautiful ghosts.

Ghosts? How many? The eagle does not reply; it just flies. Where to? I'm not sure, but it's flying in the direction of Scotland.

The Ghost

Lord James Shaw was mad as hell that his wife, Lady Shaw, gave birth to a girl instead of a boy, and he locked her up in the turret of the Ballygally Castle, from where she leaped to her death while attempting to free herself. Ever since that day, a ghost, some say three ghosts, populate the turret, where they perform all kinds of bewitching acts.

Yeah, the eagle did not lie.

The Ballygally Castle, on the Causeway Coastal Route in County Antrim, Northern Ireland, is today a hotel where humans come to vacation, eat, and enjoy captivating landscapes. The ghost, which some think is the incarnation of Lady Shaw, must be busy contemplating some devilish tricks, and I want to pay her a visit. I have been to the cities, seen the rats of Dublin; now it's time to hover in the villages, to meet the ghosts of Ireland.

Thank you, eagle.

I rent a car in Belfast and drive to Ballygally.

I enter the hotel. I walk here and there, there and here, and I see not a thing, human or spirit. Ghosts are tricky beings, I say to myself, and I better not give up until I see Lady Shaw the Ghost. I check outside, but she is not there. I check the toilets, or "lavatories," as some call them, but there's no sign of her, neither in the ladies' rooms nor in the men's. Where could she be? Is there a transgender toilet here? Nope. I continue my search, check different venues, and just as I'm ready to give up, to my disbelief, I see her. Yeah, it's definitely her. She is sitting all by herself in a huge room, with lights shining up and down from every corner, slowly and quietly sipping dark English tea from an exquisite white china cup, all the while staring at a black screen of gigantic proportions. Lady Shaw, a ghost. She looks gorgeous: she is dressed like a baroness, in seductive green, and she is more charming than the Virgin Mother of God.

Have you ever been tempted by a ghost? I have. I mean, I am, right now. I can't control the deep urge in me to jump all over this ghost. It's my first ghost, and it's love at first sight. I will promise her that I will never, ever, lock her in any room, and she'll return my love; I'm sure.

I slowly make my way to Our Lady, and the closer I get, the more of her I see! She's sexier, hear this, than Queen Elizabeth II. Honest to God!

Step by small step, I make my way to her, and with each step I hear my heart pounding, louder, stronger, faster.

When I am one half teeny tiny step from her, she opens her mouth. Just like that!

Heavenly angels can't produce sweeter sounds.

Lady Shaw, to my delighted surprise, speaks in a beautiful accent; every word coming out of her luscious lips is extraordinarily clear.

She talks to me in English.

Ghosts know English. What a delight.

She talks to me about current affairs, specifically about the Battle of the Boyne in 1690. Yeah, that battle, the battle between the Protestant King William III, also known as William of Orange, King of England, Ireland, and Scotland, and James II, the deposed Roman Catholic king.

King William, of Dutch origin, won the battle, which helped cement Protestant power for ages and ages. "This battle," the ghost says to me, "has been celebrated every year in July" in Northern Ireland. "My grandfather," she adds, "would have been part of the Orange Lodge.

"Every year, on the twelfth of July, there are marches, and there are celebrations of the Battle of the Boyne, celebrating Protestantism and the Protestant win."

What's your name? I ask the ghost.

"Michelle," the ghost answers, looking ever sexier. Yet, I must admit, something here looks fishy.

The Orange people, Irish folks who live and die with the name of King William on their lips, are often members of Orange Lodgers, like Michelle's grandpa. Only these folks are not ghosts; they are people, like Shane and Ahmad.

She's an Orange lady, this Michelle, and not a ghost. What a disappointment!

How did I get myself hooked on a ghost, me, a man who never believed in ghosts? I don't know. Perhaps I got caught up in the Irish psyche – or the Irish virus – of storytelling. They make up stories, kill each other, and then wake up to realize that the stories were just that: stories.

As Mike told me in Dublin: "We believe that the leprechauns lived here at the beginning of time. And then, suddenly, we were here."

Leprechauns. Ghosts. Rats. Whatever.

I too, for a moment or two, succumbed to the power of the Irish story-making. She is Michelle, a woman.

Michelle, who doesn't have a clue that I thought she was a ghost, is talking now. She tells me, for instance, that she used to march on the streets of Northern Ireland on the twelfth of July, in honor of the great king.

In Belfast, among the murals, people behaved as if this were the year 1960. Michelle thinks that we are in the middle of the 1690s.

Today, 1960, 1690 – it's all the same.

Michelle continues talking. She tells me, among other things, that she was raised Protestant.

Are you religious?

"I don't know. I used to be. I'm contemplating atheism."

Do you pray to God from time to time?

"Subconsciously yes."

Do you pray to Jesus?

"Jesus, God. Yeah."

Michelle feels British, very British, so she says, but she can't explain what being "British" means. What she can explain is what it means to be Irish. Irish people, she says, are warm, welcoming, friendly, laid-back and hard working.

British people, I conclude, must be cold, and very unwelcoming. Are you more of a cold British, or more of a warm Irish?

"I am Irish," she replies in the blink of an eye.

A minute ago, she felt British, very British, but that was at a different part of the story. Now she feels Irish, very Irish.

British identity. Irish identity. Protestant. Atheist. Jesus. It's all part and parcel of one storytelling, and there are many subplots being born every day.

I order a sandwich from a passing waiter, sit down, and try to grasp the mind of the Irish people. From what I have seen so far, I think that I start – start, I say, not end – to grasp the Irish psyche, including their fascination with Palestinians. It all has to do with their origin, the moment they came into being as a nation, which is around the Leprechaun Era. Oh, God, it's so clear to me all of a sudden! You see, at exactly the same time that the leprechaun fairies ruled what today is known as Ireland, brown-looking humans lived in a place that today is known as Israel. Ages later, thousands of years ago, nobody knows exactly when, the Irish people founded Ireland, and the brown people founded Palestine. Without a drop of blood being spilled in either place at the time of their founding, as everybody so well knows. Life in both Ireland and Palestine was beautiful ever after, until the dark day when the cold-blooded British arrived. They killed or maimed everyone they met, and forcibly established their kingdom in both countries, never exhibiting one single iota of mercy. And to make sure that their illegal grip on the conquered lands never gets loose, the cursed Brits flooded Ireland with Scots, and Palestine with Jews – and the rest is history.

Long live Ireland, long live Palestine.

I bid Michelle goodbye and walk around, in search of more people.

I meet Mary, a tough-looking Catholic lady. She is no ghost, not at all. Just Irish, and she cares about the Palestinian people. She talks to me about Israel and says, "I can't understand how a nation that suffered so much, such as during the Holocaust, can inflict so much pain on another people." Mary has never met a Palestinian in her life, but "Palestine" is a very nice story.

If only the Jews just disappeared, like the leprechauns, the world would have been such a nice place to inhabit.

I recall what Aidan said to me in West Belfast, that Palestine is "romantic."

I keep on driving on the Causeway Coastal Route, and I reach the village of Carnlough.

Carnlough is an interesting name, and one I don't know how to pronounce. I stop to ask the locals what the name of their village means; "a hand under a rock," one of them says.

There's a story here, of course.

A follower of St. Patrick, the patron saint of the Irish, didn't do his job right, and in remorse he cut off his own hand and buried it under a rock.

So romantic!

I look up to see if the eagle is flying anywhere around me, but I don't see a thing. I keep on driving.

I've Got Blue Irish Eyes

Driving around Carnlough is a sheer pleasure. The gorgeous land-scapes will take your breath away. Pure witchcraft! The roads are narrow, but the drive is fascinating. Try it out. Take a ride here. With the water on one side and the rocky mountains on the other, you'll feel as if you've just landed on another planet, a place with no Brits, no Jews, just leprechauns and Palestinians.

I stop at Carnlough Heritage Centre to find out more about this gem of a place.

"Carnlough's charming Victorian heritage," I read in the centre, "owes much to Lord and Lady Londonderry, who turned a quiet village into a thriving hub of history."

Lady Londonderry. Who's Lady Londonderry?

A super-rich lady, with top class friends, according to informa-tion provided by the centre, which also provides additional inter-esting details, such as a touching letter she wrote to a famous man.

Around the time of her husband's death in 1854, she wrote to Benjamin Disraeli, who would become the British prime minister some years later: "I am turned into a clerk.... I silently suck every-body's brain and go home and digest it all. I think I could manage any one subject, but I have so many to go for Estates to Docks, from draining to Railways, quarries to timber and so on till I get hope-lessly bewildered."

The Londonderry Arms Hotel, which functions to this day, used to belong to – who else? – Lady Londonderry. After her death, the property was passed on to her grandson, and later on to his son, a fellow named Sir Winston Churchill, the British prime minister who led his beaten people to victory in World War II.

That's what I've been told by a Northern Irish man. If this is not true, sue him.

As for myself, I drive to the Londonderry Arms Hotel. Churchill owned it; I shall see it.

Legend has it that when Winston Churchill was in the area, and while he owned the hotel, he slept in it, in room 114.

If Sir Winston Churchill slept in 114, why not me? It's a good feeling, let me tell you.

I relax a bit in Winston Churchill's room, room 114, and then go downstairs to meet the people.

That's what prime ministers do.

I mingle with the locals, as if I were in the middle of an election campaign. "Irish dancing," one lady tells me, "is a big part of Irish tradition, and you have to see it if you haven't already."

Before I even get the chance to say okay, eleven-year-old Keera Burleigh shows up at the Churchill Lounge of the hotel to dance for me.

Despite her tender age, Keera is strong-minded, independent, and knows exactly where she's going and what she's dancing. She dances for me the following Irish dances: slow slip jig, reel, horn-pipe, treble jig.

Don't ever forget these names!

Keera, who started dancing at the age of four, is the winner of the Leinster Championship and is qualified for "Ulster Championship every year."

When she's big, she shares with me, her dream is "to work with special-needs children." Isn't this sweet?

"Irish people," she tells me, "are stronger and more beautiful than others." Keera has brought her grandma, Nora, along. Nora is also an artist, a singer. Would you sing for me an Irish song? I ask her.

She gladly will.

She sings "How Can You Buy Killarney." Know this song? Here are some of the lines:

> How can you buy all the stars in the skies?
> How can you buy two blue Irish eyes?
> How can you purchase a fond mother's sighs?
> How can you buy Killarney?

Do you have blue Irish eyes? I ask Nora.

She comes ever closer to me, showing me her eyes, her blue Irish eyes.

You can't not like these Irish, let me tell you. They are sweeter than honey, more charming than the leprechauns.

Evening falls on Carnlough, and Terence stops by.

Terence is a plumber, for forty-two years now, and going strong. He started as an apprentice in a hospital, where he eventually stayed on as a plumber for twenty-nine years, then three years in a mental hospital, and for the past few years in a normal hospital again.

That's how he proudly introduces himself.

Do you like your job?

"I love it!"

What do you love in it?

"I love what I'm doing."

You are a plumber. You fix pipes. You fix toilets, where there's a lot of shit.

"Yes, shit. And sweet corn."

How does it work? You come in, the toilet is full of shit, and you do what…?

Sometimes, as he explains the basics of shit handling, he can just "plunge it away and it goes somewhere else. Sometimes that doesn't happen, and you have to take some of the shit. You put your hand in a large bag, you hit it, you scoop it up, and you turn the bag inside out, you tie it up and you throw it in a bin."

Terence also works in manholes, with "machines with high pressure, lots and lots of pressure."

For all his pride, Terence doesn't earn much. He works for the government, and there's not much money in it, he says. And, yet, he feels lucky. "I'm lucky I've got a job."

Politics, especially international politics, is not something he's interested in, but he identifies with the Palestinians. "They've been put down by the Israelis," he tells me.

Any other international issue that you identify with? "No, no."

I go to my car, turn the machine on, and drive on the bewitching Causeway Route.

Ahead of me is an old graveyard and one hawthorn tree. Near them is a sign with a description and an explanation. "The hawthorn plays a significant role in Irish folklore," it reads. "It was and still is said, that if you cut a fairy tree down then bad luck will befall you."

And there's more. "Some believe that Christ's crown of thorns was made from hawthorn and that this link to Christianity gave the tree healing powers."

Forget aspirin, take hawthorn. You can also try a Guinness beer or a Bushmills whiskey. Just don't forget: The Irish spell whiskey with an *e*. This is extremely important to remember. It's the damn English and the dumb Scots who spell whisky without an *e*.

When the clock strikes midnight, I am back at 114. I lie back, sip a Bushmills, and think of Sir Winston. He certainly appreciated a good whiskey, and I got the bottle.

I fall asleep. Please don't wake me up. I need lots of energy for tomorrow. You know why? Tomorrow I'm going to Bill and Hillary Clinton's place.

Yes. I swear.

Hillary Clinton, Naked in My Bed

Former American president Bill Clinton, who claims to be of Irish descent, visited Northern Ireland more than once, accompanied by his wife, former presidential nominee Hillary Clinton. A bird – which I can't name, not today – whispered in my ears yesterday that their favorite spot is the Beech Hill Country House Hotel in Londonderry. No, not the Londonderry Arms Hotel, but Londonderry the city, a city with a big history in the Irish divide, where Northern Ireland and the Republic of Ireland meet.

Off I go, to Bill's place.

As I get close to Londonderry, I notice that many of the road signs have been tampered with, and the "London" of Londonderry was painted over.

Nothing in this country, I see, takes place without fights and divisions. The Unionists, I guess, love "Londonderry," since they view themselves as British, but the Republicans favor "Derry," without the London.

"Londonderry," a young man tells me, "is the only city in the world with six silent letters." Well said.

Derek R. Hussey, a church-going Protestant of the Ulster Unionist Party, is the deputy mayor of Londonderry, and it is His Honor whom I go to see upon my arrival. "I am British," this elderly man proclaims unto me, happy like a child with a cookie. Of

course, this proud Brit has strong opinions about Brexit. Britain, he says, should get out of the European Union. The majority of the UK people voted to leave the EU, His Honor explains to me, because they wanted to preserve their identity, just as he does, and not because of some financial considerations, as many in the media claim.

His Honor likes to talk politics, and he loves to share his opinion about those he disrespects and the others whom he appreciates. Angela Merkel, the German chancellor, is a supremacist, he tells me, but he likes Israel. "We have to understand that Israel has been under a lot of pressure from Hamas and other forces within the Palestinian state," he says, and then adds: "I intend to go to Israel before I die."

What would you like to be when you grow up?

"A train driver."

We chat a bit more, laugh aplenty, and I feel welcome in Londonderry.

And now I can start moving. On to Bill's!

As I arrive at the Beech Hill Hotel, I'm shown to my room, number 59, and am told by an attendant that this is the room in which Hillary Clinton slept.

Wait a second, are you telling me that Bill and Hillary don't sleep in the same room? "That's true, they don't sleep in the same room. He is a bad boy, don't you remember?"

Yes, I do. Who doesn't? Who can forget Billy Boy and his notorious sexual liaisons while he was in the White House? Certainly not Hillary.

The best feature in Hillary's room is her super-comfortable king-size bed, which could easily accommodate Bill five times over. But no, he isn't allowed here. He must sleep by himself. Yes, Lonely Billy is not welcome here.

I love my room, but then I imagine Hillary jumping into my bed, lying naked on it, contemplating her next fundraising campaign under my blanket.

Whoosh! I need to get out of here and hook up with someone who'll cheer me up! Let me go to Roy, who, by the way, knows Lonely Billy.

Welcome to the world of Roy Arbuckle, a very talented singer and songwriter.

"I played for Bill Clinton in the White House, in Derry and in Belfast," Roy tells me. Roy, if you noticed, says Derry, not Londonderry.

Why can't these people, his people, decide who they are? I ask Roy. In Belfast, the capital of Northern Ireland, City Hall doesn't fly any flag, because of political infighting between the Unionists and the Republicans. Not to mention the government, which doesn't exist.

But Roy, a native son, tops me. "The best one is," he tells me, "most people say Good Friday Agreement, but Protestant Unionist people call it the Belfast Agreement. We can't even agree on what to call the agreement!"

I don't get it. Good Friday is not specifically a Catholic term, it's a Christian term.

"Maybe it's because *they* (Catholics) call it Good Friday."

I don't want to discuss this anymore; I want to discuss Hillary under my blanket. But, what can I say, these Irish know how to suck me into their stupid conflict. When was the last time a big bomb exploded in Derry? I ask Roy.

"Wow, a major one would've been rather in the nineties. God, there have been so many. This place, where we sit, was bombed twice."

Where do we sit? In some kind of a culture building. Don't ask for details; I don't have them. When was the last time a small bomb exploded in the area? I ask the man.

"Not too long ago. There are still some people who would use bombs, small bombs, as a statement."

When did the most recent one go off?

"I can't remember, but it was this year. And people have been shot in the knees, 'punishment beating,' we call them."

This year?

"Yeah, this year. Last week."

Who was shot?

"I don't know."

A nationalist?

"Yeah, yeah."

Shot by an anti-nationalist?

"No, no. His own people shot him."

Why?

"I don't know why. My guess would be that he had done some anti-social behavior, maybe drug dealing or burglary, and these guys, who are called dissidents, extreme nationalists, shot him."

Now, enough shootings.

If Bill Clinton invited this man three times, he must know how to sing a song or two.

Sing for me of Northern Ireland, I entreat him. Roy takes his guitar, and he sings.

> I am a northern man,
> From a northern plan,
> From where I stand, I see a northern land,
> From where I stand, I am a northern man.

I imagine Bill being with us, listening to Roy's music, while Hillary is snoring on my king-size bed.

Yep, this is what happens to you when you're too long in Ireland: dreaming of a snoring American raising money in your bed.

As we speak, the Sinn Féin is planning a demonstration not far from here. I'm going.

We Got Rid of the Jews

About four kilometers west of here, Derry's Sinn Féin is calling for a demonstration against Brexit. "The fight for rights continues," they declare. Sinn Féin is an interesting animal: it is nationalist and socialist, a combination that in some other countries would be regarded as an oxymoron. Not here.

I drive to the village of Killea, where the demonstration takes place.

Two lines of people, on both sides of the street, stand holding signs. Altogether there are around twenty people, far fewer than I expected.

The border between the Republic of Ireland and Northern Ireland passes here, and Karen Mullan, MLA (Member of the Legislative Assembly), is leading the demonstration.

I approach the lady, asking her if she could explain to me why her party is demonstrating here.

Most of the people in Northern Ireland, she says, voted to remain in the EU, and their vote should be honored.

The people of the UK – which means those of Northern Ireland, England, Scotland, and Wales – voted 52 percent to 48 percent to leave the EU, isn't it so?

"What we are talking about is a complete different island," she argues, speaking of Northern Ireland.

There was a UK vote, and the majority voted to leave.

"Yeah."

Shouldn't this vote be honored, according to simple democratic principles?

"No."

Her logic evades me.

Across from us is a gas station, and I go there.

A sign, hanging on the wall of the restroom, reads:

> GENTLEMEN Your aim will help. Stand closer; It's shorter than you think.
>
> LADIES Please remain seated for the entire performance.

I love it!

I drive back to Derry, to check on Hillary, but on the way to her, I stop by a neighborhood called Bogside in search of food.

As I walk, I notice this big sign: "Be Breast Aware. If in doubt check it out." Next to it, what a surprise, is the Palestinian flag.

What does Palestine have to do with Irish breasts? Maybe Hillary knows; I don't.

I keep on walking, enjoying the sight of the ancient walls of Derry, and then I see a bunch of Palestinian flags, all over, plus a big painting of this flag with the line "Solidarity with Palestine." There are more Palestinian flags here than I can count.

What are all these Palestinian flags about? I ask a man walking by. He doesn't want to answer.

No special meaning, another man says to me, and he comes up with a genuine explanation. The Protestants, he says, raise Israeli flags, and that's why the Catholics raise Palestinian flags.

Where are the Israeli flags? Well, I have not seen any, but there's no chance to ask this man, because he quickly walks away.

I stick around. There are more people to talk to.

Why is that big painting of a Palestinian flag there? I ask another person.

It's a "work of art," he answers.

Not bad.

I ask another guy, and he comes up with this reply: "I'm an Egyptian Jude." Jude is Jew in German, and as he says this, he's laughing, as if this were the biggest joke ever told.

Ahead of me is another sign: "Free Gaza."

What's this about? I ask a lady working in a store across the road.

"We support Palestinians," she says. "They are blown up all over the place."

Who is bombing them?

"The Israelis."

Do you mean the Jews?

"Yes."

A few feet from me is the Bogside Inn, Bar & Lounge; let's see what's cooking there. Maybe they have food. Perhaps even a Chimay Blue!

I enter.

A group of local men sit in this pub, having a good time.

I introduce myself as a German reporter and ask them about the Palestinian flags all over. You have a lot of Palestinian flags here; why?

"Because we support them," a man by the name of Damian answers. "'Cause of the fucking Jews," a man wearing a high-vis orange jacket says. A man sitting between them, Barry, is wearing a "Free Palestine" wristband. "The Israelis are scum. Killing children, killing weans," says Damian.

Are you talking about the Jews?

"Yes. They stole their land and killed the poor children."

The orange man is now complaining about Hitler because "he didn't kill enough fucking Jews."

His pals are laughing in approval, and he goes on: "Hitler didn't kill enough Jews. The scourge of the world."

What did you say?

"The Jews. The scourge of the earth." All present agree.

"Have you ever seen a poor Jew?" he asks.

Barry's laughing, his eyes shining. He's having a good time. "They all have money, they're all rich," Damian says.

Are there Jews in Ireland? "No, we got rid of them."

Now the people in the bar are laughing louder, happier ever after.

In front of a video camera, these people have no shame spewing their poisonous hatred, for the record.

I ask this righteous group if they are pro-Brexit or against; did they vote Remain or Leave? They are all Remainers, they say to me; they want to stay in the EU.

A video clip of this encounter finds its way on social media, with my name fully spelled out, and Irish people respond in writing. What do they say? Well, here's a small sample of what they write about yours truly: "We are going to need a bigger oven to cook this giant hook nose rat."

"Truly the jews are a disgusting species."

"Oy vey here comes anudda shoa again!"

"Reminds me I need to get some new lampshades, some soap too."

Initially, when I came to this island, I was looking for a cat and a rat in a church, and now that I'm about to leave, I realize that there's much more to this island than one dead rat, chased by a cat. The island of Ireland, be it the Republic of Ireland or Northern Ireland, is saturated with Jew haters, the biggest Jew haters of our time, and no dead cat will chase them away.

Perhaps I should go to see a Gaelic football game. Let me, I say to myself, experience something totally different, something that has nothing to do with Jews, Palestinians, or Hitler. In Gaelic football, or soccer, players advance the ball not just by kicking but also by hand-passing, and so no player will have free hands to fly any flag.

I drive to the stadium.

Before the game starts, I take my place and look at the field, quite a big field. And there, across from where I sit, I see it, flying high and proud, the flag of Palestine.

It's time I follow the leprechauns out of this island. Goodbye, Northern Ireland.

Hillary: I'm not going to sleep with you tonight. I'm going to Scotland. Now.

The Egyptian King

Have you seen those men wearing kilts instead of trousers? Hillary wouldn't like it. She would hate it, actually. Imagine Bill with a kilt! Can you? Wow, what he would do if he had a kilt!

With a kilt it's much easier, and faster, to go wild. In and out, before you even know the name of the lady.

Luckily Hillary is not with me to kvetch about kilts. She's busy fundraising under my blanket.

But I'm here, and next to me sits a kilt-wearing man. First time in my life that I sit next to a kilter; it's quite an experience.

He and I are on the bus to Edinburgh, and he's wearing a bluish kilt that, he says, costs four hundred pounds. It's perfect for the cold winters of Scotland, he tells me, and he advises me to buy one. If you are not a Scot and not part of any clan, he advises, get one of a "neutral" color. I'm not sure what "neutral" means, but perhaps they sell kilts that resemble the Swiss or Irish flags.

Could be. In Scotland, I have a feeling, everything's possible.

This kilt-wearing man is a musician, which most likely means that he's a "liberal," and so I ask him for his opinion about the real estate tycoon and American president Donald J. Trump, who has recently referred to himself as a "nationalist."

"I hope I find a pole somewhere, and then I'll go away. You know what I'd hang on the pole," he says, winking, seemingly very happy with himself for coming up with such an image.

I try to picture it for myself: a kilt-wearing Scottish musician hanging an American president on the tallest pole in Edinburgh.

Perhaps I should connect him with Hillary. I think that she would love the plan and finally get off my big bed in Ireland and cross over to Scotland.

You're not an American citizen; why do you care? I ask the kilter.

"Trump owns golf courses here."

How many?

"At least two."

Is that why he should be hanged?

"When he built them, he didn't hire locals!"

Yeah, let's hang him!

Is this man a normal Scot? I wonder.

I look behind me and there I see a smiling Scottish lady, and I ask her: What is the most unique feature of the Scottish personality, a quality no others have?

"Good."

What?

"We are good people."

The Irish are friendly, the Scottish are good, and I'm traveling in the midst of both.

The bus driver, a man who would never wear a kilt but is in love with big tattoos, is a proud Scot, and even prouder Brit. "I'm British," he says to me, "and I voted for Brexit." He wants Britain out of the EU, and he's upset at the politicians who want to have a new referendum, a second referendum that they call "People's Vote," as if the last Brexit referendum was voted by cats and rats, not people.

This driver strikes me as a people-loving man. What's the best thing in Edinburgh? I ask him. "A day off," he says. I like this man, my kind of man.

As of now, what my man wants more than anything is to arrive in Edinburgh ASAP, after which he'll go to a hotel, have dinner, go to sleep, have breakfast, all paid by the bus company.

He arrives in Edinburgh ahead of schedule.

Once I disembark from the bus, I buy myself a unique Scottish drink, Irn-Bru. Don't ask me to tell you what it is; it's a secret. Yes. "Bru'd in Scotland," I read on the can, "to a secret recipe since 1901." Well, this is something that's definitely unique to Scotland.

Have you ever tried Irn-Bru? It tastes a little like water mixed with iron, doesn't it? Well, whatever.

With my thirst quenched, I start walking the streets of Edinburgh.

Edinburgh, which is pronounced differently than how it is spelled, is a beautiful city; it's an old city, it's a new city, it's artsy, and it offers a great opportunity to make your wallet lighter. The hotels at the city's center are quite expensive, and if you still have money left, in the form of coins, the bagpipe players around town will be glad to accept them from you.

Once upon a time, locals tell me, there was the Kingdom of Scotland, and the bagpipe players of old served to incite people to fight in the kingdom's wars, but those days have long gone. Today it's a totally different story. Here's a bagpipe player, standing in front of the old, grand buildings of Edinburgh, and a group of Russian tourists congregate next to him, laughing.

History is cruel. One day you're a mighty king, and the next day Russian tourists laugh at you.

Down the road is St. Giles' Cathedral. If you want to take a photo inside the church, you have to purchase a "Photo Permit," which will cost you two pounds. If you want to sit on a bench inside the church, you better give a donation. If you are poor, or just stingy, the plaza outside the church is your only domain. There you'll see on the ground cobblestones in the shape of a heart, and if you spit on one, you will be blessed with good luck – a perfect solution, of course, if you happen to have cut a fairy tree down. The leaders of the church, I can see, don't stand outside spitting; they are inside, collecting pounds.

I keep on walking until I reach the Scott Monument, the tallest monument ever erected for a writer, as the locals tell me, though some Cubans might disagree, claiming that their José Martí Memorial is higher. Whatever the case, men and women are at present planting thousands of little crosses on the ground next to Scott.

What are you doing? I ask one lady.

"We are planting remembrance crosses."

Remembering what?

"People that died during conflicts."

What's the best quality of the Scot? I ask her, preferring to talk about the living rather than about the dead.

"Our humor."

Are you the funniest people on earth?

"We think so."

Tell me a funny Scottish joke!

"I'm not good at jokes."

I approach another lady, Sally.

"We do have a good sense of humor," she tells me.

Can you tell me a joke, a Scottish joke?

"Our national dish is supposed to be something that's quite humorous."

What's your national dish?

"Haggis, neeps, and tatties." Oh, gracious Lord!

A third lady, Ms. Campbell, comes by. It's a cold day today, and Ms. Campbell wears a warm scarf, a Palestinian scarf.

Where did you get this scarf?

"At Hadeel, on George Street." Hadeel, she tells me, is a shop that sells various Palestinian products. Good to know. "I stand up for the Palestinian people," she declares passionately. "They would stand for us, if given the chance. I believe in a fair and just world for everyone, not just for the chosen few."

I just arrived in Scotland, and "Palestine" is already popping up in my face. I didn't expect this, but reality has little to do with expectations.

The lady, Ms. Campbell, touches her scarf lovingly and tells me that "this is from Gaza." I've never met a person so in love with her clothes, but this is Scotland.

Have you been to Palestine? I ask her.

Not yet, but "I ran the campaign 'Scotland to Gaza,'" in which Scottish activists went to Gaza to help its residents. "King Abdallah of Egypt let them [the activists] through."

King Abdallah is the king of Jordan, not of Egypt. There's no Egyptian king.

"So, who's the other one, what's his face?"

There's no Egyptian king.

"Well, here he was, he opened the gates and he let them through, from Egypt to Gaza."

When?

"A couple of years ago."

The Egyptian king?

"Yeah."

The Egyptian king opened the gates to Gaza?

"Yeah, yeah!"

The Egyptian king?

"Of course."

No Egyptian king exists in our day and time, but she insists that there is one.

I bid her goodbye and move on, in search of Scottish humor and Egyptian kings.

But before I meet any king, let me see how the Jews, the subject of much love, are doing.

Russian Women Are the Best

On the way to the Jews, I meet Andrew, a lovely man. Would you share a Scottish joke with me? I ask him. He's got a German one, he says. Will that suffice?

Sure.

"German chancellor Angela Merkel flies into France, and as she's getting off the plane, she salutes the ground staff, and as she goes into the customs house, the customs official says to her, 'Occupation?' and she says, 'No, no, we are just here for three days this time.'"

Oh, there are some funny people in this Scotland! Will the Jews be as funny?

The largest Jewish congregation in Edinburgh, I'm told, is the Edinburgh Hebrew Congregation. I take an Uber to their synagogue.

Ahmad is my driver. He's from Pakistan, and he tells me about Muslim life in Edinburgh. Edinburgh Central Mosque, he shares with me, was built by Saudi Arabia and can hold about one thousand people. On Friday, the place is packed. Everybody comes to pray. And that's just one mosque. All mosques are jam-packed on Friday, the Muslim holy day of the week, he proudly proclaims.

Years back, when he and his family first came to Edinburgh, life was good, even excellent. The family heads built big businesses, and everyone led a comfortable life, but then one member of the family threw everybody out and took everything for himself. "He'll pay for his crime on Judgment Day," Ahmad says to me.

I join Ahmad in cursing the family traitor, which makes him feel a bit better, and he drops me off in front of the Jews.

The place looks awful, as if nobody has been taking care of it since the destruction of the Temple in Jerusalem about two thousand years ago.

I walk in and meet two Jews, officials of the Hebrew congregation, and they are eager to share with me how great it is to be a Jew in Scotland.

"In my professional life," the congregation chairman, John Danzig, tells me, "I don't recall actually at any time having any anti-Semitic comment made to me, directly or indirectly."

The rabbi, David Rose, concurs. Wonderful.

Only life is a bit more complex. According to *The Scotsman*, this very synagogue was vandalized and its windows smashed some years ago. Yet these two Jews have obviously forgotten all about it. Rabbi Rose, originally of New Zealand, paints for me a rosy picture of Jewish life in Edinburgh. Membership in his community is actually growing recently, he tells me.

And altogether there are one thousand Jews in Edinburgh, out of five thousand all over Scotland.

How many people attend services on Saturday, the Jewish holy day of the week, at this largest of Jewish temples in the area?

"Forty." Wow.

"We also have Sunday school," Rabbi Rose adds, just in case I am not impressed with the huge number, forty, who attend services.

How many students attend Sunday school?

"Twelve."

Rabbi Rose has been serving as the rabbi here for the past fifteen years.

Fifteen years ago, I ask the rabbi, did he expect that his congregation would be as it is today?

"No, actually," he answers. His congregation is doing "a lot better, it is a lot more vibrant" than what he expected a decade and a half ago.

If Ahmad heard this, he'd be exploding in laughter.

Gently, while trying to be as friendly as I possibly can, I tell them that I don't buy their rosy picture. They seem surprised, but it is at this point that Rabbi David Rose backtracks a bit and admits that life for the Jews here has not always been good. Several years ago, he offers as an example, the Church of Scotland issued a strongly worded anti-Jewish, anti-Israel document entitled "The Inheritance of Abraham? A Report on the 'Promised Land.'" The document asserted, among other things, that "Christians should not be supporting any claims by Jewish or any other people to an exclusive or even privileged divine right to possess particular territory. It is a misuse of the Bible to use it as a topographic guide to settle contemporary conflicts over land."

In the report, the Church of Scotland is concerned not only with land, but also people. They have an issue with Jews in general. Here is an example: "Jesus offered a radical critique of Jewish specialness and exclusivism, but the people of Nazareth were not ready for it."

Simply put, the message is this: If you, Jews, thought you were special, we got news for you, you are not. If you thought your home is Israel, forget it fast. Interestingly, the document relies, in part, on an American Jew who, years earlier, wrote that the Palestinians are good, patient people, while the Jews have blood on their hands. Furthermore, this document implies that Israel is an apartheid state and that the State of Israel should be boycotted.

The Church, under intense pressure, later issued a revised document to replace the original one, but that revision did not go far enough. Currently, I'm told, the Jewish community and the Church are not talking to each other. "The dialogue between us has broken down," a Jewish official, who prefers not to be named, tells me.

I hoped the Jews would be funny, but these Jews are not.

Let me go to Hadeel. Maybe Ms. Campbell will be there. She made me laugh! Maybe I'll even buy myself a colorful Palestinian scarf. I'll walk around with it, say that my name is Ahmad, and everybody in Scotland and Ireland will love me.

Great idea, isn't it?

When I get to Hadeel, I look around.

Here is a map of Palestine for sale, where the name "Israel" is nowhere to be seen. Doesn't exist. I should bring some Irish people here; they would be very happy. They won't have to invest anymore in the Palestinian cause because the Jews are gone. Alas. No more.

Why are people breathing the air of the British Isles so much into the Palestine-Israel divide? I have no clue. I don't know, for one, why the Church of Scotland would ever get involved in an issue that has nothing to do with Scotland.

Let's start dealing with Scottish issues! We're in Scotland, for God's sake! What are the Scottish issues?

Beats me, I'm new here.

Earlier today, by the way, the famous Irish singer Sinead O'Connor announced that she had converted to Islam and that she has a new name, Shuhada, Arabic for "martyr." In Palestinian lore, if you're interested to know, those who kill Jews are called martyrs.

Anyway, I'm in Scotland now. Let me see what's happening in Scotland. Hadeel is in Scotland.

There are about twenty people working in Hadeel, not all at the same time, and only two of them get paid – the rest are volunteers. The volunteers are Scots, white Scots, and they volunteer because they believe in the cause, the Palestinian cause. Khaled, the man-ager, who was born in Jordan but says that he's from Haifa, is not volunteering; he gets paid. He's no naïve Scot. He's Jordanian, like me.

Yes, today I'm Jordanian.

And we two Jordanians sit down to exchange views and feelings.

Khaled, so he tells me, dreams of the day when Israel no longer exists. On that day, inshallah, he will leave the city of Edinburgh, Scotland, and move to the city of Haifa, Palestine. Until then, he is here, and as long as he is here, he loves to chat with his *landsman*. Hadeel, he confides in me, would not exist if not for the great support of the Church of Scotland, which is the landlord of the building. The rent on George Street is very high, he tells me, but he pays very little.

The Church of Scotland loves Palestine; no need for a dialogue here.

All nice and dandy, I get myself a colorful Palestinian scarf, to the tune of eight pounds, and put it on.

Now I feel Scottish. Yeah!

I get myself into another Uber, this time going to the Scottish Parliament. A Scot like me should get acquainted with his parliament!

My driver now is not Pakistani but Romanian. He left his homeland years ago and settled in Scotland, the country of his choice. Why Scotland? Because the Scots are very friendly people, he says.

Are you married?

"No."

Would you like to marry a friendly Scottish woman?

"Oh, no!"

He would like to a marry a Russian woman, but the problem is that in all the years he has been in Scotland, he has yet to meet one Russian woman.

What a dilemma!

I arrive at my destination and take my seat in the visitors' section. The session starts.

There are many visitors today, but only fifteen MSPs (members of the Scottish Parliament) so far, all of whom seem to be very, very bored.

The parliament hall resembles a middle-class neighborhood kindergarten in New York, and I can tell that this place was not built by the Saudis.

The cabinet secretary for education and skills, John Swinney, is speaking at the moment. On the agenda today is the issue of "Primary 1 Scottish National Standardised Assessments," the meaning of which is known only to Allah and the God of the Jews. For all I know, it has something to do with computerized tests for little children, but no details are provided here. John, a man with a bald head, reads a statement from a prepared text, speaking in a perfect Scottish accent, at least as far I can tell. "Local authorities should work collaboratively with teachers," he says, and the fifteen MSPs listen, or pretend to be listening.

The visitors, on the other hand, don't bother to pretend. One by one, they leave, and soon enough there are more MSPs in this chamber than visitors. What can I say? There's much more excitement inside a small Uber car than inside the whole of the Scottish Parliament.

Next speaker is Cabinet Secretary for Justice Humza Haroon Yousaf, a man with a beard and a very nice accent. I would like to meet this man, face to face, but not in this kindergarten.

By this time, I've had enough of this place, and I depart. It's too boring.

As I leave the parliament building in my colorful Palestinian scarf, I feel like a king. I am, it occurs to me just now, the king of Palestine.

Yes!

And I, the king of Palestine, walk the streets of Edinburgh, flaunting my eight-pound colorful scarf, and the boring people of Edinburgh look at me with mushy eyes. They love me. They respect me.

Free Palestine!

Of course, not everything is boring in Edinburgh. In fact, Edinburgh is known for hosting many exciting events, drawing in hundreds of thousands of locals and foreigners. The Edinburgh Festival Fringe is a classic example. The festival takes place in August every year, lasting three weeks, and last year there were over fifty-three thousand performances in total, for which 2.7 million tickets were sold. Some 600,000 of those tickets were sold to residents of Edinburgh, an area with 540,000 people. "We are now bigger than the World Cup in terms of ticketed events and second only behind the Olympics," Oliver Davies, an official with the Edinburgh Festival Fringe Society, tells me.

Yes. King Tabbas Abdul Rahman ibn Mohammed II, my official name, has made his way to the office of the Edinburgh Festival Fringe Society.

Kings do stuff like that.

How did a relatively small city such as Edinburgh get to be an artistic world champion? I ask Oliver.

"Scotland is a nation of storytellers," he answers, and "Edinburgh has this kind of artistic vein than runs through it."

I thought that the Irish were the nation of storytellers, but I guess I got it wrong. It's the Scots! Not only that. "Edinburgh," Oliver tells me, "was the first City of Literature from UNESCO." The festival, no doubt, confirms Edinburgh as a world-class literary city.

How does this Fringe Festival really work?

The Fringe Festival, Oliver explains to me, is an organization that matches artists and venues. It does not decide what show will go up, or down, nor does it fund either artists or venues. All it does is provide a platform that matches the two and offers help and advice to both sides free of charge.

A few years ago, according to various media reports, protests erupted against a state-sponsored Israeli theater company performing in the festival. The protestors, organized by the Scottish Palestine Solidarity Campaign, claimed that since the theater company was sponsored by the State of Israel, it should be banned. As a result, the show was cancelled. I ask Oliver to tell me how the Fringe Festival handles such cases.

"We will protect the right of a show to perform," he answers, "provided it doesn't break the law, but we'll also protect the right of people to protest against that as well. The whole point of the Fringe is freedom of speech."

Did you ask the venue, in the Israeli case, to reconsider?

"It's really not our place."

The protests against Israeli participation in the Fringe, I learn, started in 2014.

That's a few years in the past. Has there been an Israeli theater company performing at the festival since? I ask him.

"I'm fairly sure there was Israeli work last year."

Was that state sponsored?

"I don't know."

Can you come back to me on that?

"I would be surprised if it was funded by the state."

Was there any venue that said, If an Israeli show is good, we'll present it?

"No."

Were there protests against any other shows, in a similar manner to the protests against the Israeli show?

"There wasn't anything that I'm aware of."

With the exception of countries like the United States, almost every theater in the world is state supported. This means, as far as I can see, that the only country not being represented here is Israel.

May Allah bless the Scots.

As a Palestinian king, I'm sure you understand, I am keen on discussing religious issues, and it is my duty to meet religious leaders. Being that I am on a state visit to Scotland, I believe it is time that My Honor meets the top brass of the Church of Scotland, the publishers of my people's most favorite report.

Stone of Destiny

Of course, life in Edinburgh, or in Scotland, is not just about Arabs and Jews, or even the Church of Scotland. No way. There are much more important issues on the table at this time. The top news of the day in Scotland, according to Google, is an American woman named Larysa Switlyk. Larysa is a hunter, or a wannabe hunter, and a few days ago she published some photos of herself, including one where she posed with a dead goat, and this created a huge storm. "Such a fun hunt!" she wrote, and the Scots went wild, demanding that the hunting laws in Scotland be amended. Scotland's prime minister, here called first minister, promptly responded on social media, writing that her government would "consider whether changes to the law are required."

In an opinion piece by playwright Ian Pattison, published in the *Guardian*, and entitled, "Why waste your social media on Yemen when Goatgate will get you more likes?" he complains that everybody cares about the goat but almost nobody cares about the dead in Yemen or the terror in Gaza. "Remember Gaza?" he asks, as if nobody does.

Well, come to Edinburgh, Ian. The Scottish Medical Aid for Palestinians is having a fundraising event at Christ Church on Morningside Road, right by the Holy Corner.

The hall in which the fundraising takes place is packed with Scots of every age, including nineteen-year-old Sonya, and they all remember Gaza.

Sonya is an atheist, despite the fact that we're in a church, and she contributes her time for the Palestinian cause.

Can you tell me, from your perspective, what's the situation in Palestine?

"The Palestinians are treated as subhuman."

Give me an example.

"Israeli kids can throw rocks at Palestinian kids, like every single time, but the Palestinian kids, when they did the same, they are taken to prison in the middle of the night."

Her grammar is a bit flawed.

I drink an Arabic coffee, which the unbelievers call Turkish coffee, and walk outside.

I look at the people passing by me. Do they also think like Sonya, and the rest of the people gathered in the church?

To find out, I'll have to ask them.

The weather today was supposed to be cloudy and cold, but so far, the sky is clear and the sun is shining brightly on the Scottish people.

I walk around.

Edinburgh is beautiful, especially when the sun is shining. The brownish buildings in the old part of the city intertwine magically with the blue sky above, and my eyes thank me profusely for the immense pleasure I give them. It is here and now that I can sense the warmth and the spirit of the city, kind of a mesh between a glorious past and a hopeful future.

Slowly, this being Edinburgh and not Cairo, the blue above disappears, replaced by ever darker clouds, and cold winds start blowing at my face.

It's time to find out what the people, non-activists, think.

I introduce myself as an Israeli TV reporter and talk to young Scots walking by.

Sadly, this doesn't work. A couple of young women I'm approaching seem to be afraid of me. One doesn't want to talk, the other sounds as if she's speaking under duress.

Israelis, you know, are frightening people. And the women are scared, because I might kill them, something Israelis do.

Let me try something different.

I stop the next young man passing by me. His name is Guri, and I tell him that I'm from the Palestinian TV. He tells me that he sides with Palestinians, but I'm not totally convinced.

I spot another young man, walking near a Tesco supermarket ahead of me, and he seems to be quite happy with his life. His name is John, he tells me, and he is a twenty-five-year-old university student.

My name is Ahmad, I'm from the Palestinian TV, I tell him.

"Oh, cool!"

What do you study?

"Art history."

What would you like to be?

"Rich."

Excellent! What would you like to say to the Palestinian people?

Raising his left hand, he says: "Free Palestine. I'm not that much of a militant, I should be more. But there you have it. That's my humble wish."

This man is ashamed that he doesn't pick up arms to fight Israel. Sadly, Sonya, not every Scot is fearless enough to fight the Jews.

The bearded politician, Scotland's cabinet secretary for justice Humza Haroon Yousaf, a Muslim, is attending, I find out, an event in the Jewish community at this very moment.

I go to meet the man.

You're Muslim, I'm Jewish, I tell him. We are cousins, sharing a great-grandfather, Abraham!

"Yeah, yeah."

Now we're in Scotland, and I'm sure you're familiar with the Church of Scotland's "Inheritance of Abraham" document.

"Right."

The dialogue between the Jewish community and the Church of Scotland has broken down. Do you have any comment about that document?

"I'm afraid I don't know too much about the 'Inheritance of Abraham' document."

A second earlier, he knew about the document, now he doesn't. To refresh his memory, I say to him that, basically, the document consists of two points. One, the Jewish people are not special, not unique; two, Israel does not belong to the Jews, from a biblical perspective. What do you think of it? I ask him.

"I probably wouldn't step into the basis of the details of the argument."

That's a justice minister, my dear. A Scottish justice minister. The man knows his job. But I'm not willing to let him off the hook easily; I want to know what this man thinks.

I steer away from the actual document and ask him instead about the ideas in it. What do you think of those two points?

Well, he avoids them. Instead, he says: "I won't comment on the substance at all. Because, as for me, I don't know the substance, I haven't seen the document. I'd never ever comment on things I don't have a detailed knowledge of."

The Jews think that the land belongs –

"For me, I don't want to go into biblical constructions. I'm more of a politician than a priest."

Let me ask you something else. We're here in Edinburgh, which is very famous for the Fringe Festival, but, as far as I know, no Israeli state-sponsored theater company can play at the Fringe, because of the protests. Does the government plan to do anything about it?

"I don't know if this has been raised with the government. It has not been raised with me."

If the Jewish community were to raise this issue with the government, he says to me, the government would deal with it.

Well, there are Jews around me here, so I ask them. An official with the Jewish community tells me that I got it all wrong. There's no boycott of any kind, and Israeli artists appear at the Fringe Festival. End of story.

Good.

When I request to film a meeting of the Jewish community, where members discuss the topic of anti-Semitism, I'm denied permission.

Two leading members of the Jewish community, both of whom reside in Glasgow but are here today, tell me that they will gladly sit down with me for an official interview if and when I'm in Glasgow.

I will, I tell them.

It'll be interesting to hear what they say, and I hope that they'll clear up for me the issue of the Fringe Festival: Is there a boycott or is there not?

It is worth noting that the early calls for boycotting Israeli artists in Edinburgh were not made just by protesters, but also by elite members of Scottish society. In 2014, for example, *The Herald* published a public letter calling for a boycott against the Israelis, signed by about seventy artists, academics, and organizations, including the organizations Scottish Jews for a Just Peace, and Jews for Boycotting Israeli Goods.

Yes, it exists: Jews who like to boycott themselves.

If I were Scottish, I'd campaign to boycott haggis, neeps, and tatties. I tried this food the other day. Awful! Having gone through centuries of history, can't the Scots come up with a better food?

Greece, with a population only twice that of Scotland, has given the world some of humanity's best cuisine. In almost every metropolitan city on this earth, there are countless Greek restaurants, but rarely a single Scottish one. It's time that the Church of Scotland, the official church of this nation, issued a serious theological document about this cultural deficiency.

I'm ready, hear me out, to wage a war, a holy war against haggis, neeps, and tatties.

Oh, Jesus of Nazareth, Mohammed of Mecca, St. Andrew of Scotland: I almost forgot all about it! I've made an appointment with a top official of the Church of Scotland, and I'm supposed to be there now, now, right now.

Run, King Tabbas II; run, Ahmad; run, Tobias.

Wait, wait! What am I supposed to be? Who am I? What name? Oh, yes. Tobias. The appointment was made with Tobias the German, me.

Good that I remember my name.

I take one more Uber and go to the Church of Scotland's office in Edinburgh to meet Reverend Dr. George J. Whyte, the principal clerk of the Church of Scotland General Assembly.

A PR lady shows me to a room where the Reverend Dr. George is, and we sit down for a talk. The lady stays in the room, and I start with some small talk which, as far as I can judge, pleases the PR lady.

First things first. This man, a well-dressed minister, loves haggis. He tells me that.

Sad, sad, sad. There's no way under the sun that this man, or this institution, would ever issue any document against haggis. Period.

What can I do? We Germans lose every war. It's in our blood.

I ask the Reverend Dr. to tell me about his church, not his haggis, and he gladly obliges.

"The Church of Scotland is a product of the sixteenth-century Reformation. It is Presbyterian, it is Calvinist, and it is Reformed. We say that we are the mother of all Presbyterian churches."

What does Presbyterian mean?

"Presbyterian means that we are ruled by elders."

Is the Church of Scotland the biggest denomination in Scotland?

"Yes, by far."

How many members do you have?

"I'd say we have 300,000 to 320,000 adult members in Scotland, out of a population of five million people in total. In the last census, maybe a third of Scots said that they are in some way Church of Scotland, but that doesn't mean they are members, nor does it mean they're coming on Sunday."

What is the average number of people attending Sunday services?

"We've never counted who comes on a Sunday, but I'd have thought that out of the 320,000 maybe 140,000 are very regular attenders; and 100,000 are irregular attenders, coming every couple of months."

Is membership increasing or decreasing in the last ten, twenty years?

"Decreasing."

What's the level of the decrease?

"We lose several thousand members a year, mainly by death."

I tell him that I have just visited the Jewish community, and their membership is also shrinking. He listens.

Of course, now that I've mentioned the Jewish community, I bring up the conflict between the two communities.

They told me, I say to him, that they have a big issue with your church, and that the dialogue with you has broken down. Do you have anything to say about it?

"Yes! I do. I'm very surprised to hear they say that the dialogue has broken down. We've been working very hard on the dialogue this year."

So, nothing has broken down?

"Oh, no. There have been tensions between us, but – "

The dialogue is continuing?

"The dialogue is continuing; the dialogue is developing! We've moved on quite a bit!"

Can you tell me anything about the … what's the name of it … "Inheritance of Abraham"? What is it about? And why did it upset the Jewish community?

"Um, well, it's, uh, it's a story in the past in many ways. But, eh, eh, eh, the … all discussion around, um, uh, where the place of Israel and how Israel … and … is, uh, eh, works … as a … a nation. And, we've a lot of interest in … in the well-being of Israel. We, eh, we invest there, we have churches in Israel, a school, eh, we are trying to … we've been involved in the Land of Israel … longer than there has been a State of Israel."

The man stutters. He's afraid, I see, to share the truth with me.

The PR lady, smelling a rat in the room, intervenes. She wants to know why I'm bringing up such an issue. I tell her not to worry, and that nothing bad was ever intended. I just happen to be German, I explain to her, and we Germans are in the habit of talking about Jews.

She calms down, and we move on.

Reverend Dr. George, a very nice man with two gorgeous blue eyes, tells me that the "Inheritance" document was just a document, and "we did not come to any great conclusion."

It's a lie, but I don't argue with him; I don't want him to stutter again. After all, heaven knows, he's not the only person with no guts in Edinburgh; the city is full of them.

We depart. A Scot and a German. Forever bound. Brexit or not.

On the street outside, I raise my eyes up to the sky, looking for my eagle, but there's no eagle to be seen. Eagle, eagle – I raise my voice, in case it can hear me – Are there no men with guts, women with spine to be found in Scotland?

My eagle does not respond. Instead, I see a crow, and the crow flies above my head until it reaches a castle.

I follow in the crow's wingsteps, until my feet touch the ground of the Edinburgh Castle. It is here, at the Edinburgh Castle, that I learn of the old folks who roamed this land.

Oh, boy, they had balls. Oh, girl, they had guts. They fought, and they died, for what they held holy and dear.

Edinburgh Castle.

This is an awe-inspiring place, powerfully transforming me into the kingly past of this country. My favorite item in the castle is the Stone of Destiny, a stone that represents the link between the land, the king, and the people. Legend has it that in the year 843 CE, Kenneth McAlpine, first king of Scotland, was crowned sitting or standing on this stone. And, a guard tells me, the next UK king or queen will be crowned with this stone by his or her side.

Who will be that lucky person? I ask the guard.

Next in line to inherit the throne, he says, is Prince Charles, the man with the big ears.

He could be wrong, of course. The next king to be crowned here could as well be my son, though not born yet, King Tabbas Abdul Rahman ibn Mohammed III.

Yeah, yeah, yeah.

But before that happens, before the Kingdom of Palestine unites with the Kingdom of Scotland under one single banner, let me first meet a Scotland Independence leader, to see if I approve of the marriage.

Let Scotland Be Free

Say a big hello to Michael Russell, Scotland's cabinet secretary for government business and constitutional relations, who dreams of the day when the marriage between Scotland and England will be dissolved.

I sit down with Michael, also known as Mike, at his office in the kindergarten, aka Scotland's Parliament, and ask him: Why would you want independence? You have been together with England for over three hundred years, since 1707's Acts of Union: Why divorce now?

"Nothing lasts forever."

Would the Scots make more money if they were independent?

"Yes. We would be far better off if we were independent. We would be in the top league of nations."

What do you, five million people, have to offer the world that would put you in the top league?

"We export more per head, for example, than any other part of the UK."

Scotland, he tells me, is "the best educated nation in Europe," and it is also UK's "number one food and drink exporter." It exports whisky, water, and even electricity.

According to a BBC report of about two years ago, "Scotland's schools have recorded their worst ever performance," but perhaps Scots get their education elsewhere.

"Brexit," His Honor tells me, "explains why independence is necessary. Scotland voted against Brexit, 62 percent to 38 percent, but what happens? We are in the process of being taken out of the EU. Surely this is antidemocratic!"

The UK is one entity, comprising England, Scotland, Northern Ireland, and Wales, and the vote was 52 percent to 48 percent for exiting the EU. That's perfect democracy!

He doesn't want to hear it. The only people who matter are the Scots, and they voted against Brexit. Full stop.

As I leave his office, it doesn't seem to me that I'll approve the union between Palestine and Scotland. But before I come to a final conclusion, let me meet the young of Scotland and see what they are made of.

No Toilet Here

The town of St. Andrews, where the Apostle Andrew's bones are buried according to legend, was founded ages ago, under this or that name, long before Jesus arrived in Jerusalem. Today, and for quite a long time, St. Andrews' crown jewel is Scotland's oldest university, the University of St. Andrews, founded in the year 1413.

In fact, Prince William, Duke of Cambridge, studied at this very university, which is one of the world's most respected institutions of higher studies, and it's here where he met his future wife, Catherine, Duchess of Cambridge.

I'm at the university, as you probably have guessed. I've arrived here to interview Paloma, the president of the Students' Association, a position which is to some degree akin to that of Shane, the student leader I interviewed a few weeks ago at Dublin's Trinity College.

Paloma, I fast find out, is not Shane, and St. Andrews is not Trinity. Paloma doesn't show up by herself, like Shane, but is accompanied by an older lady, a PR person. We meet at the university, in an open-air area known here as the Quad, and when I ask Paloma if the University of St. Andrews has contributed to any change in Scotland, the PR lady gets jittery, and Paloma has no answer.

We talk for a while, all under the watchful gaze of the PR lady, and Paloma tells me that the privileged students of St. Andrews care deeply about the needy and the sick.

This, more or less, is everything of meaning Paloma says.

When I ask the ladies in attendance, at the end of our little chat, for directions to the men's room, I'm directed to leave the sacred ground of St. Andrews University and find myself a toilet somewhere else in town. The privileged of the University of St. Andrews, I can tell, like to encourage foreigners to take long walks.

I say goodbye to the ladies, and I relieve myself at the university. I know how to find toilet rooms without the help of people who care deeply about the needy and the sick.

Relieved, I leave the university and walk on the nearby street. My mission: schmooze with the best of the privileged young, provided they don't show up with a PR person attached to them.

I first meet Jerry, a fourth-year student, who has higher than average grades.

Name for me, I ask of him, the five most evil countries in the world.

"I'm gonna get Russia Number One. I'm gonna go … oh, it's difficult! Are we talking Europe or worldwide?"

Worldwide.

"So, I'm gonna go Russia, Cambodia, I'm gonna go Iran, I'm gonna go – " He pauses. He takes his time to think, think, think, and think.

"Any hints?" he finally asks.

No. You're the student, not me.

"Okay. I'm gonna also go Syria and, I'm trying to think, and finally, Iraq."

And which ones are the five best?

"I'm gonna go first for England, I'm gonna go for – I'm not going to say the States, because I'm not a big fan of the States – um, Mexico, and Spain."

Long pause. Then: "I'm gonna say France."

What's your major?

"Spanish and international relations."

International relations. You're the perfect student to answer my question! Let me repeat it and see if you remember: Name the five most evil countries in the world.

"Okay. Iraq, Russia, Iran, Syria, and…what's the last one? Australia."

Australia?? You study international relations in the most exclusive university in the world. You should be able to answer this question easily. If not, I'm going to kick you out of the university! Now, name the countries.

"Russia, Iraq – "

What's so bad in Russia, by the way?

"They don't respect human rights."

Does China respect them? You forgot China. You also forgot Israel. Let's start from the beginning. Name the five most evil countries in the world.

"Russia, Iraq, China, Iran, Israel."

Whatever country I feed him, I see, he'll eat in no time. I gotta find myself another student. Here comes Molly, a fourth-year history major and a top grade earner.

Name the five most evil countries in the world, Molly.

"North Korea, Britain, America, uh, um, I'm not sure the other ones. Turkey, maybe. And Saudi Arabia."

You didn't mention Iran.

"Uh, yeah."

You didn't mention Israel.

"Yeah."

You didn't mention Iraq.

"Yeah."

Would you like to revise your list?

"Maybe."

Okay. Let's start again.

"North Korea, America, Iraq, Israel – for the Palestine problems – and Saudi Arabia." Molly knows about Palestine. Good!

Britain and Turkey, two countries she mentioned earlier, are no longer that bad. Like Jerry, Molly too will repeat what she's being fed.

Is that what happens to elite Scots who don't show up with a PR person?

I don't know. What I do know is that today, thanks to St. Andrews, I've learned an extremely important lesson: If you want to impress people in Scotland that you're the smartest, the coolest, and the nicest-looking, you'd better get yourself a PR person.

It's sad to watch the future generation. No Brexit or independence will help, Remain or Leave. The union between Palestine and Scotland will NOT be, this king decides. Full stop.

I drive. And drive. And drive. And then I reach Dundee, the Scottish city that prides itself for being the "UK's only UNESCO City of Design."

Dundee. Rhymes with Baby. Dundee.

Funny name. Full of humor. Full of Scottish humor. Dundee. A twin city.

Dundee. My twin city.

What, you didn't know?

Stay with me, and I'll teach you everything.

Let's Kill a Japanese Man

First things first, I go to meet John Alexander, the leader of Dundee's City Council. I make my way to City Square, where the Dundee City Chambers and Caird Hall are.

Look up, my dear. What do you see, eh? A Palestinian flag flying high atop of the hall. There are other flags flying there – all European, with one exception: the Palestinian flag.

My flag. The flag of King Tabbas II. I enter the chambers.

The interior of the building pleases my eyes much; it's gorgeous. All power to you, UNESCO!

Now, my dear, look straight ahead above the beautiful stairway. What do you see? Yes, another Palestinian flag.

What's the story? I ask His Honor, just to make sure that he knows the details.

Nablus, he answers, is Dundee's twin city.

How did Nablus get to be Dundee's twin city? What's the connection between the two?

The relationship started "much before my time," the thirty-year-old John answers. "Before I was born."

Do you know of any cooperation between Dundee and Nablus? "We have a Twinning Association," he says, and they would know.

I check the association's literature, to see if they've written anything lately.

Yes, they have. This month, they inform the public, the Dundee-Nablus Twinning Association held a meeting about the "human rights violations that occur in Israel's illegal settlements."

Very nice.

John looks at me, examines my size, and he knows exactly what to tell me. Dundee, he says, offers "the highest-quality food and drink in the world."

He knows me intimately, I can see.

And then he tells me another thing: *The Times* has chosen a local hotel, Hotel Indigo, as the best hotel in Scotland!

I make a quick calculation: The "highest-quality food and drink in the world" must be served at the Indigo, "the best hotel in Scotland." Makes total sense, doesn't it?

My belly jumps with desire, but I don't want to show it. I don't want to look like a starving putz. And so, to hide my sudden happiness, I ask him a social question: What's the income breakdown in Dundee, how many rich and how many poor?

"We have significant challenges in the city with poverty and deprivation." Any statistics on the poor and the rich?

"Roughly speaking, a quarter of the population are living in areas of poverty and deprivation."

The lion's share of social benefits given to Scotland's poor comes from UK's coffers, and John doesn't have the figures to prove that the Scottish government, if it leaves the UK, would be able to pay those benefits. But this doesn't stop John, a member of the Scottish National Party (SNP), from strongly advocating Scotland's independence.

This is not unique to John, a man who impresses me with his vivaciousness, but endemic to other proud Scots I have encountered so far. They just love being Scottish, and everything "Scottish" goes, reasonable or not. Most of them couldn't even define what being a Scot really means, if anything, other than coming up with vague, general statements such as, "We're good" or, "We're friendly." A few days ago, for example, I sat down with Ian Rankin, one of Scotland's most successful writers, and we were talking for almost an hour about all matters Scottish. But Ian, who told me that he had sold thirty to forty million copies of his books so far, couldn't come up with one convincing line that would define the meaning of being Scottish. All he could come up with was: "I feel Scottish." And as we were to part ways, he said to me that now he would go home and think about the real meaning of "Scottish."

Good for him.

As for me, and once I leave the Square of Flags, I drive to Hotel Indigo.

The first thing I notice when I enter Daisy Tasker, Indigo's restaurant, is the décor, a mixture of old and new: old-style brick ceiling, exposed ventilation pipes, contemporary lighting fixtures, and fancy Churchill Studio Prints plates. Decades ago, a jute mill factory operated in these halls, where the working class had toiled for their bread day and night, but today it's a super modern hotel and

restaurant, catering primarily to the moneyed few of Dundee. Mind you, the developers of the site are fully respecting the old poor, and that's why the restaurant is called Daisy Tasker, in honor of a female worker who started working at the jute mill at the tender age of fourteen.

I take my seat and check the menu.

Here's an example of some dishes: Blackened Carrot, Talisker 10 Cured Salmon, Cock-a-Leekie, Blade of Beef, Waldorf Salad, and Dundee Sticky Pudding.

I have no clue what any of these are, and so I order randomly from the menu: blackened carrot, fish and chips, and the Dundee sticky pudding.

The food arrives on time, praise be to Allah, and I dig in.

Oh, God in heaven! The food here is phenomenal, the environment is superb, the gorgeous servers are eager to please, and my stomach cheerfully dances to each and every bit of the chef's magical tunes.

I go to meet Daisy Tasker's head chef, a genius Scot by the name of Macca, and I thank him for making me the happiest man in Scotland. This Macca, let me tell you, understands food in a very intimate way, and human taste buds are in complete sync with him.

My taste buds are now singing a new, complete opera.

Maybe, a thought comes to my mind, I should abdicate my Palestinian throne and move here, to Indigo, Dundee.

Free Dundee! Free Dundee!

My new homeland, from now on, is Dundee. Free Dundee! Free Dundee!

As a potential new Dundee man, I go to see a theatrical performance at the Dundee Rep.

The play, if I understand what I'm watching here, is about two working-class men who plan to hijack, and then murder, a Japanese man as an anti-capitalist act. But before they murder anybody, they discuss lofty issues, such as Jean-Paul Sartre, Jews, Israel, and Palestine. They do have one problem, though: they can't find any Japanese. Makes sense? Not much. The good thing is that eventually the play comes to an end, and when it's over, two men – none Japanese – are dead on the stage, and the anti-capitalists are planning their next move.

Free Dundee of these theater people. Free Dundee! Free Dundee!

The Deprived Scots

Early next morning, after having a delicious "Three-Egg Omelette with Arbroath Smokie" breakfast at the Daisy Tasker, I drive along the streets of Dundee, back and forth, looking for people who are not Japanese, and I reach an area called Hilltown. There I see a man, his back bent, standing in the middle of the road, a bottle in his hands, paying no attention to the incoming traffic.

I'm not sure who paid for the bottle – the UK or Scotland.

I look around me, a place abandoned by the gods, and I smell acute poverty. I watch people walking by, and I see depression. This is a place, if I'm not wrong, that even rats would be ashamed to call home. Here are buildings, hell enclosed in cement, through which not one ray of hope shines out.

I keep on walking, driving, and walking again.

Along the streets I drive and walk by, I see shop after shop, and business after business, closed. Only a select few, such as the Spar Grocery Store or the old neighborhood pub, are open.

I enter the pub.

Very few people are inside, mostly elderly men, having a beer or two and schmoozing a little too. I introduce myself. Tobias, a German journalist.

Yeah, that's who I am now. If I can't find good theater in this land, I make it myself.

The people at the pub are happy that this German, yours truly, has appeared in their midst, because they want the world to know their story.

People don't have money, one of them tells me, because there are "too much drugs" in the neighborhood. Another one blames the Polish people living in Scotland, calling them "greenie poles," after the tall poles for wash lines that are no longer in use.

There used to be jute mills in Dundee, another says, but they are long gone, just like the real greenie poles. The jute mills were the biggest employers in the city, but about thirty years ago, they all disappeared.

And the people have no money since.

"Twenty-five, thirty years ago, you could buy anything here, hat to shoes, but that's finished," one of them says.

Why did the jute mills go?

"Well, because of the government."

Which government?

"The English government."

What has the English government done?

"They steal everything."

How do you pay for the beer?

"You can't sit home all day; you got to socialize."

Not all present voted for the same party, but all those who open their mouths say that the English steal their money. "For years, and years, and years," one of them says, and the bartender offers more nuance by specifying, "For hundreds and hundreds of years."

There was a referendum about Scottish independence less than five years ago, they tell me, and Dundee voted for independence. But there's no independence, because there's no democracy here. Damn the English!

Free Dundee!

The fact is that the majority of Scots voted against independence, but this means nothing for these Dundee people. Like Cabinet

Secretary Mike Russell, who sees only Scotland in the Brexit vote, they see only Dundee in the independence vote; everybody else is a dictator, and the ruthless dictators rule the world.

For them, and the way they see life, it's all dark out there.

Even the pub tradition, they tell me, is soon dying. "In ten, fifteen years, the pubs will be finished," one of them predicts, with utmost certainty.

Why?

"The price is going up, and no money is coming in."

Are the young people coming here?

"Not many. They drink in the shops."

It's cheaper to buy beer in the grocery, and then drink it at home, the bartender explains.

The people are getting poorer, he knows, and the pubs will soon go the way of the jute mills.

We talk, and talk, and after about ten minutes, one of the people here, who didn't speak until now, opens his mouth and dares to take the opposite stand. England is not stealing any money from the Scots, he says. "I am British," he declares, and blames the SNP for ruining the economy in Scotland.

It's at this point, go figure, that I think of my breakfast and suddenly have a strong urge to have an Arbroath smokie.

Arbroath is not far from here, and I drive there.

The Thumbprints of Saint Peter

Stuart, from Stuart's Fresh Fish, shows me the fish that the Arbroath smokie is made of. It's the haddock, the fish you can easily recognize by the dark mark under its dorsal fin. This distinctive mark, Stuart tells me, "was left by a human being [St. Peter], when Jesus and Peter were trying to feed the crowd of starving people." Stuart refers to the New Testament story about Jesus feeding five thousand men with five loaves and two fish, which miraculously was more than enough for all of them and their families. "There was no fish in the sea," Stuart goes on, "until Jesus totally believed there was fish in the sea and then Peter left his thumbprint on the haddock. This is the way we know it's a haddock, because no other fish in Scotland has a thumbprint on it."

So, this is the fish of Jesus?

"This is St. Peter's."

Do you really believe it?

"It's a good story," he says, but he doesn't believe it.

You don't believe in Jesus?

"Oh, yeah, in Jesus, and in God," he strongly believes, and also in the New Testament, but not in the story of St. Peter and the haddock, because it's an Old Testament story. "The New Testament is very good, but the Old Testament is just hearsay," he explains his theology to me. Stuart can't tell me where exactly the story of St.

Peter and the haddock is written in the Old Testament, but this is what he feels, and that's enough.

No doubt.

He gives me a smokie to try. I eat a whole fish, ever happy that St. Peter caught this fish and brought it to Scotland.

My belly happy with St. Peter's inside it, I walk along the harbor, and there I meet John, who has just come back from sea with his fishing boat.

John sells his most pricey booty, lobsters, to exporters in Scotland, and they ship them to France and Spain.

Today he caught enough lobster to fill one box; on better days, he fills up four of them.

All lobsters, by the way, are alive and kicking, and will stay alive until just before they reach the mouths of the rich people of France and Spain.

He picks up one lobster, quite cute, and shows it to me, up close. How old is it? I ask him.

"Twenty-five years."

I look at the lobster, I look at the man, and I ask the man: What do you think this lobster is saying to itself right now?

"Oh, shit!"

John gets £16 pounds per kilo, which makes for a total of £500 for this one box.

John is for Brexit and can't wait for the marriage between the UK and the EU to dissolve. He is not a bit worried about leaving the EU, he tells me. Scots did good before the EU, and they will do good after it.

John works twelve to fourteen hours a day, six days a week, and that's perfectly okay with him. Fishing is not a job, he says, but a way of life.

I wonder how often he eats lobster, and his answer quite surprises me: Never. This fisherman, believe it or not, doesn't like fish; he likes chicken. But yes, he could go for a haddock now and then. If it's good for St. Peter, it's good for John as well.

A strong wind now passes above us.

Oh, God! Look up, see who came to town! Yes, yes, yes. The eagle I saw in Ireland! Hello, eagle. How ya doing?

The eagle flies above me, pretty up there, and I can tell that it feels very good to be in Scotland. I think it has Scottish citizenship, if you ask me. In any case, I get in my car and drive away, following it, until I reach a place called Camperdown Golf Club, and the eagle stops flying and comes down. Should I play a little golf? I ask the eagle.

The eagle nods. My eagle nods. Yes, it is mine.

It nods again, my eagle. Eagles, if you haven't heard, love golf. Don't ask me why.

In any case, St. Andrews, as I was once told, is the home of golf. But Dundee enthusiasts, folk who believe that they're much better than the folk of St. Andrews, say that Scotland, the whole of it, is the home of golf. Either way, both camps agree that golf was invented by Scots, in Scotland, and that you should play it if you're not too busy smoking fish of any kind.

Elaine, a golf instructor, welcomes me at the course's gate and quickly proceeds to teach me the basics of the game. I love it. I hit those balls, one after another, and no ball can hide from me.

What can I say? With all humility, and I'm a famously humble man, I must admit that I was born to be an Olympic golfer.

What I love most about golf is how some golfers view the game. When Elaine is done teaching me, she takes me around the course's offices, and there I see a note hanging on the wall explaining all the reasons why golf is better than sex. Examples: "Three times a day is possible," and "foursomes are encouraged."

I get back in my car and drive on. Direction: the Highlands. My eagle, having rested enough, is flying to the Highlands. Eagles love the Highlands!

I follow my eagle. It's my GPS, I swear.

Frikadelle and Gefilte Fish

Scotland is known for Scotch and golf and is trying hard to find and export oil as well, but its greatest treasure is the Highlands.

The Highlands are in the northwest of Scotland: they have many mountain ranges, millions of sheep, and very few people.

Just gorgeous! I drive for hours, between one village and another, one town and the other, and can't stop being fascinated by the landscape. Driving is not always easy on the narrow mountainous roads, some of which are closed for traffic during inclement weather, but the landscape is so beautiful, and the roads are so unreal, that I just can't stop driving. At times, driving on a steep road leading to mountaintops, it feels as if I'm driving into the sky, reaching heights no plane has ever reached.

Look up, my dear, and you'll see St. Peter eating a haddock. You see? Yes, that's him!

After some time driving, I stop next to a herd of sheep, the cutest creatures under the sun, to get acquainted with them. They make me jealous. They roam the land, rarely stop chewing their choicest of food, grass, and I wish I were more like them. Really. I have never had it as good as them. I would love to be like them, walking lazily back and forth, up and down, and all the while having the food that I like most spread all around me, right and left, up and down. I imagine it. I imagine the ground under my feet filled up with the food I like: vanilla-strawberry ice cream, New York cheesecake, German frikadelles, Jewish gefilte fish (yeah!), Diet Coke, apple strudel, Viennese schnitzel, Turkish coffee, "Three-Egg Omelette with Arbroath Smokie" – to name just a few – all mine for the asking. What a perfect life!

If only I were a sheep.

Following in the footsteps of Her Majesty, the Queen, I stop at the village of Braemar, not far from Her Majesty's castle, where she vacations on a yearly basis. Accompanied by her son, the Prince of Wales, she opened the Duke of Rothesay Highland Games Pavilion just last month. The Duke of Rothesay is the prince of Wales, only here he is called the Duke of Rothesay. Don't ask me to explain. Nobody in Braemar could, and they are the locals. I mean, kind of. Out of five hundred residents of Braemar, only about twenty-five have their roots here; the rest are all kinds of UK people who have come to this place to work in the hospitality business, as this is a very touristy place. The tourists come here to hike, to ski, and to go distillery hopping – there are countless distilleries in the Highlands.

The Highland Games, having their own stadium, take place once a year. Today, for example, nobody is playing anything, but the office is open, and already tickets are sold for the next game, eleven months from now. This whole operation, as you might imagine, is one huge waste of money, but since the queen often honors the game with her presence, every penny wasted is worth it. It makes no sense to me, but a whole lot of sense to Braemar's residents.

At the moment, by the way, no Palestinian flag flies in Braemar or anywhere near it.

I drive around the streets of Braemar, a nice village with a castle of its own, but can hardly see a human being anywhere. The hiking tourists, it turns out, have already left; winter is upon us, and nobody in his or her right mind enjoys hiking in the rain. At the same time, the skiers have not arrived yet. No snow has fallen thus far, and nobody likes to ski on snowless mountains. The village residents, on the other hand, are either sleeping all day long or have gone somewhere else, maybe Brazil. In short: the streets are empty, save for one or two humans who pop in and out occasionally, following a dog or two. If you don't like people, this place, Braemar at autumn's end, is the perfect place for you. In fact, I've just met a German lady, from Munich, sitting all alone in a restaurant that's still open in the village's center. She tells me that she loves Scotland, and that she comes to the Highlands once a year. Doesn't it bother you that there are no people around? I ask her. Not at all, she says, because she prefers not to have people around her. There are birds flying above, all kinds of them, and that's enough. She doesn't mind one or two human beings near her, it seems, and she talks to me nonstop.

Before we depart, she asks me if I plan to stay in Braemar or go somewhere else. If I plan to move on, she says to me, she can suggest a great place. Grantown-on-Spey, says the Munich lady, is really cool.

I don't know about you, but when Germans tell me to do something, I run to do it. It's a Jewish habit. When the Germans tell us to do something, we do it. Don't ask questions; it's too complex.

I get into my car and drive on. To Grantown-on-Spey.

Time to Watch Birds and Ants, Cats and Rats

As I drive, I ask myself this inevitable question: What kind of people go to Grantown-on-Spey other than the Munich lady?

Surprise, surprise, the answer is: Victoria. Yes, yes. Queen Victoria, the great-great-great-grandmother of the Duke of Rothesay. According to her own journals, in an entry dated September 4, 1860, she stayed in an inn, today known as the Grant Arms Hotel, and she liked it. Here is what she wrote: "We went up a small staircase, and were shown to our bed-room at the top of it – very small, but clean – with a large four-post bed which nearly filled the whole room."

I reach the hotel, and I'm shown to Queen Victoria's room. I stayed in Churchill's room, and in Clinton's; it's high time I connect with a queen.

I lie down on the reddish-pinkish four-post bed, imagining myself to be Queen Victoria, and think of my princely great-great-great grandchildren. They are all very healthy, learned, loving, beautiful, gorgeous, smart, sexy, and none of them is called Charles.

I don't know why, but I don't like the duke.

In any case, soon enough I get up, get out of the room, and view my new surroundings, be it the hallway or the staircase, and I notice endless pictures of birds hanging all over.

This hotel, I soon find out, specializes in bird-watching activities, and many bird-watchers come to this Grant Arms to roost.

Bird watchers! What am I to do with bird-watchers? I've got an eagle, I don't need to watch any birds!

Well, I'm here already; let me try to get into the groove.

It's evening time, and the bird-watchers, who have spent the day watching birds, gather for a meeting with an expert, a bird expert. I join the gathering, sit down with the bird-watchers, and ask the expert if he could, please, explain to me the psychological makeup of bird-watchers. What drives them? Why are they watching birds and not, let's say, cats, rats, and ants?

Bizarre, bizarre, the bird-watchers are not amused by my inquiries.

They leave. One by one, except for one Englishman. The English people, perhaps, have thicker skin and don't get offended so quickly.

Well, not so sure. The Englishman stays, but for a purpose. He argues with me. Bird-watching is a great activity, he says, and no psychological analysis is required to explain this hobby.

Thinking that he might be a great conversation partner, I bring up an issue that the English media is obsessed with these days, and which is known in this island as the "anti-Semitism row."

What is the anti-Semitism row?

According to the media, the mainstream Labour Party, and its leader Jeremy Corbyn, appear to harbor deep anti-Semitic feelings. How do they know it? The Labour leader, and those below him, were found to have made, for quite some time now, racist comments that betray infectious hatred of Jews.

Any thoughts on this issue? I ask the Englishman.

That's not a new issue, he retorts. Anti-Semitism is not unique to Labour, or even Britain, but exists all over the world. Consequently, he goes on, some members of the Labour Party, since they are part of the world at large, are anti-Semitic. But Jeremy Corbyn is no anti-Semite. Period.

Why do people hate Jews? I ask the Englishman.

Because of jealousy, he replies. "Jews are excellent money managers, and people are jealous." Let him watch more birds.

Outside the hotel, I meet a bird-watching guide, a man you can hire for £200 a day to help you watch birds. I ask him if Scottish birds have any opinion about Brexit or about Scottish independence, two timely issues that need an in-depth examination. The guide, a Scot of no humor, doesn't think this is funny and runs to the hotel manager to complain about me, Stasi style, requesting that I be excluded from any bird-watching activities run by the hotel.

Don't you worry about that, my eagle whispers into my ears. You have me! Hey, you, eagle: Have you always been here, or did you just come?

My eagle doesn't answer this question.

If you want to understand the Scottish people and mentality, it whispers above my skull, you have to visit the site of the 1746 Culloden Battle, near the city of Inverness. They have a great museum there, and I would benefit much by visiting it, it assures me.

Now, I'm curious. I check the place on Google, our era's supreme maven. Three people's reviews immediately pop up. The first recommends coming to the museum, because, "Sandwiches, pie and sausage roll were fresh and tasty." The second writes, "A great inter-act history lesson which the whole family enjoyed." The third says, "The cafeteria is clean, and offers a variety of foods."

Don't pay attention to them, my eagle tells me. Just go to the bat-tlefield. I drive to the Culloden battlefield.

The Diet Coke Is Great

The first thing I see is not sandwiches, sausages, or any variety of any food. What I do see is a field, green grass all over, and flags – red flags and blue flags. The red flags denote British forces, the blue flags denote the Jacobites. And there's a museum building too. The museum's literature reads: "On 16 April 1746, the final Jacobite Rising came to a brutal head in one of the most harrowing battles in British history. Jacobite supporters, seeking to restore the Stuart monarchy to the British throne, gathered to fight the Duke of Cumberland's government troops. It was the last pitched battle on British soil and, in less than an hour, around 1,600 men were slain – 1,500 of them Jacobites." There's also a four-minute movie here, projected on four walls in an otherwise empty room, that presents a reenactment of the battle.

It's not fun.

I meet Raymond, a museum employee, and he's dressed like a "Highlander gentleman" of the period, with a pocket watch, breeches, and swords.

We go out to the battlefield.

What would you do to me if we met in this battlefield and, let's say, I have forgotten to bring my sword?

"I would probably split your head open."

What a nice image. What would you do with my body?

"Leave it where it is."

And you are a gentleman. What does it mean to be a gentleman?

"Top of the class system. You own property, you have a lot of money."

We talk a bit more. After this battle, Raymond teaches me a chapter of Scottish history. Laws were put into place by the British government that targeted the Highlanders. These laws allowed the British government's soldiers to march throughout the Highlands and steal everything from everybody. As a result, in just four years after the Culloden battle, "thirty thousand men, women, and children died from hunger-related illnesses."

He speaks about it as if it were yesterday. Well, to an extent it was.

Raymond, a Highlander in real life, tells me that from 1746 until 1950, the Highlands people have been suppressed and oppressed by the British government. His own grandmother, he tells me, was punished after she was heard speaking Gaelic in school.

That's not fun.

It is at this particular moment that I start to better understand the Scottish people, a people who for generations have been subjugated, belittled, and punished for speaking in their tongue, for wearing their kilts, and for being who they are – whatever that is. It's a sensitive spot, I guess, that refuses to heal.

"Today only 1 percent of the people speak Gaelic," Raymond tells me, trying to convey the message, the fact as he knows it, that 99 percent of the people don't speak their ancestors' tongue.

I go to the cafeteria and talk to the diners. What does it mean to be Scottish? I ask them. Pride, they say, and a great sense of humor.

I'm not laughing.

I get myself a sandwich, a cup of coffee, a piece of cake, and a Diet Coke. The Diet Coke is great.

I'm done here.

As I'm about to leave, I learn that the Highland Council, the council responsible for the Highlands, has just informed the public of "an opportunity for everyone in Highland to come together to mark the centenary of the end of the First World War by joining a candle procession from Inverness Cathedral to the Old High Church and to attend a special commemorative service."

The Scots, or at least these Scots, love to celebrate battles, wars, and armistice.

Personally, I don't understand why they're celebrating the end of World War I, a war that was followed by World War II, which was far worse, but I'm intrigued by their commemoratory mood, and since Inverness is a short drive from the Culloden battlefield, I drive there.

Send Her Victorious, Happy and Glorious

It's early afternoon in Inverness when I arrive for the procession, and here I see men and women dressed in traditional clothes, plus four horses, marching from one church to the other, carrying a candle. The candle was lit four years ago at the Old High Church, after which it was transferred to the Inverness Cathedral. In remembrance of World War I, which lasted for four years, from 1914 to 1918, the candle is now coming back to the Old High Church, four years after initially being lit. How could a candle keep burning for four years? Reverend Peter Nimmo of Old High Church, which is part of the Church of Scotland, tells me that it's been "spiritually" burning for four years.

Once the procession is over, I go to the church.

Here I hear the national anthem, "God Save the Queen."

> God save our gracious Queen!
> Long live our noble Queen!
> God save the Queen!
> Send her victorious,
> Happy and glorious,
> Long to reign over us,
> God save the Queen…

The service itself incorporates readings of select biblical passages that include the following verses: "Behold, he that keeps Israel, he slumbers not, nor sleeps," and "For out of Zion shall go forth instruction, and the word of the Lord from Jerusalem."

These Church of Scotland people must love Jews, I say to myself, and following the service, I sit down with the reverend for a chat.

What does it mean to be Scottish? I ask him.

"We are people who believe very strongly that everyone is equal. We have a phrase, 'We're all children of the same God.'"

The idea of "we are all equal" is what you always hear in the US of A. It's an international concept; it's not Scottish.

"I would argue that the American ideas of democracy and equality come from the Scots, at least partly."

If being Scottish means belief in the idea of equality, let me ask you: Here in Scotland, you have a Jewish community that is fading, declining –

"Indeed."

– partly because of the fight they had, and still have, with the Church of Scotland. They were extremely offended by the church document, "The Inheritance of Abraham" –

"Yes."

Say something about that document.

"That document came out a few years ago, and it did cause a good deal of offense. It was an attempt by the Church to deal with the realities of what was happening in the Holy Land, and there were things in that document that shouldn't have been there."

Biblically speaking, do you think that the State of Israel belongs to the Jews? Here the reverend asks me to stop recording our conversation.

Did you see what just happened, eagle? My eagle doesn't answer.

Take My Wife, Leave My Whisky

Today, the eleventh day of the eleventh month, at eleven o'clock in the morning, on a day known as Armistice Day, over one thousand people gather at the Inverness War Memorial to commemorate the one hundredth anniversary of the end of World War I.

Loud and clear, in a voice that can be heard from one side of the River Ness to the other, a woman tells the crowd, "When you go home, tell them of us and say, For your tomorrow, we gave our today."

George, a true English gentleman, is not going anywhere. He stays at a nearby hotel and won't attend the ceremony. Had he been in London, he says, he would have attended the commemoration – but not in Scotland.

Why are you, Brits, commemorating an event that took place one hundred years ago? "To remember the fallen. It's also good for tourism – this way we make more shekels."

Shekels? Are you Jewish?

"No, I'm English."

Why do you say shekels?

George doesn't answer, and I can't answer for him. But long ago I began to notice that some people use the word *shekel*, which is the Israeli currency, when they talk about money, since – as we all know – Jews are very good with money.

George is doing very well financially, thank you for asking. He has a chauffeur, and he makes his living in real estate. He buys here, and he sells there. Life's good. Years back, he used to have a hotel, which he owned together with a partner, but then his wife got romantically involved with the partner, and the two lovebirds threw George out.

"What are you doing in this part of the world?" George asks me.

I'm trying to figure out British culture.

"In Scotland? Britain is England. The others [Scotland, North Ireland, Wales], they came off the back of the lorries."

George loves Queen Elizabeth. He would give up his life for her, he tells me. He can't stand Prince Charles, who's next to the throne, because Charles is not a "man's man," and is also an idiot on top of it. But if the queen dies and Charles takes over, he would give up his life for King Charles. "They would announce: The queen is dead, the queen is dead, long live the king."

Will you still be thinking of her, after she has passed away?

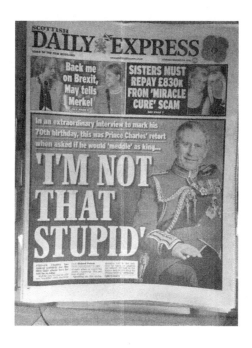

"No."

How could you erase from memory a person that you were willing to die for?

"You have no queen," he says to me, and that's why I can't understand an Englishman's relationship with his queen. You gotta be a Brit to understand these things.

I walk over to the gathering at the war memorial site, a five-minute walk from where I am, and join the people who are already there.

I meet Galvin, a seventeen-year-old pupil at the Culloden Academy. What do you know about the Culloden battlefield?

"A little bit."

Tell me about the Culloden battlefield.

"I don't know for sure."

Ahead of me I see four young soldiers, three males and one female; one of them serves in infantry and the rest in maritime.

Is serving in the UK Armed Forces compulsory? I ask them. "No, no; it's on a volunteer basis," the infantry soldier replies.

If you volunteer to serve in the American army, you get free education, salary, and, supposedly, they take good care of you, including paying your university tuition. Are you getting something similar?

"I'd say, yes, it's reasonable. They do support you in terms of education, but I wouldn't say it's a pop star's wages. But it's enough, it's reasonable."

At this point, obviously upset, one of the soldiers walks away.

I ignore him and continue to chat with the infantry soldier. Is that what made you serve in the army? I ask him.

"Yeah, yeah. That, and obviously, patriotism as well."

What does this day mean for you?

The female soldier responds: "Remembering everyone that fought for us, giving their lives for us to be here today."

The event today is for soldiers who died one hundred years ago. They didn't even know you.

Hearing this, the infantry soldier tells his comrades that I am "left wing" and quickly walks away; the others follow suit.

If these people are indicative of Scottish society, Scotland better forget its independence dreams, because they won't be able to make it.

Don't tell Bruce, a passionate Scottish journalist, what I just said. Please don't.

I meet Bruce in a pub, where he sits with six other musicians, all playing traditional Scottish music. In between the songs, he shares with me how angry he is with Westminster, and with England in general. England has subjugated Scotland for centuries, and it's time to end this shame. The English people hate the Scots, and Scots should not sing "God Save the Queen." The British anthem used to have a sixth verse, which called to crush the Scots. The English people don't sing that verse anymore, he explains to me, because it's against the Zeitgeist, but the hatred of the Scots is still there.

What's the sixth verse, Bruce? Well, here goes:

> Lord grant that Marshal Wade
> May by thy mighty aid
> Victory bring.
> May he sedition hush,
> And like a torrent rush,
> Rebellious Scots to crush.
> God save the King!

This verse, Bruce says, was first sung "when Bonnie Prince Charlie set foot on Scottish soil." Bonnie Prince Charlie, aka the Young Pretender, was defeated at the Battle of Culloden.

Bruce is steaming.

At another table, another flaming Scotsman plays a song about the Scots' love for their whisky. Here goes:

> Take our jobs
> Take our homes

Take anything else you will
Wife, family, and friends
But leave us our Glens!

George, the shekels man, would have a blast if he were here.

After I leave the Scots, Maggie, an old English lady, comes my way. In her youth, she was a stewardess, and she remembers her flights overseas, especially to Beirut. "I saw the Palestinian refugee camps. It was sad to see the poor families, people who lost their homeland."

Yep.

My eagle shows up, for a less-than-a-minute visit, kicks me in my buttocks, and whispers to my torso: Go to the monster! And immediately it flies away. What's the emergency? Where is it flying to? I don't know. Maybe to Palestine.

I drive to the monster.

My Wife Is a Dragon

About six years before the birth of the Prophet Mohammed, founder of Islam, and about a millennium before the passing of Martin Luther, founder of Protestant Christianity, St. Columba, an Irish missionary, encountered a beast in a place called Loch Ness. Centuries passed, everybody heard of M&M, but nobody heard of the beast, and St. Columba's miraculous sacred sighting was about to be erased from the face of the earth.

But then, like always when bad is about to befall the good, another miracle happened, and the beast decided to reappear.

The exact date of the beast's reappearance is April 14, 1933, at 3:00 p.m. sharp, and the *Inverness Courier* newspaper duly reported the sighting of the beast by Aldie Mackay, a local hotel manager. The paper named the beast "monster," and ever since that day, nobody says beast, and everybody says monster.

Year after year after year, people come from all over the world to Loch Ness, hoping to catch a glimpse of the monster, whose name is Nessie, and the numbers do not abate. Last year alone, one million people came to Loch Ness, excitedly searching for Nessie. The people of Loch Ness, of course, are extremely happy. Last year, a man by the name of Willie Cameron tells me, Nessie tourists generated £41 million to the local economy. Willie, who is "into marketing, sales, development of Loch Ness," works for Cobbs, a company "whose portfolio contains everything you could ever want from Scotland," which includes cafés, restaurants, and also four hotels in the Loch Ness area.

The truth is, there's no better place for a monster than Loch Ness, a gorgeous, long, deep-blue lake, surrounded by picturesque mountains and kissed by multi-shaped clouds in the cold nights. There are rough winds flying from every corner of the lake, and animals are roaming freely alongside its banks. This is, as you can see, the perfect abode for demons, fairies, dragons, and a monster.

The Irish have leprechauns, the Scots have a monster. Why not?

Nessie, locals tell me, is not a he or an it, but a she. Yes, Nessie is female, a female monster. No male monster, I am assured by some Scots here, would have survived thousands of years in Scotland. Forget it.

They say, they know.

Ian, a tour guide on a boat carrying Nessie worshippers along the lake, is a real expert on Nessie.

Have you seen the she-monster? I ask Ian. "Yes, every morning. She's my wife." Your wife?

"Well, no, not really. My wife is from Wales, she's a dragon." There you go: I finally found a Scot with a special sense of humor.

Across the street from the harbor, a port of entry to Nessie's world, is the Clansman Hotel, where you can get everything Nessie. Dolls, dresses, cups, and all kinds and sorts of other *bopkes*.

Outside, just before you go in, you can see Nessie in the flesh. Kind of. It's a statue of her. She is a creature of the sea, half fish, half animal, and the rest of her is what you make up of her.

I go to the Clansman to chat with Willie, the EU's top Nessie salesman, over a cup of coffee, a glass of Diet Coke, and two cookies in the shape of Nessie. When I ask him when Nessie first appeared in the waters of Loch Ness, he has no problem citing the exact date: before Christianity, in 500 AD.

I tell him that 500 AD is after Christianity. Do you mean 500 BC? I ask the man.

Yes, he says, 500 BC. No, he also says, 500 AD. What's the difference? BC, AD, AD, BC. It's all the same. Five hundred here, five hundred there, and £41 million are flowing.

This Willie should be the EU's or the UK's chief Brexit negotiator, I think. With him at the table, Brexit will be much more entertaining. UK, EU, EU, UK, who cares?

Do you believe that there's a monster in Loch Ness? I ask the potential Brexit chief. "Without a shadow of a doubt," the chief answers without one iota of hesitation.

Have you personally seen the monster?

"I have. I have seen something very, very strange; I have photographed it."

What did you see?

"Something under the surface of the water. The wind was going in double directions, west to east and east to west, but this object was crossing underneath the water, about midway across the Loch, and it was creating a delta wing shape as if it was breaking the head of the water, and the water was coming back, very large, and it was heading across the water. I took a short video and we sent it to the marine laboratory, and they said they couldn't identify what it was."

His words might make no sense to you or me, but they are good enough to generate £41 million.

I ask Willie to show me the video. Well, he can't do it right now, he says, but will send it to me later on.

Will he? Time will tell. As far as I can see, he'll first send it to the Egyptian king for approval.

Meanwhile I want to know more details about the monster. Monsters, like human beings, come in pairs, right? I ask Willie.

"Yes."

So, Nessie must be making love sometimes to another monster, right?

"Well, I'd think so."

She has sex, right?

"Yes."

Who's her husband? Where's her husband?

"I don't know. Down there in the deep silts."

Where exactly?

To locate him in an exact area will be a huge task, Willie tells me, because the lake is of immense proportions. "The silts down there is an area that's 250 meters deep, it's twice as deep as the North Sea, it's twenty-four miles long. It's a lot of bloody space out there."

Video or not, Willie says that he has taken a photo of Nessie as well.

Could he show me the picture?

Well, yes.

It's a photo of the lake, a body of water, mostly gray, with practically nothing that looks like anything unique. I look at it, I stare at it, examine it over and over, but I can't find a single trace of a monster.

Could it be, you might ask, that Willie and company wear the Emperor's new clothes and are simply lucky enough to have no child crying out that they are naked?

Willie doesn't entertain this kind of question. Just the other day, he tells me, he was in an island in the South Andaman Sea, in a small colony of Buddhist monks. One of the monks was smoking a cigar while polishing a coral with a little grinding wheel, and when he heard that Willie was from Loch Ness, "he took his cigar out, laid it down, and he said, 'Huh, Monster!'"

Bingo!

And I am thinking: People pay a fortune to come here, believing that here they'll see Nessie. Are they not out of their minds?

Well, this is Scotland. The Scots sell you Nessie and they sell you Palestine. You can buy both, if you want.

Why did my eagle want me to come here? Why did it want me to see all this? I don't know.

I spend the night at the Clansman, in a room with a great view of the lake. I stare at the lake for a long time, again and again, digging deeper and deeper in my mind, and just before the night is over, I miraculously see Nessie! Yes, I swear. Nessie, be it known to all, looks exactly like Diana, Princess of Wales. To be more exact, Nessie *is* the Princess of Wales. Definitely female, definitely British, definitely princess, definitely monster. She is swimming magically over the waters of the lake, smiling graciously, winking with her left eye, and sending her sweetest of kisses over the water's surface. Oh, how beautiful is my Nessie!

Look, look, look, look, look who's flying above! Look, take a look! Oh, yes.

When morning arrives, I drive to the Loch Ness Centre and Exhibition to meet a man whom the BBC had called "Loch Ness expert," a man by the name of Adrian Shine. Adrian has a beard, a long beard, much longer than Jesus', and the centre is his domain, his kingdom, his Jerusalem.

Officially, he is the "leader of the Loch Ness project." In short: Jesus Plus.

Last night, I tell Jesus, I personally spotted the monster, and it looked exactly like Princess Diana.

Jesus is not impressed. "Generally speaking," he tells me, "Loch Ness monsters are not as beautiful as Princess Diana."

This man is an atheist Scot!

Far away from here, in London, dark clouds are hovering above 10 Downing Street. Prime Minister Theresa May is facing a revolt in her own party, after many Tories rejected her draft Brexit withdrawal deal. The government is in one huge mess, MPs are roiling, cabinet ministers are quitting, and the media is topsy-turvy with the rapidly heating political landscape. They, like Adrian, are all atheists.

In Loch Ness, on the other hand, there are no atheists. Loch Ness is an island of believers, the best place on earth. Here we have a monster, a good monster, and soon a much younger monster, circa 2021 BC or AD, will arise. That's the date, more or less, when I'll be back in Loch Ness, introducing my own monster. New dolls will be out for sale, all in the image of the princess, and cookies too, for fanatic believers who prefer the monster in their mouths. Long live Princess Di, long live Nessie Di, long live the Monster Princess. Bon appétit.

But before I become a tycoon, the copyright owner of the Di cookies, Di dolls, Di shoes, Di knives, Di condoms, and Di drinks, I've got to go to Glasgow, to meet the Jews who would love to see me. It's a bit of a schlep, I know, but I said I'd meet them, and I want to keep my word. When I'm a tycoon, I know, I won't have time for Scottish Jews. They're too big of a headache for a tycoon, so it's either now or never.

Are you ready? Let's go!

Luscious Lips in Buchanan Street

Hidayatullah is a nice man, and when we first meet, he's all smiles. I told him that I'm a Muslim, and he's happy to keep company with a fellow believer.

Hidayatullah is not a regular Scottish man. Actually, he doesn't even like Scots. The Scots don't like him, he tells me, because he doesn't look like them, and he returns the favor.

Hidayatullah, who has been living in the UK for ten years, was born in Pakistan and got a visa to the UK because he's a "highly skilled" man.

His job?

To put it succinctly, he's my Uber driver.

I myself, a highly skilled passenger, am going to be very busy today.

Back in Edinburgh, as you may recall, I met two top leaders of Scotland's Jewish community, and they invited me to interview them in Glasgow.

My highly skilled Uber man will take me to them.

And, indeed, in due time Hidayatullah drops me off next to the Jewish center in Glasgow, a complex of buildings that seem to have had much better days before I was born.

A security guard promptly comes to check who I am, but I answer him in Yiddish, a language he clearly does not understand.

He lets me enter.

Members of the community, including the two leaders, are just about getting ready to sit down for a Sabbath meal in a hall on the ground floor, and I join them.

There are twelve tables in the hall, each seating about seven white-haired people. On each table, there's a cheap plastic tray, plastic utensils, and plastic cups.

On the tray, there are a few herrings of medium quality, a few pieces of carrots, small slices of brined cucumber, a little hummus spread, and small cubes of cheese. In addition, there is a plate of small pieces of cake.

All in all, the right amount of food for a newborn dog.

"We usually don't have such an elaborate selection of food," a woman sitting next to me says. "It's a special day today because tomorrow is Mitzvah Day, when members of the community will come to the synagogue with bags of food to donate to the food banks in Glasgow."

What's a food bank?

"There are food banks all over the UK. A food bank is a place where the poor can pick up free food, provided they have the right certificate from the government."

I write a note for myself to check food banks. I should see them.

A bottle of Diet Coke stands on a table at the hall's entrance, and I go there to pour myself a cup. There's not enough money, I'm told, to have a Coke on every table.

When I am back, cup in hand, I sit down and sip my Diet Coke while listening to the synagogue's guest speaker, a woman from the charity organization Mary's Meals. She tells the old Jews that they can save the children of Malawi from certain starvation, provided they, the old Jews, donate £13.90 per year, per Malawian child.

Following her speech, the two Jewish leaders I was supposed to interview disappear from sight, each having left without as much as saying goodbye to me.

Why have they run away? I ask a member of the congregation.

"They don't want to talk to you."

Why?

"They are afraid that they would lose their NHS," National Health Service, the British universal health insurance.

What does talking to me have to do with NHS?

"If they say something wrong, they could lose their NHS."

What??

"Look, here we are all pro-Israel, but we keep quiet. We are afraid. You have to understand something: Scotland's Jewish community is the last remnant of the Holocaust generation."

I take an Uber out.

Abdul of Pakistan, my second Uber driver of the day, has been living in Scotland for twenty-seven years, but he doesn't like the Scots.

Why, then, are you here? "Money. Here I make money." Driving an Uber???

Well, not really, not yet, but one day he will be rich, and he will be shopping on Buchanan Street, Glasgow's beloved shopping street.

Umm. I have never been to Buchanan Street. Will you, ya Abdul, take me to Buchanan Street? Yes, Abdul will.

Abdul does. He drops me off about a hundred feet from an Apple store, a company whose merchandise I admire.

Let me go to Apple. It's time I shop, isn't it?

As I approach the Apple store, I see a bunch of Palestinian flags right before the entrance door. A man and two ladies hold big Palestinian flags, trying to convince passersby that Palestine, the greatest place on earth, is threatened by devilish Zionists.

Behind them is a stall, manned by Scots who say that they are pro-Israel and pro-Palestine. Inside their stall, a gazebo structure with a table in the middle, there are small flags of both Israel and Palestine, a mishmash of colors designed to confuse both you and me.

I look around, just to make sure that I'm actually in Glasgow and not in Bethlehem, Glasgow's twin city.

Yes, you didn't know? Twin cities.

I look, look, and look, and then, up the road on my right, I spot another stall, with big Palestinian flags.

Must be Bethlehem.

I walk up to them. The people of this stall, I'm told, are from the Scottish Palestine Solidarity Campaign.

Must be Glasgow.

Inside the stall, in big letters, the following is written: "Anti-Semitism is a crime. Anti-Zionism is a duty," and "Don't play ball with Israeli Apartheid." What's that about? I ask. In a few days, they reply, a football match is scheduled to take place, Scotland versus Israel, and they want the game to be cancelled.

They are planning a big demonstration on game day at the stadium. I'll come by, I tell them.

As for now, I leave them and go down Buchanan Street, and within a couple hundred feet I see another stall, with more Palestinian flags.

Who are these people? They are, as is written on their stall, members of the Glasgow Palestine Human Rights Campaign.

There's not one stall in the Middle East, not a single one, about Scotland's independence. No one in the Middle East, not a single soul, cares a hoot about Scots. Why do these Scots care about Palestinians?

It's more than just caring, at least in this stall. The Scots in this stall are so much into "Palestine" that they fly to the Middle East back and forth, and don't mind losing a limb or two in the process. "I lost my hearing," one of them tells me, "when an Israeli sound bomb fell next to me." I don't know what a sound bomb is, and so he shows me what he claims is part of that bomb.

And he's damn proud of it. If only he could lose another limb or five for the Palestinian cause, there would be no happier man than him in the Western world.

As of now, though, he's not a very happy man. In fact, none of the Scots married to the P Cause is happy. If you are looking for happy

people on Buchanan Street, you have to walk a little bit more, to the stall advertising itself as "Free Qur'an." I can feel their happiness from afar, as their happiness is shedding a big ray of light on Buchanan Street.

I walk over to them.

The Free Qur'an stall is a place where not one Scot is present, not one white man or woman. This stall offers the passing Buchanan Street shoppers an opportunity to get something for free: the Qur'an. Here they don't talk about Palestine, Israel, or bombs. Just Qur'an. They are from Pakistan, Kurdistan, Egypt, and Iraq, and they are here to spread the gospel of Islam every Saturday.

How many passersby pick the free holy book?

"In the winter months the average number of people who take the holy book is between twenty and twenty-five. In the summer months, fifty."

For passersby interested in reading shorter literary materials about Islam, there are various colorful pamphlets to pick, all free of charge.

What's written in these pamphlets?

"A woman in Islam is more respected than in any other community. Islam says that there's no right for terrorism under any conditions. The Bible prophesied the coming of Mohammed, peace be upon him, as the last prophet."

Where did the Bible prophesy this? What book and what verse?

"Song of Suliman [Song of Songs], chapter 5, verse 16," the guy from Kurdistan answers.

Give me the verse!

"The original verse is in Hebrew."

Do you know Hebrew?

"No, I don't know Hebrew, but I can get the verse for you. It's very easy."

He searches for the verse on his iPhone. He searches, searches, and searches. And, finally, he finds a verse he says is about Mohammed. He hands me his iPhone so that I could see for myself. I look at the screen. He doesn't know that I can read Hebrew, and I don't tell him.

I read the verse, Song of Songs, 5:16. "His mouth is full of sweetness. And he is wholly desirable. This is my beloved and this is my friend, O daughters of Jerusalem."

Nothing about Mohammed, and everything about a man of luscious lips.

I look at them, a collection of various Muslims. There are striking differences between this group and the Palestine-loving groups on Buchanan Street, too many to count, but one is outstanding: the Free Qur'an people are full of life. There's no hatred coming out of their mouths, only laughter and words of faith. They are, I believe, the happiest bunch in Scotland. And none of them, let me tell you, is afraid to lose his or her NHS.

I keep on walking, and ahead of me I see a communist stall. I approach them. They are, be it known, sworn enemies of all capitalists. But as much as they hate money, they still try to make a few pounds here and there. What do they sell here? All kinds of *schmontzes*, like pins. The largest and biggest pin here is a Free Palestine pin.

Palestine again.

Well, this is the land of Nessie, isn't it?

Nessie or not, I've had enough of the fake Scottish Palestinians and the real Scottish Jews, and I go to see *Still Alice*, a stage performance piece about a fifty-year-old linguistics professor suffering from early onset dementia, who progressively forgets more and more words as the days go by. *Still Alice* saw life as a novel, then a film, and is presently playing at the Theatre Royal Glasgow. As a theatrical piece, it fails to rise to any level of drama, but as a stage documentary, it achieves what its creators probably envisioned: theatergoers turning into captive eyewitnesses to a painful journey of a woman sliding from her top seat in academia to a bottomless pit of powerlessness.

It's a depressing stage piece, an exhibition of the fragility of man, and a reminder that we are all human beings, made of the same matter, be us Remainers, Leavers, Gentile, or Jew.

Tomorrow I'm going to a food bank.

Do You Have Toilet Paper?

Food Allocation Form: One Person – YELLOW

Cereal – 1 small.

Soup (can/packet) – 2 standard. Beans/spaghetti in sauce – 2 small/1 std. Tomatoes/pasta sauce – 2 small/1 std.

Fish – 1 small. Meat – 2 small/1std.

Or vegetarian – 2 small/1 std. Vegetables – 2 small/1 std.

Fruit – 1 standard.

Rice pudding/custard – 1 standard. Biscuit – 1 small packet.

Pasta/rice/noodles – 500g.

Tea or coffee – 40 bags/small jar. Long-life juice – 1 litre.

Milk UHT – 1 litre.

Extra items when available:

Sauces (CONDIMENTS) – 1 packet. Chocolate – 1 small bar.

Jam (if available) – 1 jar.

Sugar (if needed) – 500g.

Potatoes (ONLY if available) – 1 small. Toilet Roll (only if needed) – 1 roll.

Client signature to confirm food received: X 7.3.R2 One Person Packing List.

Glasgow NW Foodbank.

This is the form that will be filled out by a volunteer at the food bank I'm visiting before a recipient, here known as a "client," will get a bag or two of food consisting of the items listed above. Clients won't get everything listed above, since all items depend on availability. Fresh food, for instance, is seldom available.

It was at the Glasgow synagogue that I was first told about food banks, and now I am in one such bank. The meal they had there and the food items here are a testament to the pockets of extreme poverty in this country, the world's fifth-largest economy by nominal GDP.

Food banks, I'm told by a manager, are meant to give food to the poor only in extreme circumstances, and the giving is not to exceed four times within a six-month period. Also, people cannot just walk in and ask for food, but must have a referral from a social worker, a doctor, the job center, or other agencies catering to the poor, before they show up. Referrals are good for one time only, which means that clients must meet the approval of a professional social worker each time before they ask for food.

What a humiliation.

In the food bank, inside a local church, I see about ten clients waiting for their turn to meet a volunteer who will decide if they are to come out of here empty-handed or with plastic bags containing canned food, toilet paper, or whatever is available today. The average age of the clients, if I judge correctly, is thirty-five. In appearance, none of them betrays their financial hardships, as all of them are dressed well, though modestly, and look healthy as well.

To fill out the form, a volunteer interviews the prospective client and then decides which items to check. I observe a few interviews, the last of which is with a young man.

> – Do you want coffee, tea? Yes.
> – Do you need shampoo? No.
> – Do you have toilet paper? Yes.
> – Toothpaste? I'll take.
> – Milk, do you want milk? Yes.

Today, lucky him, this food bank has toothpaste to offer.

At the end of the interview, the young man receives a yellow slip, and the now filled-out form is sent to the next room.

As he waits for his food bag, he's given a cup of hot tea and two slices of toasted white bread.

The whole process is done in dignity and respect, and the clients seem satisfied by the way they're treated. But it's heartbreaking to watch, and I decide not to interview any of them.

I talk only to the manager instead.

About 20 percent of the clients here, he tells me, come more than four times in six months – some even twice a week. The food bank will serve everybody who comes with a referral, no matter how often the client shows up. This particular food bank is open for two hours, twice a week, serving on average twenty-five clients.

The volunteers working here offer additional assistance to the poor, such as advising them on how to apply for Universal Credit, the government's social benefit payment program, which comprises various social benefits under one roof. On a separate table, there are leaflets and pamphlets, mostly dealing with issues concerning the poor. Here I read, for instance, that "13 million people live in poverty in the UK, including 3.6 million children," which translates to a poverty rate of almost 20 percent. If this figure is correct, it is a high rate indeed. In the United States, in comparison, the poverty rate is 12.3 percent, according to the latest available data from the Census Bureau.

I try to imagine what these people must feel. Oh, God.

What will happen to the poor of Scotland if the country becomes independent? I ask a Scot I chance to meet outside the food bank. "We'll be in a big hole," he says. "We get a lot of money from the UK under the Barnett formula," a formula for distributing money between the four nations in the UK, "and if this money dries up, we won't be able to make it."

Is he right? I don't know.

I go for a walk on Glasgow streets and get myself a "sticky toffee pudding," a popular dessert here, and when evening approaches, I slowly make my way to watch the EUFA Nations League game, Scotland versus Israel.

I told the folks of the Scottish Palestine Solidarity Campaign that I would come, and so I do.

The game takes place at Hampden Park, "Scotland's national stadium," in front of an audience of about twenty thousand people, who fill up fewer than half the seats. The audience includes around 150 Hebrew-speaking fans of the Israeli team, some of whom have come here directly from Israel.

Outside the stadium, there are about twenty-five pro-Palestine demonstrators who call for the cancellation of the game. Twenty-five, that's the total number of people that the Scottish Palestine Solidarity Campaign, an organization with an impressive presence in the local media, could muster to bring here. Four years ago, this same organization succeeded in stopping Israeli artists from performing at the Fringe Festival in Edinburgh, but not here. Scottish football associations are not theater companies, and they choose to ignore the boycotters.

So easy, if one only wants it.

Before the game starts, the anthems of both countries are played on the loudspeakers. "Hatikvah," Israel's anthem, is played first, followed by Scotland's anthem. Kind of. Here they don't play "God Save the Queen" but "Flower of Scotland."

> O flower of Scotland
> When will we see
> Your like again
>
> That fought and died for
> Your wee bit hill and glen
> And stood against him

> Proud Edward's army
> And sent him homeward
> To think again…

The Scots, some with kilts, rise up to sing along. This is their protest against England, and they are damn proud to have their own song.

No bother, as they say here.

The game starts well for the Israelis, who kick the first goal during the first ten minutes, but in the end, Scotland beats Israel 3-2. Watching the game live, you can see that both teams are mediocre at best. Neither of them is Bayern München, not even close, but the Scots are better than the Israelis, who play with a staggering lack of skill. "This is too big for us," an Israeli journalist told me before the game even started, and he is right.

Without much fanfare, the game ends after just a bit more than ninety minutes, and the audience quickly spills out of the stadium. All in all, the game lacked professionalism, and the evening was boring at best. Yet, surprisingly, the BBC refers to the game as "a dramatic and angst-ridden night," a description that makes me question the veracity of everything else the BBC reports.

It's time for me to leave Glasgow, a city of beautiful sandstone buildings, residents who speak their own brand of English, five stalls, and one toothpaste. But I'm not leaving Scotland yet. Scotland, my eagle once whispered in my belly button, is the place for love.

Is it?

Let me go until the end of Scotland, less than a hundred miles from here, to find out.

The Kissing Gate by the Motorway

I drive south, direction England, and stop in Dumfries, a town where Scotland's "Greatest Scot of all time," also known as Scotland's Bard, once lived.

This Greatest Scot is none other than Robert Burns, a man who passed away in 1796 but whose memory is alive and kicking to this very day. It was just nine years ago that Scottish TV channel STV asked its viewers to name the Greatest Scot of All Time, and they named Robert Burns.

Robert composed many poems and songs, in both Scots and English, including the famous *To a Mouse*.

> Wee, sleeket, cowran, tim'rous beastie,
> O, what a panic's in thy breastie!
> Thou need na start awa sae hasty,
> Wi' bickerin brattle!
> I wad be laith to rin an' chase thee
> Wi' murd'ring pattle!

The Irish can't take their eyes off rats; the Scots are in love with mice.

Yes, of course. This a lovely poem, no denying it. The man was a great bard, no doubt.

Lover of alcohol, our bard used to go to an inn at the town's center whenever he felt the need to drink or the desire to mate.

That inn is still standing today, and so is the chair on which Robert sat drinking at the inn's bar. Naturally, I go to sit on his chair. Kenny, who works as a communication manager for the town's council, blurts out just before I sit down: "If you sit here, you won't see next week."

I sit, feeling like a bard myself, and then I go upstairs. What's upstairs?

Upstairs is a room, with a bed in it, and that's where Scotland's national treasure mated with his ladies. Bill Clinton would love this room. I enter the room, looking for a ghost of a lady or two, but I can't find any. This is an inn, not the Ballygally Castle.

I go out, looking for my eagle, but I can't see it. Is it in the Highlands?

I don't know, but I talk to it still; eagles have good ears. My eagle: Scotland is soon over, where's the love?

From far, far away the eagle sends words to me. If your soul yearns to meet young women in love, it says, go to Gretna Green, near the Anglo-Scottish border, and there you'll find some of the best.

For hundreds of years, says the eagle, young English teenagers in love would run to Gretna Green, Scotland, to get married. In those days, the legal marriage age in England was twenty-one, but in Scotland it was sixteen. Lovers younger than twenty-one who could not contain the fire of their desire would cross the border into the of village of Gretna Green, the first human habitat on this side of the border, rush to the first Scots in sight, the blacksmiths working in their shop, and get married by a blacksmith. Back then, long before Apple, Brexit, and Theresa May, all you needed to get married was someone to marry you off, and two witnesses.

Would you like to marry me? my eagle asks me.

No, eagle! In the future, when doctors are more advanced and they can perform trans-eagle operations, the procedure that changes humans to eagles, maybe then I'll marry you.

No problem, answers my eagle; enjoy Gretna Green. I'm trying.

Life was good and simple in the old days, I think to myself. But, like all good things, the good and the simple had to end. In 1940, an old lady passing by tells me, the English lowered the legal marriage age, a change that made eloping to Gretna Green obsolete.

Well, not exactly. At some point in time, some visionary businesspeople in Gretna Green found a way to make Gretna Green more successful than it had ever been.

Their idea was absolutely genius, yet simple. Since historically, as well as in various literary works, Gretna Green was known for eloping couples, why not build on that past and rebrand the village as the place of love and romance?

And so it became.

I want to witness how this works in real life.

I enter Gretna Green in my car, and right away I notice the big coach buses in the huge parking lot. People, it seems, come here in droves. Just this morning, I'm told, two thousand people came by to bathe in the river of love of "Gretna Green, the Thrill of the Chase."

The "Thrill of the Chase." Whoever came up with this line should be awarded the Nobel Prize for creative writing.

With such genius of simplicity, no wonder the tourists flock in.

What can they do here? Well, many things; they can eat, drink, shop, and kiss.

Would you like to exchange a kiss? There's a perfect spot for you to do so at this very village. Seriously. If you walk a few steps away from the current tourist-oriented blacksmith shops, you'll reach "The Kissing Gate," a spot just underneath a motorway, where you can kiss and be kissed.

Isn't it romantic to kiss your beloved to the loud sound of passing semitrailers? Yeah!

Some people come here to get married in the former blacksmith shop, which now sells only marriages, in a ceremony to be officiated by a justice of the peace.

Not one of them is sixteen years of age, in case you wonder.

I watch a marriage ceremony of a middle-aged couple in a room that ages ago served as a blacksmith shop. The groom is in traditional Scottish gear – kilt and the rest – and the bride is dressed in white. I don't know why, but she reminds me of Camilla, the Duchess of Cornwall; maybe because these two ladies share a brand of beauty that I can hardly comprehend. In any case, the groom is sweating mightily, repeatedly rubbing his face and forehead, and the bride is expressionless and motionless, as each repeat what the justice of the peace is dictating to them. When this legal part is over, the groom and the bride put their hands on an anvil and a man, a tourism professional, hits the anvil with a big hammer.

Outside Gretna Hall Hotel I meet a young couple, a Scottish man and an American woman. They have come here because it was the easiest way for them to get married, they say to me. They paid for a package deal that includes accommodation, minister, witnesses, rented kilt and dress, registration, wedding cake, wine, and meals.

Noticing the fact that I, unfortunately, have no Scottish accent, the Scot asks me, "Where are you from?" Israel, I answer. This gets him going. "Israel," he says to me, "is a great place, but people don't understand this. People think that Israel is connected to Zionism, which is totally false. Israel has nothing to do with Zionism!"

I don't know if you've noticed by now, my dear, but the Scots, just like the Irish, love to make up stories that have nothing to do with reality. That's who they are, that's their inheritance. And that's why my eagle loves them. Yeah.

Don't tell a soul what I'm about to tell you now. I bought a kilt. Yeah! I pack it nicely, put it in my car, and drive to England. I've got to meet the naked men of Sheffield, and I can't wait!

Adios, Scotland. Hello, England. Here I come!

Asian Women Are Nice

What's here to see? I ask an Englishman as soon as I arrive in Newcastle-upon-Tyne, my first stop in England.

Newcastle-upon-Tyne, Newcastle upon Tyne, and just Newcastle are all the same thing. It's just that the English people, I suspect, want to confuse the rest of us. They think it's funny, I guess.

I'm in Newcastle's city center, between the Tyne Theatre and a place called Help Centre on Westgate Road, and the Englishman points left as he gives me directions. "Up the road, over there, are the foreigners."

If I thought I was on my way to meet the naked men of Sheffield, this man has got some news for me: the foreigners are fully dressed.

I light up a cigarette, quite an expensive commodity in the UK, when a deliveryman on a bike – who seems to me to be Muslim – approaches me.

"Did you order pizza?"

Not yet, my dear. Maybe tomorrow I'll order, inshallah.

"Are you Muslim?"

What else could I be?

"Welcome, brother."

What are you doing here, in the land of the infidels?

"Money."

Money for what?

"I want to get for myself an Asian wife and take her with me to my home, to Turkey."

Those Asian girls, brother, are expensive! Did you save enough money?

"I worked for five years and I saved £10,000, but I don't have it anymore."

What happened?

"Last year I took my savings of five years, £10,000, and played slot machines in the casino. After two hours, I lost all my money."

No Asian lady for you, my brother.

"I'll work another five years, get an Asian woman, and go back home. Asian women are nice, ah?"

Very nice!

The Turkish man mounts his bike and moves on. I go to the Help Centre. I'm curious.

The first thing I see as I enter the centre is five words in big gold letters, "Jesus Christ is the Lord," prominently displayed on the front wall. There are about two hundred seats in the hall, but fewer than ten participants at the moment, mostly black people. Is this an African church? No, it's a Brazilian church. Our base is in Brazil, one of the attendants tells me.

I join the service. Why not? The pastor, who speaks English in a foreign accent, encourages us to read a couple of verses projected on a screen: "Or do you not know what the Scripture says of Elijah, how he pleads with God against Israel, saying, 'Lord, they have killed Your prophets and torn down Your altars...'"

I take a photo of the screen, and the pastor tells me that taking pictures is not permitted at this establishment. I apologize and take no more photos.

The pastor goes on. He tells us that if we really want to succeed in life, we should give to the church, meaning him, 10 percent of all our earnings.

This Help Center, I see, is geared to help the pastor.

I get up and walk to the exit, but just before I reach the exit door, I'm stopped by an employee of the church, who demands that I erase the photo I took. "Right now, in front of my eyes," he orders me.

What's the problem?

"You photographed me."

No, I did not.

"I want to see the photo."

I show him the photo.

"Erase it!"

I walk out.

Across the street from the church is an Amnesty International bookstore, Books for Amnesty. I go there.

A poster hangs on the wall at the entrance: "Millions of Palestinians will be DENIED human rights today and every day. Help stop 50 years of suffering and oppression for Palestinian families."

Ireland, Northern Ireland, Scotland, and now England: Palestine rules supreme. Don't these people have anything else to occupy their brains with? How about Brexit, my sweeties?

Brian, the man in charge of the store, takes his time to talk to me.

What's bad in the world and how do we fix it? I ask him, just so, as if he were the secretary-general of the United Nations.

"I don't know," he answers, and immediately adds: "It's human rights, about people being criticized for their gender."

I want him to give me more than just gender issues, and so I ask him: Which is the worst country that needs to be – ?

"I can't say which is the worst country."

Give me the five worst countries that have to change, I ask of him, as if he were one of those students in St. Andrews.

He gives me three: China, Uganda, and Turkey. "China has executed a lot of people; being gay in Uganda is illegal; the chairman of Amnesty in Turkey was arrested lately."

This is the Zeitgeist. Human rights organizations are being put on pedestals, and gay rights are humanity's highest goal. Not that I have anything against gay rights but, with all due respect, there are more important issues in our world. As we speak, tens of thousands of people are being tortured inside Turkish prisons for no crime whatsoever, including journalists and judges, but that's not as important as Mr. Chairman. Hundreds of thousands of people are being slaughtered in Syria, Sudan, and Yemen, but that's not as important as two penises on the same bed.

That said, I do understand why Amnesty needs chairmen, but why does it need a bookstore? To raise money, Brian explains to me. How does it work? Very simple. People donate books to the store, other people buy them, and Amnesty gets the pounds.

Are all book donations accepted? No; racist books won't be accepted. How about Adolf Hitler's *Mein Kampf*? Yes, *Mein Kampf* will be accepted, because it has historic value. *The Protocol of the Elders of Zion*? That too, for the same reason. But no porno books.

What's the story with the "millions of Palestinians," Brian?

"Amnesty has very close ties with the PSC, Palestine Solidarity Campaign."

Tell me about it.

"I don't want to talk about the Palestinians, it's too complicated to get involved with."

He has statements hanging on the wall about the Palestinians, claiming that they are being denied human rights today and every day, but it's too complicated to discuss.

I leave his store and go to visit the lord mayor, the Honorable David Down, at his chambers in the Civic Centre of Newcastle-upon-Tyne.

He might be less complicated.

On the short corridor leading to His Honor's chambers, I spot the coroner's office. Why, in heaven's name, do you have the coroner's office next to you?

"With the budgetary cuts to the City Council finances," His Honor replies, "there are various areas of the Civic Center which can be used by other agencies, such as the coroner's. We do get requests to be very quiet when we're walking through because, of course, the coroner may be sitting and listening to an inquest about the cause of death of an individual, which is a very traumatic event and occasion for families and therefore there's need to concentrate on the inquest and not be disturbed."

I love how this man answers a simple question! Is this the British way to answer a question? Go figure.

What's special about Newcastle? I ask this Brit.

"We welcome people. We welcome refugees and asylum seekers."

"Up the road, over there, are the foreigners," the Englishman told me upon my arrival to this city. They must love foreigners here, or maybe they just pretend. Allah knows.

What's the level of poverty in the city? I ask His Honor.

"It's quite high. The increase in need for food banks has increased greatly in the last few years." What's the percentage of people in Newcastle who live below the poverty line?

At this, David asks me to go off the record. This question, he says to me, is a political question and he, as the lord mayor of all the people, should be apolitical.

Why would such a question be treated as a political issue?

I'm not sure, but this is my guess: In 2010, the Tory-led government introduced an austerity program, which aimed to reduce the national deficit through reductions in social spending and an increase in tax collection. The Labour Party, and others, have argued that the austerity program, which the present Tory leader Theresa May only recently pledged to end, is responsible for the high level of poverty in the country. The Conservatives, on the other hand, argue that poverty would have been much more severe had Labour been in power all these years. It is within that political framework, perhaps, that the issue of poverty in this country could be construed as a political matter.

Too complicated.

Excluding the poverty issue, the lord mayor is happy to talk about any topic there is. For example, his city. Newcastle, he says, is a great place for art and culture. I should, he tells me, visit Theatre Royal and Tyne Theatre.

Another issue he'll gladly discuss is casinos, one of which I noticed on my way to His Honor, a stone's throw away from a pawnshop.

"The government is now agreeing to reduce the maximum bet you can have on the slot machines from £100 to £2."

What else should I discuss with the lord mayor? I ask myself. Nothing much is happening in Newcastle, as far as I can tell, other than a Turk dreaming of an Asian, a Brazilian in search of my pockets, and an Amnesty devoted to penises and Palestinians, P&P for short.

Newcastle, not being London, does not usually feature on international news pages, but a couple of months ago, it actually did. It happened after protestors had stormed a meeting of the Newcastle City Council, a rare occurrence as far as I know. According to the *Daily Mirror*, the protesters "opposed Newcastle City Council's adoption of the International Holocaust Remembrance Alliance definition of anti-Semitism." As defined by IHRA, "denying the Jewish people their right to self-determination, e.g., by claiming that the existence of a State of Israel is a racist endeavor," is a form of anti-Semitism, among some others. The protestors, pro-Palestinian Communists, tried to prevent the council from adopting such a definition.

Council leader Nick Forbes was quoted by the BBC as saying, "Many of the councillors felt intimidated, several were in tears."

His Honor knows about this story firsthand.

"I was chairing the meeting. The City Council, along with many other councils in the country, were asked to consider and vote on whether they accepted the IHRA's definition. When we began debating, the protestors began making a loud noise and protesting in the public gallery, and on the advice of the legal officer to the Council, the meeting was adjourned." Twenty-five minutes later, the Council resumed the meeting and decided unanimously "to accept the definition as set out."

Why is such a resolution, about anti-Semitism, being put to a vote now?

"There's been a rise in anti-Semitism in the country quite markedly in many places in the last three to five years."

The lord mayor, let me share with you, has official clothes for special occasions. No, it's not a kilt, but clothes much grander. They include a black three-pointed hat, a beard made of cloth, gold necklaces, a blood-red gown, a sword, and some other gimmicks. I put his hat on my head – I can't resist it – and he gives me the rest of his accouterments to try out. I put them on. What a feeling! I've never

felt English, until now. And as far as I can tell, I look much better than Prince Charles. Really. This attire, let me share with you, is very theatrical. A moment ago, I was a normal human being, but now I am a mayor. Yeah!

Could it be, I ask myself, that English actors are such good performers – at least as far as I know, mostly from past years – because they are surrounded, from birth, by high class costumes?

As I've already mentioned on these pages, years back I used to fly to London for a couple of days at a time just to see theater. How come, I asked myself again and again, English actors are so good at pretending that they are what they are not? Hopefully, now that I'm in this country for a much longer period of time, I'll discover the root of their immense talent.

Come evening, I'll try to attend a performance in one of the theaters His Honor recommended.

As of now, the sun is shining, and it's time to explore the mayor's assertion about anti-Semitism. Gateshead, a town of over 100,000 residents, is across the Tyne River from Newcastle. It is also the abode of one of Europe's most renowned Jewish rabbinical semi-naries, the Gateshead Yeshiva, and it will be interesting to see if the Jews living there indeed experience anti-Semitism.

Sheffield can wait, I think. I'll get there sooner or later.

Jake, who studies biomedical science at the Newcastle University, prepares me for the road.

A few months ago, he tells me, the Mechanical Engineering Society at Newcastle University distributed white T-shirts to its members, and students were encouraged to write whatever they wanted on their T-shirts or on their friends' T-shirts.

What did they write?

"Swastikas and anti-Semitic hate slogans."

Oy Vey, a Boy Looks at a Girl

Centuries ago, the Prophet Mohammed called the Jews the Nation of the Book, so naturally the first place I'm looking for once in Gateshead is a bookstore.

Not an easy task. I look left and right, up and down, and all I see is a bakery here and a barber there, this store and that, but no bookstores. Zilch. Nada.

Was Mohammed wrong?

Well, not really. There is a bookstore, a fourteen-year-old boy tells me, right ahead of us. I look for it but see no bookstore, not even a trace of one. The boy suggests that I follow him, which I dutifully do, and in a few seconds, he and I are inside a bookstore. The exterior of the bookstore does not resemble a bookstore, or any store whatever, as the shutters are down, and there's no sign of anything in sight. As strange as it might sound, the owners of this bookstore are doing everything they can to hide the store by all means possible.

Why would any business owner hide the establishment? This is a bookstore, not a heroin distribution center or a pedophile entertainment complex. Why hide? I ask the salesperson, a religious Jew wearing a hat and sporting a beard. "Because we live in the Diaspora," he tells me.

People here don't like to talk about it, and some will deny it altogether, he says, but anti-Semitic acts are routine in this area. The
shutters of this bookstore are down because otherwise the store
would be vandalized by anti-Semites. Just a couple of days ago, a
book shopper wandering in the store tells me, someone yelled at
him "Dirty Jew!" Another customer says he was violently pushed
aside when walking on the street the other day, and the attacker
yelled "Jew." People here are afraid and ashamed, a young Jewish
man tells me, and only very few admit what's going on in this part
of the world. "You won't see any of it in the media," a young man
outside the store tells me, "but anti-Semitism is a big problem here."

The boy who accompanied me to the bookstores, wearing a black
yarmulke on his head, stands in front of me now and gives me the
Heil Hitler salute.

He thinks it's funny.

The Jews I meet in Gateshead are religious, members of the
Orthodox branch of Judaism, and they eat only kosher food. The

grocery in the center, selling expensive kosher food, offers many goods imported from Israel. The non-imported food, such as their English gefilte fish and cookies, which I try out, are for the most part less tasteful than sand.

I walk over to the Gateshead Yeshiva, the most prominent British yeshiva, but I can't walk in. Unlike similar rabbinical seminaries I've visited in the United States and in Israel, this one requires a passcode at the entrance door. I stand outside, looking at the young people coming in and going out, and within minutes, a number of students start gathering around me. They want to know what this non-Jew, yours truly, wants from their life. I answer them in Yiddish and Hebrew, and immediately they calm down.

We schmooze, about this and that, and they tell me about their way of life. No student is allowed to have or use a smartphone, but there are landline phones in the yeshiva for students to make calls. Smartphones offer temptations, God save us, and Satan hides inside them. Yeah. But beware: even if no iPhone is in sight, Satan still roams around, especially in restaurants. Not in Gateshead, of course. There are no restaurants in the Jewish part of Gateshead, because in a restaurant, God forbid, boys could look at girls, God save us, and dream of them at night, which could potentially stop the sun from shining in the morning.

Before long, the head of security approaches me. He was called in, he tells me, to verify my identity. "Here we must be careful," the man says.

Suddenly, there's a big commotion among the students. The door of the yeshiva opens, and the *rosh yeshiva* (rabbinical dean), an old man carrying books, comes out. The students clear the way, in awe, to make room for their leader to pass through. The rabbi stops next to me, shakes my hand, and looks at me with his two penetrating eyes. I ask him how life is in the UK. "We are living in the Diaspora," he responds, and his face turns sad.

I ask the students what "living in the Diaspora" means. What happened in the past, they say, can happen again. What happened in the past?

In 1190, they tell me, the entire Jewish community of York, 150 people, were massacred. The butchery, known as the York Pogrom, took place at Clifford's Tower, located near an area known as Jewbury.

Jewbury. What a word.

One hundred years later, in 1290, the students go on telling me, King Edward I issued an Edict of Expulsion, expelling all the Jews from the Kingdom of England. This edict was overturned only 367 years later.

That's the story of the past. The Jews of the present day, mindful of the constant news about anti-Semitism in Britain's mainstream party these days, are living in fear, ever afraid that they will be slaughtered once more.

Meantime, they eat their horrible food that tastes like sand. What a curse!

Do I feel pity for them? Not at all. They have the choice, every day of their lives, to move out of here, but they don't. "Life is comfortable here," they tell me. As far as I can tell, they need a psychiatrist.

I return to Newcastle and go to the one still-functioning Jewish house of prayer. The synagogue, which takes me some time to find, doesn't look like a synagogue but like a high-security prison. Actually, worse than that. First off, there's a big, high fence surrounding it. This is not to prevent any prisoner from leaving the compound, but to prevent those outside from breaking in and damaging the place. Then there's the synagogue itself. There's no name on the building to identify it as a synagogue, not even a Star of David. Just stones, steps, and walls. The Jews here, you see, are hiding. A temple doesn't look like a temple, a bookstore doesn't look like a bookstore, and the food stinks. What a comfortable life!

Have you ever seen those people, Lord Mayor? They are your neighbors, people living in a cage of their own creation, spending their days in denial, finding their comfort in the deepest halls of darkness, shutters down.

I leave the Jews and go to Theatre Royal, to attend a performance. I know not a thing about this theater, but its exterior, which resembles a palace, is awe-inspiring. Definitely not a Jewish house of prayer; the Royal folks are very happy to publicize their building.

What's on this evening? *Goldilocks and the Three Bears*, which is the name of one of England's best-known fairy tales. Is this a fairy tale performance? According to the Royal, *Goldilocks* is "the greatest panto on earth."

Goldilocks and her bears, I'm told, is actually a Christmas show, a British Christmas show, of the British pantomime genre.

I walk in.

The Broadway-size theater is packed with adults and children. *Goldilocks* is not a play, nor a musical, but a genre all its own. At this particular production, the audience is entertained by circus-style performances, including breathtaking motorbike races, classic comedy routines, special effects, and various hair-raising acrobatics.

All in all, this show is a far cry from the original fairy tale, but nobody here cares. The audience, young and old, love every second of it.

Text-wise, *Goldilocks* is very weak. Performance-wise, it's acting at its best. The people on this stage can sell you anything, twenty dead bears and the Brooklyn Bridge, and you'll never know you've been duped.

I watch the actors onstage, overwhelmed by their brilliant ability to infuse meaning and emotion into the most banal of lines, and it dawns on me that their forefathers, the world's colonizers, must have had the same talent. No wonder, it now occurs on me, that Amnesty International was founded in this country. If anyone knows how to create mountains out of thin air, it's the people born here.

Who are these people? Who are the English people? Do they stand for anything unique?

Maybe, maybe not. In any case, there's a big shopping heaven about one hundred miles south of here, in Leeds, and nobody there has their shutters down. What a relief! Let me go there, let me please my eyes with images of shops well lit and well displayed.

Yeah. Let's witness the miracle of normalcy! Sheffield: I've not forgotten thee.

Santa Claus's Wife

With each passing day, I get more and more used to driving on the left side. It's a learning process, just like trying to understand the various accents and dialects of English-speakers on this island. I'll never forget my struggle to understand a Scottish guy who kept talking to me about his *aursh*.

What's an *aursh*? I kept asking him, and he kept answering, "*Aursh. Aursh. AURSH!*" It took me a while, but then I got it: horse. The funny thing is that when a few days later, someone talked to me about a horse, initially I didn't get what he was saying. What's a horse?

Same thing in driving. I'm getting used to driving on the left, and it makes perfect sense to me, but I hope that I won't drive on the left back home.

I don't constantly drive. When I'm in big cities, I leave the car in a garage and use Uber; it saves me time because I don't have to find parking places. Do I enjoy Uber here? I'm loving it, as the McDonald's ad goes.

At the moment, I'm driving. I have a Hyundai i800, and it does the job.

One of the pleasures of driving is the freedom to be guided by your nose. I "smell" something, I drive there, and then I stop. At this very moment, I stop in Durham, not far from a group of ladies wearing yellow stars. Who are they, and what are they doing? Are they waiting for some trains to take them to certain camps?

I ask them.

No, no; they have nothing to do with "that" yellow star. Their yellow star, they tell me, is the logo of Rock Choir, of which they are members. I ask them to sing something for me, and they gladly do.

> Noel, Noel, Noel, Noel
> Born is the King of Israel!

The people of the British Isles have a little obsession with Israel and Jews, be they religious or atheist, but I must admit that I enjoy listening to these ladies. They are so lovable!

We chat for a while, and one of them asks me if I've already been to the romantic city of Richmond. The Richmonders, she also tells me, have a great Christmas market.

I'm a sucker for anything romantic, and I'm back in my driver's seat faster than a Tomahawk missile.

Santa Claus, I imagine as I drive, will show up with his wife in romantic Richmond's Christmas market. To see her will be a great honor for me, of course, since Santa's wife is the one Christian who was never, ever reported, at any time whatsoever, to have said or done anything anti-Semitic.

I can't wait to see her.

I arrive in Richmond before any missile, but armored vehicles have arrived before me. Yes.

There's no Mrs. Claus around, I sadly notice. In fact, Mr. Claus is nowhere in sight either. What I see instead are soldiers from the 5th Regiment Royal Artillery (the Yorkshire Gunners). They are in romantic Richmond, at the Christmas market, together with their armored vehicles, and they invite me to mount their armored toys so that I may feel how great it is to serve the country.

Next to them are soldiers from the Royal Dragoon Guards, some of whom have served in Iraq and Afghanistan, but they can't tell me what exactly they were doing there that changed anything.

A few feet away, I see a man taking photos of soldiers.

What do you think of these soldiers when you look at them?

"They make me feel safe."

Did you tell them that?

He looks in their direction with admiring eyes, and says, "They know it!"

Paula, an English lady walking by, tells me that she's very proud to be English. No, she's not proud to be a UK citizen, she emphasizes, because she doesn't see herself as a UK woman. She is an Englishwoman, and that's what she's proud of. English. England. Period. She couldn't care less about the Irish or the Scots. There are English morals out there, but not British morals, and she loves English morals. No, she's NOT British, she's English. English people are ethical, possess high morals, and have the greatest history. Full stop.

I make a little detour on my way to Leeds, as I've done with Sheffield, and drive to Clifford's Tower in York, England's ancient capital of the North, to examine English morals up close.

Funny Dead Jews

Clifford's Tower, an imposing structure surrounded by green grass, is situated on top of a very high hill. At the base of the hill, to the left of the many steps leading to the tower's top, I spot a memorial tablet, a plaque, which is quite easy to miss. It was installed in 1978, and it reads as follows:

> On the night of Friday 16 March 1190 some 150 Jews and Jewesses of York having sought protection in the Royal Castle on this site from a mob incited by Richard Malebisse and others chose to die at each other's hands rather than renounce their faith.
>
> ☒☒☒☒☒ ☒☒☒☒☒☒ ☒☒☒☒ '☒☒ ☒☒☒☒☒
> [Let them give glory to the Lord and proclaim his praise in the islands.]
> Isaiah XLII 12

The story, as described here, is one version of many about what really happened in this place. What all versions of the story agree on is the fact that 150 Jews were forced to meet death by the people of York. This happened long, long ago, but was kept in the dark for many, many years. It took the people of York 788 years to share this chapter of their history with the public, and when they finally did, the memorial plaque they have produced is of the kind that most people wouldn't stop to read.

Why are Yorkies hiding a centuries-old story? Don't ask me.

A gentle-looking English couple is passing by. Do you know what this is? I ask them. "A castle on a hill," the woman answers.

I point to the plaque on the left, and they come over to look at it. The lady reads and tells me that she has never read this before. "I've been here two or three times, but I've never seen it."

What do you feel, now that you've seen it? "Something to think about," she says and walks away.

I approach another couple, walking down the steps, and I point to the plaque. The man walks over and reads.

Any feelings, any emotions? I ask the man, once he's done reading.

He smiles, and then says: "Not particularly."

Do you feel nothing about it?

"Not really."

Another couple passes by, and I guide them to the plaque. Would they read the plaque and tell me what they think? I ask.

The man reads, word for word.

"Wow," he says when he's done reading.

Did you know about this story?

"No."

How do you feel about it?

The man, native of Manchester, answers: "Bad, innit?" (Bad, isn't it?)

He goes on: "No one should die for the belief in their faith. Regardless. Should they?"

This is part of the history of York; they killed all the Jews here.

"I didn't know about it."

They didn't teach it in school?

"No. They only teach you what they want you to know."

What do they teach you in school?

"They teach you history, but they don't teach anything like that. Not once." He looks at the plaque and says: "It's quite sad. No better than Adolf, was it?"

Do you know that the Jews were banned from this country for hundreds of years?

No, they never heard anything like that.

"We know about Hitler," the woman says, "but we don't know about our country."

Are you English? I ask a man walking around with a camera.

Yes, he is.

I get him to read the plaque and ask for his thoughts and feelings.

"It's interesting," he says, with a little smirk on his face.

Does it say anything to you?

"Not really."

Another couple passes by. I ask them to read the plaque. And they do.

What do you think?

"It's a nice thing to do," the man answers.

Does this make you feel anything?

"It puts us to shame, as British citizens," the woman says.

"Um, what is this about? 150 Jews that died?" the man asks, smilingly.

For him, I guess, this is a funny joke.

I wonder: Is this what Paula of Richmond meant when she spoke about English morals?

What happened in the past, the Gateshead students said, can happen again. Meantime, though, it's time for shopping.

Shop Till You Are Cremated

Late at night in the first week of December, the temperature reaches zero Celsius, but the young ladies of the prestigious University of Leeds parade in almost Full Monty in front of the Marriot Hotel in Leeds, where they are having a big party.

All told, counting female and male, there are 277 of them; all are white, skinny, and seemingly rich, and they are celebrating their various achievements of the year about to end. They are laughing louder than Nessie, shouting louder than anyone in Bogside, and they are drunk. With their bikini-like clothes, the young females show off their white bodies, while the young males are showing off their tailored suits. As the clock keeps advancing in the freezing night, some young males "scoop" some of the girls the way fishermen catch lobsters, while others get busy fondling a girl's breasts.

These students are, let there be no doubt, the elite of England.

Two blocks away, at a McDonald's restaurant, I see a group of young teenagers. They are all black, and not one of them is showing off skin.

That's my introduction to Leeds, in black and white. Are there more colors in between?

The next day I go to chat with Judith Blake, the leader of the City Council.

Judith, a member of the Labour Party, tells me that Leeds is seeing a "dramatic growth in private sector jobs. We have opened two significant shopping centers, Trinity and Victoria Gate," in addition to the other four shopping malls that already exist in the city center. Leeds, Judith wants me to know, has "one of the most significant shopping centers in the country."

How many people in Leeds live below the poverty line? I ask her. God knows why this particular question came out of my lips.

"I'm sorry, that figure is not in my head," she replies.

I understand that you have a strong interest in the Middle East. Is that correct? (Truth be told, I've no such information; it's just a wild guess.)

"Yeah. How did you know?" she answers, really surprised. "I spent quite a lot of time in the Middle East, after I left the university. I spent a lot of time in Egypt, Syria, and Jordan, and I traveled a lot to Israel recently as well. So, it's a personal interest."

There are people here, I can tell by the shape of their eyebrows, who have nothing better to do in life than be busy with Palestine, Israel, Jews, Egypt, Syria, Jordan, and then one more round of Jews.

Anyway, since she's interested in the issue, let me ask her about it.

From your perspective, I ask the leader, whose fault is it that we don't have peace in the Middle East? Is it the fault of the Israelis or of the Palestinians?

Her Honor refuses to answer this question.

There's one thing I don't get about many UK people: their lack of spine. Instance after instance, one person after another, I keep encountering gutlessness. Be it a reverend or a soldier, an artist or a scientist, a student or a politician. And then there is Ephraim Mirvis, the chief rabbi of the UK, who is another brave man. He won't meet me because his schedule is "stacked up for the coming months." The former chief rabbi, Lord Jonathan Sacks, won't meet me either, because he, too, refuses to be interviewed by me. Both rabbis are afraid, I was told, that I would expose them. Expose what? Are these two rabbis parading naked in some decrepit factory in Sheffield?

Maybe. I'll see soon.

The affable Gerald Jennings, of the Leeds Chamber of Commerce, is different. He's a busy man – he sits on all kinds of boards in addition to being busy with his own real estate business – but he feels confident enough to sit down with me.

We talk about trade and commerce, Britain and the world, and he tells me that the malls in the city center of Leeds are frequented by thirty million visitors a year. Wow! That's thirty times the number of people who go to visit Nessie. I think I should open a store here, Princess Di Sweets & Kisses.

I get intrigued and go to the malls. A tour guide, provided by a city agency, is accompanying me.

We walk around, here and there, one mall after the other, and at some points my guide even helps me shop. I want new shoes, I tell him, and he asks me how much I want to spend. Money is no issue, I say to him. Take me to the best of the best!

He takes me to a Church's store.

An elegantly dressed Church's salesman shows me some shoes, with the average price of £1,000 a pair.

I own a pair of Clarks, I tell the salesman, and I love them. They cost me £89. What does Church's offer that Clarks does not?

He looks at me as if I were from some undesirable and untouchable caste in India, and says: "If that's your category, then – " and motions with his hand downwards, direction garbage, to show me my place.

My guide smiles. He would pay this kind of money for a car, not a shoe.

How did the malls of Leeds start? I ask him. Who started the malls, and who opened the first store?

The answer – listen carefully – is this: A Jew and a Jew. Yeah. This is not a typo. A Jew and a Jew. Two Jews. Thus says the guide, a man who is a complete gentile.

He tells me the story as we enter Kirkgate Market.

It all started right here, with a Jew named Michael Marks. Michael was very good with money – he had a natural talent for it– and he was also an excellent salesman. One day, this brilliant moneyman had an idea: Why not create an entity that sells various products, all at the same price, one penny? Thomas Spencer, a non-Jew, realized the extraordinary money talents of Michael Marks, and he invested in him.

Thusly started what later would become the miracle of marketing, the Penny Bazaar.

Have you seen, my dear, those pound, euro, and dollar stores? Well, they all started as a thought in the head of a Jew.

Michael put his merchandise on a wheelbarrow, walked around with it, and shouted: "Anybody want to buy something for a penny? Everything here's one penny!"

The wheelbarrow soon became a stall, the stall turned into a store, and the store into a chain – the world-famous M&S, Marks & Spencer.

Yep. Now you know!

The Jews, my guide tells me, were the biggest traders in Leeds. They were smart, and they understood money. They concentrated on men's fashion because men's fashion doesn't change much and is easy to tailor. They let the traders of Manchester, known gentiles, deal with women's fashion.

Smart Jews! Do you hear me, Jeremy Corbyn?

Who is the second Jew of Jew & Jew? I ask my guide.

Arnold Ziff, he says.

What did AZ do? Well, the first shopping mall in Europe was founded, in Leeds, by Arnold Ziff. He went to America, saw the malls there, built by other Jews, and he brought the concept here.

Ahead of us, as we walk the shopping malls of Leeds, is Next, a British retailer. Next, my guide points out to me, is owned by the billionaire Sir Philip Green, a Jew involved in financial scandals.

We reach the Victoria Gate mall, where I can buy the Maserati Levante Gransport, starting at only £69,425.

If you already own a car, how about a handbag? Louis Vuitton's high-priced store for bags could be the answer to your prayers. I notice something interesting here, by the way: all shoppers are white, and two guards, both black, stand at the door to keep the undesirables out. This is diversity at its best.

The most frequented mall is the Trinity, which is adjacent to a church.

David Madison, Trinity's general manager, tells me that this mall is geared for people with a disposable income of £800 a month.

All in all, the malls are great places to be while in Leeds. Some of the malls, especially the older ones, are an architectural delight, and all offer a great and magical excuse to buy more or to dream of more. What a wonderful tribute to the Jews of old.

Are the Jews living in Leeds today the same as their ancestors? Intrigued, I go to visit the Jewish Community Centre in Leeds.

When I arrive, the Jews are having a party; there are thirty of them altogether, with the youngest being about seventy years of age. The song "All You Need Is Love" is playing on the loudspeaker, and here is this lady, older than God, dancing with her walker.

It's one of those rare moments in life when I don't know whether to smile or to cry.

I talk with some of the old Jews, and they tell me that they feel very welcome by their fellow non-Jews.

Great.

When talking with them more at length, however, they change their tune. "It's inbred in them [non-Jews] to hate us" is how one lady puts it to me.

These Jews are quite similar to the Jews of Scotland. When you start talking to them, they tell you that everything is great. But if you continue talking to them, they tell you that everything is a disaster.

When I talk with them even more, they tell me a story about Bradford, a neighboring city.

A few years ago, four or five, a Bradford politician by the name of George Galloway declared Bradford an "Israel-free zone," demanding that no Israeli visit the city.

What's so great about Bradford, I wonder, that Israeli Jews would lose by not showing up there? Do they sell the higher-priced Maserati Levante?

Let's find out.

Driving from Leeds to Bradford in the evening hours, I can tell where one city ends and the other starts. There are fewer lights on the streets of Bradford, the infrastructure is of a lesser quality, and the smell of poverty enters my nostrils to immediate effect.

I get out of the car.

Most of the stores in front of me are closed, but a music shop, where one can buy or repair various instruments, is open.

Nobody is in the store except for one man, Malcolm, who'll sell me a functioning accordion for £300 to £600, depending on make, size, and quality.

Seventy-five percent of the stores in Bradford, Malcom tells me, are permanently closed. People live in destitution; everything's down except for unemployment, crime, gang membership, and drug availability.

I leave the depressed man behind and stroll the streets of Bradford.

What do I see? Shuttered stores, but inside them are no books. This is not Gateshead, where the Jews fill the streets; this is Bradford, where no Jew or Israeli is welcome. Muslims, by the way, are quite welcome here, and many actually call the place home.

I keep on strolling until I find businesses that are still in operation: casinos. These are casinos for the poor, like the Turkish pizza deliveryman in Newcastle. Here the poor can bury the little money they have.

For the "native" residents, those who are not Muslim, there's an open shop here: a crematorium funeral home and services. Yep. "The very best funeral care at an affordable price," as the owners claim.

In case you're interested, let me share some details with you. You can be cremated here for £595, much cheaper than a Maserati. This service is called Purely Cremation and includes the following: "Dignified and private funeral, no mourners or celebrant, straightforward funeral with minimum fuss." You can upgrade to another service, called Cortege to a Place of Worship, which will cost you only £1,900 to £3,455. Your fee will cover the following: "Hearse to transport your loved one to an address of your choice for onward cortege to the crematorium, our attendance at the place of worship and the crematorium or burial place, family conveyed to home or venue of your choice after the funeral."

If you're an Israeli Jew, find yourself another place to be cremated.

There's another store, if this can be classified as a store, that's open: UK Armed Forces recruitment station. If you don't plan to die soon and are fed up with the crime and darkness around you, you can join the armed forces of the United Kingdom.

A "Be a Yorkshire Warrior!" poster hangs high on the wall inside. Yes, lemme be!

Starting yearly salary: around £15,000 – good enough for fifteen pairs of shoes at Church's.

The officer stationed here tells me that he can't wait for his pension to kick in, two years from now, after having served the best years of his life protecting his fellow citizens.

How much will you get? "About £1,000 a month."

This translates into a disposable income of zero, which effectively makes Leeds a soldier-free zone.

God bless the Queen.

The rain starts pouring down mercilessly on the streets of Bradford, and I need a food break. Is there any restaurant around here, between the warriors and the cremated?

A Pakistani man crosses the street to my left, and he seems to be in a hurry, but my belly recognizes no manners and strenuously demands that I stop the Pakistani to inquire about food.

Excuse me, is there any Pakistani or Afghani restaurant around here?

Hearing the urgency in my voice, the man stops despite the pouring rain. He looks at me, examines my face, listens to my belly, and asks: "Are you Muslim?"

Certainly!

He looks at me again, examining my face a bit closer to see where the Pakistani starts and the Afghani ends.

He can't find the resemblance.

He thinks. Then an idea comes to him. "Are you an Arab?" he asks.

Can't you tell? I'm Arab pure!

"Would you like an Arabic restaurant?"

Only if it's halal!

"Halal, halal! Come I'll show you." I follow him.

We walk a bit, getting ever wetter, and suddenly he stops. I see no restaurant.

"Upstairs," he tells me. "The restaurant is upstairs." I walk upstairs.

What can I say? None of the people at this restaurant is a Yorkshire warrior, and they will never be, but oh, boy, do they know how to cook!

I stick around with the Arabs for over an hour and enjoy my meal, every bit and bite. Price tag, which includes the fee for half a chicken, two cans of icy Diet Coke, extra hot tea, and sweets: £4.50.

With my belly full, it's finally time for the Full Monty, the original!

The Full Monty

PM Theresa May is to present her Brexit Withdrawal Agreement at the House of Commons tomorrow, or so she says. The probability of its approval by the MPs is 0 percent, but until today she has said that she would present it anyway.

Well, not really. Today, facing the reality of zero success, and 100 percent humiliation, she decides not to present it.

The House of Commons is boiling. MP after MP rises to say that the prime minister has shown disrespect for Parliament, and for the MPs, because they especially came to London to vote on Brexit, and she is denying them their right to do so.

These MPs, mostly of the opposition, are pissed off that she made them show up in their place of employment, the Parliament. Christmas is coming, and they could have been somewhere else, in Richmond perhaps, but they are in London.

To watch them complain about the PM, as if she had emotionally and physically abused them, is to witness a theatrical performance in a kindergarten.

They behave like babies.

I think they all should relocate to the Scottish Parliament building, where the main hall looks like a kindergarten. It'll be such a great fit!

Most of these babies, as you might have expected, just want to vote No. That's all. They are too small to come up with anything else.

Theresa May's 585-page Brexit proposal, *Draft Withdrawal Agreement*, was made available to anyone wishing to read it a month ago. Her detractors, including those in her party, have each come up with a Brexit plan zero pages long.

The drama in the House of Commons goes on and on, and at times it takes bizarre turns. One of the babies there, for example, Labour MP Lloyd Russell-Moyle, takes an extra step to register his frustration at Mama for making him show up at work. He picks up the mace, the ceremonial item in the House that represents the queen, something he knows he shouldn't be doing, and tries to walk away with it.

Is all this for real, or is it just a show for TV, where I'm watching it all?

A short while later, act II, scene I, members of Theresa May's own party call for a no-confidence vote in order to unseat her. The way she handles the Brexit issue, they argue, is disastrous, and she must go. Now.

The British media, happy to have such a big story to tell, are having a feast. Every day they report a new Brexit crisis, and sometimes two, and in between they report another amazing story about the American president, Donald Trump, who got elected to the presidency because – so they learn from their American counterparts – he colluded with Russian agents to influence naïve Americans to vote for him. The similarities are obvious: Leave voters and Trump voters are naïve idiots, and it's up to us, the elite British and American media, to void their votes.

If those stories do not suffice, the British media is also busy, very busy, with stories about anti-Semitism in the Labour Party. Every day, there's another anti-Semitic vignette to tell.

That's life in today's Britain.

The Brexit issue, it is important to note, did not start today, or yesterday, and will not die in the years ahead, no matter what happens on Brexit Day. British politicians, as well as journalists, will be talking about it long after Jesus' Second Coming. Some people, who are neither politicians nor journalists, would like both of them, politicians and journalists, to just shut up, already.

"I voted Leave," a chef in a Sheffield restaurant tells me, "but now I'm totally fed up with it. I want it over, I don't care how. It's enough!"

Yes, I've arrived in Sheffield. But this chef is fully clothed.

Meg, a student in Sheffield Hallam University, tells me that the English people "still view ourselves as the British Empire, that we're all high and mighty, but we're a tiny little island at the end of the day."

Island or not, Meg is not naked either.

Did you watch the last session at the House of Commons? I ask her and her friend, James, also fully dressed.

James did.

What did you think of it?

"It's a joke, it's embarrassing. Grown people shouting at each other instead of doing things."

Was it a real anger or just a show?

"A show, for the media."

I'm looking for another show, of course.

I've come here, as you know, to see the naked children of England. Will you and I get the chance?

Hopefully any day soon.

Sheffield. I like the name. Don't you? It's so romantic. Yeah, really.

Once upon a time, Sheffield was the queen, the British queen, of the steel industry. In those days, the city was shining in full glory, business was booming, and the people were full of pride in their city and their work. But those days are long gone. The steel industry collapsed, and the imposing factories, brimming with work and pride, turned into mountains of despair. Today, when driving into the city, one cannot avoid the sight of deserted factories and abandoned buildings, the once-glorious structures that are today's massive eyesores.

The knowledge and skill of working with metals, gained through centuries of steel manufacturing in the area, is not lost. Mass production of steel is gone, but specialized steel is still manufactured here, as well as research into other metals. The University of Sheffield, together with big and small corporations, has joined in conducting research relating to metals, automation, robotics, and AI (artificial intelligence), in the Sheffield area. I visit the Advanced Manufacturing Research Center (AMRC), a research institution where professors and CEOs marry mind and money, and I listen to scientists explaining how they work together with the private sector. Boeing, they cite as an example, wanted to use more titanium and less aluminum in their planes, but struggled with effectively cutting titanium, which is quite different from cutting aluminum.

There are some robots here. All naked! It's a good sign, innit?

Much of the work done at AMRC, an esteemed professor tells me, is in the field of digital research.

Digital research, like artificial intelligence, is something I have a keen interest in.

At some point in the future, I ask my professor, when I meet a beautiful woman and have "dirty" thoughts, will she be able to read them?

"It's not for me to comment on that."

But will she?

"No."

Never?

"Never is a long time."

This means, in scientific lingo, that if I come to Sheffield again, let's say in ten or thirty years, I better not be looking at any beautiful woman in the city, dressed or not.

The professor tries to calm me down.

"The government," he says, "has set up the office of AI to look at these ethical and moral dilemmas."

Can you point me to the person in charge of that office, since I'd like to talk to him or her?

"I think her name is Theresa May, and I think that she has got other things to worry about at the moment."

He's talking about Brexit.

AMRC, which is jointly funded by the UK government and the private sector, works with European companies as well, such as Airbus. Will you be out of business if the UK is out of the EU?

Surprisingly, the answer is No, with a capital N.

Yes, the learned people here tell me, personally they might have voted to remain in the EU, but this has nothing to do with research and trade. If we offer a better product, they say, everybody will buy from us.

Are they sure?

Yes, they say, because it's always been like that, even before the queen was born. That's what trade is all about. Foreigners bought and sold from and to the Brits for centuries.

These scientists make me think.

The financial world, according to the media, predicts economic chaos if Brexit is not stopped. Do they report the truth, or have they simply selected Remain financiers to tell them what they wanted to hear?

As far as I can tell, while driving around in search of naked English folks, the Brits are having the time of their lives. Hotel after hotel, restaurant after restaurant, is packed to capacity. If everything is down, how come everything is up?

Ask the babies at the Commons.

In any case, Sheffield is not just about science, but also about nightlife. Like in many a British habitat, there are pubs all around.

I visit a pub, the traditional living room of many Brits. The food stinks, but the company is great.

The company, if you're curious, is composed of three former cops who are lucky, so they tell me, to have entered the police force when the pension contracts were great. They get close to £2,000 a month, they brag, and it pays very nicely for many a beer in life. They are also very happy, they add, that they are part of their generation and not of the present generation, the "snowflake" generation.

Why snowflake?

"The young people melt very fast; they're afraid of everything."

I'm afraid he's right. How do I know? Most often it takes me quite some time to find young people willing to talk on the record. "Is it going to be political?" a student asked me just earlier, when I introduced myself as a journalist writing about the UK.

Snowflakes. Yeah.

May I ask you a stupid question? I ask the ex-cop. I've been thinking about it a lot. Are you, English citizens, passionate people?

"Yes, but we don't show it. English people don't show emotions."

Why?

"Showing emotions is a sign of weakness."

Yet, there is one place, so I hear, where the English show emotions. Where?

At concerts.

I go to a club called Leadmill, where three different bands play on the same evening. They might be playing – hold your breath – the female version of the Full Monty set to music.

What makes me think the ladies might play the Monty? I have a dream, my dear.

The music starts. Loud. And louder.

Band after band after band.

Yes. All three bands are loud, louder than steel, and in no instance can I comprehend the lyrics. I ask locals to help me out, but they can't understand anything either. Fans, mostly snowflakes, stand for hours drinking beer and listening to the music. Some move their heads, right and left or back and front, and then drink ever more.

All singers and musicians are fully clothed. No Monty.

At the entrance, there are blank papers on a table, for fans to write down their email addresses, in case they want to be notified when and where their band will be playing next. Some fans write their contact info, others write other things. I read: "Rich suck hard cock + hates blacks." The word "blacks" is crossed out. At the bottom of the page I read this: "I hate Jews."

Thanks for showing emotions, kiddo.

The next day, as I'm getting ready to leave the fully clothed Sheffield, I hear the muezzin summoning the believers to pray and I, son of a German priest and a Jordanian nurse – or something like that – abide by the call.

Yeah.

I go to the Burngreave district, where many a Muslim resides, and I meet Jamal of Yemen. He invites me to join him for a prayer in the mosque, a good place for a Muslim like me.

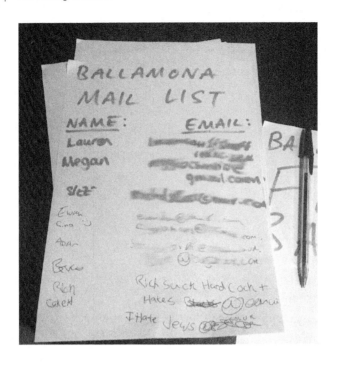

God blesses the queen; Allah will bless me.

We take off our shoes– and only our shoes – say hello to Allah, and then we go to sit down in his nearby office in order to get acquainted.

Jamal, who buys and sells fragrances in Saudi Arabia and England, is also the muezzin, the man who summons the people to prayer five times a day. "I make the adhan" is how he puts it to me, referring to the call to prayer.

Can you do one for me, a private adhan? I ask His Fragrant Holiness. He happily does.

"Allahu Akbar, Allahu Akbar, Allahu Akbar, Allahu Akbar. Ashhadu an la ilaha illa Allah. Ashhadu an la ilaha illa Allah. Ashadu anna Muhammadan Rasool Allah…"

It's gorgeous. I love it!

How do you, a Muslim, feel in the UK? Do you feel welcome? I ask my new brother.

"We are very happy in England. There's no problem. Islam is very strong here in the land, and the government is top with the Muslims here. If there's any problem, believe me, the police come many times to me and say: 'If you have any problem, call and we'll help you.' We are very, very happy here."

Praise be to Allah.

"Praise be to Allah."

How about the rest of the people – not the government – how do they, the white community, treat you?

"No problem, no problem in this area, because the community here is all Muslim. All are Muslims here, from all over the world. Yemen, Somalia, Algiers, Tunisia, Iraq, Syria, Egypt. Muslims from all over live here. There are some white people who live here, but we are happy together. No problem. In Sheffield, it's okay, except in Burngreave."

In other words, where he and I sit.

How many people, Muslims, live around here?

"Plenty, plenty."

How many?

"In Sheffield, more than 200,000."

The man might be exaggerating, but who am I to dispute his figures?

Some people, I say to him, told me the other day that this area, Burngreave, is infested with crime.

"Some people say that, because the young people, some people, sell drugs. They make problems. They are not here. They stand in the corner, next street. Not any problem in the day, only at night. They come at night."

How do you feel about the other people living around here, like the Jewish community? I don't know if they live here. Are there Jews in the area?

"No, there are no Jews here."

Praise be to Allah.

"Praise be to Allah."

We talk more, and he says more. There's crime, tons of it. Nights are dangerous in this place. Young Muslims in this area – not all, of course, but enough – sell drugs and commit murder. His own son was shot dead right next to where we sit.

That's life in the Western world, another Muslim tells me. Drugs and death. You can die in Yemen, and you can die in England. Your choice.

May Allah grant you health.

As I leave Jamal, I think: I met some Jews in the UK, but not where most of them live, Manchester and London. Here I met Muslims who live around many other Muslims. How do the Jews of Manchester, for example, feel in Manchester, where there are many more of them around?

Maybe I should go to Manchester and see. Praise be to Allah.

The clock moves, one hour is coming as the other is going, and before it's all done, Theresa May survives a no-confidence vote in her own party, 200 to 117.

I wouldn't want to be in her shoes these days. Imagine how she must feel watching her own party members trying to depose her. All because of Brexit.

This makes me think of the Brits and their Brexit. The Brexit story is going to take a long time to solve, if ever, but what's really underneath it all? There must be more to Brexit than just the UK's relationship with the EU. What is it?

Hopefully, I'll find out sooner or later. Meantime, jump into my Hyundai, for I'm about to be driving to Manchester. The weather is quite harsh at the moment, and I might stop along the way, if it gets gloomier than this.

Jeremy Loves Irony

Slowly, slowly I learn about the English people, but it's a slow process. Unlike the Scots, the Irish, and almost everyone else, the English are hard to crack. They are polite, seldom raise their voices, and it's easier to meet a passionate pretzel than a passionate English man or woman.

At times, they are a study in opposites. Take, for instance, the people and their representatives in the House of Commons.

The English, when they are not drunk, are the politest humans on the planet, but their chosen leaders are the exact opposite. Watching how happily members of Parliament jump on one another, ever ready to swallow the other alive, makes me wonder if the Englishman, Charles Robert Darwin, suffered from extreme dementia when he wrote *On the Origin of Species*. How could he ever entertain the idea that man comes from the ape? I have never ever seen a monkey so loud, so thirsty for blood, and so disrespectful as the MPs of this land.

Charles Darwin was born in Shrewsbury. I think I should visit his birthplace, one day or another, and try to figure out what made him make such a mistake.

Yes, granted, he lived before Brexit. Lucky me, I live in the middle of it, and no matter how the Brexit story ends up, the road to Brexit is sure to expose much more than anybody wants.

It is on these days, when the Brits, led by England, are about to leave the European fold, or not, that the raw nature of these polite people threatens to reveal itself in all its glory, or shame. Will we, the rest of mankind, finally be able to see under the skin of the polite English?

The rain falls hard. It looks like a storm approaching, and so I stop, in Losehill. I like the name. I like many names. Sheffield, Newcastle, Gateshead, Glasgow, Dublin, Belfast. And now Losehill.

They have a lovely little English hotel in Losehill, where a night will make you £500 lighter, and that's where I'm going to stay tonight.

I got a good deal; don't worry about me.

Jews know how to get good deals, don't you know? Yeah!

I'm a happy man today, let me tell you. It's cold and wet outside, but warm and comfy inside – can I complain?

It is here, let me share with you, that I meet David and Belinda, a medical physicist and a teacher, and they are a very nice, elegantly dressed, and outstandingly proper English couple. I'd love to get to know them, wouldn't you? Well, you might not believe it, but just as these two lovely birds are about to retire to their room, I ask them: May I take up your time to get to know you?

Being the polite English that they are, they offer to sit down with me for as long as it takes. God bless England!

We sit down for a chat in the lobby of the hotel, where, I hope, they will share with me their thoughts about the English character, Brexit, and democracy.

I'm ready to learn.

The essence of the English character, David tells me, is this: "We are fairly polite, we queue, we rely on queues."

Only an English physicist could be so precise.

I hope nobody is queuing outside now, in this stormy weather.

Belinda, a soft-spoken lady, defines the English character thusly: "We are quite good drivers compared with, say, the Spanish or the French. On the whole, I think we're quite good on the roads. I think we're quite tolerant as a nation, on the whole."

That's an English teacher for you!

The two of them hope, very much, that the Commons will kill Brexit, even though such a move would be against the vote of the people. "I don't feel they really know the situation," Belinda says of the people who voted to leave the EU. The referendum, she believes, must be annulled.

"They are stupid," David says of the Leave voters, and their vote shouldn't count.

But what about democracy, does it not apply to Britain?

"Democracy has its limitations," Belinda says.

There is a democracy here, David insists, because "we do allow people to vote." People can vote, but this doesn't mean that anybody has to abide by their vote.

I love it!

Russia's leader, Vladimir Putin, who understands dictatorship better than the rest of us, is all too happy to catch fake democrats. Speaking about the Brexit drama earlier today, he remarked: "Was it not a referendum? Someone disliked the result, so repeat it over and over? Is this democracy? What then would be the point of the referendum in the first place?"

For a change, the man is right, even if he has some ulterior motives here.

David, on the other hand, sees no fake democracy anywhere in the UK. "We have a democracy, a representative democracy. We elect professionals, people who are committed to politics, who understand the nuances of politics, and then we delegate the responsibility to them. That's how it works."

There was a referendum, and the people, stupid or not, voted to leave. Why can't you accept it?

David gets a little irate. "You're using a particular definition of democracy which is a fairly simple one," he tells me. The people who voted to leave, he lets me understand, like to "upset the applecart."

I love the way the higher-class people express themselves in this country. They have a beautiful way of using language, often coupled with colorful idioms, to turn basic concepts into meaningful nothingness. And they do it in the coolest way possible, rarely showing emotions.

I tell them that.

"I think that our society, on the whole, is a very phlegmatic society. It doesn't get very heated," Belinda muses.

Why is that?

"That is part of the English culture. We are a fairly calm race. We are not easily excitable like the French or the Spanish."

I'm not sure I fully understand her, so I ask her: Do you mean that the English suppress their excitement or that they don't have any excitement to start with?

"Well, I don't know if it's suppressed or that it just isn't there, I can't tell you." What she can tell me is this: "I don't think the English are particularly passionate."

The English people, she tells me, are "probably" actors. "Don't forget: the highest artistic expression in this country is theater. We have more theaters in London probably than any other capital. The high point of our culture is, really, theater."

In other words, the highest point of your culture is lying, pretending that you're someone else.

David: "Yes."

Belinda: "Probably. And we're probably quite hypocritical."

For years, I've wondered why English theater is so good, and this Belinda is not wondering at all. If this is a society of actors, it makes tons of sense why their actors are so good on stage.

That said, I still struggle to comprehend these two. Their logic, especially when it comes to the question of Brexit, makes absolutely no sense to me.

I wish my eagle were here to explain it all to me, but I think that eagles don't like England. I'm sure – I mean, I hope – that in case of emergency, it will come to help me no matter where I am.

Of course, these two people are not the only ones who make no sense to me. The British media is full of arguments just like the ones they make. Article after article, all written in proper English, giving me one huge headache. What happened to plain, basic logic? I hear myself asking, again and again.

As I've already mentioned, Brexit is not the only issue occupying British media. Jews pop up in the English media on an almost daily basis as if the Jews were the majority of citizens in the UK. For as long as I'm here, whenever I read British papers, I see story after story about Jeremy Corbyn, the Labour Party's leader, each story with a juicier anti-Semitic flavor than the one before.

Not that all of those stories took place this year, but until now they were kept under a dusty carpet, buried deep down. Here's a story that pops up on my iPhone right now. It has to do with a speech Jeremy Corbyn gave a few years ago. In it he berated "Zionists in the audience" who, despite "having lived in this country for a very long time, probably all their lives, don't understand English irony."

That's anti-Semitism Plus, and it tickles a certain intimate cell deep inside my psyche, making me want to meet this Jeremy face to face.

I'll need to find people who know him, tell them that I'm a pure German who is in love with him, and get them to introduce me to Lovely Jeremy.

At the moment, I don't know anybody who knows him, but I have time. I might not have irony, that English irony, but I've got time.

We Jews got time.

My smart iPhone, hearing the word "Jews," notifies me that the Jews star in yet another story now, this one without Jeremy Corbyn in the middle.

"British politics has worst record for antisemitism in Europe, poll says," the *Guardian* reports. Quoting from a poll taken by the EU's Agency on Fundamental Rights, it adds: "The survey found that 75 percent of Jewish people in the UK perceived antisemitism to be generally a very big or fairly big problem, up from 48 percent in 2012, with 29 percent having considered emigrating." The headline in the *Telegraph* is: "Four out of five British Jews believe anti-Semitism has infected UK politics."

Pretty heavy.

Put your seatbelt on, my dear. Next stop: Manchester.

We Are Economical with the Truth

The weather is okay, no more storms, and I'm driving.

First, I go to Prestwich, which I've been told is a "Jewish" part of town. I get out of the car and look around me.

What do I see? In front of me I see a big synagogue, with a Star of David on the front. The Jews here, it seems, are not hiding like the other British Jews that I met before.

How many Jews live in Manchester? I ask the first Jew I meet. "Five thousand," he answers. I walk a bit more and meet another Jew. How many Jews live in Manchester? I ask him. "Thirty thousand," he answers. A third Jew I meet adds up the two numbers: "Thirty-five thousand, at least." Then I meet another Jew, a Jewess actually, and she says that there are forty thousand Jews in Manchester.

If this goes on, by the end of the day I'll be told that six million Jews live in Manchester. I stop asking.

I read in the paper, I say to a fifth Jew, that anti-Semitism is on the rise in Britain and that about a third of the Jews in the UK are considering, or have considered, leaving the country. Any comments?

"What paper did you read?"

The *Guardian*.

"Oh, the *Guardian*! They don't sell enough papers, that's why they write such stuff. They want to excite the people, to get them to buy their paper."

Are you saying that it's not true what they are writing?

"No way."

Good.

I walk a bit more, and then I meet one of the rabbis in the area.

Claims of anti-Semitism in Britain are an exaggeration, Rabbi Joseph tells me, sorry to disappoint you. He repeats this statement, in various phrasings, for the next thirty minutes. In short: the stories in the media are fake news.

Well, if that's what the Jews say, it's probably the truth. It's about them, after all.

It's time to eat.

It takes me about twenty minutes to settle in a kosher restaurant, and I'm ready to swallow a cow.

Before I order anything, I chat with a waiter. Is it true, I ask the man, that anti-Semitism in this country is on the rise? He looks at me the way one would look at the biggest idiot in town and tells me that he doesn't know what I'm talking about.

Do you have a cow?

No.

What do you have?

Pizza.

I order a white pizza.

Believe it or not, this is the best pizza I've had so far in the UK.

Miracle of miracles. Jews might not have a sense of irony, but they know how to bake a pizza. I believe, though I'm not sure, that even Jeremy Corbyn would like this pizza.

Now that my belly is full, I take a few moments to chat with a married couple sitting at a table next to me. I introduce myself as a European journalist and ask: Is it true that there's a growing problem with anti-Semitism in this country?

I don't know why I don't let go, but I don't.

The woman, mother of four, tells me that she had never experienced anti-Semitism, whatsoever. Her husband, a heavy man in love with kosher pizzas, agrees with his wife. Have they ever heard, I ask them, of any anti-Semitic act happening anywhere in Manchester?

No, they say. Never. Full stop.

The husband and wife are not alone in the restaurant. Their children, four of them, are sitting at the same table. I ask one of the kids, the one sitting closest to me, if he has experienced anti-Semitism. The kid, about eight years old, tells me a story. He and his friend were walking on the street the other day, and they were pelted with eggs because they're "Jews."

I look at the father, and he lowers his eyes. "Oh, yes," he says, "I forgot that."

Your son is not old enough to lie.

This comment gets to him, and he opens up.

"What do you want me to do? If I tell you about the anti-Semitic attacks that we experience here, you'll write about them, inviting copycats, and more people will attack us. If I tell you that everything's good, hopefully it will be good."

I leave the Jews and go to my hotel, DoubleTree by Hilton, at the city center. I love this hotel, especially because of its floor-to-ceiling windows in the guest rooms, and because on the left side, I can even open a little window for fresh air.

Oh, the fresh air of Manchester! It's so good, innit?

I sit at my desk and stare at the endless Uber cars down below, most of which are driven by Pakistanis. The right-wingers of this land complain that the "foreigners" are stealing their jobs, a claim I've heard over and over. But these Pakistanis prove them wrong, because they take nobody's job. Everybody can work for Uber; all it takes is a little will.

Tomorrow, and for the duration of my stay in this big city, I'll use Uber.

When I wake up the next morning, I take an Uber to the Jews once more. I sense that I missed something yesterday and decide to take another approach today: I won't talk to any rabbi, and I'll introduce myself as Jewish. Will be interesting to see what people will tell me.

A few steps up the road from where I had my white pizza yesterday, there's another kosher restaurant. I approach Michael, the owner, and chat with him in three languages: English, Hebrew, and Yiddish.

He talks.

He tells me that his restaurant was relaunched earlier this year, after being closed for nine months. Why was it closed? Well, there is a story behind it. "Last June," says Michael, "somebody tried to break in, smashed the window, dropped a petrol bomb through the window, and caused us a tremendous amount of damage."

Was it a burglary?

"No. They wanted to cause damage to a Jewish property."

The restaurant was set on fire, and it had to be rebuilt from scratch to the tune of half a million pounds.

Did you expect something like this to happen?

"Unfortunately, you have attacks in this area, where anti-Semites shout and say things to you in the street, but I didn't expect a petrol bomb."

What do they shout?

"You awful Jew. You *f* Jew."

He says *f*, just *f*, because in his community people don't say the *f*-word.

When did they shout at you last? I ask him.

"Last month."

Shouting is not the only thing the Jews here have to tolerate from some of their non-Jewish neighbors. At times, Michael tells me, Jews are being pelted with eggs.

A five-minute walk from Michael's restaurant is another kosher restaurant. Chayah, the owner, tells me a similar story. Her restaurant was set on fire as well, days apart from Michael's restaurant. The attack took place on Friday night, when kosher restaurants are closed. The police, I'm told, have classified both arson attacks as "anti-Semitic hate crimes."

Why was I told a totally different story yesterday? I ask a local Jewish lady.

"We are economical with the truth," she answers.

But why lie?

"Because it's painful to admit that so many people hate you."

A Jewish Labour MP from this area, Ivan Lewis, has just resigned from the Labour Party. "It is for others to determine whether you are anti semitic," he writes in his resignation letter to Jeremy Corbyn, made public moments ago, but "I could no longer reconcile my Jewish identity and current Labour policies."

I think I should meet this man.

May I Touch Your Leg?

Once upon a time, actually eight years ago, a man allegedly stroked a woman's leg with his leg and invited her to his house. The woman said no, and the man went home alone. During the night, so the rumors go, the man dreamt about both her legs.

The man is an MP, a former member of the Labour Party, and a Jew. Jews might not have a sense of English irony, but they have a sense of touch, and their libido seems to be quite high.

Over a year ago, Labour suspended MP Ivan Lewis, issuing the following statement via a party's spokesperson: "The Labour Party takes all allegations of sexual harassment extremely seriously. Ivan Lewis is currently suspended from the Labour Party pending an investigation." In response, MP Lewis denied the allegation and issued his own statement: "I strongly dispute the allegations and intend to cooperate fully with the Labour Party's investigation."

More than a year has passed since that suspension, but the Labour Party has yet to engage in any investigation. The man has been waiting for his name to be cleared, for hundreds of days, but the party had more important things to attend to. What were they? Well, for months, the Labour Party has been busy trying to answer this one question: Who's an anti-Semite? Yes, a very important question, isn't it?

During these months, Jeremy Corbyn fought like the Most Righteous King Edward I to give every Brit the right to believe that Israel has no right to exist. Like the Palestinian Communists in Newcastle, Jeremy wouldn't accept the IHRA's definition of anti-Semitism, and he wanted to make sure that the Labour Party wouldn't accept it either. Brexit? He has no time for that. Israel? Day and night.

And MP Ivan Lewis, the Jew, watched from the bed in his lonely bedroom how the anti-Semitism row was destroying the image of his beloved Labour Party, but he couldn't do much about it because of a leg.

The party would neither indict him nor clear him, and all he could do was stay in bed or resign. And so, he resigned.

That was yesterday.

Today he's not in Westminster but in Manchester. The story of his resignation stars in the most important British papers, but he's here, sitting across the table from me in a local kosher restaurant, a restaurant that has not been set on fire.

The anti-Semitism problems in the Labour Party, Ivan tells me, started three years ago, when Jeremy Corbyn was elected as the party's leader. It was at that time that "I wrote to my party members a letter why I could not support Jeremy Corbyn, who in the past has chosen to support individuals who have been undoubtedly responsible for anti-Semitism. My letter to my members appeared on the front page of the *Daily Telegraph* and the *Daily Express*, and it said that I've accused Corbyn of being an anti-Semite. I actually challenged them because I didn't accuse him at that time of being an anti-Semite. I said he had supported and associated with people who undoubtedly engaged in anti-Semitic rhetoric."

And now, today, would you say that Jeremy Corbyn is an anti-Semite?

"If the definition of modern contemporary anti-Semitism is denying the right of the Jewish people to self-determination, then the answer is yes. The debate is: Is that anti-Semitic?"

This definition, if I'm not wrong, has finally been accepted by the Labour Party.

"Yes, yes."

Is he an anti-Semite?

"If you're asking me, do I believe that Jeremy Corbyn believes that Jews have a right to self-determination in the state of Israel – I do not believe he believes that."

In your mind, then, is he an anti-Semite?

"I've answered you in my way. You have your answer. Using the definition, then he would be."

If I understand you correctly, I can write that you believe that Jeremy Corbyn is an anti-Semite.

"Using that definition."

So, he's an anti-Semite then.

"If that's the definition."

That's your definition too. Right?

"Yes."

So, I can say that you say that he's an anti-Semite.

"You can say that based on the definition I've just given to you – "

– he's an anti-Semite.

"Hm. It has to be contextualized in that definition."

And so our chat goes. Ivan tells me, again and again and again, that what Jeremy Corbyn says, believes, and does, for years and years and years, is anti-Semitic, but not once is Ivan willing to call Jeremy an anti-Semite. According to Ivan, denying Israel the right to exist is anti-Semitism. Jeremy, Ivan says, is denying Israel that right. Yet, Ivan wouldn't utter the obvious corollary that "Jeremy Corbyn is an anti-Semite."

I ask myself: Is MP Ivan Lewis a brilliant politician, ever careful not to kill alliances even with the bitterest of enemies, or is Ivan'ke just another frightened Jew who'll never say anything negative about a goy?

Or, perhaps, MP Ivan Lewis is a true Englishman and politician: ever polite, never direct.

The leg, if it happened or not, is not the whole story, at least not in terms of Ivan's story with the Labour Party and Jeremy Corbyn.

When Jeremy Corbyn "became a leader, I was the first person that he sacked from the shadow cabinet, and he sacked me by text message."

Here in Britain, unlike in many other countries, the opposition party establishes a "shadow cabinet," a cabinet that will be real, maybe, if the government, the one with the real cabinet, falls. In Ivan's case, he was the shadow secretary of state for Northern Ireland before being sacked.

How long did it take Jeremy Corbyn to sack you, from the time he became the leader? "About three days."

Why did you wait until yesterday to resign?

"I've been discussing my anxieties and concerns and my conflicts between my Jewish identity and my Labour politics for a long, long period of time. Okay? And it really reached a stage where there was nothing left for me to do."

Was there something that happened yesterday, a straw that broke the camel's back, that made you decide to resign specifically on that day?

He wanted to resign before, he tells me, but he hoped to have his name – you may say, his legs – first cleared by the party. But recently, when he realized that the party was not willing to "facilitate a fair process of any kind," he finally acted on his feelings and resigned.

Ivan strikes me as a nice guy, a nice guy who walked himself to the wrong place, party, and legs at the wrong time. Will he recover from it all? If he runs in the next election, and I think that he should, we will probably have the answer.

I need a break from the Jews; I wouldn't mind even meeting some Nazis. Well, why not? Let's see them.

Haben Sie Gehört das Deutsche Band?

Broadway stages used to be the home of brilliant American Jewish creators such as Mel Brooks, whose record-breaking musical *The Producers* delighted thousands upon thousands of theatergoers in the Big Apple and was garnished with twelve Tony awards. Those creators have long gone, and the Broadway stage today is but a shadow of what it once was, but Broadway's musicals of old, like *The Producers*, have not disappeared, nor will they soon.

The Producers, a show within a show, tells the story of two shysters who scheme to defraud investors with a surefire musical flop, *Springtime for Hitler*. If the musical, a love story to Adolf Hitler, fails on the stage, they calculate, they will close the show on opening night and fly to Brazil, with the investors' money that they have not yet spent, and live happily ever after in Rio. To their horror, *Springtime for Hitler* succeeds beyond anybody's wildest imagination, winning rave reviews from both audiences and critics, and no closing date is anywhere in sight.

Goodbye, Brazil. Hello, England.

The Producers is currently playing at the Royal Exchange Theatre in Manchester, and I'm going to see it. I saw this funny musical quite a few years ago on Broadway and am intrigued to see how the English will bring it to life, especially since the Royal Exchange is to present the show on its theater-in-the-round stage.

Like any comedic writing, the far-fetched plot of this musical requires brilliant actors to pull it off in any meaningful or convincing way. Otherwise, as is the case with any brilliant comedy, it will fall flat on the stage, and even worse than that: it'll turn into a horror show, offending everybody in sight. Luckily, the actors of the Royal Exchange know their job.

The two principal characters, the shysters, are played to great delight by Stuart Neal, as Leo Bloom, and Julius D'Silva, as Max Bialystock. Dale Meeks, as the German Nazi writer Franz Liebkind, is brimming with talent.

The musical numbers "I Wanna Be a Producer" and "Haben Sie Gehört das Deutsche Band?" bring down the Manchester house, as the English audience members can't get enough of it, and they rock with pleasure. The cute Little Old Ladies, Max's money angels, remind me of the old Jewish lady in Leeds, dancing with her walker, only here it's so, so funny! And when they join the musical number

"'Til Him" with the two crooks, Max and Leo, the audience falls in love with them all. What a beautiful and emotional moment.

True to Mel Brooks's text and intent, the actors here present the Nazis, including Adolf Hitler, as the funniest creatures in the national zoo. They are so ridiculous, these Nazis, that it's delightful to watch them. Can anybody compete with such talent?

This production, undoubtedly, far surpasses the one I saw on Broadway. How do these actors achieve such a feat?

We are in Manchester, not in New York, but the actors here pull off their roles not only in exact American manners and accent, but they also keep faithful to the era in the States when this was first presented. Not for a moment there did I suspect that these actors are anything but native New Yorkers. Amazing.

How do they do it?

I examine the actors' faces and body movements up close, and I notice their sheer joy when acting out their roles. I also watch the actors when they have no lines, but are still onstage, and am taken by the way they observe those in action and how they react to them, as if the story unfolding on the stage were totally real. These actors are dedicated to their characters more than to the audience, to craft more than to ideology, and they are totally engulfed by the fake reality that they create on the stage, moment by sweating moment. They are, and I say this with full respect, the perfect liars. And it works on the stage like magic.

When I see the performance of these actors, I think I understand the Leave people better: they love their English culture and don't want to be Europeanized. No other European theater, at least to my knowledge, can replicate such a performance. And if that's what it means to be English, I am – selfishly, of course – all for Leave.

Well, nothing is just black and white, as every liberal and leftist ever born will tell every conservative or right-winger the moment they open their mouths. And they are right, because life has more colors than just two. A case in point: yes, it's great to preserve

English culture, and the acting is brilliant, but there are other facets to English culture, such as their horrible cuisine.

Let's destroy that culture, I say.

Not so fast, an Englishwoman tells me. You don't know our food yet, says she. Just here in Manchester, there are excellent restaurants. Would you like to try one of them?

Yes, say I. I want, tomorrow morning, to have a great breakfast in Manchester. Well, let's see what tomorrow brings.

All-Glass Restaurant over the Motorway

What's Manchester for you? I ask a young man, born and raised in Manchester.

"Ten months of gray and rain," he answers, on this gray and rainy day in Manchester.

I'm on my way to Evelyn's Café Bar, for my breakfast research.

Yes, I don't eat for eating's sake; I eat for the sake of research. Didn't you know? Welcome, my dear, to Evelyn's Café Bar in Manchester's Northern Quarter.

The place looks nice and homey, and skinny waiters offer smiles from here to Honolulu. Can a man ask for more?

For a menu, of course – which is speedily delivered to me by a skinny.

I start reading.

1. Buddha bowl, avocado, grains, pumpkin, carrot, greens, watermelon, sesame.
2. Avocado, poached egg, seeds, avo oil, sourdough.
3. Moroccan mushrooms, apricot couscous, chickpeas, cinnamon, poached egg, sumac.
4. Merguez lamb sausage, beans, fried egg, sourdough.

Buddha bowl. I'd rather have a Moses bowl. What's avo oil?

I ask a super skinny if she could recommend a calorie-rich dish. That's like asking Jesus for the best verse in the Quran, I know. She is vegetarian or vegan, I'm not sure which, but she says that she thinks the Merguez would be a good choice.

I go for it. I choose number 4.

In moments, super skinny number 2 rushes to my table and serves me my chosen dish. I like how the fried egg looks, reddish-orange surrounded by milky white.

I bite into the food, as the super skinnies observe me from afar. Oh, Mama, this is good!

Every bite, be it egg or sourdough, merguez or beans, is utterly delicious. The food melts in my mouth, every bit Bingo, and my tummy whispers a loud thank you.

Finally, someone who can cook almost like Macca of Dundee! Yes, I must admit: British law does NOT forbid tasty food.

What a wonderful discovery!

The skinnies and the super skinnies keep strangely quiet. I have to meet the chef, at my taste buds' request.

Could you tell the chef, I ask a lovely super-super skinny, that I would love to chat with him? She rushes to him, and in seconds he rushes to me.

Everything is done fast, in the café of the skinnies.

Did you make this delicious sausage? I ask Chef Jimmy Carr.

This Jimmy, for the record, is a serious guy, not to be confused with the stand-up comedian by the same name.

"No, the butcher did; we actually made it together, we made the recipe together."

What butcher, which butcher?

"Jack Wood, in Failsworth. It's local, five miles off the road. Together we came up with the sausage, the right mince and the right skin. We use lamb belly skin, for the wrapping, and inside are lamb's shoulder and lamb's leg. The belly skin gives the crispy feel, the shoulder has tenderness that melts nicely in the mouth, and the leg is flavored. We use paprika, fenugreek, and cumin."

I also had this green stuff on the plate, what's that?

"Salad, made of kale, fennel, pomegranate, and citrus dressing."

I want to talk about the fried egg. I've had thousands of fried eggs in my life, none as good as this one. How do you do it? I mean, fried egg should be the easiest food to make, yet in almost every restaurant that I've been to, the chef –

" – failed."

Correct. How come you didn't?

"You can buy eggs from anywhere in England, but I get my eggs from Clarence Court, a company based in London, where they specialize in the rich egg yolk. Their chickens have the freedom to roam, really free range, and so their eggs are of a better quality. Obviously, when you taste the egg you get the richness."

In every supermarket they sell free-range eggs. What's the big deal?

"When they say 'free range' it can be anything, from a small and narrow place to a really big place. Our chickens have really big places to roam, and they are being fed with better quality food. They live better than other chickens. If the chickens have a happy life and are enjoying their life, the eggs they produce will be better."

What oil did you use for the fried eggs?

"Grapeseed oil, which gives the egg a little bitterness, but obviously it's a nice balance."

I've been traveling in this country for some time. With minor exceptions, nothing on this island tasted good so far, not even the bread. But your bread, which totally surprised me, is excellent. Absolutely delicious.

"In England, it's all about money, about cashflow and making a business running, operating. Nobody focuses on the product. My bread I source from Kendal, from the Lovingly Artisan Bakery, which is like sixty miles down the road. They specialize in bread. Only. That's all they do."

Your bread comes from sixty miles away?

"Every day."

Let me ask you this: You are surrounded by tons of restaurants that are tasteless, you grew up in a land where people are born with dead taste buds, and yet you've come up with such delicious food. What's your secret?

"When I was growing up, I wanted to be a lawyer, and a computer engineer. And while I was in college, I had a little part-time job in a little Italian restaurant, and I saw the happiness you can deliver to a customer as a chef. So, when I was seventeen, my dream was to own a restaurant across the motorway, all glass. Can you imagine it? People can see inside, people can see outside. Everything glass: the floor, the table, the chair, and you see the cars 'pffff' underneath."

I like that!

"When you dine, you know, even if the food is bad, if the scene is great suddenly the food becomes better. Would you like to try our pancakes?"

Why not?

"Dining is also theater," he tells me with a smile, before he goes to prepare the pancakes.

Yeah, I'm in England. Everything here is theater.

The pancakes arrive soon and I, loving every second at this restaurant, start thinking of the kosher restaurants set on fire.

Who set them on fire?

Should I go to the Jews once more and see if they have another tale to tell? Well, why not?

With breakfast done, I schlep myself to Prestwich.

I present myself as a foreign journalist with an assignment to write a story about the Jewish community.

The Jews gladly talk to me. What do they say?

Manchester, they say to me, is the greatest place for Jews to live.

On the sixth day, I read yesterday on walls in this city of gray and rain, God created MANchester.

On the seventh day, they should add, He created Jewish liars.

I've heard, I tell the Jews, of two kosher restaurants that were set on fire by Jew haters. Isn't that true?

No, they say; it's not. The two kosher restaurants were set on fire by the owners, for the purpose of collecting insurance. "Did you see how nice the two restaurants look today? Guess who paid for it!"

They have no proof, but they would rather accuse their fellow Jews of theft than accuse non-Jews of arson.

And then I meet another Jew, a man who knows that I'm Jewish, and he talks to me in a quiet voice, so that no-one will hear the secrets he reveals to me. "Do you know Golders Green in London?" he asks, referring to an area where many Jews live. "There are many restaurants there; five of them are kosher. All five, at one point or another, went up in smoke. But not one of the non-kosher restaurants. Don't be naïve, these are our Jews."

Yeah. Damn the Jews.

Who is telling the truth and who's lying?

I proceed to interview an official of the Jewish community, and he tells me of anti-Semitic attacks in Prestwich.

Were you also attacked?

His little son was.

He was walking with his son a few weeks ago, he tells me, when white kids approached the boy, grabbed the yarmulke off his head, and threw it into a puddle. Anti-Semitism is on the rise, he tells me, and it's frightening that Jeremy Corbyn, whom he classifies as certainly anti-Semitic, is heading a mainstream party.

"What I said to you," he tells me before I leave, "should not be made public."

What's the problem with what you said?

"If you make it public, I'll be fired."

Wait a second. You represent the Jewish community. Are you telling me that they will fire you for saying that –

"We are not supposed to say that Jeremy Corbyn is an anti-Semite."

Is he?

"Definitely."

But you can't say it?

"No."

Can you share your opinion, your personal opinion?

"I'm sorry for taking up your time. I have a family to take care of, and I can't afford to lose my job."

That's Jewish life in Manchester.

Manchester has the second largest Jewish presence in the UK, after London, but numbers don't add to confidence. The Jews of gray and rain live in fear, continuously attacked, ever protected by their own lies. They behave like rats, tremblingly hiding from Sir Cat, until dead inside an organ of a Dublin church, having nobody to blame but themselves.

This story of anti-Semitism, of perpetrator and victim, is missing from the British media's constant reportage of anti-Semitism in the Labour Party. The anti-Semitism in Manchester, as in other places where I've been in this land up to now, has nothing to do with Labour and Jeremy. It is much mightier. The anti-Semitism in Labour can be eradicated by purging anti-Semitic members, and Jeremy Corbyn can always be sacked. And there you'll have it. But the anti-Semitism in the street, the anti-Semitism in people's hearts, is a totally different ball game. It's a virus, a virus that resists all known antibiotics.

Will I continue to encounter anti-Semitism as I make my way through England? Time will tell.

As of now, as of this minute, the people of Manchester are busy with one Jew, a famous Jew. Do you know who he is? No, not Michael Marks. The other Jew. Yes, Jesus Christ.

It's Christmas time.

And I'm sticking around for the holiday.

On the next day, away from the Jews, I get to experience Christmas in the city of gray and rain. What a beautiful sight it is! Go outside your home, my dear, look at the endless roads of Manchester, and you'll not believe your eyes. Empty roads, hardly a car anywhere. Manchester, known as the world's first industrial city, is eerily quiet today.

Where I am at the moment, the Piccadilly area at city center, very few have shown up, save for the homeless and the beggars. According to the UK's Vagrancy Act of 1824, it is an offense to "sleep rough" or beg in her Majesty's Kingdom. But the poor, as you might imagine, are not well versed in matters legal.

Officially, according to the *Mirror*, "there are 4,751 sleeping rough in the UK," in addition to the estimated "320,000 homeless people living in temporary accommodation."

I go to McDonald's for a warm cup of coffee, amidst the gray and the rain.

In front of me are two old beggars. I observe them and eavesdrop on their conversation. Neither of them has taken a shower since the days when Queen Victoria ruled over this land, but yet they are a study in humanity. They are strangers to each other, as they have just met, but they treat each other like brothers. One of the old men, who obviously has spent the day collecting food, all kinds of food, shares his collection with the other. A piece of cake, a slice of bread, a half can of soda, and some spices. "I also have a few pieces of chocolate. Would you like? It's not healthy, but if you want, I'll give you."

It's so sad to watch, making me want to cry, yet it's so heartwarming.

Tomorrow I'll be going to Liverpool, on my way to London. I've got to see if I can finagle meeting Jeremy Corbyn, and perhaps some lords and a few MPs.

You may ask: Why Liverpool now? Well, Liverpool is the city of the Beatles, a very British thing, and I want to crack the British soul, the English soul, and perhaps Liverpool will offer a clue or two. Besides, there aren't many Jews in Liverpool, and nobody to get on my nerves – at least not yet.

Happy holidays.

You'll Never Walk Alone

I register in my new hotel, here in Liverpool, and check the news. What's new in Britain? I ask my MacBook Pro. The first news item, from CNN, states: "Anti-Semitism is so bad in Britain that some Jews are planning to leave."

Damn it.

I close my computer and go out.

Is there anything special, or unique, about Liverpool? I ask a Liverpool man, walking past me.

"Yes," he says, "the people."

What is it about the people?

"Liverpool people are very friendly."

What's going on with the people of this island, who think so highly of themselves? I don't know of another people so in love with themselves as the English and the Irish and the Scots. One after the other, Irish, Scottish and, so far, English as well, tell me that they are the friendliest, warmest, loveliest, and most humorous creatures on earth. If I'm not mistaken, in the last century the Germans had a similar notion about themselves, and the Brits almost evaporated from the face of the earth as a result. Of course, the Germans went one step too far: killing those who were not as great as they thought themselves. The Brits wouldn't go that far. The most they do is Brexit, if at all. They enjoy their own friendly company so much that they don't need anybody else around them.

It'll be interesting to find out what the Welsh think of themselves.

This evening the friendly, good people of Liverpool flock to the Liverpool Playhouse to watch Charles Dickens' *A Christmas Carol*.

I join them.

The Spymonkey theater group, whose actors play the *Carol* here, welcomes the friendly English people to the Playhouse. An actor playing Dickens shouts: "Good people of Liverpool!" and they answer back with loud oohs and aahs.

And then the show begins.

Everything idiotic you can think of or imagine is part of this show. On this stage you can hear Charles Dickens analyzing Jeremy Corbyn. Yeah. Got more stupid ideas in your head? These actors would love to hear from you. Can you come up with the biggest lie ever invented? That lie belongs on this stage. These actors utter the most bizarre lines they can come up with, insisting that Dickens put the words in their mouths, and the audience loves them and believes them.

Why not? We are in Liverpool.

This *Carol* is the stupidest and yet most refreshing, brilliantly ridiculous theater presentation I've seen to date. Bravo!

The good people of Liverpool, you must admit, deserve a good show.

While the good people of Liverpool flock to the theater, lesser people from around the world flock to this city, filling up hotel rooms and giving the rest of us, like me, a huge headache just finding a hotel that costs less than a new Mercedes. Why do they come here? Sporting events and music, to cite two motivations.

This week, for example, Liverpool is playing against Arsenal at the Anfield stadium, and soccer fans want to watch it live. Then there are other fans, or groupies, who flock to this city, the birthplace of the Beatles, to hear the Beatles once more. They go to the Cavern Club, where the Beatles played in their early years, and they feel as if they are part of history.

The last time the Beatles played at the Cavern was 1963. The club has been rebuilt at least twice since, but the fans have no doubt that right there, on that floor, the Beatles can still be heard, at least spiritually. Day and night, whatever the time, the fans are wandering around the Cavern. They stroll on Mathew St., Victoria St., Temple Ct., and everything in between and surrounding. Cashing in on the Beatles craze, the area is packed with music clubs, gentlemen's clubs, slot machines, pawnshops, beggars, and yet another gentlemen's club.

Liverpool today is totally different than what it used to be in the days of the Beatles. A port city once known for providing hard life to its residents is today a thriving city with gleaming multistory buildings shaped like huge ships, countless hotels, and millions upon millions of pounds earned by selling memories to generations of lost souls, who look for guidance in a guideless world.

The Beatles fans don't restrict themselves just to Mathew St. and Temple Ct. You can spot them in the thousands wandering around in other parts of the city, such as that gorgeous place where stone and water meet to form a magical mirror display, known as Albert Dock. Oh, sorry, Royal Albert Dock. We are in England. If anything is gorgeous enough on this island, a member of the monarchy will show up sooner or later to grant it a royal stamp of approval.

It's on Albert Dock, before it became royal, that Sir Winston Churchill would drop by to drink, eat, drink again, and spend quality time with the loveliest dames of Britain.

I slept in the man's room, at Londonderry Arms Hotel, and it's time I follow him once more.

The Royal Albert Dock is also well geared for Beatles fans. The Beatles Story, one of a number of Beatles museums in Liverpool, provides a walk in the belly of the earth through various Beatles moments.

I walk the walk.

Since I'm not a fan, and certainly not a walking Beatles encyclo-
pedia like some others here, I only now learn of their history, which
has evaded me since my birth. There would have been no Beatles, I
learn here, if not for a Jew named Brian Epstein, son of Malka. Yes,
the Beatles played at the Cavern, but that was pretty much it. Until
Brian appeared. Brian signed up to be their manager, taught them
how to present themselves onstage, and made them the superstars
that they became.

No break for me from the Jews, alive or dead.

Did the Beatles sweethearts appreciate the man who made them?
Most likely, but not necessarily every aspect of him.

When they were recording the song "Baby, You're a Rich Man,"
"Lennon corrupted the song's chorus as it faded out. Instead of
singing 'Baby, you're a rich man too,' he sang, 'Baby, you're a rich
fag Jew,'" according to John McMillian, as published by *Newsweek*.

John Lennon.

The Beatles Story dedicates a nice chunk of their property to John Lennon. Written all across a wall facing me at this very moment, is John Lennon's *Imagine*, a song that inspired – nay, made – a generation, the generation of Peace and Love, and its influence still rings loud in our day and time.

There's a special room in the Beatles Story for "Imagine," one of the most touching, humane songs ever composed. John singing "Imagine" is playing softly in the background, intertwining with the written lines on the wall.

It touches every chord in my heart. But then my eyes catch the photos.

John Lennon's photos are lovingly hanging in a tasteful order on a neighboring wall. Here you can see the man walking in New York, delicately dressed in top fashion, just coming out of or going into his luxurious abode at the Dakota, on the Upper West Side of Manhattan.

I know the Dakota. You must have tons of money to have your body surrounded by the Dakota walls.

The man is super, super rich. I listen to him sing,

> Imagine no possessions
> I wonder if you can
> No need for greed or hunger
> A brotherhood of man
> Imagine all the people sharing all the world –

as I watch the photos.

The photos and the lyrics don't live comfortably next to each other, and I feel cheated. Either the singer or the photographer is not telling the truth.

John, baby, you're a rich liar.

I've never thought of it. It's only here and now, where image, words, and sound are juxtaposed against possessions, *heavy* possessions, that I see through John's English-designed mask. And I imagine. I imagine a pedophile priest praying for the welfare of the little children.

I share my thoughts with Victor, a local Liverpool man, and he tells me that he knew John Lennon personally. "I went to the Quarry Bank school, which was a very good grammar school in 1956, and one of the things that the school was famous for was the girls' school next door.

"There was a dividing wall between the boys and the girls. I was eleven years of age, and I was very pleased to go to the school until I realized that there was a certain group of very aggressive students, led by John Lennon, who took great delight in knowing that young boys don't really like girls at the age of eleven. They went to the classroom of the newcomers, which they called 'newts,' and they would get a hold of newts and throw them over the wall to the girls' school, much to our disgust and horror. We didn't know what the girls would do to us. It was very frightening, and John Lennon took it upon himself to lead his friends in throwing as many newts over the wall as possible. That was my first meeting with John Lennon, who I would describe as a bully. I was only a little kid, in short trousers, and John Lennon picked me up and threw me over the wall. I was screaming."

Imagine, said John, and I imagine. I imagine the little boy screaming. Hey, John!

We live at a time when people follow musicians and actors, putting them on pedestals and making gods of them. We tend to forget that they are artists, not spiritual leaders, and in democracies we should follow no one, making no one a god. And it is here that I see it clearer than ever.

This doesn't mean that there are no good people in the world. There are. For example: a lovely German by the name of Jürgen Klopp.

I take an Uber and go to see him.

Have you heard of the man, of Jürgen Klopp?

Jürgen, just so you know, is the most likable and most beloved German in England.

Jürgen Klopp is a football (soccer to Americans) genius who in the past had led the Mainz and Dortmund football clubs to great successes back home in Germany and is now repeating that formula right here in England as the manager of Liverpool FC (football club).

Under Jürgen's capable hands, Liverpool FC is winning game after game in the Premier League, and today they're getting ready for the next big game, Liverpool versus Arsenal. This is the real deal, mind you. This is not Scotland versus Israel. Oh, no!

Jürgen is about to give a press conference in Liverpool FC's training ground at Melwood, and I've come here to ask him a few questions.

You're probably the most beloved and admired German on English soil, I tell him.

"That's only because of the alternatives, ah."

How does it feel?

"I don't feel that. I don't feel as a German in the daily life, to be honest. The reason for that is that we are pretty similar."

Not totally so, but almost.

"English people," he fast corrects himself, "are much better in taking the weather like it is. If not, they will not be able to be happy here. That's pretty much the only big difference."

He goes on to tell me that his life in this land is pretty much divided between field and home, and not much in between, which means that he doesn't interact with many people. "I don't know how the people in England think about me," he says, and then adds, "Go to Manchester and ask again. You'll find a few, I'm pretty sure…"

The truth is, and don't tell it to any member of the English tribe, the English are partly Germanic. In fact, the four nations making up the UK are one big mix of origins: Celtic, German, Viking, and God knows what else. That said, however, it is amazing how the English love and admire Jürgen, aka "The Boss" and "The Normal One." The other day, I asked a twelve-year-old Jewish boy what's more important to him, Jürgen or God?

"That's easy," he said. "Jürgen Klopp."

Bill Shankly, the man who over a half a century ago lifted Liverpool FC from the deep bottom to the mountaintop, is quoted as saying, "Some people think football is a matter of life and death. I assure you, it's much more serious than that." Paraphrasing this quote, I ask Jürgen: There's a saying that English football is not a question of life and death but much more than that, and my question to you is, Do you see any difference between the English fan and the German fan? Are the fans here more into football than in Germany, or anywhere else in the world?

"Yeah, I'd say so."

How does it come about? How do you see it?

"It's more intense here. It's more important for the people if your team is winning or not."

Why is that? Do you know why?

"I think that the British people bet much more!" He erupts in loud laughter after saying this.

When he finally calms down, he tells me that in Dortmund, "a lot of people already said [football is] kind of a religion. That's probably true. But then you come to Liverpool and it's the next level. That's how it is. It's everything. You only meet a supporter of Liverpool or a supporter of Everton. That's all."

Kind of more Catholic than the pope...?

"Yeah, probably. It's more intense. It's nice. The atmosphere in the stadium is different. In Germany, we have this constant singing around the football games; here people are really in the game. That means, if nothing happened in the game, it can be really silent. It's not better or worse, it's just different."

Jürgen, despite the fact that he's not Liverpool born and raised, is a very friendly guy. Yeah, I swear.

Of course, I have to see this miracle of quiet fans firsthand.

I'm going to see the game at the Anfield stadium, which seats well over fifty thousand. No seats are available for sale, unless you're willing to buy from scalpers at exuberant sums. Lucky me, I got my ticket thanks to Liverpool's press office.

Look at the thousands here! Babies who just started to speak and *alte kackers* who can hardly speak. Common denominator: Liverpool fans. From birth to death.

The game's about to start.

The crowd stands for the anthem. No, not "God Save the Queen." No queen here, only Jürgen. The anthem they are singing here is Rodgers and Hammerstein's "You'll Never Walk Alone."

> Walk on, walk on
> With hope in your heart

And you'll never walk alone
You'll never walk alone...

This is one of the most difficult of Broadway songs to pull off, and these fans are no Judy Garland or Doris Day, who knew – oh, how they knew! – to sing this one in their heavenly voices. Still, for these fans, "You'll Never Walk Alone" is much more than lyrics and music; to them, it's their very being. When singing, many close their eyes, as in prayer to their god, Jürgen Klopp.

Jürgen himself is down on the field, directly below where I sit, and I can see him in action. He's excited when the players do the right thing but gets upset when they don't. For much of the game, his hands are interlocked behind his back, in the fashion of Jerusalem's holiest rabbis, and he walks back and forth like a yeshiva student trying to solve a complex philosophical question. Maybe I should send him to Gateshead. At times, this Klopp yells to his players, though it doesn't look like they hear him, and then he moves his hands in all kinds of directions, like a drunk conductor, until finally he holds his ass tight with both hands – something very un-rabbinical.

Bottom line: This man, let me tell you, loves the game.

Liverpool and Arsenal are both Premier League teams, and they know how to put on a show. Oh, boy, they do! Both are highly professional, up to speed, and understand balls. In this game, the Arsenals are outstanding in passing the ball but, for some reason, they don't know how to hit a ball into a net. This part of football art is almost entirely controlled by the Liverpool guys. They walk on, on, on, on and on. When the game's over, it's 5-1 Liverpool.

Were the fans quiet for the past ninety-plus minutes? Not for a minute. Jürgen is dreaming. Yet, shockingly surprising to me, once the game's over, the fifty thousand-plus fans leave the arena in an extremely orderly manner. No one is shouting, no one is pushing, no one is misbehaving. I stare at the stream of people, the fifty thousand-plus souls, and I just can't believe my eyes and my ears. It's extraordinary.

Who, in God's name, created these friendly people? I don't know. What I do know is this: Liverpool, according to what I'm told, has some very interesting people, not people who have already died, but people who are still alive. Who are they? Many, and I wish I could meet them all. I can't, of course, but I would love to meet four people I've heard a little bit about: a dame, two millionaires, and a gangster.

Yes, it will be interesting to see them, for they are part of the puzzle I'm trying to solve.

Dame Commander of the British Empire

Remember the hottest news on CNN? Well, don't even mention it to Labour MP Louise Ellman of Riverside, Liverpool, whom I'm about to visit. She is riding high these days, or so it seems.

She just came back from Buckingham Palace, a place she had never been to until last week. She went to the palace for the investiture ceremony by Prince Charles, son of the queen. The prince – listen to this – presented our lady with her damehood at Buckingham, and from that day forth, hear me loud and clear, our lady is legally permitted to refer to herself as the "Dame Commander of the British Empire." Yeah. Louise, a Jewish woman married to Geoffrey, Jeff for short, is a Dame Commander of the British Empire. No less. That's an honor that will make every woman happy, not to mention a Jewish woman in this age of anti-Semitism in Britain.

I order an Uber, and in minutes I am with the Dame Commander of the British Empire. Yes, I'm again with a Jew. A Jewess.

Stuff happens.

As far as I can tell, she deserves this title. Louise, you see, has a clear, direct voice, and you can count on her to tell you the truth even if it hurts. In a recent speech she gave at the House of Commons, speaking about her own constituency, she didn't hide the bad news and told her listeners the naked truth. "Forty percent of children in Liverpool, Riverside, suffer poverty."

It ain't easy for a politician to admit such a horrible fact about a constituency that she represents. She didn't stop there.

"Three wards in Liverpool, Riverside – Kirkdale, Princes Park, and Riverside – contain some of the poorest areas in the whole country."

Painful, probably truthful, and she said it.

The dame is a flaming liberal, and a sworn Labour member. She has been representing Labour for decades and is a sharp critic of the Tories. For this and other reasons, she is admired by many.

Not by Jeremy Corbyn. According to rumors published in British media, Jeremy regularly refers to her as "the Honorable Member for Tel Aviv."

Her crime? She's a Jewess who supports Israel.

The dame welcomes me at her home with a big smile, as if I were the long-lost brother she has not seen in years. Jeff, the lovely husband, serves me a delicious lemonade, and I enjoy every sip.

Life couldn't be better.

The Commander of the British Empire and I talk.

I'd like to ask you a question, I tell her, and please answer me with a yes or no.

She laughs.

Is Jeremy Corbyn an anti-Semite, yes or no?

"I do not know what is in his heart," the Honorable Dame responds, "but I do know that he has presided over the growth of anti-Semitism in the Labour Party."

The dame, being a dame, does not answer yes or no. So, I try a different tactic.

Is a person who is presiding over a growth of anti-Semitism, whether in the UK or anywhere else, an anti-Semite or not?

"He – "

Forget Jeremy Corbyn. I asked a general question about a person presiding over anti-Semitism.

"It raises a big question."

Beyond raising a question, is that person –

"I think he [Jeremy] has a blind spot understanding leftist anti-Semitism."

He said something to the effect that Jews don't have a sense of British irony, which sounds anti-Semitic to me. Is he an anti-Semite, yes or no?

She says, "Mmm-hmm," which might be a yes, but it's not an explicit yes. So, I try something else.

He also doesn't believe that Jews have a right to their own country, Israel. Is that correct?

"Correct."

According to the accepted definition of anti-Semitism, denying Jews that right is anti-Semitism.

"Mmm-hmm."

I don't think I should let her off the hook on this one. So, I repeat by rephrasing my question: Would you agree with the definition stating that denying the right of Israel to exist is anti-Semitic?

"The definition is correct."

Is it true to say that Jeremy Corbyn denies Israel the right to exist?

"I think that's what he believes."

Now, let's add the two statements – that denying the right of Israel to exist is anti-Semitism, and that Jeremy Corbyn denies Israel that right – and the conclusion is: Jeremy Corbyn is an anti-Semite. Simple arithmetic. Would you now state, clearly, that Jeremy Corbyn is an anti-Semite?

She can't bring herself to say this. Instead, she says: "He's acting like an anti-Semite."

I think the British Empire is in deep trouble.

Her husband, Jeff, who sits with us, is laughing. Even he doesn't get it.

I ask Jeff if Jeremy Corbyn is an anti-Semite, and he has no problem answering it: "Yes, he is."

I ask Jeff: When you talked to your wife last time about it, did she tell you that she thinks that Jeremy Corbyn is an anti-Semite?

"Yes."

At this point our dame feels a little stupid, obviously, and she does what politicians do in such a situation: arguing that not taking a stand is far better than taking one.

"I am fighting anti-Semitism at the Labour Party, which I've called out, very loudly indeed, for which I've been attacked for by other members of the Labour Party who wish to get rid of me and will, no doubt, manage to get rid of me for the next general election. I will not be reselected."

So, you have nothing to lose. Why, then, wouldn't you say in public what you believe, that Jeremy Corbyn is an anti-Semite?

She doesn't budge.

I sit with her for over an hour, and not once will she say what she thinks. It's bizarre, because it's obvious what she thinks – her husband just said it – but she won't. No chance. It will be easier to get a dog to speak Yiddish, I conclude, than to get this Jewish dame to call a spade a spade.

As far as she's concerned, if I understand it correctly, you can't say that a person is an "anti-Semite" unless that person publicly declares, "I am an anti-Semite." If, on the other hand, that person says that Jews have no right to breathe, for example, you can say, at the maximum, that he or she "behaves" like an anti-Semite.

Adolf Hitler, you can safely conclude, was not an anti-Semite.

I leave the lovely couple and go to meet the millionaire hotel owner Lawrence Kenwright.

Lawrence, one of the most successful real estate people in Liverpool, drives me to a homeless shelter that he finances out of his own pocket.

We chat on the way there, and I learn a little about him.

Lawrence is an interesting man, one of a kind. He loves doing business, he cares about his city, and most deeply he cares about poor people, especially the homeless. "I'm a Scouser," meaning a real, tough Liverpudlian, this millionaire tells me when he introduces himself to me. But he's much more than a Scouser. He is, let me tell you, one of those angels you have heard of or read about but rarely if ever seen. He owns many buildings, some of them quite grandiose, and he is in the habit of converting some of his properties to shelters for the homeless. Sadly, though, Prince Charles is not planning to invite him to Buckingham Palace any time soon, and there are no queenly plans to award him a lordship of any kind. He gets no thanks from city officials, either. On the contrary. City officials constantly threaten him with lawsuits, he tells me.

Homelessness is the city's domain, they argue, and he should stop getting involved in their business.

It doesn't make much sense. Well, maybe it does.

The more we drive through Liverpool, whose elected officials are almost all Labour, the more poverty I see. And given the common thinking in the liberal UK that Conservatives care for the rich and Labour cares for the poor, I ask myself: How come Labour presides over such poverty?

Admittedly, I do understand Labour's dilemma. If the poor become rich, they probably calculate, the newly rich would run to vote Conservative.

That said, and whatever their reasoning, it seems to me that Labour politicians love the poor as much as they love the Jew.

Time is moving slowly, but we finally reach the shelter, located in a God-forsaken Everton street. We go to the first floor, a huge floor, and in it I see a number of huts, kind of little houses. I check one of the huts, geared for one person, and inside it I see a bed, a little TV, a heater, and a corner for the private belongings of the homeless. They like to have their own stuff just like anybody else. As for food, it's available around the clock in the shared space. As Lawrence puts it: I'll do everything I can to feed their bellies, not their veins.

Bless him.

We chat, Lawrence and I, and when the homeless see him, they come over to hug him. They are so thankful.

The weather outside is below the freezing mark, and if not for this man, the poor here might have frozen to death, courtesy of the Labour Party.

Tell me, Lawrence: Do your people, the English people – officials or not – say what they really think when they open their mouths?

This is the last question I should ask in this place, but in my mind's eye, I can see the officials "politely" threatening him, and it drives me bananas.

"Everything comes from above, from high up. We are raised to be polite, and we learn to embellish the truth. Politicians lie, and in our society, in England, we have an entity that's above the politicians, I mean the monarchy, and they lie all the time. We learn from them that this is the honorable way to behave."

Wow!

Slowly, it does take time, I start cracking the nut called England.

Lawrence drops me off at my hotel, owned by a man named Marwan, another rich boy.

Marwan, a self-made millionaire, was born in the Middle East, and has been living in Liverpool for over forty years. "You can't tell what they think," he says of the English people, "because they are cold inside. No heart. Except for my wife."

Tell me your story, Marwan.

Would You Like to Try Our Presidential Suite?

I know of Marwan Koukash by chance.

My journey through the islands requires extensive travel, which means constantly changing abodes. And since I happened to be a spoiled man, I like to stay in American hotels from time to time. I have slept in many hotels, from zero to five stars, and have learned that American hotels – not always, but often – offer what I need most: a good desk, a good writing chair, and a refrigerator. European hotels don't always offer that. Some of them, for example, offer beautiful bedrooms, with imposing pillars intended to make you imagine that you are King David, but there's no refrigerator, and the desk is a beautifully engraved mahogany masterpiece that lacks any inkling of comfort.

I want comfort.

When I was in Manchester, I stayed at the DoubleTree by Hilton and really enjoyed it. The room featured windows floor to ceiling, a great desk, and a comfortable chair, and a refrigerator for my sweet Diet Coke and my bitter lemonade. I need that!

When moving to Liverpool, I chose another DoubleTree. And, yes, they have a refrigerator! Not only that, but they also have a heated smoking area and a cigar shop, in case my soul craves fine Cuban cigars.

Can't ask for more.

In my first hours at the hotel, before I checked CNN, I roamed the lobby, and something in the hotel looked different, very different. All around I saw paintings and photos of horses, and in general the décor seemed a bit Mediterranean.

I went to the reception and asked the person at the front desk if this was a genuine DoubleTree by Hilton or a private hotel whose owner is paying Hilton a nice fee to use their name, a practice called "license."

"Almost all hotels in Liverpool are by license only," he answered me, "including this one."

Who owns this hotel? I asked him.

"Marwan Koukash."

Who's Marwan Koukash?

"He is a Palestinian millionaire, multi-millionaire, and he's very famous in Liverpool."

I asked another clerk, just to be sure, and he told me that Marwan was actually a Lebanese, a very famous Lebanese.

I got intrigued and decided to check out this Marwan. Not an easy task.

The *Manchester Evening News* claims that "Dr Koukash was born on December 3, 1958, on the West Bank in Palestine. When he was seven years old his family's farm was bombed and his mother walked him and his seven siblings for three days to sanctuary in Jordan. On the way they were forced to hide in a cave outside his home village of Burin to shelter from aircraft attacks.

"He became a refugee for a second time when his family was forced to leave Jordan for Kuwait."

Family farm. Bombed. Who bombed the farm? It doesn't say. Walked for three days, with a stopover near Burin. What's that? Sounds like the biblical story of Ishmael. And then they were forced to leave Jordan. Who forced them?

The *Echo* has a similar story, plus a detail about "three years."

"After reaching Jordan, the family spent three years in a refugee camp before being forced to leave Jordan for Kuwait."

The Sun has a more "polished" version.

"He walked with his mother and seven siblings for three days without food until they reached the River Jordan. They were then forced to spend three years in a refugee camp before moving to Kuwait."

"Without food." That's a nice touch. But no "sanctuary" in Jordan, just "forced" to be there, but not "forced to leave."

Wikipedia has a more detailed story, this one involving the Israelis.

"Koukash was born on the west bank of the River Jordan in December 1958 in Palestine. When he was eight years old, the family farm was bombed, due to rising escalations with the Israeli military in Palestine and the family crossed into Jordan before settling in Kuwait."

I wanted to meet the man. I said to myself: Almost everybody on these islands has Palestine on their mind, and right here under my nose is a real Palestinian, a Palestinian living in Britain. Let me meet the man. And so, I went to the concierge and asked to deliver a short message to Marwan: "Your cousin would like to meet you."

Yes, we are cousins, from biblical times, in case you didn't know.

Nobody got back to me, but then I saw the man in the dining room, and we had a little chat, as relatives often have, and we decided to meet for coffee later on. Cousins love coffees.

The Later On is now, and the coffees are ready. Tell me your story, Marwan.

"What do you want me to tell you?"

Your life story, from the day you were born up until this very day. Marwan does.

Brace yourself, my dear, because I suspect it's gonna be long, but I bet it will be interesting; my cousins are not boring people.

"I'm a Palestinian. I grew up in the West Bank village of Burin, a few miles from Nablus.

"I wasn't born with a silver spoon in my mouth. I started working when I was four or five years old. My father was employed by the Jordanian army, but in 1965, when I was seven years old, he resigned and went to work in Kuwait, where he got a job as a clerk, because he wanted to make a better life for himself. I was the eldest son, and now I had to work even more. We had a lot of land in Burin and a lot of olive trees, and we lived off the land. We also had a lot of cactus trees. In the morning, I remember, I'd wake up early to collect cactus and then take them to the market and sell them before I went to school.

"Life was not very comfortable, but it was nice. It was simple.

"And then something changed. You see, I've never seen planes, but in 1967, I suddenly saw planes, war planes. They bombed a Jordanian army base near Nablus, I don't remember the name of the base, but I remember the sound of the planes, the thunder. I looked up at the planes, and I saw them dropping bombs. It was scary.

"No Israeli soldier came to Burin, but the fear of the planes made us leave the village. We walked, I think, for three days until we reached the King Hussein border, and then we crossed into Jordan.

"We went to a cheap area in Zarqa, where many Palestinians lived, and there we rented a little apartment in which we lived for the next three years. In those years, the young people were recruited by the PLO [Palestine Liberation Organization] and trained by them. I was trained to carry a Kalashnikov rifle, the AK-47. We spent a lot of time training in PLO camps because, as they said to us, one day soon, we'd go back and fight the Jews and get back our land. But the relationship between the PLO and the Jordanian government soon went sour. In 1970, in what is known as the Black September, Jordanian army units started attacking the PLO positions in Jordan.

"The bombing started at four o'clock in the morning.

"We were living on the first floor, but as soon as the bombing started, everyone in the building went down to the ground floor, about fifty or sixty people in total. Initially, we thought that the bombing would last a day or two, but the bombing by the Jordanian army went on, and on, and on. They were firing bombs, not bullets. We lived at the edge of Zarqa, and when we looked out, we could see the tanks. We suffered heavy losses. There was a bus next to our place, I remember, and it was bombed. A lot of people got killed on the street. Every day we would go and collect corpses, carry them, and then put them in the bus. When the stench from the dead bodies became unbearable, we released the brakes of the bus and pushed it downhill.

"One day I had to go to the toilet, but I couldn't use the toilet on the floor because there was only one toilet there for all the people, and others were using it. I went outside to relieve myself, and I got shot in my behind and in my leg. You want me to show you? Here, look, you can still see the scar. Look at my leg, here. You see? When that happened, I said to myself: Don't ever give up, Marwan! Fight!

"In many ways, I think, Black September shaped my life.

"There was a house next to us, a fancy house with a garden, which the Jordanian army took over, and I could see what was going on inside. Every day there was food being delivered to the soldiers. We were starving, we hardly had anything to eat, but they were fed quite well.

"During that time, we had many grenades at our disposal because many of the men had left and didn't take the grenades with them. One day, when the soldiers sat down to eat their food, four of us children threw some grenades at them. They ran away!

"And we took their food!

"If you don't shoot, you know, you'll get shot.

"After this happened, we had to move out. We knew that the Jordanian army would come looking for us.

"My mother contacted my father, and he arranged for us to come to Kuwait. By that time, my father was doing very well; he became a partner in the same company where he worked as a clerk.

"It was then, when I was in Kuwait, that flashes of the war started haunting me. When you are in it, when you are carrying corpses, when you see mutilated bodies, you just live it. It's only afterward, when you are away from it all, that you start recalling the images, that you have the time to fear and be tormented by what you've seen. From the moment I arrived in Kuwait, I couldn't fall asleep with the lights off. I was so scared. If the lights were off, and the room was dark, I would see mutilated bodies and corpses.

"I went to school in Kuwait, and after I graduated, my father sent me to London to study English. And so, I boarded a plane to London.

"After we landed, I took a taxi out of Heathrow Airport to Piccadilly Circus, to see some animals. Yes, animals. Circus is the place of animals, no? But there was a problem. When I arrived at

Piccadilly Circus, I saw different kind of animals: women with miniskirts, sorry for my rudeness, and boobs sticking out. I was a virgin. I'd never seen women's legs before!

"I looked at the women, and I got very excited, if you know what I mean. It was so embarrassing! I didn't know where to hide myself.

"Two nights later, I managed to solve the issue of my virginity. I lost it. I don't remember how that woman, my first woman, looked like, but I know she was a woman.

"In London, I studied English for three months, and before flying back to Kuwait, I went to Liverpool, to visit Palestinian friends who lived in the city. But when I arrived in Liverpool, I couldn't find them. In those days there were no smartphones. So, I went to a club instead. There I met a lady, and she came with me to my hotel room. I called up my father and I begged him: Can I stay in Liverpool?

"I registered in a university in Liverpool, where I studied electrical and electronic engineering, and when I finished my studies, my father said to me: 'Come back to Kuwait.'

"But I fell in love with Liverpool, and I wanted to make my PhD in the city. My father didn't like the idea, and he said to me: 'If you want to stay in Liverpool, you will have to finance your stay, because I will not.' That was a hard blow for me. I had to find ways to finance myself, which was not easy, but I managed. I excelled in my studies, and I earned my PhD at twenty-six, and then I became a professor at the university.

"My PhD thesis was about 3D image recognition, a technology that I created, and one day I got a call from a friend of mine in Kuwait, and he said to me that the Iraqis were looking to create a facility to manufacture integrated chips. He arranged for me to be invited to Baghdad, and I agreed to come.

"I arrived at Baghdad Airport, where I was welcomed like a bloody VIP. I got a car, and a guard, and I was taken to Al Rasheed Hotel in Baghdad. The best hotel, you know. The next day I was taken to what looked like a military facility, and I said to myself: This is not what I've signed up for!

"I was sitting in this room, when twelve high-ranking military personnel came in and started talking about electronic technology and image processing. They wanted chips. We were talking for a while and, eventually, I understood what they were looking for: image-processing technology to guide their missiles.

"If I gave them what they wanted, I knew, I'd become a multimillionaire.

"I flew to the UK and talked with my university about it. We agreed to create a company, where I would own the majority shares, and together we signed up on the deal with the Iraqis. Of course, because of the sensitivity of the material we were about to export, we had to get export licenses, one from the DTI, the British Department of Trade and Industry, and one from the American Department of State, because some of the equipment was made in America.

"We got the licenses from both governments.

"I flew back to Iraq and landed in Baghdad.

"I was accompanied to a Mercedes car with darkened windows. The driver didn't stop at any traffic light. He just drove, non-stop. I started fearing for my life.

"The car was accelerating. We were now outside of Baghdad. That's it, I said to myself, they are going to kill me.

"As we advanced, there was a security check every few miles. Why's that? The car finally stopped, and I was taken to President Saddam Hussein's palace.

"Saddam Hussein put his hand on me and asked whether I was treated well. He cared about me.

"Saddam was a warm person, and genuine. Forget about the politics. Person to person, he was fantastic. I isolate politics from the person I meet. When I meet the queen of England, whom I've met many times, I look at her as an old grandma, not as a queen. I see her as a person. Same with Saddam Hussein. When I met him, I found him very charming.

"Then I left Iraq and flew back to London. A day later Iraq invaded Kuwait.

"My contract became null and void, as all deals with Iraq were outlawed.

"As if this was not enough, I also got blacklisted by the American government because of my dealings with the Iraqis, which meant that nobody could do business with me.

"I was depressed. I had lost everything. I didn't have money. And I started drinking. Heavy drinking.

"I protested for being blacklisted, because I had the documents with me, the licenses that I got from both the American and the British governments.

"It took some time, but at the end the British took me out of the blacklist and offered me British citizenship to pacify me, so that I would just shut up and not continue to complain. That's how I became a British citizen.

"But by now I had no money left. I couldn't pay for anything.

"It was at this time when I met Mandy, my wife to be. She was a waitress and she gave me free drinks, and then free food.

"She saved my life.

"We started a business together.

"We set up a corporate training company, bringing in profession-als from the West to the Gulf states to teach intensive, on-the-job training courses. To beat the competition, since other companies were also doing this, we did the on-the-job training not in the office but in a five-star hotel. We brought in American speakers, because the Americans are warmer and more personable than the British. We didn't tell anybody that this was our first event!

"Since those days, I have been involved in more businesses. I got involved in aviation, I owned a rugby club, and now I am involved with horse races – I own about seventy horses – I own the

DoubleTree hotel in Liverpool, which took me almost nine years to build at a cost of millions of pounds.

"Would you like to try our presidential suite? I invite you. On me." Thus spoke Marwan. Interesting, innit? I told you!

Marwan's story is not exactly as the traditional and social media have been telling us.

No "family farm bombed," no "forced to spend three years in Jordan," no "rising escalations with the Israeli military," and no stopover in Burin. All of them, by the way, ignored the main story: corpses, mutilated bodies, a leg and a bullet, and the stench. The British media, perhaps, find it hard to report dead Palestinians not by the hand of a Jew.

Marwan the Palestinian is a warm creature in a sea of cold Brits, a little child who buys fast-running horses that help him forget the mutilated bodies that won't move, a kid who buys a hotel to hide from shooting tanks, and a grown-up man who insists on his right to be a child again.

It's time for a cigar.

The gangster is next.

If You Dress Well, Women Will Love You, Even if You Are a Killer

Why am I meeting a gangster?

Because there's more to this island than Jews and Brexit. Gangsters, for example.

Charlie Seiga, born in 1940, is the real McCoy, and he's more of a Dapper Don than most of them. He says he's Irish, half Irish, and that half of Liverpool is also Irish. In fact, according to him, Liverpool has very little to do with England, because its people are Irish and Welsh and God knows what else, but not English. Charlie is also half Italian – at least that's what he says. He's dressed like a lord, and he's cleaner than Mr. Clean. No spot on his clothes, no crumb after he eats, and no dirt anywhere in his world. He can't stand dirt. And he can't stand dirty people. His iPhone is cleaner and more spotless than on the day he bought it. So are his pants, shirt, scarf, and suit. The man likes everything clean.

The other day, the story goes, someone was sitting in his kitchen for a bite of clean food and was fatally shot in the process. "The blood was flowing on his hand, on the expensive jewelry," is how Charlie remembers it. Who shot him? Charlie says it was not him but somebody else. Stuff happens. Charlie hired a "Jewish lawyer," and the jury, mostly females, acquitted him. "Women like a well-dressed man," Charlie says to me.

Charlie, son of Liverpool, has been in and out of prison, and today he enjoys life in Wales. I meet Charlie in Liverpool, where he has come to visit me at my hotel, before I leave for Chester. Not that I plan to go there. Charlie asked me where I go next, so I said Chester. Just came out of my lips. "In Chester, you should stay at the Grosvenor," he tells me. "You'll have to pay a bit more, but it's worth it."

Well, maybe I will go to Chester. If the gangster likes it, I definitely should try it.

Thanks, Charlie, I tell him. I'll try. But before I go, I'd like to hear about you. Tell me your story!

"I'll start with my family history first. I did come off a crime family."

Good to know that he's not the son of the pope.

"I didn't realize that until I was about twelve years of age."

Is he such a slow learner? I'm not sure, but I'm here to listen to his story, in his authentic accent, including the "me" that stands for "my."

"It was during the war. England was getting really battered by the Germans. We were getting bombarded all over the city, and we had to move out, so they placed us on the outskirts, for safety. We had a house, we had a lovely house. We had everything as children. Best toys we could ask for, best food, everything was coming into our house. Contraband was coming in. 'Cause me dad, me old fella, he was very active in crime, believe it or not, and so was me three older brothers. I come off seven brothers, and we were the four youngest."

He stops for a second there.

"Should I talk about my parents first?"

Yeah.

"'Cause it's interesting."

Yeah, of course.

I say yeah to this man because you never know what happens when you say no to a character like him. I don't want the blood to flow on my hand, "on the expensive jewelry."

Charlie goes on.

"Both my parents were staunch Catholics. Most people are in Liverpool. But they came off two different backgrounds. Me dad was like a, what they call them days, a scally, he was like lowlife, keep away from them, don't harbor them. Me mother come off a decent side of me family, her family, and they were businesspeople. Honest and upright citizens. But not me old fella's side. Unfortunately, well, I don't know if it is unfortunately, but they fell in love. They met at a dance hall, and me mother was telling me that years ago, when he was a young man, he was always smartly dressed and, you know, he was a nice-looking fella and all this. Me mother was eighteen, he was nineteen, I think."

This is gonna be a long story, I see, but I say nothing. Charlie wants to talk, Charlie will talk.

"People were safe in them days, women and everything, not like it's now, where women are getting mugged and everything now. There's no law and order now but in them days there was. They decided to get married because me mam's parents disapproved of me father. 'Cause they realized the reputation what he had round the area. 'Cause obviously the parents on me mother's side were pretty clever and they'd done a checkup. You know, they wanted to see who their daughter was going with, like you would do, and found out about his reputation and they said to her, 'You're not going with him.' They forbade them to go together. But they married in secret in a registry office, which is a sin to do if you're a Catholic. It should be in a church, married in white. He took my mother home to her house, even though they were married, and he went back to his mother's house. They never even consummated the marriage. They were still like young teenagers, never slept together or nothing. 'Cause that was a ... You know, you had to be married properly. Anyway, the Catholic priest found out and exposed it to both parents so there was all kinds of arguments going on with them, but they decided now to marry properly in a church. So they got married in a church. I'm not boring you, am I?"

No, no. This is very interesting!

"You sure?"

Yes, sure!

"So they got married in a church, and he went to work, me old fella was a seafarer, you know, a free spirit, so to speak. And kids were getting born, you know."

I like the way he phrases things. "Kids were getting born."

"We had a lovely time when we were kids, because during the war years, things were harsh and people were starving, but we weren't."

War. Lovely. The man is brilliant.

"We used to go to school, and the teachers all respected us 'cause we looked good. We were dressed nice, clean. Other kids would have no shoes on their feet, some of them. And the teachers,

Mr. Johnson was ah, me mam used to say, 'Give Mr. Johnson an apple and an orange.' That was hard to get a hold of during the war, you couldn't get them, you know."

That's a clever mama.

"Me old fella, he had a back room, like an office in the back of the house, a parlor, that was it. You couldn't go in that room. Doors were always shut. He was always doing business with his cronies or the people he's involved with. 'Cause the contraband coming from the States was getting torpedoed and everything, a lot of people were reluctant to go back to sea over that. So I remember seeing all this contraband going into the house. Like a black shiny car used to pull up with me uncle in it, me dad's brother, and all kinds of bags of stuff going into the house. You couldn't go near this room."

If I get him right, everybody in his family is a super criminal, but I say not a word.

"One night we were playing, like kids do, and I was getting chased by me three younger brothers, and I burst open into this room. As I burst open that room, I couldn't believe what I'd seen. My older brother, I didn't know it was him at first, 'cause he had a mask around his face and a gun in his hand. He pulled it away quick and tried to smile, like that. I had burst in on a robbery they were planning. A jewel robbery. Me older brother was testing this mask out in the mirror, you know, this is the way they planned things, obviously. But he was a bit stupid, a bit boisterous. He wanted to see what he looked like, like did he look like a gangster. Then me mother burst in and seen all the commotion and she grabbed us, and she said to me old fella, 'Not in front of me children, I've told you before.' 'Cause she had the other room, with her friends, when they were having their teas and biscuits."

How lovely!

"This all came in the papers, headlines in the Liverpool *Echo*.

"Our house, all the lovely stuff in the house, was getting sold off because there was no legal aid to represent criminals them days. You know, you had to find your own lawyer, especially a good one in a high court. So, me mam sold all her jewelry and everything else, and we went right down in it."

He's emotional now. I hope he doesn't carry a gun, grenade, or knife. When people like him get emotional, it doesn't always end up nice.

"Imagine going into school like that. And the worst part about it was in Christmas time, and so the teacher said, 'Everybody, bring something in for the party.' I had nothing to bring, there was nothing in our house, we were completely poor. Gone from being rich to poor. Me old fella was taking to the drink, 'cause me three brothers had just been sentenced to ten years, five years and three years. I was only a little kid. It was a big blow."

Charlie looks me straight in the eye, very intense, trying to elicit sympathy.

"All the little kids were bringing in little parcels with a lovely little cake on them, some little thing you know, biscuits or something. I went home and said to me dad, 'I need to bring something in, I must bring something in, I don't want to be the one left out. It's bad enough them not speaking to me.' You know what I mean? You know, 'cause we were ostracized. I remember me dad getting a loaf of bread and there was no such a thing as sliced bread then, you had to cut the bread yourself. Me dad cut the bread. I said, 'What are you giving me?' He said, 'Bring the bread. Couple of rounds of bread with something.' I don't know what he put on the bread, some stuff, but he cut his finger as he was cutting the bread. He wrapped it in some brown paper, and it looked terrible. Me offering looked terrible, you know. I went to school, seen all these lovely little parcels with ribbons on, and just before the class started, you know, I stuffed mine between them all. So the teacher comes in and goes, 'Oh, this is beautiful, whose mam made this?' Then he gets hold of me offering, the bread, and he throws it in the wastebasket, in the waste bin. And he looked at me. Later, when the party got started,

I went to pick one of the little homemade cakes. And the teacher went, 'That's not yours, Seiga; that doesn't belong to you.'"

It's at this point, portraying a hurt little child, that he does get my sympathy.

"I said to meself, 'This is the last Christmas I'll ever have like this, I'm going to make sure.' This is when I turned to crime."

Oops.

"We moved to a new neighborhood. It was a bit low class, but I was happier there because people accepted us. They had nothing themselves, so we were all thrown into the same boat sort of thing. That's when I first started robbing."

The interesting thing about Charlie is that he tells his life-in-crime story and he's pretty proud of it, as if the word *crime* is a badge of honor. And as far as I know, he actually penned a number of books detailing his criminal history and is presently looking for a publisher.

"I was new in the neighborhood, and the kids confronted me, about five or six of them. They said, 'You're not from round here, are ya? What are you doing around here?' I said, 'Well, we're new round here.' There was this little scruffy fella, with his pants all ripped and all that, and he had a high-pitched voice, and he went, 'Go on, curly, show 'em what you can do, put your fist up.' So it was me and him were gonna have what you call a straightening, a fight. And I battered him, I won. Got him on the floor, and he started crying. They couldn't believe that their gang leader was done by me and I turned to walk away, and he come running back and he said, 'Hey, wait a minute. What's your name?' I said, 'I've got to go shopping for me mam.' They said, 'What's that? We don't pay for no shopping. We rob it, we'll steal all your stuff for ya.'"

I wonder where these humanists are today.

"Me bag was full up with all good gear!"

Charlie, believe it or not, sometimes has self-doubts. Like right now. "Is that boring to ya?" he asks me.

No, it's very interesting, I answer.

He drinks hot milk, whole milk, with honey, from a white mug, which is next to his white iPhone.

"Me school days were bad. Teachers wouldn't speak to us or nothing. The bullies were in school. I had to fight for me kids, you know, for me brothers. I formed me own gang, I've got me own gang. And we would bang others into shoplifting, that was the start of it all. People were buying anything in them days, anything cheap we'd rob. And do you know what was one of the greatest things to rob and steal? Coal. 'Cause people couldn't get coal for the fires. So we would raid coal yards. You know what I mean? You're sort of like a provider, you know, twelve years of age, you're out on your feet, you can run. We used to have chasers in the street all in a line, running to the next lamppost, who would be the fastest. Do you know what that's for? Not to prove to yourself, that was 'cause we could run faster than policemen, 'cause in them days policemen were on the beat, and they were big runners, they could run. And they were all six-footers, not like now, little tiny stubby fellas are sitting in police cars, can't arrest anybody. Do you know what I mean?"

Yes.

"This was the way we were surviving. See, it'll take me days to tell you all this, you know. It'll take me days. I haven't even started yet, and I don't know whether you're getting bored with it. Are you getting bored?"

No, I love it!

"Are you sure?"

Yeah.

"Do you want something to drink or something?"

Soon. Did you spend time in jail?

"Very, very serious time."

How much time altogether?

"I went through a Borstal, that was about twelve months, that's a training, youth training center. Twenty months in a jail. Eighteen months in another jail. And that was it."

And that was it?

"Yeah, but I've done things what you would never believe. I was the first man in England, I'm talking about England, to be the first safe blower in England."

To be what?

"Safe blowing. Blowing safes open with dynamite, and detonators, explosives."

Charlie is my man. Here's a Brit with a spine, a Brit who says whatever he wants to say. No games. No hiding. He's a safe blower, a wages snatcher, and he says it like it is.

A cat on a mission. I love it.

Charlie sips his milk, and he calls me "mate." Yeah.

Well, I met my man, and now it's time for me to go.

To Chester Grosvenor Hotel. Where else?

Five-Star Homeless

The Chester Grosvenor Hotel is nice. You can tell it's five-star even before you step in. Here, you see, you can keep your energy for better uses than opening doors, because here you have people who do that for you. Not only the entrance door, but also the door to your room or suite, depending on how many pounds you're willing to shed. You'll love the reception area, I'm sure. It doesn't look like a reception. There's a young lady sitting at a desk, facing two empty chairs – your chairs. And you chat. You chat about the weather, about the queen, about whatever you want. Don't worry. She knows your name, and she knows exactly what room you will be in. Not only her. Remember the guy who opened the main entrance door? He also knows your name. "Welcome, Mr Tenenbom," he said when our eyes first met.

In any case, as you probably understand, the card key is a bit heavy, and so the young lady will carry it with her, as she accompanies you to your room, suite, or whatever. She will open the door, she will show you where the lights are, where the desk is, where the bed is, the sofa, the bathtub, the chairs – just in case you got stricken with a momentary blindness.

Charlie has exquisite taste.

Across the hotel, I notice when I go out to smoke, homeless people prepare for their night's sleep.

This dichotomy, between the haves and the have-nots, couldn't possibly be sharper. Come morning, I walk the streets of Chester.

Chester is beautiful. The city walls, built two thousand years ago, I'm told, give the city a historical aura, reminding you that the people living here have a huge history behind them. The cathedral, originally built in 1093, according to an employee who encourages me to donate five pounds for the upkeep of the church, is a miracle of architecture and design. It's Godly, to put it succinctly. It costs to maintain, per a sign at the entrance, £5,500 per day, and I immediately realize that my five pounds won't make an iota of difference. I stick around for a while, to watch how many visitors, good English folks, drop the pounds in the dedicated box, and can't spot a single one in about ten minutes.

Luckily, the day is young.

I'm no Christian, but I love cathedrals. From my perspective, this is Christianity's biggest contribution to mankind, for which I'm ever grateful.

Outside the cathedral, I meet a dance student. Yes, there are people who go to university to study dance. I ask him if he's for or against Brexit. "I voted Leave," he says, "and I would vote Leave again." He is the first student I have met so far who is pro-Brexit. He shares with me many of his thoughts, as this going-to-be-dancer loves politics. "Israel is an aggressive state, treating the Palestinians quite unfairly," he tells me, "but I recognize that it's also impressively multicultural, and that's why I prefer the Israelis to the Palestinians."

How did you find out that Israel is multicultural?

"What? Didn't you see that big mosque in Jerusalem? That's impressive!"

When I was his age, I went to university to study mathematics, computer science, literature, and God remembers what else. So stupid of me. I should have studied dance! I could have a career in dance. Imagine me as a ballet professor or a belly dance doctor. Life would have been so much fun! I'm not the only one missing his profession, by the way. Jeremy Corbyn, I know for sure, would have made an excellent belly dancer. I can see him on the stage, dressed like a University of Leeds female student, going by the name of Mohammed, and dancing with the Parliament's mace over his head at the top of Clifford's Tower in York.

That would be a show!

Back to earth, I would like to attend a cultural event in Chester, but nothing interesting is happening in Chester these days. There are no theater performances going on, no dance, and no music. There are stores, all open, and people are buying. My hotel has no more empty rooms available, and a pub I walk into is packed, not one seat available. I chat with people I meet on the street, friendly English citizens, and they empathize with the Palestinians. How do I know? I ask them, and they tell me.

I have nothing better to do, so I go back to the Grosvenor. I roam in the hotel, here and there, and the employees never fail to open doors for me. I feel like a respected gangster. I wonder how many gangsters are in the hotel today, but I don't ask.

I sit down, order tea, cake, and more tea – I'm in England – and I watch the rich. I eavesdrop here and there, like a little spy, and hear no one uttering the word *Brexit*.

Done with the tea, I go to my room. I paid enough for it, let me enjoy it. I turn the TV on.

Nice TV.

I watch BBC. The topic today: a special about Brexit. Then the news comes, and it's Brexit again.

I fall asleep.

I spend another day at the hotel, enjoying the door rituals – I walk in and out, this door and that, back and forth, forth and back – and the day passes.

When the novelty of having people open doors for me and show me where the floor starts and where the ceiling ends wears off, I get into my car and drive to Shrewsbury.

Yes, Shrewsbury. It was between Sheffield and Losehill that I said to myself that I'd try to go Shrewsbury, and Shrewsbury, guess what, is not far from here.

Shrewsbury is the Bethlehem of the atheists, the Jerusalem of the unbelievers. No Jesus walked there, on water or dry land, no Mohammed flew there, and no King David danced there. Just Darwin.

I check into the Lion Hotel, where I see a photo of finches from Galapagos Archipelago. Have you not heard of those finches?

They are the finches that "made Charles Darwin develop his theory of natural selection," the man sitting at the front desk of the Lion Hotel proudly tells me.

The Lion Hotel, sorry to disappoint you, is no five-star hotel. Far from it. But this hotel has something to offer that none other has. It was right here, at this very hotel, that Charles Darwin started the journey that would end with the publication of *On the Origin of Species*, the theory of evolution that changed the world.

Charles Robert Darwin was born in Shrewsbury, a fact that many people celebrate to this day – especially businesspeople. There's a shopping center named after him, not to mention a restaurant, and soon – hear this – a Darwin chocolate. Yeah, that's what I am planning to do next year. Princess Di cookies in Scotland – I hope you've not forgotten! – and Charles Darwin chocolates in England. In Austria they have Mozart chocolate, and I think it's only proper to have a chocolate named after Darwin. Atheists would love it; they would be eating chocolate all day long, and I would be richer than the Duke of Westminster, buried at Chester Cathedral, ever was.

I walk the streets of Shrewsbury, joyfully taking in the beauty of this old city. Oh, heaven! Once upon a time people knew how to design well, how to build well, how to paint, and how to dream. It is such a pleasure to walk in the streets here, some of which have hardly changed in the last hundreds of years, and here I can breathe history with every step I take. It's so powerful.

Walking these streets, I'm trying to solve my old question: Did Mr. Darwin suffer from extreme dementia?

Maybe I should ask the people here; they might know.

I stroll around until I meet Alex, a local young man. What do you think of Brexit? I ask him. I can't believe I did it. I was supposed to ask him about Darwin and dementia.

Maybe that's what happens to your brain when you have servants opening and closing doors for you all day long, and then show you where your bed is, where is the floor and where is the ceiling. Damn that Charlie gangster who made me do it! Now I got stuck with Brexit.

"I voted Remain, but if there's another referendum, I'll vote Leave," Alex answers.

Yep, now I have to be polite and continue on subject.

Why? I ask him.

"I had more time to check the facts, and I've concluded that the EU is a globalist manipulator and a danger to our future."

What??

"They constantly lie. One thing is immigration. We are never told the truth about immigrants and crime, and the relationship between them."

Alex cares not only about domestic issues but also about international issues.

"When was it? Not long ago. The Israeli army killed forty Palestinian children in just one day."

Does this mean that you identify with the Palestinians?

"That's hard. I don't like what the Muslims do either."

Pick a side.

"I think that the establishment of the State of Israel was wrong. They came in and took over a country. Yes, this is a difficult story. Figuring this out is a rabbit hole."

What do you mean?

"The Holocaust is a big rabbit hole. History is always written by the victors, so you can't really tell. Did the Germans kill the Jews?

Not all agree. Did Hitler order to kill the Jews? There's no evidence for that. And if some Jews were killed, how many were they? That's another rabbit hole."

So, you support the Palestinians?

"Not necessarily. I mean, now that the Jews are there, I'm kind of, I think, more on their side. Hard to say."

The beaks of the finches were different, and Darwin thought that the better beaks were a result of evolution. What's interesting is that the mouths of people who don't particularly like Jews are never really evolving, and I'm not sure why. I try to get Alex – who reads a lot about Israel, as he tells me – to develop an interest in other trouble spots, like Kurdistan and Sudan, maybe Turkey too, but he's not interested. Why aren't you interested in other trouble spots? I ask him.

His reply? "It's interesting, and I never thought about it. I read a lot about Israel, not about the others. I think you're right – why am I not interested in the others? I'm just not. I don't know why."

I like this Alex, friendly and honest.

As far as I can tell, there's one feature that he shares with Charles Darwin: a screw in the brain that doesn't work properly, creating a slight imbalance in their logic circuitry.

The NHS will have to solve it, not I.

This is the ceiling. This is the floor. How are you? I light up. Cigarettes are good for the brain.

I stroll a bit more.

I like this city. Old, charming, beautiful, full of character, and a place that is anything but evolutionary.

Down south from this charming city is the town of Stratford-upon-Avon, the birthplace of another Englishman whose name is engraved in the very soul of the Western world: William Shakespeare, the world's most influential theater man.

Yes, I have to crack open this thing called English Theater, the forefather of the Brexit Theater. I enter my car and drive south.

The Most Tolerant and Academically Inquisitive Religion in the World

I move to a hotel steps away from "the site of Shakespeare's family home from 1597 to 1616," excited to have finally reached the nerve center of the English theater. I've heard so much about Stratford-upon-Avon, a holy city of the Western theater, and the home of the world-famous Royal Shakespeare Company, RSC for short.

I can't wait for the evening to come so that I can attend a performance by the RSC.

Time, as is always the case and not only in England, flies fast, and evening is descending on Stratford right in front of my eyes.

I am at the RSC. The play to be performed this evening is Molière's *Tartuffe*. Molière, one of my most favorite playwrights, is the funniest of them all, and *Tartuffe* is one of Molière's best, deepest, and funniest.

Yes, I was hoping to see *Hamlet* or *Macbeth* this evening, but *Tartuffe*, a delightful comedy about religious hypocrisy, is an excellent choice as well.

Moments before the lights go down, I buy a copy of the play at RSC's bookshop. This *Tartuffe*, I read, is "a brand-new version of Molière's provocative classic, relocated to present-day Birmingham's Pakistani Muslim community."

What??

Yes, it's an adaptation. In other words: This *Tartuffe* was not exactly written by Molière. Let me check what kind of an adaptation this is.

I read from the book:

> Amira: Please, I hope I haven't offended you.
> Tartuffe: Why? What have you done?
> Amira: My hair. My head's uncovered.
> Tartuffe: And?
> Amira: I should have worn hijab.

Oh, Jean-Baptiste Poquelin, look what they have done to your masterwork! I read more.

> Khalil: I'm just making the point that far from science and learning and the quest for knowledge being a western invention, it was actually thanks to Islamic scholars that the knowledge accrued by the ancient civilizations…
> Tartuffe: Colin, Colin, Colin. That was the old days. Things are different now.
> Khalil: How did we get to a point where the most tolerant and academically inquisitive religion in the world ended up being hijacked by people like you?

Amira stands for Molière's Elmire, and Khalil is a new character.

The text is super politically correct. Who else, other than flaming theater atheists of our time, will frame Islam as "the most tolerant and academically inquisitive religion in the world"? I never met Muslims using such a phrase.

I read a bit more, but then the lights go down. The play starts.

Sounds, deafening sounds, and lights, blinding lights, accompany the actors as they enter the stage. I can hear Molière screaming from the depth of his grave: Is this the best way to start a comedy?

As the play progresses, I realize that the initial moments of blitz were the most professional of the evening. The actor playing Orgon (herein called Imran), the man who blindly follows the hypocrite Tartuffe, is excellent at screaming, but that's about it. The actor playing Orgon's son, Damee (Damis), is a good rap singer, but that's it. The actor playing Tartuffe seems to love his long, fake beard, but shows little understanding of an inner character.

I'm watching the actors, and I get the impression that none of them is here to play, and that all of them are here to preach.

This is a cardinal sin in the world of theater.

The worst of it all, the creative team behind this *Tartuffe*, who sadly lack any sense of humor, end up depicting Islam, and Muslims, as a bunch of total idiots. There's a thin line that separates humor from horror, and their failed attempt at humor leaves the characters – all Muslim – in the worst light possible. This *Tartuffe* is a case of politically correct words that, spoken aloud, expose a reality that betrays the racism underneath the letters. Islam as presented here is paper thin, lacking the richness of an ancient culture and the nuances of a living religion. Despite all the politically correct praises of Islam and the Quran on the stage, it is evident that no one involved with this production has even read the Quran, and if anyone did, he or she is obviously dyslexic.

How disappointing. I expected to see the best of theater here, but I ended up seeing the worst. The flawless English theater that I admire is but a faded memory here. This is a case of failed artists who try to inject an ideological belief, correctness, into an art form, theater. Theater is not the House of Commons, and a stage does not tolerate ideologies.

The theater is packed, but anybody who expected to have Pakistanis come see this play would be extremely disappointed. I see only one theatergoer who's non-white, and almost all are old. The Pakistanis don't need the atheists of RSC to patronize them. Oh, no.

I follow their lead and leave at intermission.

Where is my eagle to direct me when the English confuse me? Will it ever come again to guide me? I have a feeling, though I'm not sure, that my eagle doesn't like England. I haven't seen my eagle for a long while now!

Where are you, my eagle, king of the birds? You should be here, in this England, land of kings and queens!

Being on my own, I talk to myself: Are London theaters also infused with PC? I shall see soon, I guess.

Oh, how I miss *The Producers*!

Before I head to London, I decide here and now, I shall visit Oxford. I want to see if political correctness has also infiltrated the famed halls of England's house of knowledge.

In case you hear me, my eagle: Is it a good plan?

A soft wind blows in my face, perhaps caused by my eagle's wings, and it sounds like a yes.

Donald Trump Is a Man, Yeah

Oxford University is one of the most elite institutions of higher learning in the world, whose student body is made of the brightest of the bright in the human species. Members of the student body of this institution are assured the best jobs on the market upon graduation, a fact that makes this group of young people some of the most privileged in British society.

A walk in the streets along the various colleges that make up Oxford University reveals one of the finest environments for students, combining pristine gardens, ancient libraries, imposing architecture, and enough space to feel like a lord or a baroness. I walk where they walk, and I am taken by what I see: so much beauty, so much richness, so many pounds.

But wait, here's something very interesting. On my right is a beautiful building, probably a dormitory, with a Pride flag sticking out from a window sill, and a big photo of an older man covering the length of the window. The man is far from being a sex symbol, and so I assume that this photo is intended as a statement of some kind. What is it?

I check around and slowly find out. This is the story.

Hundreds of Oxford students are accusing Professor Emeritus John Finnis, a legal philosopher, of homophobia, primarily because of a speech he made in 1994. They are demanding his immediate removal.

The part of the speech that is irritating them most reads as follows: "The standard modern position involves a number of explicit or implicit judgments about the proper role of law and the compelling interests of political communities, and about the evil of homosexual conduct. Can these be defended by reflective, critical, publicly intelligible and rational arguments? I believe they can."

Years back, privileged students could be seen marching against the slaughter in Darfur, Sudan, but that cause is too old to excite the young of today. They need something new, more refreshing, something with a flag, something with many colors.

The man in the window is John Finnis, and this photo is meant to deride him.

I keep on walking, and suddenly I hear shouts for "justice." I walk in the direction of the Justice sound, and when I get there, I see a group of people demonstrating against the Sudanese president, Omar Al-Bashir, accusing him of the brutal atrocities in Darfur. The protesters, among whom I can't spot one white person, are Africans. They are probably trying to get the privileged students to join them, but so far to no avail.

Today it's Finnis the others care about, not Bashir. I keep on walking.

Let me chat with the folks of the City of Dreaming Spires, aka Oxford, I say to myself.

My eyes catch sight of a young lady who is tremendously enjoying her cigarette, and I approach her. Her name is Beth, she tells me, and she's a writer. She's well dressed, well made up, and is in the process of lighting up another cigarette. She has big dreams, she has an agent, and soon her first book will come out. She is English, or as she calls herself, "Brit," and she's equipped with all the politeness that can be found in the British book of manners.

How does she feel about Brexit? Well, she thinks that the people who voted to leave the EU are, in a word, stupid, and their vote should not count.

As a general rule, she informs me, the Brits are stupid. Yeah.

"We are British, of course we are. We are completely uneducated."

Around us are some stores operated by well-known charities such as Oxfam, among others, and I wonder how much people like her care about the charitable.

Is there any cause, an international cause, that you champion? An issue, or a place in the world, that you care about?

"I haven't got a clue."

But Beth has got more than just a clue about her fellow Brits. The Brits, she tells me, have nothing to talk about when they meet one another, except for the weather. "Whenever I meet another person, it's, 'Oh, nice weather today,' or 'God, it's bloody miserable today.'" Brits, according to her, are also the biggest liars on the planet. "I say 'sorry' after everything. I can walk down the street, I won't even bump into someone, but I'd say sorry. Why am I doing this? I don't know. It's this inherent politeness that we can't seem to get rid of."

When you say sorry, doesn't it mean that you care?

"No, I don't care. I don't care at all. No, I'm not saying sorry because I care about their feelings; I'm saying sorry because that's what I've been taught to do. You always apologize."

That's a very tough life to live, isn't it?

"It really is. That's why I like to go abroad so much, to meet new people and pretend that I'm not British."

Beth, like some other English people I've met, feels confident enough to laugh at herself. Self-deprecation, I slowly learn here, is a by-product of people who think highly of themselves, like many an English person, and of the privileged in society.

Oxford, of course, is a headquarters for the more privileged of the privileged.

Many a student walks on the streets of Oxford, most with their noses up to the sky. They are young, they are sharply dressed, they are a happy bunch, and they are quiet. Kind of quiet. I speak to a number of them, and most won't say a word for the record about most anything political. They have no clue, so they tell me, about anything happening anywhere outside of Oxford. Bosnia, what's that? Palestine, where is that? Israel, what is it? Donald Trump? That's a man, right?

Is this true? Not exactly. It would be safe to bet that quite a number of students here are enamored with the Palestinians, for example. A case in point is Oxford Union. A few months ago, the prestigious debating platform of Oxford Union invited Palestinian prime minister Rami Hamdallah as a speaker, but that's not enough for them. Palestine is a huge country, as we all know, and next week the Union will host a "Palestine Debate."

Love's love.

But they wouldn't admit it. At least not today.

Later in the week the Malaysian prime minister, a man who is on record as saying that the "hook-nosed" Jews have "an instinctive sense of money," will be hosted by Oxford Union. They know whom to honor.

Yeah.

Often it takes time to get English people to clearly say what they think, and it's much more so in Oxford. When I push harder, the Oxford students tell me that the reason they don't speak their minds is that they have been taught in their university not to comment on any issue that they have not thoroughly researched. Others explain to me that they, the Oxford students, are ambitious people, and they are worried that if they said anything political, it might risk their future employment. In other words, they are what the Sheffield cops call "snowflakes."

There's one thing, though, that they have no fear talking about: Brexit. This item, Brexit, they know back and forth, up and down, right and left, and every corner of it. Almost all them are firmly against it. There was a referendum, correct, but the vote shouldn't count. It's totally undemocratic, the geniuses say, to abide by the result of the referendum. Accepting the verdict of the voter is absolutely undemocratic, they argue with passion. Full stop. End.

These are the young.

Of course, not only the young breathe the air of Oxford.

Not far from me is a nice café, inside which a baroness is waiting for me. Yeah. Can you believe it?

I go to meet her.

"Where are you staying?" she asks me.

Now, this is an extremely important question in Her Majesty's land. If I stay, let's say, in a Holiday Inn, that would mean that I'm not worthy of anybody's time in Oxford. For hundreds of years, close to a millennium, this city has been the abode of royalty, scholars, and of the moneyed few, and only they matter, only they count.

I'm staying at the Randolph, I tell her, a five-star hotel. She's pleased to hear this.

Some years ago, she tells me, the hotel caught fire – but everything's okay now.

I can't avoid it, but after what I learned in Manchester, all I can think of is: Which Jew owns the Randolph?

Should I ask the baroness for the name of the Jew who set the Randolph on fire? No, I don't think it's a good idea.

Instead I ask her a simpler question: Is our meeting here on the record or off?

Like all great politicians, the baroness is a strong lady who makes quick decisions. "I'll tell you more," she says, "if you don't quote me." She surveys the café, up and down, right and left, and then changes her response. It doesn't matter, she now says, because everything is bugged in this café.

But she is a baroness and she wants to talk anyway, on the condition that whatever she says is not for attribution.

What does she tell me that's so sensitive?

1. Brits are superficial people.
2. Jeremy Corbyn is an anti-Semite.
3. British society in general is becoming more and more anti-Semitic. If she were young, she tells me without looking at my face, she would have left this country and moved either to Israel or the United States. She never thought that Britain would become anti-Semitic, but now that it has, she regrets not having left this country when she was young.

She's Jewish.

I go to my hotel. I must find out which Jew owns the Randolph.

I approach a hotel employee and ask her: Was there a fire in this hotel at some recent point?

Yes, she says. The fire started in the kitchen and spread upward, and the hotel was closed for about six weeks for renovation.

Do you know the name of the family that owns the hotel?

I expect to hear a name such as Dreyfus, Cohen, or Disraeli, but that's not to be. The owner is a company by the name of Macdonald, she tells me, and they are Scots.

Not Jews. What a disappointment!

Before I go totally nuts, I need a break from reality. And that's where I'm heading next.

There's Daggers in Men's Smiles

Right by my hotel is a theater by the name of New Theatre Oxford, where the Royal National Theatre production of Shakespeare's *Macbeth* will be performed tonight. This *Macbeth*, as far as I can tell, is not adapted to any Pakistani family and does not take place in Golders Green either. Just Brits. Stupid, superficial Brits.

I go to the theater.

The set is dark, with many black drapes all over and one huge black ramp in the middle. The other dominant color on the stage is red, symbolizing blood and royalty. The witches of this *Macbeth* are young and agile, and Macbeth speaks in a Scottish accent that I fully understand.

I'm damn proud of myself, by the way!

The play goes on.

Strange, but for me, this is the first time that Shakespeare on the stage sounds reassuringly clear, smoothly evoking mighty emotions, and the text sounds amazingly simple.

It's here, on this English stage, surrounded by Brits, that I experience Shakespearean theater in its purest form. Shakespeare, what a discovery, is not complex literature but rather emotional storytelling. Yes, really.

Shakespeare took huge artistic license interpreting facts, but the core of his stories is based on reality. British reality.

And here I can see and sense it.

Watching and listening to the actor playing Macbeth brings me back to Scotland. When I hear the name of Inverness, where Macbeth's castle is located, I say to myself: I know that place! And when I listen to the witches, Nessie jumps in front of my eyes.

It all sounds so familiar, so British.

Shakespearean theater, it dawns on me during this performance, is first and foremost about the people living here, including the hundreds of Brits surrounding me at this very moment. It's about their history, about their complex relationship to monarchy, about their struggles with one another, about their bloody fights all over this island, about themselves. The audience watches how those on the stage talk ever so nicely to one another, My Lord and Shmy Lord, but then stab each other to death – and the audience looks at the mirror.

"There's daggers in men's smiles."

The House of Commons that we see on TV actually started here.

My Honorable Gentleman, My Honorable Friend, they say with their tongues as the poison drips from their lips, now as then.

Sorry, Beth says, but she means not.

These are my English people. On stage and off. Acting all the time.

My break from reality is actually *the* reality. Funny.

In London, in the House of Commons, MPs vote down Theresa May's Brexit deal, 432 to 202. Is it time to head on to the capital?

Maybe, but let me stay at the Randolph one more day.

Israeli Embassy Plants a Spy in Labour Party

During the height of the anti-Semitism row, a Labour Party veteran accused "Jewish Trump fanatics" for creating the row and said that he would not be lectured by those Jews. Many people, including some Jewish leaders, demanded his immediate expulsion from the Labour Party.

Their demand was rejected.

The veteran, a close friend of Jeremy Corbyn, is a member of Labour's National Executive Committee (NEC), the governing body of the Labour Party, and Secretary of Campaign for Labour Party Democracy, a Labour Party activists' group. He is, in short, still in power, and his detractors can fume as much as they want.

According to the *Guardian*, this obviously powerful man later "apologised, saying he was 'of course aware of appalling instances of antisemitism in the party,' that he was 'wholly determined to rooting it out of our movement' and that he would undertake equalities training."

Who is this man? His name is Peter Willsman, and according to the *New Stateman* he "is the true face of Labour's anti-Semitism problem." The *Guardian*, in a separate article, argued that his "rant points to a Labour party still blind to antisemitism," and asked, "How much more poisonous will Labour let this issue become?"

I read about him some time ago and almost forgot about him. But now it all comes back.

It's late evening, the following day, and I hardly had anything to eat today. I was walking the streets of Oxford, talking to people and looking for my eagle as well, and all I could find of interest were figurines of the queen and other members of the monarchy, £3 each. But now my belly calls. The Randolph restaurant is soon closing, but they still have some food for me, their starving guest.

Awesome.

The restaurant is almost empty of diners, except for one person who sits by himself at a corner table, reading a paper.

I sit down a couple of tables in front of him and order a sandwich, which is the only food the restaurant is serving at this time.

How's the sandwich at this five-star hotel? Well, it was not prepared by Macca, but for now anything will do.

As I eat the sandwich, I examine the paper-reading man. He looks awfully familiar.

Isn't he, I ask myself, the man of power behind the anti-Semitism row?

If so, if he is Peter Willsman, he could be my key to Jeremy Corbyn's door. That would be a wonderful, wouldn't it?

What's your name? I ask him.

"Peter. Red Pete."

He doesn't give out his last name. Why? I don't know.

He continues to talk.

"I am the spider at the center of the web. They call me Corbyn's enforcer, but I don't want to be called Corbyn's enforcer because enforcers have no sense of humor. I'm more like Corbyn's protector, because he never looks after himself, he never defends his back."

Why is that?

"He's not interested in himself. He just wants to change the world. Not only that, but he sees good in everyone. I tell him they're not all like that, they're fucking bastards. But he sees good in everyone.

They want to stab him in the back, but it's not something he's going to bother about. He never considers it. It's me who has to stop people stabbing him in the back."

Should I tell him that I once envisioned Jeremy Corbyn as a belly dancer wearing a bikini and carrying the mace?

I don't think that this man will appreciate it.

I order a drink, my usual Diet Coke, and ask him to join my table. He does.

And he continues to talk.

"You stay in this hotel, where the posh people live. Five stars. Your eyeglasses, they are John Lennon's glasses!"

This man is funny, let me tell you.

I tell the man that he can call me John Lennon, if he so wishes, but that in reality I am a German journalist. Hearing this, he starts doing a PR job on me, selling me his favorite man: Jeremy Corbyn. Where does he start? From the beginning, Jeremy's parents.

"The Battle of Cable Street was in the late thirties. There was a big fascist movement in London, based around a guy called Mosley, who supported Hitler and so on. The trade union stood up, and there was a fight between the fascists and the trade unions for two days, and the fascists were driven out. Jeremy's mother was on that battle, and Jeremy's father was very left wing as well.

"They met at a left-wing demo. The minute Jeremy was born, he was born to be Jeremy. When he was only eight, he was told by the headmaster that he had to do military practice because it was not long after the war in the fifties. He refused to do it. So, from the age of eight he was sweeping the playground when the other kids were marching up and down. Now, how many kids at eight would have done that? He did it because he was born to be Jeremy Corbyn."

The man now jumps many years ahead.

"Jeremy is an atheist like me, but he shares many Christian views, meaning that everyone should be together and all that. He wants to see all the world, all of the decent people, all coming together, ending wars and all wickedness."

Can you arrange for me to meet him?

"I'll send him a note. But you have to tell me what I should tell him that you want. You got to ask him something that he'd be interested in. He'll do it for me because he's my friend."

Great. Thanks. By the way, do you think that he'll be prime minister one day?

"They're going to move heaven and earth to stop him, aren't they? If you're rich enough, you can move heaven and earth. You know the rich control the papers, the rich control everything. And the rich know he's going to make them pay taxes. They'd move heaven and earth if they could. One of the things about anti-Semitism is they're using it to whip people up. They use anything. Any lies. All types of lies. And they just whip it up. I'll tell you who's behind all that anti-Semitism against Jeremy."

Who?

"Almost certainly, it was the Israeli embassy."

Really?

"Yeah, they caught somebody in the Labour Party, and it turns out that the person was an agent in the embassy. Nothing to do with the Labour Party."

Can you prove it?

"I'll tell you, it was in the paper. But that was an obvious one. But the thing is that the people who are in the Labour Party doing it are people who are linked. One of them works indirectly for the Israeli embassy, and my guess would be that they're the ones whipping it up all the time.

"They've always done it, so it's nothing unusual. Now in the *Guardian*, not long ago, we had sixty-eight rabbis, obviously organized by the Israeli embassy, sixty-eight rabbis saying, 'Anti-Semitism in the Labour Party is widespread and severe.' Widespread and severe. That is the fucking rubbish they're coming out with. And people are getting whipped up by it. People are just being whipped up. Sixty-eight rabbis signed the letter in the *Guardian*, saying that anti-Semitism in the Labour Party is widespread and severe. The most we found in the Labour Party is seventy examples of anti-Semitism so far, but we've got 600,000 members. Is seventy out of 600,000 widespread and severe?"

If I could get Jeremy Corbyn to say it, that would be a perfect statement!

"Oh, Jeremy doesn't want to get involved in it. Jeremy's above all that."

I am also interested in his life story.

"Jeremy is totally unique in British history."

Explain.

"Look, Theresa May would get about a hundred people coming to see her if she gave a talk, Churchill got five thousand. A year and a half ago, Jeremy gave a talk in Durham. How many did he get?"

I don't know.

"Quarter of a million. That is the most ever in British history. Jeremy wants to change the world!"

How?

"Well, first of all, we've got greater inequality in this country since 1910. We have got more people sleeping in the streets than we've ever had. The Tories have thrown people out of their homes. We've got massive inequality, massive poverty, and masses of people sleeping on the streets. Jeremy is going to transform the lives of millions of people. And he will never give up. Jeremy never, ever gives up, all right?"

You are Peter Willsman, aren't you?

"How did you know? Somebody for the first time in a hundred years recorded what I said. Illegitimately. Illegally. And of course, I was having one of my rants. It was this one here, that I done to you, because I'm so angry about it. Where it said 'widespread and severe' and there's only seventy examples out of 600,000. I really went angry. I wasn't attacking the rabbis, I was attacking the unfairness of it. I couldn't give a fuck whether they were Jehovah's Witnesses, the fucking pope or what. But of course, they said I was being anti-Semitic. And they used it. Jeremy stuck up for me and told them to piss off. So it didn't matter. But that will be all in there. Somebody rung me up on New Year's Eve. They said, you're on News of the Year, or something. And they played my ranting. I rant all the time at these meetings. Bunch of dickheads, attacking Jeremy? You think I'm going to sit there and put up with it? Bollocks, you know what I mean? And of course, they don't know how to handle these things. Thirty-seven years I've been ranting at them. And so, recording me and trying to do me in was ideal for them. But they didn't do me in because Jeremy told them to fuck off. Although Jeremy would never say 'fuck off.'"

I know. Will you open for me the door to Jeremy Corbyn?

Peter Willsman, impressed that I've found out who he is, gets a notepad and a pen. He'll write a note to Jeremy, he tells me, asking him to meet me. The question is, what should he write in the note? Holding the pen in his right hand, he wonders aloud.

"Jeremy won't respond unless we present a good question. It has to be something that looks… Well, we've got to think. Should I say that I'm in a hotel with a German journalist?"

Are you for real or are you just a teaser?

"I might tease you, but I will never deceive you. I will write a proper text." He starts writing and continues to talk at the same time.

"What I could write is that 'I'm having a – having a drink – having a meal,' I'd say, because he's not a drinker. Well, we're not having a drink anyway, are we?"

A sandwich.

"'Having a meal, having a cup of tea.' That's more Jeremy. 'Having a cup of tea with a journalist in Oxford.' I won't say I'm here, at the Randolph, because he'll say, What are you doing in a posh place like that? 'In Oxford having a cup of tea with a journalist from Germany – '"

You can tell him that I'm a big fan of his.

"No, he doesn't like being flattered. He wouldn't believe it anyway. Are you writing about British politics?"

Yeah.

"Okay. ' – who is writing about Britain and British politics, about modern Britain and their politics. Surprise, surprise, he is fascinated by the JC saga,' or 'by the rise of JC or by the – ' What do we call it? Phenomenon, I think, is better than saga."

Okay.

"' – by the JC phenomenon. He's particularly interested in trying to strengthen the…' What do you call it, the bonds, the international bonds or – "

Perhaps: International bonds between Britain and Germany.

"What's another word for it? You're trying to build up a, not just bonds, sort of a warmer type than bonds. Trying to strengthen the... It's not just bonds. 'Trying to strengthen the – '"

The relationship.

"The *solidarity* relationship. Yeah. ' – trying to strengthen the solidarity between...' We better say 'progressives,' he'll be more responsive. 'Trying to strengthen the solidarity between progressive forces.'"

I suggest: In the UK and Germany.

"' – between the UK and Germany.' Yeah, that's very good. He'll like that. ' – Obviously, your views would be vital to him. He's given me his number, what do I do next?'"

Sounds very good.

"Let me just read what I wrote so far: 'I'm in Oxford having a cup of tea with a journalist from Germany. He is writing about modern Britain and our politics. Surprise, surprise he has said he is fascinated by the JC phenomenon. He is here until end of March. He is particularly interested in trying to use his work to strengthen the solidarity between the progressive forces in UK and Germany. He has given me his telephone number. What do I do now?'"

Very good! Let me ask you a personal question, Peter. Are you married?

"I was married, yeah. I see my wife a lot, ex-wife, we're still best friends. When we got married, we said we wouldn't have children. I'm not ready for children yet. I'm too immature. But she wanted children thirty-five years ago. So, we decided to split up, 'cause I'm not ready. I'm not ready for children. I'm too immature. I still go night clubbing. I go night clubbing twice a week. I love children, but I like to be able to hand them back after a few hours of playing with them. You know what I mean? I'm not ready. I'm not mature enough. I could not be a proper father. Should I tell you how Jeremy met his wife?"

Go ahead.

"It was told to me by his wife's best friend. There was a Spanish woman who came over to him and told him that she had met some chap from Eastern Europe or something, they had a baby and he ran off with the baby; she was in a terrible state. Jeremy went to Interpol. He pursued it ruthlessly. He didn't rest and eventually the Interpol tracked the kid down and she got the kid back. She couldn't believe it, what he'd done for her. She went back home, to Mexico, and she told her sister that she'd met this amazing man who got her child back. And the sister said: I'll go and thank him. She didn't speak any English and Jeremy didn't speak any Spanish. But she came to see him, and she was using a dictionary to communicate with him. Later they started corresponding, and one day she asked him: Would you like to come to Mexico to see my family? What do you think Jeremy did?"

Took a plane to Mexico.

"Well, yeah, but he was an MP, and Parliament was still sitting. He wouldn't leave Parliament, he's obsessive about his work. What did he do? He went to a night school every night until he learned perfect Spanish. Then, about two or three months later, he went to see her, and he spoke Spanish with her. Of course, they fell in love."

One hour after another comes and goes, and Peter can't stop talking about Jeremy. Before I depart, he shares with me one more story about his real love: Jeremy Corbyn.

"Jeremy goes to this café, a workers' café, where he sits at a table and makes notes about all the effects of the benefit cuts and what it means for people. Suddenly the door opens – he told me this story – and this bloke comes in, a great big bloke, a working-class bloke, bald head, covered in tattoos, and he presses his index finger on Jeremy's nose for about ten minutes as he says to him: 'You fucking cunt, you cunt fucking cunt.' That bloke is obviously a fanatical UKIP supporter. Now, if someone came into a room and did that to you, what would you do? I would just say 'piss off.' What did Jeremy do? He took a chair and sat him down and he talked to him for three-quarters of an hour. I said: Jeremy, you can't do this, you're the leader of the Labour Party, you can't talk to every dickhead for three-quarters of an hour. Jeremy looked at me completely horrified and said: Pete, I've known you for forty-two years, I can't believe you just said that!"

In short: Jeremy is a saint.

If Peter is indicative of the people around Corbyn, or his supporters in general, this might point to a cult worship existing deep inside the very soul of a liberal party, a fact that not even the most imaginative fiction writer could have invented.

As we depart, I realize that Peter's famous apology is totally fake. His "equality training" belongs in the fiction department, if anywhere, and if anything changed, it's in the other direction: now Peter accuses the Israeli embassy of igniting the flames of anti-Semitism in Britain. It's absurd.

But that said, one cannot deny Peter's good sides, and they are not few. Peter is smart, funny, warm – actually one of the warmest people I've met so far in England.

Will he get Jeremy to meet me, his biggest German fan? We'll see.

On the morrow, my dear, I'm going to London. You see, sometimes it's good to be in a posh hotel.

I guess I better find myself a nice hotel in London!

May I Bother You by Asking for a Lighter?

London is not just the UK capital, it is also a global financial center. London: where money, politics, and art intermingle in a hidden trinity.

And I'm here. Yes, I've arrived in London!

First things first. I check in at my new hotel, the Park Plaza Westminster Bridge, right by the Westminster Bridge.

And I am going for a little walk. Where? On the Westminster Bridge.

Have you been to Westminster Bridge?

Brexit or not, millions of tourists flock to Her Majesty's land, including countless thimbleriggers, known to locals as "Romanians," who love to congregate on Westminster Bridge. Here they, the thimbleriggers, swindle naïve tourists out of every pound they have, and no local law authority is anywhere in sight to stop them.

I'm taken by what I see here: Big Ben and the Palace of Westminster casting their shadow on the bridge and its shell gamers, forming a bizarre and fascinating dance of politicians and thieves.

The Palace of Westminster holds both houses of the British parliament: the House of Lords and the House of Commons. It's here, in the Commons, that the future of Brexit will be decided.

The no-confidence vote designed to force Theresa May down fails in the Commons, right here, as the saga of Brexit goes on, and on, and on.

The abode of Prime Minister Theresa May, 10 Downing Street, is just around the corner.

Yes, I'm in the midst of the nerve center of this nation, one of the most powerful nations in the world. I am so excited!

It is here, at the center of a global military power that will save us from the evils of the world by smashing to the ground our bitterest and toughest of enemies, that the authorities are powerless in the face of a few thimbleriggers.

That's a beauty, innit?

I stick around for a while, but when evening comes, I go to the famed National Theatre, which is not far from my hotel, to get educated on an issue that I've been dealing with lately: the Labour Party. *I'm Not Running*, Sir David Hare's new play spanning twenty years of Labour Party history, is playing at the NT's stage tonight. Ticket prices in the stalls are £68 a seat, below Broadway prices but the most expensive of the shows I have seen thus far in the UK. David Hare is extremely well regarded – according to the *Washington Post* he is "almost certainly the premiere political dramatist writing in English" – and no amount of money is too high to see his work.

I take my seat, close to the stage, and I am excited like a baby with the cutest doll. Curtain.

Play starts.

It's moving at a brisk pace for the first three minutes but goes all the way down from there. Two and a half hours of boredom. The actors are doing their best, and at times they shine, but the text is so bad that despite their hard work, this play cannot be saved. *I'm Not Running* is packed with expositions but short of a clear story line. The language is mediocre and the drama, or humor, is in extremely short supply.

Have I learned anything new about the Labour Party? Not a thing. When a play is this bad, nothing in it is enlightening.

When the play is over, I smoke a cigarette outside the theater, breathing in the air of London and the smoke of my cigarette. It's a nice, cool evening, and as I look around, an elegantly dressed English lady approaches me. "May I bother you by asking for a lighter?" she asks me. I give her my lighter, and she says, "Thank you very much. It's magic," and lights up her cigarette.

I love these English people and how they use language. I've never heard an American speaking such a delightful English in decades of living in the USA. For me, this short exchange made my visit to the National Theater worth it, all £68 of it.

It's not just the way they use the English language. There's more to their English than can be put to the page; it's the sound of their English, how they enunciate every syllable, which gives added meaning to every word. I listen to them speak, and I'm in awe of how every word that crosses their lips comes out so clear, with its unique intonation. It's such beautiful English! Of course, I also like the way they dress, both men and women. Some of them, believe it or not, look like museum pieces. I'm not kidding! And then, forgive me for saying it, the makeup that the ladies here use is something else. Superb! And there you have it: sound and image forming impressions of words.

They are aware of this, their uniqueness, and often they walk the streets of this earth with their noses up in the sky.

And they are damn proud of their theaters, their cultural monuments that live on and on, for hundreds and hundreds of years.

Cultural life in Britain, of course, is not happening only onstage. The TV, for example, is another major creator of British culture. One such creation is *Naked Attraction*.

From Auschwitz to Gaza, Labour Style

Have you ever seen the dating show *Naked Attraction*? No Brexit and no clothes, just flesh, the naked flesh. The real Full Monty, nudity from top to bottom, unlike the fake Monty of Dublin. Here, playing for your pleasure on Channel 4 TV, you will see breasts, thighs, penises, vaginas, behinds, arms, calves, hands, toes, fingernails, and armpits – at times unshaved – as well. This is a human meat market on screen, where each body part is for sale, piece by naked piece.

If you are not familiar with *Naked Attraction*, a quirky British cultural event, let me explain it all to you. *Naked Attraction* is a TV dating program where men and women get to see each other naked before they go on a date. The naked bodies are revealed in stages from bottom to top, and a prospective mate gets to choose who to date based on his or her special affection for different organs of the naked individuals. The suitor, fully dressed, shares with us, the viewers, his or her assessment regarding size, look, shape, weight, atmosphere, color, and appearance of smoothness of the body part just exposed. Once the decision is made, the suitor takes off his or her clothes, and we get to see the couple in their most natural selves.

Channel 4 is not just about nudity, of course. On the other side of their spectrum is a show called *Countdown*, a game show of words and numbers, which is copresented by Rachel Riley, the "maths expert" of the show.

Rachel describes the show to me as "brainy maths on telly," meaning TV.

Rachel is an attractive blond lady in her early thirties, who joined *Countdown* ten years ago and has since also appeared on various other programs on British TV. She is a British celebrity, skinny like many of them, and as of this writing, her Twitter account has more than 600,000 followers.

Rachel, who looks even younger than her young age, is a cool lady. We meet, guess where, in my hotel room. Yeah.

It's good that I have this expensive hotel. You see?

Rachel likes my room, let me tell you. It is on the eleventh floor of the hotel, and it has a big window directly across from the Palace of Westminster. If we ever get tired of looking at each other, we can look at the palace, which provides for a pretty sexy view. Yes. One hundred percent. If I didn't know that this building is the home of the British parliament, I would have said that it is the home of island fairies, all having great fun in Full Monty. Really. From the outside, I swear, this palace looks like one big, sexy fairy tale.

The main thing is this: Rachel likes it.

A graduate of Oxford University, where she studied mathematics, Rachel knew somehow that her family had some Jewish roots, but it didn't mean much to her since she is anyway an atheist; the only thing she believes in is Manchester United. "My mom is Jewish, my father is Manchester United," is how she explains to me her cultural roots, and she's Papa's daughter.

Recently, and only recently, she started getting in touch with mom's side of the equation, the Jewish part.

How and why did she even bother? Because of Labour and the anti-Semitism row.

"I didn't realize that anti-Semitism was a problem in Britain. I thought it was dead. Personally, I didn't quite know where I fit into being Jewish because I'm not religious, and I lived in an area where there were few Jews. To me, when I was growing up, I knew when we were singing hymns in the assembly not to say the Jesus bit, but I was confused as a child. But I've always been brought up know-ing about the Holocaust, knowing about persecution, and knowing my grandparents' history. My family came over in the late 1800s running from the pogroms somewhere there in Ukraine, Russia, Poland. So, in 2018 when I saw on the national news a bunch of British Jews standing outside Parliament with placards, you know, complaining against anti-Semitism, that was a big surprise to me. So, I started reading things, I started looking at articles, tweets here, posts there."

That's when the Jewish bug in her head was born, and it's been growing ever since.

One day, when she was on a two-hour train ride to London, she read an article. "Jews in the news. Always moaning, smearing, just negative in some description." It bothered her. "I never see a posi-tive news story about Jews."

Later that day, on the set of *Countdown*, a colleague told her a nice story about a Hungarian Jewish baker who moved to New York, opened a bakery, and then gave away bread to the hungry and their families.

That's a positive story about Jews, she said to herself, and she posted it on Twitter. The response was swift, from accusing her of anti-Semitism to calling her Bloody Jew.

That's how she got sucked into the anti-Semitism row, on the opposite side of Peter Willsman. And that's where this blond atheist, smart and attractive, is spending her energies these days: fighting a war she never imagined existed. Never before had she heard of the IHRA definition of anti-Semitism, she tells me, but now she's deeply involved with many aspects of it.

The ether is full of smears against her, accusing her of the worst under the sun, but all she wanted was to tell a nice story about a loving Jew.

Rachel is not a political person, she is not a member of any party, and only recently has she started seeing Labour as the address that offers sanctuary to her abusers.

Do you think that Jeremy Corbyn is an anti-Semite? I ask Rachel.

"Personally, yes. I think he is. The abuse that I received, on the level of top politicians, is disgusting, and anyone that can allow this kind of abuse and persecution and lies and smears to exist – he doesn't care about Jews."

So, he's an anti-Semite.

"Yes."

Can you give me examples of the anti-Semitic abuse that you have been getting?

"I've been speaking up against anti-Semitism, specifically in Labour, and I've been called a white supremacist, an anti-Semite, a Nazi sympathizer, that I'm not a real Jew, that I'm a bully, that I'm a Zionist scum."

The usual stuff.

"The usual stuff, and there are more and more elaborate conspiracy theories."

Give me an example of the conspiracy theories.

"That's potentially going to be a legal issue, so I can't, really."

Can't you give me an example?

"I want to sue these people, so I can't."

On what grounds can you sue these people?

"Because the people that spread these malicious lies are top-level officials, or unofficial spokespeople for Labour. The spokesperson for the Shadow Transport Secretary tweeted to his followers that I was a bully, and a troll, and I am using this [issue of anti-Semitism] to smear my political opponents, as if I have political opponents."

So basically, the anti-Semitism in the Labour Party is not just Jeremy Corbyn –

"No, no, no. That's the problem. The Labour Party is institutionally anti-Semitic."

These are strong words, but as Rachel sees it, "It's time to call a spade a spade."

She is the first Jewish public figure, as far as I know, to possess the mental muscles to stand up for her rights, fearlessly accusing a major British political party and its leader of virulent anti-Semitism.

Rachel is a British Jewess who didn't grow up Jewish, a celebrity blond whose faith is Manchester United, and her subconscious does not contain fear of non-Jews.

As she gets ready to depart, she tells me, in case I have some doubts about Jeremy Corbyn: "He's the guy who spoke at the event 'Never Again, from Auschwitz to Gaza,' comparing Israelis to Nazis."

This is one of countless stories about Mr. Corbyn, a man in love with Hamas and Hizballah, two groups whose stated mission is to murder every Israeli alive, and he's the one who also laid a wreath on the graves of Palestinians who masterminded the murder of Israeli athletes in Munich, Germany, in 1972. These stories that have come out as of late paint a portrait of a man obsessed with Jews. And this man, go figure, is the leader of the Labour Party, a liberal party that seems to be anything but liberal nowadays.

I want to see the man.

Hopefully, Red Pete will make it happen.

Will be nice to have Jeremy Corbyn in my hotel room, belly dancing on my big bed!

Rachel leaves, and I feel like going to a theater. For God's sake, I'm in London, the theaterland of the Western world!

I go to the West End, the address for London's biggest theaters.

I stroll in the streets of London's celebrated theaters and settle on a commercial theater, a musical by the name of *Thriller Live*.

Thriller Live is playing for the tenth year at the Lyric Theatre, featuring the songs of the late Michael Jackson, or, more accurately, "Featuring the songs of Michael and the Jackson 5."

Ticket price: £72.50.

Let it be.

I settle in my seat and am ready to take in whatever the stage will graciously offer.

What does it offer?

As the show progresses, it becomes abundantly clear that what *Thriller Live* offers is a concert. Kind of. There's no story line, just songs and projected video images.

This is a sold-out performance, and the members of the audience are having the greatest of times. They sing along and occasionally get off their seats to move their asses to the music.

Whoever is producing this show is a genius. Very little art, no headaches of creating something new, digital set that doesn't need to be moved, and songs with an excellent track record.

The makers of this show, producers and what have you, seemingly assumed the audience to be of the liberal variety, and they cater to it accordingly. For example, at the climax of the show, we see the word PEACE in big letters and a parade of American liberal celebrities, from Martin Luther King to Barack Obama, projected on the stage.

I observe the people sitting next to me, and then I look on the stage. What an interesting study in opposites: while the actors on the stage are mostly black, there are no blacks in the audience. In London's supposedly classless society, the blacks entertain themselves at McDonald's – which is where I saw many of them on my way here – and the whites entertain themselves at the West End, watching blacks playing black music for them and making them feel like liberal, modern, black-loving whites.

I smell the odor of racism entering my nostrils.

No, not that the show in and of itself is racist, but the attempt to impose a "liberal" message on a show about Jackson, a man suspected of pedophilia and not of sainthood, is nothing but manipulative. It's intended to make these whites feel that they are "inclusive" by the fact that they are listening to black music.

Nu, really.

Had this show been about a white singer, would we watch the big PEACE and a parade of American presidents, from Reagan to Trump?

They love blacks here, I suspect, as much as they love Jews. I wanted a break from hate, and I got a Thriller. Live.

> They're out to get you, better leave while you can ... Just beat it, beat it, beat it, beat it, beat it.

I feel cheated. I came here to see a show, but I ended up being part of a society that is blind to racism within its own ranks. The fact that no black is here, because most of them can't afford to come to the theater, bothers me. There's no love of minorities in your heart if your eyes don't cry at this sight. You can clap as much as you want when you see the word PEACE on the stage, but to me it means nothing.

I light up a cigarette outside.

A perfectly dressed, nice-looking man stands next to me and asks: "May I pinch one of your cigarettes?"

I LOVE the way these people use language!

I give him one of my precious cigarettes, and we chat a bit. Tell me about your people, the English people, I ask of him. "We are a class society," he says as he blows smoke in the air.

Under the headline, "Revealed: the poverty pay behind the charity slogans," the *Guardian* writes today: "Spice Girls T-shirts sold to raise money for Comic Relief's 'gender justice' campaign were made in a factory in Bangladesh where women earn the equivalent of 35p an hour during shifts in which they claim to be verbally abused and harassed."

Walk on the streets of this blessed land, especially the High Street part, what the Americans call Main Street, and you'll see charity shops – Oxfam, Amnesty, etcetera – and you'll think that my Brits are the most charitable people on earth.

Are they? PEACE.

As is my habit in big cities, I use Uber for rides in the city. My driver this time is a thirty-five-year-old black man from Congo. Initially he lived in Italy, but Italy, he tells me, is too racist for his taste, so he moved to Britain, to London. He has two university degrees, in political science and in business management, but can't find a job in either field.

How do you feel as a black man in London? I ask him. Is Britain less racist than Italy?

"Definitely. I don't feel racism here."

Why, do you think, can't you get a job in your field, or fields, in London?

"What you have in London is 'institutional' racism, and that's why I can't find the good jobs here."

What do you mean?

"London is very competitive, and one thousand people apply for the same job. When your name is Muteba Mulumba and the one next to you on the list is Charles Wellington, the HR people are going to choose Charles Wellington. Wellington is a name they're familiar with, Muteba is foreign to them. That's kind of racism, but not in-your-face-racism. I mean, in Italy people said to my face, 'Get out of here, fucking black,' but nobody in London said such things to me."

I just saw a show about Michael Jackson. The actors are mostly black, the audience is all white. How do you explain that?

"A theater ticket costs £200, that's £400 for a couple – and that's with no restaurant before or after, and no transportation. The average salary for one week is £300. Can I spend £400 on two hours in the theater? No. We don't get the good jobs, and we cannot spend like those who have the good jobs. That's life for us. One day, I tell you, I'll go back to Congo. Much better weather, much better food."

PEACE.

The People with Hooked Noses

Looking for a better thrill in life, I go to the House of Lords.

Oh, what a majestic place!

The Palace of Westminster, as I already mentioned, is home to both the House of Lords and the House of Commons, and each of them has a different color motif: Lords are red, Commons are green. I love the red. The carpets here are red, the chairs are red – and the heart is red too. Yeah!

The visitors' section of the Lords, where one can watch the sessions in the Lords Chamber, is not called "Visitors' Section" but "Strangers' Gallery." We are in England, and here they use elevated English, because they are the real English unlike the rest of us. Very few lords are around, similar to the number of MSPs I saw in Scotland's parliament – politicians are the same all over – and right smack in the middle is a man wearing a wig. I have no idea what his job is. I ask the people working there, but I get different answers, from chair to clerk. So, whatever.

The lords stand up and talk, one by one, each facing either the void or a couple of about-to-fall-asleep fellow lords. Still, they go on, and on and on as if thousands of people were listening and applauding. The Lords Chamber, like the Commons, has rows of benches facing each other, like in a Quaker church, and it's quite funny, at least to me, to watch people talk to empty red benches. Naturally, the staff working here are bored as well, but they at least try to do something about it. They walk here and there, there and here, and then one of them stops next to me. I happen to have a hat on my head, and this servant of the lords asks this stranger to take it off. No hats in the House of Lords. This is a Catholic church, not a Quaker church.

The esteemed lords, in case you're curious, are presently discussing amendments to Brexit. They try to impress each other, or maybe the handymen and the floor cleaners, that they know everything there is to know about Brexit. But when, a few moments ago, I paid attention to what they were saying, I realized that they actually know nothing.

Well, if I were a lord, I'd probably behave exactly like them. You can't just be a lord and say nothing; it doesn't work like that.

Yeah, yeah, yeah.

Hey, eagle, can you hear me? I'm in London now. Do you know what I'm doing right at this very minute? I'm not driving anywhere, just sitting at the House of Lords watching old lords moving their lips.

Look at them, King of the Birds. What do you think?

The eagle is quiet. My eagle, I think, is now flying over the Highlands, amusing himself with the sight of kilt-wearing Scots.

And I'm here, staring at the creatures around me.

Would there be lords and wigs, I ask myself, if there were no queen and princes? Probably not. God save the Queen. In fact, I think, much of what I – and maybe my eagle as well – see almost everywhere in this land has to do with the monarchy. It's all about hierarchy, kind of a class system. Queens, kings, eagles, crows, princes, dukes, lords, sirs, barons, baronesses, earls, and parakeets. The letter delivery service, fittingly enough, is called Royal Mail.

Oh, if only I were the Duke of Wellington! Imagine me, a Jew with an accent, becoming the Duke of Wellington! I'd be the best duke there is.

I certainly missed my calling.

A few years ago, a young man by the name of Hugh Grosvenor became the Duke of Westminster, a frightfully rich man, and I think it's only fair that I be the Duke of Wellington.

Well, if that's too hard to pull off, I wouldn't mind being Earl Tenenbom. At least that.

But no. I'm a Stranger, in the middle of the Strangers' Gallery, and I'm getting totally bored with the lords.

Time I meet a baroness.

She's somewhere in this palace; I just have to go and find her.

Oh, here she is, on the ground floor not far from the entrance, sitting on a red armchair. Here's a woman who, unlike me, did not miss her calling: woman, Jewish, and religious.

Life ain't fair.

Her name is Baroness Rosalind Altmann, and she is an economist by profession, a former work and pensions minister, and she sits at the House of Lords as a Conservative, aka Tory.

What shall one Jew ask another Jew in these days in London? Well, the obvious thing: Is Jeremy Corbyn an anti-Semite?

This woman is one tough cookie, my eagle once told me; let me see what answer this tough lady, a baroness no less, will give me.

"I believe Jeremy Corbyn is an anti-Semite."

You can tell that she's religious. She starts with "I believe."

And she goes on and on because, like the lords, she's giving a speech, not just an answer: "I believe he must be anti-Semitic, because I cannot believe anyone could misconstrue the cartoon that he endorsed."

What cartoon?

"There was a cartoon which portrayed Jewish, moneyed bankers, money lenders, playing Monopoly on top of the backs of poor people. The classic trope of Jews being moneyed people, the money men. It is Jews with hooked noses. All of the characteristics that put...the classic signs."

When was that?

"This was a cartoon that he endorsed, it was…I don't exactly remember where it was, I can look that up. But they wanted to take it down, and he said that would not be appropriate, because one has to be able to express one's opinions, and it's art. But I'm afraid there is a distinction between what counts as art and what is merely incitement to hatred. And there have been so many examples when he was endorsing views that are anti-Semitic and then trying to distance himself from them. I believe that he is anti-Semitic and that he believes in the classic anti-Semitic tropes of Jews being the evil capitalists, the bankers, and those medieval – or even further back in history – stereotypes that are so damaging and dangerous, and that, of course, are entirely wrong. Jews come from all different parts of the social spectrum; they have all different political beliefs. Some may be capitalists, some are unquestionably socialist or communist."

I posed this question to many Jewish leaders and Jewish officials: "Is Jeremy Corbyn an anti-Semite? Yes or no." You are the first one to say, on the record, that he is an anti-Semite.

"I'm afraid I might get into trouble for it, but I'm the kind of person who says what I think. If I believe something, I will say it."

I congratulate you for saying what you think.

"I don't feel in any need of congratulations. I'm very sad that I need to say it, and I'm also very sad that for the first time in my lifetime I feel threatened as a Jew for my future in this country. I have never felt that before. Indeed, I have always felt so fortunate to be living in a country which has been so tolerant. The government, of all different parties, I'm not just talking about the Conservatives, I'm talking about whether it's Labour or Conservative, for the last umpteen decades has been led by people who were not anti-Semitic, people who were religiously tolerant and have created and fostered a society which has promoted the interests of Jews, promoted the interests of Muslims, all faiths and none, with respect for each person's beliefs as an individual. For the first time in my life, I believe that there is a serious threat that one of our major mainstream political parties may take power and be against Jewish interests."

I hear her, look at her, and it is startling to witness: a lady in a position so high, fearful of the ultimate fall. Here's a woman who has achieved one of the highest levels of society, a member of the House of Lords, a baroness, but the abyss deep below is staring at her.

She's not the only person fearful that her fortunes will turn 180 degrees. There are non-Jewish Brits fearful of a similar fate, if and when Lady Brexit is born.

What does this baroness think of Brexit?

As an economist, what's your position on Brexit? I ask her.

"I am deeply concerned about Brexit, I am opposed to Brexit. I would accept leaving the European Union if I could be convinced that it is, indeed, what the majority of the people in this country want. If it is, that's okay. You know, I'm a democrat."

I don't understand this logic.

"What don't you understand?"

There *was* a referendum, and the majority decided, 52 to 48, to leave the EU.

"Yeah."

Period.

"I don't believe that we really have to obey those instructions."

Why not? That's democracy.

"No. It's not. It was an advisory referendum."

The majority of people –

"Hang on, hang on! Seventeen point four million people voted to leave the EU on the basis of promises and assurances that were false. Both sides of the campaign were terrible, I agree. But if they had been told that leaving the EU would mean losing all our free trade, and all the trade deals we have, and that leaving the EU would certainly mean that we would be worse off, at least for a time, I'm not convinced that they would have voted to leave."

That's patronizing, patronizing the Leave voters, which in essence means disrespecting their ability to think for themselves. But she's not the only one thinking so. Most in Labour, and most so-called liberals, think the same. Those Remainers can't believe that they lost the vote, and they kvetch. Fittingly enough, some British tabloids refer to the Remainers as Remoaners.

Good use of English!

But the baroness, like her colleagues, just can't stop.

"I come from the world of pensions, okay, if you promise somebody that if they buy your pension they will be much better off and there aren't any risks, that's called mis-selling, and that person would have the chance to change their mind or get some compensation. The premise on which people voted, and we don't know how many of them believed it, was that they would be better off, have a lot more money, and would also keep all the benefits without losing what we already have. That isn't true."

Maybe we should also invalidate the Good Friday Agreement referendum –

"Let me tell you something."

If you invalidate one referendum, why not invalidate the others as well?

"It's a very important point. A few years ago, there was a refer endum on Wales. Okay? Zero point three percent swung the vote. Theresa May, who is currently saying this referendum is sacrosanct, campaigned to have another referendum to overturn that one. We are even going to lose our nuclear safeguards, we're going to lose our security. Nobody explained that to people."

For an economist, who should be good with numbers, she got the number wrong. It was 0.6 percent difference, not 0.3. In addition, that referendum, despite the low figure, was accepted, and the Welsh Assembly was created as a result.

At the end of the day, if I'm to judge by the people I've talked to, the Brexit vote was more about emotions than about logic. Remainers feel European, Leavers feel British. The Rs want to be part of the globalized world, the Ls don't. It's not about "the economy, stupid."

I'm not British, and I don't care either way, remain or leave, but I'll never get the logic of the Remainers, who try every excuse in the book to skirt basic democratic principles – and facts. It's a talent I usually encounter in the intellectual world, mostly on the left side of politics, where facts and logic matter not. But she's an exception: conservative, religious, and senseless.

We talk more about this, the baroness and I, but then I drop it. There's simply no point in arguing with people who come to the table with a religious zeal against, or for, Brexit. You can't argue faith.

At least this baroness had the guts, the nerve, and the courage to say the obvious about my belly dancer, Jeremy Corbyn, unlike many of her coreligionists who lack the ability to stare truth in the eye and call a spade a spade.

Jeremy Corbyn, the man who may be – if he plays his cards right – the next prime minister.

What does it mean to play your cards right in today's Britain? I don't know. Maybe hate Jews a bit more.

In any case, I want to see this saint, already! Should I bother Red Pete?

Yeah, why not?

I send him a message, reminding him that "John Lennon" is waiting to meet JC. He promptly replies. Isn't he sweet?

He says that he's going to meet JC in a few days, and that he'll try. If this materializes, he says, it will be after an NEC meeting taking place in London next week.

Never, ever have I thought that one day I would be called John Lennon. But all's possible in the world of Jeremy Corbyn.

The baroness did not surprise me when she mentioned the anti-Semitic cartoon. Often when I talk to people about JC, they share with me all kinds of juicy anti-Semitic stories in which JC is the protagonist. If I lived permanently in London, I'd have already created an anti-Semitic musical, *JC and Me*, incorporating all those stories. *JC and Me*, I'm sure, would be a West End smash, the highest-grossing musical of all time.

I'm not sure yet, but maybe in one scene I'll have him a trans, dancing with a pink bikini, eating Princess Di cookies and licking Darwin chocolates.

In another scene, I think, I'll have him strolling in Gateshead with a kilt, looking for a bookstore. Won't it be funny?

JC and Me. Tickets are available now at your local Jewish banks. I can't wait!

I stroll in the palace, from the House of Lords to the House of Commons, and I pass the Royal Gallery, whose walls are decorated with two enormous paintings. One is *The Death of Nelson*, depicting the Battle of Trafalgar, and the other is *The Meeting of Wellington and Blücher*, depicting the Battle of Waterloo.

Two new thoughts come to my mind. First: the Duke of Wellington doesn't look like me. Second: Will a Jeremy Corbyn portrait hang on these walls one day?

I close my eyes and I see a painting hanging on the wall next to me: the head of the British Labour Party and the Malaysian prime minister standing on top of a mighty hill looking down at frail, hook-nosed Jews exchanging currencies just before they die.

That painting will hang here tomorrow if the Brits don't crush their anti-Semitism today. My eyes now open, I leave.

The Horrible Bastards of England

I don't know if anybody has ever told you, but the Palace of Westminster has the tendency to numb human cells after being in contact with it for over two hours. Nobody has told me, not even my eagle, and I got numbed. If I didn't immediately leave the palace, I suspect, I might have died there, and maybe even been buried there. Can you imagine? JC and me. In the same palace.

Luckily, I left before it was too late. I jumped into an Uber, and the driver – a really great person – took me as far away as Uberly permitted. Yes.

I'm presently in Surbiton, in a pub that once was a synagogue. I'm not kidding. I swear.

You don't believe me? Jump in an Uber and come here; tell the driver to drop you off in front of Coronation Hall pub. What do you see when you look at the pub? Yes, a big Star of David.

No, I've not come here to pray; I came here to drink, as far away from the palace as possible. What do I drink? Diet Coke.

A sad story, isn't it? A man sits in a pub and drinks Diet Coke. Well, that's life, my life.

At a table next to me I see Bob and Colin, Tory and Labour pubgoers, respectively. They are normal people: they have beer.

And both of them are pro-Israel. So they tell me. Why?

Because of the Holocaust, they say. The Jews have suffered too much and they, as Brits, identify with them.

It is flattering for a Jew like me to meet two total strangers having such a deep commitment to Jewish people, except that in this pub nobody knows I'm Jewish. I told Bob and Colin that I'm Jordanian. Yeah. I am, to make it perfectly clear, a Hashemite, like King Abdallah of Jordan. In other words, I am a direct descendant of the Prophet Mohammed.

Yeah. Me.

As a Jordanian, I'm sure you'll understand, I'm very offended that these two Brits support the Jews. How could you, I ask them, not support my Palestinian brothers and sisters, who suffer under the illegal occupation of the Israelis?

But they won't budge. They are pro-Israel. Period. Stubborn Brits.

I ask them, these two Jew lovers, to share with me their feelings about the anti-Semitism row in their country, especially in light of the media's constant reports about anti-Semitism in the Labour Party.

Well, that's what the media say, but that's not true, they argue. The media are owned by Jews and those Jews spread such news.

I listen to them talking, and I can hear Peter Willsman: "You know the rich control the papers, the rich control everything."

What a small world.

Wait. Correction. Everything is owned by Jews. They elaborate.

Colin: "The Jewish people run all the businesses, they make the money. They have an ability, they come together... all the richest people in the world are Jewish."

You agree with that? I ask Bob.

Bob: "Yeah."

Colin: "They have a business acumen."

Bob: "I've once been to Bethlehem, and it happened to be on December 25. In the Manger Square was Arafat. The Christmas tree and the religious part was Catholic, but all the money, all the lights and everything, were done by the Jews, and by the end of Christmas Day, they were fighting each other."

And the Jews made the money?

"Of course!"

These lovers of Israel, go figure, are classic anti-Semites.

I ask myself: Is that what happens when you scratch a Brit, find an anti-Semite underneath? Maybe.

It's the people who put Jeremy Corbyn on top; he didn't do it on his own. I go out to smoke and check on my smartphone what's new in the world.

I watch a clip of the event with the Malaysian prime minister at the Oxford Union. Shamelessly, the man repeats his anti-Semitic trash, claiming it's his right to say whatever he wants to say about the hook-nosed Jews, and the audience applauds him. Not that the audience is made up of Muslim Brotherhood followers, by the way. When he speaks negatively about gays, nobody applauds him.

What's going on in Oxford? Jesus knows.

And here's a *Guardian* editorial, under a photo of an armored vehicle somewhere on earth, with soldiers shooting – or about to shoot – to death a lone demonstrator. It's horrifying. In the article, the *Guardian* editors tell us about a brutal regime that murders innocent people who have "little more than rocks in their hands and slogans on their lips."

Beautiful English, isn't it?

Now guess who the horrible people are.

Yes, Jews, aka Israelis, meaning the Jews of Israel. Who else?

If only there were no Jews, the world would be a paradise.

I'm going to the Ivy Club in London, "An exclusive members' club" above the Ivy restaurant, to meet a smart British man who, potentially, could explain everything to me.

Have you been to the Ivy Club? The prices are sky high. But I am a guest of the smart man, a member of the club and a famous London lawyer, so I am in.

This famous lawyer, let it be known, doesn't want to have his name revealed. Okay.

Is Britain anti-Semitic? I ask him.

"Britain has always been anti-Semitic. Perfidious Albion."

This man talks high English, and if you don't understand him, that's your problem.

"Have you been to York? Have you been to Clifford's Tower, where they burned the Jews to death?"

That was in the year 1190, but this lawyer won't let it go. He's building a case. That's what he does for a living.

Swiftly, to confuse the enemy, he jumps to the present.

"There are stories coming out every single day about the Labour Party being anti-Semitic and, yet, according to the polls, 40 percent of the people are supporting Labour. I won't say that all these people are anti-Semitic per se, but this 40 percent is made up of people who are either anti-Semitic per se and those who are not bothered about other people being anti-Semitic."

All I have to do is add up the far right, a number of capitalists, some non-political Jew haters, and you get an impressive number of Brits who won't let me become a duke, lord, or earl.

I need to be cheered up. How about going to see a show, a funny show?

A few minutes' walk from here is the Criterion Theatre, where Mischief Theatre's production of *The Comedy about a Bank Robbery* is playing. Why not go there? Yes, why not?

I wonder if I will find similarities with my gangster safe blower, Charlie of Liverpool. God bless Britain for giving us, the rest of us, so much theater to choose from.

I go to the theater.

Lights down.

Curtain up.

The play starts in a prison, and from the curtain up, I can't stop laughing.

Here are two examples of short dialogues between the first characters appearing on stage: a warden, Cooper the guard, and Mitch the convict.

> Warden: Weight?
> *Silence.*
> Warden: Weight!
> Cooper: I'm waiting, sir.
> …
> Warden (*to Mitch*): So, are you enjoying your time here at British Columbia Penitentiary?
> Mitch: I'm having a ball.
> Warden (*to Cooper*): Tell me about his sentence.
> Cooper: It was kinda sarcastic, sir.
> Warden: No, no, how long is the man's sentence?
> Cooper: It was four words, sir.
> Warden: No! How long is his jail term?
> Cooper: Ten years, sir.

And this is just the beginning. As time moves on, the play becomes ever funnier, quite more intricate, and totally believable – even though I, the viewer, know that nothing on this stage is real. It's a miracle how this works so well, but it does.

The actors, God Bless the Queen, are superb!

I'm the luckiest man in the world: I'm in Britain, in London, and I get to watch this genius of British theater. God bless England.

This kind of amazingly funny evening should have taken place in *Tartuffe*, but it didn't. Here, as you can tell, nobody's trying to preach to anybody.

At play's end, I go to my hotel, the Park Plaza Westminster Bridge. Before I get to my room, in the plaza downstairs, I meet Thomas, a Scot from Glasgow on a business trip to London. He's a bit drunk, and his tongue is a bit loose. "I hate the English people," he says to me. Why do you hate them? "They're horrible bastards who think they're still an empire."

Who owns this hotel? I ask at the front desk, just before going to my room.

In response, he whispers: "An Israeli Jew."

What's his name?

"Eli Papouchado."

That's my luck. I go from a Palestinian named Marwan to a Jew named Eli. They might be killing each other in the Middle East, but in England they make hotels.

I settle in my room and look out the window. What do I see? Yes, the palace. I ran away from it, but now I miss it.

That place, I think, is addictive.

I have to crack open that place and make it my own. I've got to conquer it. The question is: How?

JC and Me

I am at the moment at the Queen Elizabeth II Centre, across the street from Westminster Abbey. The occasion: Holocaust Memorial Day, organized by the Holocaust Memorial Day Trust. The Holocaust Memorial Day, which takes place on the day the German concentration camp Auschwitz-Birkenau in Poland was liberated, is a Memorial Day not just for Jews but also for gypsies and gays as well as other peoples who perished in other tragic circumstances, be it in Sudan, Rwanda, Myanmar, Bosnia, and so on.

I have attended a number of Holocaust Memorial Days in the past, mostly in the USA, commemorating the murder of six million Jews in World War II, in what is known as the Holocaust, but this is my first Holocaust Memorial Day commemoration where various tragedies are joined into one. Why is it so here? I think that this Holocaust Memorial Day originated with the UN, and as such is intended to commemorate all genocides. If that's the case indeed, I think they should call it Genocide Day.

Sitting in the first rows are some of the most esteemed people of British society. This lord and that, this lady and that, this leader and that – including Britain's chief rabbi and the leader of the opposition, meaning Labour.

Yes, Jeremy Corbyn is here. He is surrounded by a number of ladies and by two anti-Zionist Hasidic Jews, one of whom escorts him to the toilet and back.

He might be a saint, but he also needs to urinate. And who better to help him relieve himself than an anti-Zionist Jew?

Jeremy Corbyn. Right here. Brought to me on a silver plate by the angels of the Holocaust, not by Red Pete of Oxford.

Here, in the least likely place for me to find the man, I can finally stand next to him and stare into his eyes. Deep inside.

I approach the man. Yeah. I approach my dream anti-Semite.

What should I say to him? I ask my eagle, hoping that it can hear me, wherever it is. I think, but I'm not sure, that the eagle tells me to eat him.

No, eagle! You can't tell a Jew to eat a gentile during a Holocaust Memorial Day service! The two Jews here will kill me!

Well, what am I to do? I look JC deep in his nose, to see if it's a bit hooked, and I introduce myself as a German journalist.

I give him no name. Had he asked, I'd of course say Adolf. But he doesn't ask. He looks me in my eyes, examines my face, my nose, my lips, and decides, I think, that he likes me.

Would you mind giving me an interview? I ask him.

"We'll do that," he says, and directs me to one of the ladies, whom he calls "the most efficient. She has German levels of efficiency about her," he says to me.

We connect, Satan and yours truly. And we chat.

We talk about cities in Germany, and I tell him that Hamburg is the media city, Berlin the culture city, and Frankfurt the money city. He likes that. This is "much better than Britain," he says, because "Britain is too dominated by London. We need to make Leeds and Manchester and Newcastle much stronger."

Between you and me, I don't care one bit, but I tell him that I totally agree with it, and he tells me that his government will invest in different cities. "I realize the importance of improving regions."

I, the German city planner, agree with every word he says. Yeah.

We also talk a bit about education. "What I admire about Germany," he tells me, "is education and the way you invest in education. I'd be happy to talk to you about all of these things."

Jeremy Corbyn, my Jeremy Corbyn, asks "the most efficient" of ladies, his Chief of Staff Karie Murphy, to arrange a meeting between us. I give Karie my name, to her I give Tobias, not Adolf, and she promises to arrange the meeting at the earliest possible time.

It is at this point that Jeremy and I hug. Yes, we do.

Two souls unite.

I look deep into his eyes, two penetrating eyes, quite similar to the eyes of the Gateshead rabbi. Are they siblings?

This Jeremy, a thought comes to me, could have been a rabbi. Rabbi Corbyn of Gateshead. What an irony. What an English irony.

I didn't expect it, but this is what it is.

Jeremy Corbyn, up close, projects warmth few politicians do. His lips betray a man in search of good food, and they seem to be ever ready for a laugh. He is meticulously dressed, he is soft-spoken, friendly, and a gentleman, an English gentleman.

I like the man.

This reminds me of Marwan, my Palestinian cousin from Liverpool, and what he told me about his feelings when he first met Saddam Hussein: "Saddam was a warm person, and genuine.... When I met him, I found him very charming."

In short: if I got it right, my Jeremy is a really nice man who really doesn't like Jews. Oy vey, as they say in Yiddish.

The memorial service is about to start, and all assume their seats, including JC and Me.

Laura Marks OBE, a British Jewess who's the chair of the Holocaust Memorial Day Trust, welcomes the participants: "This year we have seen a significant surge in hate crimes against Muslims, the LGBT community, immigrants, refugees, Jews, and other minorities."

You know she's a British Jewess because she mentions Muslims first and Jews last. You gotta be a British Jew to feel comfortable only if you are at the bottom of the ladder.

Addressing Jeremy Corbyn, without mentioning his name, she continues: "I have to tell you that for the past few months people have questioned our trustees over today's guest list."

I don't get it since, as far as I know, Jeremy Corbyn's participation has been kept secret and never advertised.

Anyway, she goes on.

"We were asked if it is appropriate to continue to welcome some representatives, knowing that this may cause a distress of local survivors and refugees here in this room. We know, from independent study, that people who attend Holocaust Memorial Day events learn more, empathize more deeply, and go on to do more to build a better future. It is our sincere hope, therefore, that everyone at our ceremony today, including politicians of all levels, will actively challenge anti-Semitism."

This is, at best, tasteless. If she wants to attack Jeremy Corbyn, she doesn't have to invite him and then preach to him in front of everybody. And if all she wants is to persuade him to her side, there are better ways of doing it.

The service goes on.

A number of countries are repeatedly mentioned, but Israel is mentioned only once, and even then, more as an afterthought. This is the Holocaust Memorial Day, Britain-style.

There are songs here as well. About gays, Rwanda, and a Jewish cantorial piece, in Hebrew, which a speaker explains is usually followed by fundraising. Don't ask me to explain this weird remark but, for the record, it's just not true.

The speaker now adds that the Hebrew cantorial piece is not just about Jews but also about gays and friends. This is as true as Prophet Mohammed being mentioned in Song of Songs.

Remember that one?

Finally, thank God, the event is over. The two anti-Zionist Jews accompany Jeremy Corbyn out, and soon enough I leave as well.

Outside, in Parliament Square, I meet a woman with a really big cross hanging from her neck and a man who seems to be older than her. They are the president and vice president of the Methodist Church, Reverend Michaela Youngson and Bala Gnanapragasam, respectively. Their church has 200,000 members, they tell me, and they have just left the QE II Centre, where they attended the memorial service. I ask them if they could share with me their thoughts about the event, and they politely agree.

Great.

What do you think about the fact that the organizers invited Jeremy Corbyn? I ask them.

Michaela: "I think it's very important. Jeremy Corbyn is a political leader who represents a party with lots of views. He said very publicly that he's against anti-Semitism, so why wouldn't you? We need people in the same room to talk – "

From what I read in the British media, including on the left, he has been accused of being anti-Semitic, supporting anti-Semitism, or refusing to deal with anti-Semitism in his party.

Bala: "He is very clear that he's against that, and people who accuse him of being anti-Semitic are wrong. Because he said it, several times. How often has he got to say this, before people would accept it?"

I heard some stories –

"You heard the wrong stories. Why shouldn't he be here? He's the leader of Her Majesty's opposition, the official leader! He's an important person. Not Jeremy Corbyn per se, but the fact that he's the leader of the opposition."

Michaela gets a bit testy, her politeness gone: "I thought we were going to talk about the event, not Jeremy Corbyn. Are you going to ask us another question about the event, or shall we go?"

Go, my dears, go.

It's early evening in Parliament Square, and I stare at the sky above and ask the angels: Angels of the Holocaust, can you give me Jeremy once more?

Neh, Neh, Neh

Lord Stone of Blackheath is spending much of his time in the House of Lords, and if I want to see him, and I do, I have to go to the palace.

The men of the older generation used to say, when talking about women: You can't live with them, and you can't live without them. That's what I say about the Palace of Westminster: You can't live with it, and you can't live without it.

You tell me: Would you pass up an opportunity to meet the Lord Stone of Blackheath? No way, right? Lord Stone of Blackheath. That's a name, isn't it? It's like Baroness Statue of Liberty, isn't it? Something you won't miss. Ever.

Now, there's a little problem here, a small one. We're in Britain, the land of language. This means, hear me out, that Lord Stone of Blackheath is just an official name, a British title, not a real name. It's all a show. Shakespeare. What is the real name of this creature? His real name is Andrew Zelig Stone. No Blackheath and no Shmalackheath. Once a person becomes a lord or baroness, you see, he or she turns into Lord of the Garden, Baroness of the Sea, Sir of the Fire, and Dame of the Wind. Or something like that. That's the way it is. When I become a lord, hopefully quite soon, I will be Lord Tenenbom of Piccadilly Circus. Sounds nice, doesn't it? I love Piccadilly Circus, especially at night when thousands of lights shine on the majestic buildings in the area, giving it the aura of a kingly neighborhood. This is one of those areas in London that look more inspiring than the biblical Garden of Eden.

Lord Tenenbom of Piccadilly Circus. Marwan, the Palestinian of Liverpool, will come to visit me in search of horses and elephants.

It'll be nice to meet again.

In any case, Lord Stone of Blackheath waits for me at the Peers' Entrance of the House of Lords, then walks me around the place, room by room, until we enter the Royal Gallery, decorated with giant paintings of battlefields on facing walls, where the bodies of dead people pile up one upon the other.

Yes, I've been here before. Here's where I imagined that awful image of JC and the dying Jews. Would you like to sit here? Lord Stone of Blackheath asks me.

Yes, I'd love to.

I've become a polite Englishman, I see.

That's the last place I'd like to sit, but I won't say that. We sit down and talk.

He used to work in M&S, he tells me.

What was your position when you left?

"Managing director."

Is that the top position at Marks & Spencer?

"Number two."

And now you are a lord. How did you become a lord?

"Okay, I am not educated. I left school when I was fifteen years old because I was dyslexic. I worked on a street market for ten years in the gutter, and an uncle of mine was very kind to me and said…"

He stops for a moment, collecting his thoughts. Then: "You know, I thought I was stupid. My two brothers were very clever, they were logical, linear, linguistic, but my brain works in a different way. And my uncle said, 'Look, you're very clever in a different way, in a different way to most people. And retailing is really good, and you should go and join somebody who is a great retailer rather than in the gutter as a market man.' And then I was very lucky that another Jew, Sir Marcus Sieff, who was the chairman of Marks & Spencer, liked me."

This man is a Jew, I see.

He continues to talk.

"He saw me misbehaving on the one hand but being sort of clever on the other. And he took me as his personal assistant. He taught me how to behave, how to behave in a different way. And eventually I became managing director. I was managing director of Marks & Spencer in the '90s and – "

How many years did it take you to become a managing director?

"Well, I joined in 1966, and I was managing director by 1994. About thirty years. But that's a different story. What happened was, in the late '90s, the Labour Party was getting more and more popular, and Tony Blair and his team wanted to change the House of Lords. In the old days, the House of Lords was made of heredi-tary peers; they were the son of the son of the son of the son. He changed that in 1998. You don't have to be the son of the son of the son. In 1998, after fifty years of discussions, they said, 'No, no. We can make a lord for life for something a person did in his life, not because he's the son of somebody else.'"

A little pause. Then:

"Every law goes through the Commons and then comes to the Lords and then goes to the queen. Tony Blair and Gordon Brown said, 'No, no, no, no, no. We're not gonna pull it down. We're not gonna get rid of it. It's good to have two houses, because one is for short-term, for five years, and one is for long-term, for life. One looks at the long view, one looks at the short view. One is elected and one is appointed.' So, he said, 'We're gonna put our own people in there, and we will get rid of the hereditary peers. Make me… find me thirty lords.' They had people who were lawyers, people who knew about politics and everything, and he said, 'Oh. I want to show that there are people in business who are also socialists, who believe that everybody has a fair shot.

"'Get me David Sainsbury, and the chairman of Marks & Spencer.' They said, 'No, you can't have the chairman of Marks & Spencer. The chairman of Marks & Spencer is Sir Richard Greenbury, he's a Tory and he's autocratic and he's not our type of person.' He said, 'Well, there must be somebody there.' They said, 'Oh, there's this guy, Andrew Stone. He's a bit mad, and he waves his arm around when he tells a story, but he and his wife really believe in what we do.' So, he said, 'Okay, fine.' They phoned me up and made me a lord. That's how I became a lord."

Do you have to be appointed by the prime minister to become a lord?

"The prime minister recommends a person to the queen, and the queen then appoints that person for life. The prime minister gets some, the opposition gets some, each year they – "

But they're all appointed initially before the queen grants –

"Yes, yes, yes."

Appointed by a political party?

"Correct, yes."

Do you like your job as a lord?

"That's interesting. I've been here for twenty years. You ask, 'Do I like it?' I don't like confrontations. I don't like arguments. I don't like tribal stuff. When I came in, I was appalled to see that it was like being in a schoolyard with people like, 'Neh, neh, neh,' they're on the other side. And they were using nefarious, horrible tricks, political shenanigans, and I don't like it. I wasn't very good at it, and I'm not a minister, I'm not on a Select Committee. But there are a number of things that I'm really interested in. Peace in the Middle East, some charities, education. And what is great about this place is you've got the greatest people in the country here. At the moment, we've got about 750 lords, and amongst them are the greatest architects and lawyers and doctors and whatever (including twenty-six bishops, also known as Lords Spiritual). If I want to get anything done, I don't need any money because I've got a pension. I don't need any status because I'm a lord. I don't need any ego, or I've got a bit of an ego, so I don't need anything. And people know that if I come to them and say, 'Look, there's something really important, will you help me?' then they'll help me immediately. And, therefore, it's a fantastic network. And that is how I get things done."

Can you give me an example of what you've achieved, something that you're the proudest of, in the last twenty years?

"Okay. I mean, it hasn't happened yet, but I've been working… In 1967 I went to Israel as a volunteer in the Six-Day War. I was there for a year. I realized that we have our Jewish narrative that this is the country that we deserve to have, and the United Nations made it for us in 1948.

"But on the other hand, the Palestinians feel that we came and invaded their country, and they have their narrative. I don't hate them. Even Hamas, they hate us but I understand where they're coming from. They've been brought up in a different way. And I've always tried to talk to both sides – as I say, I don't like confrontations – to see whether there's something that is a win-win situation."

I should have brought with me some people from the IRA, the kind of folks that for years enjoyed bombing London, just so to see if he would understand where they're coming from as well, but I don't think that IRA fighters would come to meet a Jew. Too bad.

The lord continues to talk.

"A few years ago, there was an organization called Two States, One Homeland, who had the idea that you could have a state of Palestine and a state of Israel and a confederation. And that that confederation could be run by Palestinians and Israelis, and we could do ecological and economic and education and health across the border. I liked it very much. I spoke to the Palestinians, I spoke to the Israelis, and I came back saying, 'Well, that's what I'm gonna promote.' And all of a sudden I saw Lord Woolf, Lord Harry Woolf, who was the most senior judge and Master of the Rolls in this country. He's a great lawyer. I said, 'Harry, look, I've been talking in

Israel, and there's this idea of having a confederation. Can you have a constitution for a confederation?' He said, 'Those are two very big words for a retailer, Andrew. What do you mean?' So, I explained to him what I was saying. He said, 'Andrew, this is fantastic. I want to help you. Sir Jeffrey Jowell is the greatest constitutional architect in the world. I will get him, we'll pay for it and we'll go there, and we'll try and work out how we can do this constitution.' So, I said, 'Great!' They started to work on that. Then a few steps later I saw Lord Dear, who was the head of the Metropolitan Police and advised our government on policing. I said, 'Oh, Lord Dear, Geoffrey, can you do police, police, and police?' He said, 'Andrew, this is what I advise on all over the world.' I told him what I was doing, he said, 'I'll do it for nothing.' What I'm saying is, now, and they're working on these sorts of things."

Anything happened out of all this?

"Well, they're still working on it, still working. Here's another thing, which is the first. I don't even know if I should publish it at the moment. With all these groups there is a guy called Dan Hart who is running a new thing called Tracks of Peace where he wants to get all these various things that are going together to come together as one. So, there are people on the ground and charities, there are NGOs, there are businesses. There's government, there's the people. And all these people are doing good things across Israel, Palestine, Egypt, Jordan. Now, Tony Blair has got an organization called ALLMEP, which is Alliance for Middle East Peace. And he's talking at the uber-government level. Then Tracks of Peace are talking about it with the charities level. The thing I told you about, Two States, One Homeland is talking at the municipality level. And Klaus Schwab, who is the head of the World Economic Forum, would really like this to happen. Who knows? I mean, it's gonna take a long time. In 1948, Israel was formed, and maybe in 2048 we'll find a settlement."

I understand why you have an interest in this issue, since you are Jewish, but I don't understand why the other ones, those you've mentioned and many others in this land, have an interest in the Israeli-Palestinian conflict. That part in the Middle East is a little dot on the map. Almost nothing. A little drop in the sea of troubles around the world. There are killings in so many parts of the world, genocides, extreme human rights violations – but everybody wants to focus on the little dot. Look what happens, on a daily basis, in China, Russia, Afghanistan, Pakistan, even Turkey. Kurdistan does not even exist. And this is just the short list, very short. I mean, there are so many horrible things happening in the world, but nobody cares. Why are people, so many people, the brightest people of the land, getting involved in Israel?

"I don't know."

Thank you very much.

"I've got a flat in Jerusalem. I go there six times a year."

Let me ask you something else. You are a member of Labour. For months now, there is this anti-Semitism row in Labour. You hardly have Jews in this country; why is Labour even bothering to deal with Jews? Why? Here, you have a beautiful House of Lords. Look how gorgeous it is. You can't dream of anything more. London is a beautiful city, one of the richest in the world. There are so many things, so many great things. Yet the Brits have nothing better to do than talk about Israel and have that anti-Semitism row. What's going on here?

"I'm not gonna answer that question. I mean, anti-Semitism has been around forever. I was born in 1942. They were killing six million Jews. When I went to high school, in assembly they would sing some Christian stuff, prayers. And then they would make some announcements. The 'Jew boys,' of which there were sixteen out of six hundred, had to go to the 'Jew room,' and three of them were me and my two brothers. And so there was anti-Semitism. When I used to work on a street market, there was anti-Semitism. I mean, I don't know the answer to why, all the way through the history of Jews, there has been anti-Semitism. It's not a question I'm gonna answer."

Are you surprised with all the anti-Semitism in the Labour Party?

"I don't wanna be interviewed on that."

But how do you feel about it? Personally, how do you feel?

"I have a bag which I carry everywhere. In it I have my passport and twenty-seven different currencies. If I had to leave tomorrow, I'd go. I'm seventy-six and I've lived here for seventy-six years and I'm a member of the House of Lords and yet."

That's why you carry the passport?

"Yeah. And that's why I've got a flat in Jerusalem."

I'm shocked, and touched, by his response. Here is a man who achieved it all – money, power, and prestige – and he's scared of being deported from this country, a country in which he is a lord, because he's a Jew. The year is 2019, the city is London, and this Jew, member of the House of Lords, is carrying his passport, plus twenty-seven different currencies, fully prepared to be kicked out by his countrymen at any time, any day.

The Holocaust has not yet ended, and it belongs to Jews only. Lords too.

They Are All Asian over There

While everybody who's anybody in Britain gets involved with the Israeli-Palestinian issue, and everybody has an opinion about it, almost nobody knows anything about the Pakistani-Afghani story, despite the fact that millions of Pakistanis and Afghanis live in the midst of English society. Untold numbers of people are being murdered, raped, mutilated, arrested, and abused these very days in Afghanistan by members of the Taliban, which means "students," who are financially and militarily aided by Pakistan.

How do I know?

I talk to Pakistanis and Afghanis, not to mention Indians, Bengalis, and Kashmiris, on a daily basis. They are my Uber drivers, they are my cooks and waiters in "Asian" restaurants, and at times I just meet them on the street, and we chat. The Afghanis tell me horrifying stories; the Pakistanis tell me sad stories; then there are the Kashmiris and the Indians who can't stand one another, and the untouchables of India, and then the Bengalis who get screwed by people and the weather – and I talk to them all.

The average white English person doesn't even recognize these people as unique, separate groups. The English here put Pakistanis, Afghanis, Indians, Kashmiris, and Bengalis in the same pot, calling them all "Asian." As in: What restaurant do you prefer, Chinese, Japanese, or Asian?

A few years ago, the residents of London voted in a Pakistani as their mayor, a man born in London to a Pakistani family. His name is Sadiq Aman Khan, and "his father was a Pakistani car driver," a young Pakistani, my Uber driver, tells me. "Once he became a mayor," the young man continues to tell me, "he changed his skin to white. We, the brown people, will never vote for him again. He cares only for the white rich, not for us. He made a new law, charging a Congestion Tax for every day we drive in London. Every Uber driver will have to pay it. Who drives Uber? We do, the brown people. He's a liar."

He drops me in the West End, and I go to the theater. What show? *The Play That Goes Wrong*, another production from the school of Mischief Theatre, playing at the Duchess Theatre.

Like its sister comedy about the bank robbers, *Play* is a comedy that requires English actors to pull it off. It's a play within a play, complete with dead people, murderers, lovers, death inspectors – to mention just a few professions meeting on the same stage. Only the dead actors of *Play* don't really like to be dead, its killers don't know how to kill, its inspectors can't inspect anything, loving couples have no clue how to love, and everything else on the stage, such as walls or a lift, falls down and breaks on the actors at the most delicate moment. In short: to act on this stage, you have to be a born liar with a sharp sense of the comic and with German timing. If your great-grandparents were a mix of Anglo-Saxons and Vikings, you'll most likely be an excellent candidate to play any of the characters on the Duchess stage.

The audience goes wild; they love every minute of it.

Sadly, at some point the show ends, and I have to leave the theater.

Outside the theater, snow is falling. Finally. I've read about the coming snow in the British media for months, but for the most part, the weather refuses to collaborate with the British forecasters. Not so today. Snow is here, finally for real.

Two blocks down I see homeless people, lying under assortments of clothes, paper, and plastic intended to protect them from the cold and the water, a sight that freezes me.

You have to have a heart made of stone and iron not to be affected by this sight. So much richness just steps up the road, and hardly a penny down the road.

According to Britain's Ministry of Housing, Communities and Local Government, "the total number of people counted or estimated to be sleeping rough on a single night was 4,677," out of which 1,283 were in London. This is a lower number than the one I've mentioned before on these pages, but perhaps this is more up to date.

The numbers, if they are correct, are not big – especially when compared with cities like New York or San Francisco in the United States, but each suffering person is one too many.

I slowly move away, knowing that there's not much I can do to help these people. There are quite a number of charities in this country, some having stores in the most expensive shopping districts, who are supposed to raise money for the homeless and the needy, but are they doing it?

I don't know.

Back in my hotel room, I go online to see what Oxfam, one of the biggest UK charities, is busy with these days. Well, for as little as £100 I can buy a book from Oxfam about "the history of Palestine and its turbulent formation in 1948."

What Palestine was founded when? Is this another play by the Mischief Theatre? Is Oxfam just another show? Well, when it comes to Palestine, everything goes.

Incredibly Delicate Subject

Next to my hotel, come morning of the following day, I meet a man who tells me that there must be another referendum on Brexit, because the first referendum took place over two years ago, which means that young people who have come of voting age just now are deprived of any say in the matter, and that's totally wrong. The people who voted to leave, he passionately argues, are old people, who are going to die soon anyway, and the people who want to remain, the young people to whom the future belongs, will have to pay the heavy price of divorce from the EU. It's bloody undemocratic, he tells me, to accept the referendum.

He's talking about the snowflakes.

In the old days, older people showed the way to the younger; in our modern day, there are intelligent people who believe that the older generation shouldn't count because they are going to die soon anyway.

How cruel.

Good that the House of Lords exists, I say to myself, with its older folks.

The man is an educated man, part of the aristocratic elite, and he hates with passion each and every Leave voter.

I cross the bridge to the other side, the palace's side.

There's a demonstration outside the Palace of Westminster, where people of all sides try to make lawmakers change their votes, only it's hard to tell which of the demonstrators is for Brexit and which is against, because the posters and signs intermingle.

Are you for or against Brexit? I ask a demonstrator who tries to shield herself from the rain.

"Very much against," she says. She's originally from Spain, she tells me, and she feels that "my identity has gone."

"Rubbish," says another lady standing next to her. "What this lady is saying is rubbish."

Are you pro-Leave?

"Of course! We voted to leave, because we wanted to take back control of our own country. We also voted that we don't want to go where the EU is going." The history of many European countries is grounded in dictatorships, while Britain is the nation that invented parliamentary democracy, and Britain shouldn't be in bed with the EU.

That's what she thinks.

Many Remainers argue that you, the citizens who voted to leave, did so because you have been fed lies, that you did not understand the implications of leaving, and that's why they want another referendum, another vote, the People's Vote. What do you think?

"If they haven't done their research, they are really beyond help. We love Europe, we love traveling to Europe, but we don't want to be ruled by Europe."

The two ladies now confront each other, and I watch.

Next to them stands a man, well dressed, and I ask him for his opinion.

"We should have good control of immigration coming into the EU, and we should be terribly afraid of creeping EU militarization, which means that we could get police forces controlling events like this."

This man is, obviously, pro-Leave.

A man wearing a hat that resembles the EU flag, carrying the Union Jack flag and wearing a jacket with the EU stars, says that there must be a People's Vote because the first vote was based on lies, and the people who voted Leave didn't know what they were doing. I ask him to tell the two Leave people next to me that they are idiots, but he won't do it because he's a polite man.

"They think we're stupid," the Leave woman says, "but we are not."

Are you a proud British citizen? I ask the lady.

"I am, yes."

Do you think that Britain is one of the best countries in the world?

"Of course I do!"

The Remainer guy with the flags says: "I'm very proud of my country, and I'm also proud of the EU."

I talk to some more people, and what transpires is this: Those who think Britain is unique, better than the rest, want to leave the EU, and those who think that the EU is just as good as Britain want to remain in the EU.

And then we have the snowflakes, of course.

The snowflakes are known anti-Brexiteers. Don't even mention the word to them.

With the help of Uber, I move my body from Westminster to Hackney, an area where there are many hip, "free," and really cool people and places all around. You know you've arrived in a cool neighborhood when you see men who look like women, women who look like men, straights who look like gays, humans who are double-trans, teenagers who smoke hashish, restaurants that look like flower shops, vegetarian and vegan preachers roaming around, men who march with funny hats and women who parade on recycled high heels, and people who grow pink and blue hair. They want to remain within the EU, to unite with all other pink and blue hairs of the EU, and maybe even the world. That's, at least, what they tell me, and very proudly so.

Here's a cool man, James, walking with two friends, and they love Europeans. Especially me, the fat German.

Great.

We chat a bit, having a really good time, and then I ask James to share with me what he thinks of Jeremy Corbyn.

Oops. That was the wrong question.

One of his friends immediately tells me that he has to leave, sorry. Suddenly he remembers that he's actually busy, very busy. The one next to him also suddenly remembers that he must be somewhere, somewhere else, away from me. James, obviously, suddenly remembers that he, too, must go. Somewhere. Anywhere. Just not here.

All because of a question about Jeremy Corbyn.

They remind me of the soldiers in Inverness. They, too, ran away one after the other, at the exact second they were asked a question that they didn't feel safe enough to answer.

In short: snowflakes.

Red Pete is sending me a message. I see, he writes, that you found JC on your own.

Yes, I did. Advise him to meet me, I reply.

He will, he says.

JC and Red Pete, I see, are discussing me. It's a good sign. In a day or two or three, I say to myself, if I don't hear anything, I'll call Jeremy's office. Sometimes, in the age of snowflakes, you gotta push.

I walk around here and there, there and here, and soon I reach a gentrified area, which means that old residents, the artsy and the poor, were made to leave, and the young well-to-do are moving in.

Twenty-five-year-old Tom describes himself as a "young professional" and in the next election will "probably" vote Labour. Like most Londoners, he wants to stay in the EU, but adds that "it's very easy to be in the London bubble, to be in this very cosmopolitan vibrant city with so many different languages and cultures. But I guess across the country there is a feeling of being left behind," which is why the majority of people in England outside London don't see eye to eye with the Londoners.

I ask Tom for his opinion about anti-Semitism in Labour.

Suddenly, there is a major change in his speech pattern. He stutters: "I mean, ah, eh, that's a very, that's incredibly, em, eh, it's an in-, incredibly delicate subject, I guess. Hmm, there is, there has been a lot in the press about Labour and an influx of anti-Semitism, ah, and – "

And sure enough, after a bit more struggling with it, he tells me that he has to go. Yeah.

I tell him that the interview is over and ask him if he could explain to me why he, and others, run away the moment I raise this issue.

Well, he's willing to talk, and he does. Now he has time. Sadly, I can't quote him.

For weeks I've been in England asking its people what's unique about them. Maybe, just maybe, today I found what's unique about them: the fear of saying what they think, what they really think. And maybe, just maybe, there're all snowflakes, not just the young.

I need a break from these people, from the fearful Brits.

I take an Uber to Edgware Road, near Marble Arch, an Arabic-speaking area of town, where people behave differently, listen to different music, play different tunes, aren't reserved, don't know what the word *queue* means, are not sure what *polite* means, are proud of themselves and their culture, and have much better food than in the rest of this huge city.

My kind of people.

The Muslim Uber driver, thanks be to Allah, drops me next to a restaurant. He knows what a man needs in life.

I look around, examining my environment. Should I share with you what I see?

Well, I will.

Shop signs in this part of Edgware Road are in Arabic and in English, and if you have been to the Arab world, you'll feel at home in this place. Here you'll see women dressed in niqab, only their eyes shown – what the famous British Tory politician Boris Johnson once referred to as "letter boxes" – and, of course, those who are dressed in hijab, which these days is a common sight in Britain's big cities.

A young Pakistani, who knows me as a man who eats only halal food, recommends the Lebanese restaurant Maroush. There are two Maroush restaurants, one opposite the other. One is a normal restaurant, whatever normal means, and the other is Maroush Express. And since my belly demands food right away, I go to Maroush Express and order a shawarma.

Well, this part of the world is Middle Eastern, and my shawarma arrives express, which here means close to two hours. Lord Stone, and the rest of his esteemed white folks, will never understand it, but luckily, reality needs no understanding. The food here, if you would like to know, is good. Not as good as in Jordan or Qatar, but better than in most other restaurants in London.

Next to Maroush Express is a place called Euro Gulf Ltd., a very interesting place. Would you like to know what Euro Gulf is selling? I'll tell you: international properties, Rolex and Cartier watches, property rentals, diamonds and gold, translation services, and they also have a nutritional therapist on location. In other words: nothing.

That's the Middle East, my dear. No Stone or Woolf will ever comprehend.

And suddenly I think of Brexit. Again. Will these Arabs still be here if Brexit materializes? It will be an immense loss to this country if they leave.

I order coffee and meantime check on my iPhone what's new in England at the moment. I read.

"Board of Deputies of British Jews President Marie van der Zyl has accused the Labour Party of 'treating the Jewish community with contempt' following the readmittance of three party members suspended on charges of antisemitism," according to an official statement issued by the board.

I know this lady.

Marie van der Zyl, whom I met personally, refused to grant me an interview. It's all too "sensitive," she told me. The same as the former and the present chief rabbis of this country, who both won't meet me.

They are my Hiding Jews.

I drink my coffee and leave the Middle East. I go to the West End.

Company, a 1970 musical by Stephen Sondheim (lyrics and music) and George Furth (book), is playing on the West End, £95 per ticket, after being slightly rewritten for the cool people of Her Majesty's Kingdom. The leading role of Bobby, a thirty-five-year-old man looking for the perfect female, was changed to Bobbie, a thirty-five-year-old female looking for the greatest male, and the couple Amy and Paul, a man and a woman, were changed to Jamie and Paul, both men.

It's politically correct, but not in-your-face, preachy PC. And it works.

Everyone onstage, including the actors who are British-born, reminds me of New York. It's so New York here! Speech patterns, manners, movements, tics, neuroticism, sound and look, feel and atmosphere – all are 100 percent New York. Even the Jewish humor of Sondheim comes out perfectly well here, as if the actors onstage were New York Jews. Brilliant!

God bless the Brits.

Back in my room, I look at the palace and I realize that I have not yet been to the House of Commons. Tomorrow, I promise myself, I'll go there. For up to two hours, of course.

Mice in the Palace!

Nicolette Peterson is a lovely lady who has been working in Jeremy Corbyn's office for many years and is an ardent believer in the man and a true follower of his preaching. Some years ago, according to *The Sun*, she "urged Labour supporters not to vote for MPs who appeared in Jewish newspapers," but today she is very nice. We meet next to a gift shop across the street from Parliament, and she "smuggles" me into the House of Commons through an underground passage which, it seems to me, only insiders know, in order to save me the time it takes any other flesh-and-blood creature to enter the palace.

She knows me by the name of Adrian, she thinks that I'm French, and she loves my French accent.

Don't ask.

The House of Lords is much nicer than the House of Commons. The red benches in the Lords, and the shining gold, are more impressive than the green benches of the Commons. But the Commons is a much more powerful house, and the future of Brexit depends on the MPs.

The session in the chamber starts with a prayer, the way sessions start here, but that's for members only, not for French tourists. Sorry, even the biggest love has a limit.

Prayer done, I go to the Special Gallery, which in the Lords is called Strangers' Gallery, and I start feeling very special, whatever special means. The gallery is enclosed by floor to ceiling glass, which means that I can't yell at MPs the way that the House Speaker does. And he does!

On the agenda today: education, knife crime prevention orders, US withdrawal from nuclear treaties, and Nissan in Sunderland.

This place is a must-visit for everyone wishing to become a politician, a diplomat, a lawyer, or a criminal. Why? Because here you can learn how to lie, through your nose, but still give the impression that you're the nicest, kindest person out there.

Watch, listen, and learn.

Here are MPs asking a minister various questions, but whatever the question is, the minister gives, more or less, the same answer. 'I thank the honorable gentleman/lady/friend for his/her comment,' blah, blah, blah, 'and I'm sure that the honorable gentleman/lady will support the government motion,' blah, blah, blah.

And, believe it or not, it always works, like a Swiss clock. The answer, whatever answer, always sounds so good, so real, so honest, so straight, so reasonable, and ever unique. In reality, though, Mr. Minister says nothing.

Once all problems about education have been solved, members are ready to discuss the nuclear issue.

The average question in this part sounds something like this: Did the Minister notify the American government of the UK position?

Excuse me? Listening to this question, you'd think that the UK is a superpower and the US is an island somewhere.

I watch this, firstly in disbelief, but soon I get used to it. The delivery is so impeccable that it becomes believable.

Yet, something is missing in the House.

Unlike what I saw in the House of Lords, no one here wears a wig. I miss it!

But don't worry, for there is still plenty of entertainment here, most of which is graciously supplied by John Bercow, a bigmouth whose official title is Speaker of the House of Commons.

Look at him. He sits on a huge, kingly green chair, under something that looks like an ancient royal canopy, and he is the MC of the House.

He is better, let me tell you, than any actor in the West End.

He does not speak, he sings. He does not talk, he hums. He does not say, he roars. His mouth, a London miracle, is louder than an aircraft.

This man has two mischievous eyes that at times seem like two eyes of a cat approaching a rat, and he also two lips that seem to always be at the ready to suck you into his belly.

Unlike Speakers all over the world, this Speaker is not a Speaker, not really, but an actor. More precisely: midway between actor and cantor. As far as he sees it, the House of Commons is an opera house – no more, no less.

Listen to this Speaker asking a Minister to answer.

"M-I-N-I-S-T-E-R!" he roars and sings, like a drunk man in a Wagner opera. Look at him and see how is literally full of himself – and that's, probably, his power. He's proud as hell, I think, for being the only man in London who's capable of creating a whole song out of one word.

John Bercow – formerly Bercowitz, as I'm told – is just another Jew in Westminster who would have loved to be a king but, sadly, will never make it. The closest he will ever get to the monarchy is the mace, which represents the queen, lying on the podium just a few steps away from him.

Nissan Motor Manufacturing was supposed to manufacture its new model of the X-Trail in Sunderland, but a couple of days ago it announced that it wouldn't – and this is the next issue to be discussed in this chamber.

Nissan insinuated that its decision was made because of Brexit, but many believe that the real reason had nothing to do with Brexit. Nissan, they say, was not able to sell enough X-Trail SUVs to Londoners, who prefer smaller cars in the narrow London streets, but instead of telling the truth, Nissan preferred to come up with an excuse.

It's not the first time, I guess, that a car salesman is selling tales.

In the chamber, more and more MPs enter, mostly Labour MPs, and many of them want to talk. I stick around for a while longer, but when I spot John Bercow about to fall asleep, I leave.

I walk around here and there, this building and that, until I reach the Jubilee Room. It is there that a strange visitor makes an appearance: a big mouse. Yeah. A live mouse running all around. "We have a problem with mice here; it's an old building," one of the guards confides in me.

They have a mice problem in the palace. Look at this one.

Unlike the rat in Dublin, this London mouse is alive and well, and no cat is coming its way. The Irish, I think, will be very happy to hear about the mice of England.

Meantime, according to the BBC, "Labour MPs have unanimously passed a motion urging the party leadership to do more to tackle anti-Semitism." In addition: "MPs accused general secretary Jennie Formby of refusing to give answers."

Does it mean anything? Probably nothing, but it sounds good.

Across the Atlantic, a new star of the Democratic party in the US, Congresswoman Alexandria Ocasio-Cortez, had a phone chat with Jeremy Corbyn, after which she tweeted: "It was an honor to share such a lovely and wide-reaching conversation with you." For his part, Jeremy tweeted the following: "Let's build a movement across borders to take on the billionaires, polluters and migrant baiters, and support a happier, freer and cleaner planet." Alexandria and Jeremy would make good bedfellows, no doubt. The other day, going through an attack of righteousness, she accused Israel of perpetrating a "massacre" against Palestinians.

Well, whatever that is, I see that Rabbi Jeremy is not that busy. If he has time for Alexandria Ocasio-Cortez, he should have time for me.

I call his diary manager, a lady by the name of Ayse. She knows me by the name of Florian, not Tobias. It's good to have two names, because if Tobias is denied an interview, perhaps eventually Florian will get it. I tell Lady Ayse that I met Jeremy and that he wants to meet me. How long will it take to arrange a meeting between us? She asks me to shoot her a message, and she tells me to be patient because it will take her time to find the time for Jeremy and me to meet.

Good.

I leave the palace.

Outside the palace, right by Parliament Square, there's a restaurant that looks very nice from the outside with hardly anybody inside.

The restaurant's name is Roux, which sounds French to this newly French person, and I walk in.

I wish Nicolette were here, to witness with her own eyes her beloved Frenchman inside the Roux.

But I'm happy to be here in any case. I love the atmosphere in this place. It feels unique, aristocratic, diplomatic, secretive, sinful, and expensive. My cup of tea. I was born for riches, my dear!

It's a different class here.

The waiters, for example, give the impression that all they want out of life is to serve me. And to be honest, I feel like a lord. I'm not sure if a Tory or Labour, perhaps an independent, but what I do know is that I'll never tell JC or Red Pete that I've been eating here. Oh, no!

I could've ordered wine, Shiraz, for only £75, but I order water, San Pellegrino, for £5. I just saved £70. We Jews know how to do business. Spectacular!

The menu arrives.

After a long consultation from the waiting crew, and a session of personal meditation, I choose the following items. For starters, I choose "Celeriac: Goats Cheese, Lovage, Hazelnut"; for main,

I choose "Cod: White Beans, Morteau Sausage, Three-cornered garlic"; and for dessert, "Treacle Tart: Pear, Stem ginger." I have no idea what any of them are, but they all sound so good!

Result? Outstanding. Don't ask me to explain to you what Celeriac or Morteau are. Just come on in and give it a try. You won't regret, I promise. This is the best restaurant in the UK, at least according to the taste buds of this Frenchman, a class above Daisy Tasker. I ask the head chef, Steve Groves, to share his secrets with me, and he gladly does: multiple experiments, continuous tasting, fifteen-hour workdays, great teamwork in the kitchen, and best available suppliers.

I try to imagine John Bercow dining here. G-I-N-G-E-R! C-E-L-E-R-I-A-C! G-I-N-G-E-R! If you have not been here yet, Mr. Bercow, you should come soon. You'll love it.

When the bill arrives, service charge is not included, unlike most other restaurants I've frequented. But it does include an interesting item, "Charity," for £1. This pound, it states in accompanying literature, goes to help homeless people.

Yes, John Bercow, you can spare a pound.

Bercow is not a bad name. It has a nice ring to it. If I had a dog, I'd probably call it Bercow – and I love dogs, in case I never mentioned it. There are other names, though, that I don't connect with quite so fast. Like Nigel Farage.

Have you heard of Nigel Farage?

The Corrupt Mayor of London

There are people who don't mind – and perhaps even cherish – having the strangest-sounding words serve as their names. One of them is a man known to all as Nigel Farage, a name that I think is certainly a code name for somebody else. Who is that somebody? It's a secret, and nobody knows.

What everybody does know, as so wonderfully told in Tim Shipman's *All Out War*, is that if not for this man with such a strange name, former PM David Cameron would not have declared a Brexit referendum, and there would have been no Brexit to start with.

Nigel Farage, the leader of the Brexit Party and former leader of the UK Independence Party (UKIP), is a member of the European Parliament and chair of Europe of Freedom and Direct Democracy Group. In 2014 the UKIP Party, under his leadership, won twenty-four seats in the European Parliament, more than Labour (twenty seats) and Conservatives (nineteen seats), making it the biggest UK party in the EP.

David Cameron wanted UKIP voters, whose main reason for living was to get the UK out of the EU, to vote for the Conservative ticket instead of UKIP, so he promised them a Brexit referendum, hoping that the general public would vote Remain and the referendum would result in Britain remaining in the EU. Hope springs eternal, they say, and David followed hope, but his genius plan backfired. The majority of the British people wanted out, voting Leave, and he promptly resigned. Theresa May took over, and that's how and why we are where we are.

Long before I arrived in Britain, I heard the name Nigel Farage quite often. Who has not? Rivers of ink and oceans of digital letter have been poured for years in an attempt to decipher the man called Farage. What has not been written about him? Almost everything. That he's a schmuck, that he's horrible, that he's a selfish bastard, that he's a nutcase, that he's a racist, that he's a genius, and that he's an anti-Semite.

Yes, before anybody outside Britain heard of Jeremy Corbyn the anti-Semite, everybody already knew that Nigel Farage was.

Like President Donald Trump of the United States, Nigel Farage also comes from the business world, and both of them have one more important point in common: they are hated by the educated and left-oriented classes of the Western world. Yet one cannot deny the fact that these two businessmen-turned-politicians are shaping our world, and humanity's future, for generations to come. For even if they don't achieve any of their goals, Donald and Nigel have succeeded in giving a voice to majorities in both their countries, a voice of the common people charging loud and clear against society's elites and its leaders.

It's time I meet the man behind the name.

Nigel Farage's office, to put it succinctly, is nothing to brag about. The average bathroom in any of Donald Trump's properties is a hundredfold more impressive, and costlier, than the whole of Nigel Farage's office.

His office is located in central London, in what seems to be a residential unit. There are a number of rooms in the unit, where a few employees are half-busy working, and then there's Nigel Farage's room, all the way in the back, and this room has an exit to a backyard that serves Nigel's smoking habit.

Nigel knows everything intimate and important and personal about me, namely that I'm a German journalist by the name of Tobias.

Brexit or not, every Londoner loves a fat German with red eyeglasses and a funny accent.

Nigel, a smart businessman, wants to make me, the German, feel comfortable with him, the Englishman.

"We're more rule-obsessed than the Germans. We are! We really are," he says to me as we sit down, in an attempt to "admit" that the English are worse than the Germans.

Is your family from Germany? I ask the man, because I have nothing better to ask at the moment.

"Well, my wife... we're separated... she's from Hamburg. But the other German connection is my father's mother. My father's mother's father was from Hamburg, as well. There are lots of Hamburg connections."

Welcome, brother!

"They say that Hamburg is the most English city in Germany, don't they? What interests me about German politics and about German life is that, when I first started going regularly to Germany, it would be the late 1980s. There were very, very, very few parts of the Rhineland and the Ruhr that I haven't been to because I was in the metals business: copper, aluminum, zinc. I always felt Germany was much more family-orientated. That it was a much more, in many ways, calmer place than here. A more traditional family-type structure. And maybe this is why what Mrs. Merkel has done in terms of changing the population of many of those cities [by opening the gates of the country to somewhere between one and two million refugees] has come as such a shock. You want to know what type of democracy it is: an elected dictatorship.

"Anyway, you want to talk about Brexit."

About Brexit, about you, and about everything. So, first of all, why do you want to get out of the EU?

"About nearly thirty years ago, I began to understand what the European Project was, not what we had been told it was. We were told it was about trade. We were told it was about being good neighbors in a world of postwar reconciliation. But I realized, after the Single European Act of 1986, which was the creation of the Single Market, that actually, economics was being used as a means of bringing in a European political union."

How did you realize that, when nobody else did?

"It wasn't very difficult, because all you had to do was to ignore every single British politician, because they would all lie, or they'd be ignorant, or they'd pretend: oh, no, no, no, no, no, there's nothing to worry about. All you really had to do was to listen to what was being said by the European Commission president, who at the time was a very able, talented man, Jacques Delors. Delors was incredibly talented. My one regret about my years in Parliament is, I didn't go head-to-head with Delors. Because that would have been great. That would have been really...

"Because he was brilliant in many ways. But all you had to do was listen to Delors. And so, yes, I realized that this was about the creation of the state. I thought, as far as we [British people] were concerned, we'd very much be a square peg in a round hole. We'd never fit this model. I mean, our legal system, our patents of trade around the world. For all of those reasons, I never, ever thought we'd fit. But I also thought that, economically, it is insane. Why would you want to tie yourself economically just to Europe? The world's changing. And I could feel globalization was happening. China was beginning to make economic strides."

Are you saying that the idea about the EU is not trade but, rather, a political, ideological move to create –

"I realized that economics was being used as an argument to try to build a new global power, and that it was being done without the consent of the public."

What was their reason to build a new global power?

"Because that's what mankind does. Mankind creates empires."

In other words, the Europeans are missing their old empires and they want to have them back, one way or another.

"Well, there have been many attempts to take that – "

Would you call it colonialization?

"It's a form of that. And, by the way, I'm not blaming Germany for this."

No, no. It just –

"But there is no question in my mind: Men seek to build empires. All through history, men seek to build empires. But then, every empire comes crashing down. I think the best guarantor of peace is the nation-state as a functioning, mature democracy."

It is here and now that Nigel tells me why he's against globalization:

"In the end, human beings are individuals. And every attempt at corporatization or collectivization of the human soul ends in disaster. We rebel against it. And what's interesting is, I mean, from the birth of man, we've chosen to live in tribes. In a sense, the nation-state is our modern-day adaptation of what a tribe is. And that doesn't mean that we're offensive to our neighbors, I mean, far from it. Goodness me, I might work for French companies, and I married a German woman. I'm not anti-European at all. But I just felt that there was something intrinsically wrong with what they were trying to do. And then, I looked around amongst the politicians in this country to see how much of an appreciation there was, and what I discovered, very, very few people had even thought about it. And those that had and were concerned about it, well frankly, weren't brave enough to fight it. So, I decided, I'm going to fight this."

Well, personally, I haven't found many brave people in England. You are one of the few who stands for what he believes and says it.

"We have lost our courage in many, many ways."

When did this process start? You used to be an empire.

"I know."

You controlled a third of the world.

"I think when we look back in a couple of hundred years on what happened to the English, particularly the English, I think that Suez was an incredible watershed moment. I think that after Suez, 1956, our ruling classes gave up."

He refers to the 1956 nationalization of the Suez Canal by then Egyptian leader Gamal Abdul Nasser. In response, Israel opened a military offensive against Egypt, later joined by Britain and France. The Soviet leader, Nikita Khrushchev, threatened Western Europe with nuclear missiles, and the American president, Dwight Eisenhower, threatened economic sanctions against the three nations. All three eventually withdrew their forces from the canal.

"The Suez Canal crisis where we, within twenty-four hours of military victory – the Americans pull support. The pound collapses on the exchanges. The prime minister is forced to resign. We're humiliated. And there was a realization, or a feeling, after Suez, that we're no longer a great country. And frankly, ever since that moment, with the brief interruption of Mrs. Thatcher, it's been managed decline. That has been the official policy of the government, of the civil service, managed decline."

The people too?

"Yeah, I think we've lost confidence. And I think our leaders have totally lost confidence in themselves."

As he sees it, that phenomenon is the modus operandi of the present British leaders.

"Think about the arguments that have run up to the referendum, during the referendum, and are still being run post the referendum. The chief argument of the Remain side is that we're not big enough. We're not good enough. We're not strong enough. It's all talking ourselves down. And I would argue that despite all that's gone wrong, hey: we're still the fifth-biggest economy in the world. London is the sexiest city in the world."

Sexiest city?

"Of course, it is."

What do you mean sexiest?

"Well, where do the young people want to go in Europe? Berlin, for a weekend; Paris, no one wants to go there; Rome, a little bit. But it's London. This is where the music is. This is where the culture is. This is where the future is. And you feel that. We've got a language that now dominates the world. We've got a Commonwealth that the Queen is the head of, with 2.4 billion people living in it. So I think we are good enough. And in a sense, I suppose that is what drives my positive agenda of saying, 'Look, we can do this.'"

Some argue that the Leave campaign lied to the people. They say that people voted Leave because of promises given them about NHS, and other issues mostly related to the economy and money, but all of which turned out to be a lie, and therefore the referendum should not be binding.

"That's what a professional spin master does. A spin master accuses the other side of doing exactly what he's been doing. They've lied to us for fifty years, fifty years. My parents were told, 'This is just a common market.' There's no politics. Don't worry your little head. I warned the country that there's going to be a European army. Oh, he's lying, they said. Let's be clear: people voted Leave because they wanted to leave. It's as simple as that. It was an assertion of sovereignty. An assertion of we don't want to be governed by Monsieur Barnier [Michel Barnier, European Union chief Brexit negotiator] or Mr. Juncker [Jean-Claude Juncker, European Commission president]."

Or Mr. Tusk (Donald Tusk, president of the European Council).

"What a frightful bunch of people! I mean, to think that half a billion people are being governed by people we can't vote for and we can't remove, but we call that progress! Yeah, yeah. So, to me, and once I got to the European Parliament, the thing that really changed me was in 2005.

"They devised a European constitution. The French voted no. The Dutch voted no. And they, then, rebranded it as the Lisbon Treaty. They boasted that because it wasn't called a constitution, it would not need to be put to referendums and rammed it through. And that was the day when my mission changed. I started off wanting to get the United Kingdom out of the

European Union. Since 2005, I now want to get Europe out of the European Union."

How would you solve the problem of a border between the Republic of Ireland and Northern Ireland, which seems to be the main issue?

"If we went to that border right now, if you and I flew there right now, do you know what we'd find from one field to the next? Different income tax rates, different corporation tax rates, different duties, and a different currency. Why is there no hard border there now? Because the whole point about the peace agreement is that it's a compromise. The whole point about that border between us and the Republic is that it's been a free travel area anyway for decades and decades and decades. So why, if you add it to that list of economic differences, and you put a bit of tariff on, would it need a hard border? It's a hoax."

I was there a few months ago, and I remember it as if it were yesterday – and Nigel is right about the different currencies, etcetera, etcetera. What I don't get is this: If there's no hard border out there, only a soft one, meaning there'll be no police, soldiers, gates on either side, then goods would be coming in and out, which means that the EU border will be totally porous. Is that what he wants? I ask him to explain to me how he visualizes a soft border that's actually functioning.

"We have the same product specifications. On the day we leave the European Union, we will be on exactly the same rule book as the rest of the EU. There's no need for hard border, whatsoever. Everything about Ireland, for the last hundred years, has been a compromise. At times, a very difficult compromise, alright? But look, when you drive into London, Boris [Johnson] made this point, the authorities take your plate number and take £10 out of your bank account. So, what's the difference?"

The problem is about taxing the goods that cross the border.

"If we have a free trade deal, the whole argument's finished. Finished. Finished."

Why, then, do you think the Europeans make such a big deal about the border?

"Oh, look, I think what…I mean, during the referendum, this issue was hardly mentioned. I think that what Barnier and those devious minds in Brussels did, was to devise a trap for Mrs. May. And she jumped straight into it."

Let me ask you another question. Yesterday, after a videotape emerged of Jeremy Corbyn's anti-European outbursts, it's been reported in the media that you recommended for people to vote for him if he comes out in public for Brexit. I don't know Jeremy, I met him only once, but according to media reports, he and the NEC, and the people who rule Labour today, have been shown to be anti-Semitic. Doesn't it bother you?

"Look. I think, probably, I've been more critical of Jeremy Corbyn than anybody in the country consistently. Just that yesterday we saw his true colors on one issue, which is the most important issue of our time. He is, at heart, a Eurosceptic. He is at heart a Stalinist. Look, I think the anti-Semitic direction that the Labour party has been going in is not just under Corbyn. This has been going on for a long time."

But it came out just now.

"I saw it under Ken Livingston [former London mayor]. I saw it when Cherie Blair [wife of former PM Tony Blair] has made comments in the past, saying that she understands why Palestinian suicide bombers do what they do. This has been going on for a long time."

Why is that? How did we get there?

"I think it goes with the whole globalism side of it. The Trotskyites are globalists. Trotskyites in the Labour Party see the European Union as a prototype for a bigger form of global government. And one of the countries they hate the most is Israel. Not just because they're Jewish, but because they are the manifestation of a nation-state that seeks to protect itself and defend its borders.

And these people believe in global government and total free movement. These people actually want to get rid of nation-state. So, it isn't just the religious thing."

Hungary is also a nation-state, especially under Victor Orban. Does the Labour Party say anything about the Hungarians? Hungary has ten million people, more than Israel. Why the fascination with Israel?

"There is an obsession with Israel. I'm personally very supportive of Israel. And I think if you are surrounded by a group of countries that want to obliterate you, you probably do defend yourself."

Now it's time I hear his thoughts about the English people, his people.

How would you describe the English character? You are an Englishman. You know the people. What would you say is the characteristic of the English?

"Generally, quite laid back. Generally, quite slow to anger. Generally, fairly unemotional in public. We tend to be a little bit quieter about how we feel about things. But yes, generally, very slow to anger. But when they get angry, they get very angry. And I think we're witnessing that with Brexit. I think what you're witnessing is because of the way Parliament's behaving, you're witnessing a growing upwelling of very, very strong feeling. And I would like to think of my country…I would like to think that we have a fairly good sense of what is right and wrong."

If Brexit happens, you will have to leave the European Parliament. Will you miss it?

"I won't miss the corridors, the grayness, the appalling people. It's just so awful. What I'll miss is the theater. It has been fantastic for me. I mean, look: Who could have scripted this? How is it that I've got seat number 20 on the front row when Jean-Claude Juncker is in seat number 21. Who did that for me?"

The man is happy, couldn't be happier, and laughs loudly about his seating arrangement as I make my way out of his office.

He's probably surprised that I treated him nicely, maybe too nicely, during our encounter. Many a European journalist, especially German, wouldn't do that. Instead, they would try to trick him into saying something stupid, or preach to him. To me journalism is not activism, and there's no point in tricking anyone into saying anything unless you suspect that your interviewee is playing you, lying to you, or trying to hide important facts from you.

That stated, I actually agree with one essential element of Nigel's arguments, and I can't emphasize it enough: there was a vote, a referendum provided by the British government and sanctioned by the British Parliament, and the powers that be refuse to abide by its result. That's undemocratic. Nigel, the figurehead of the Leave campaign, represents the belittled, often patronized majority, and for this he has to be respected. Not because of his ideas or politics, but because of what he represents, the people, the will of the people.

The day is not over. I move on.

I take an Uber to the House of Lords. There are some lords there I haven't met yet, and why not do it today?

Minutes into the ride, the Uber car can't move anymore. Black taxis, aka London taxis, are striking, and they block traffic leading to Parliament. God knows how many taxis are here, at least as far as my eyes can see, and they don't move.

I get out of my Uber and walk over to the striking drivers. What are you demonstrating against? I ask them.

"The corrupt mayor of London," comes the reply.

I ask for specifics, but they direct me to Parliament Square, where, they say, I can find their union leader, and he'll explain it all to me.

Did you vote for the mayor?

"I'll vote for someone to kill him," comes the second reply.

What they do tell me is that they lose much money because of Uber, and that they are extremely upset. They tell me that Uber got its license to operate in London thanks to corrupt politicians, including David Cameron and a number of ministers, and that the commissioner of police said that there is "nearly one rape a week by Uber drivers."

If I remember correctly, over 80 percent of "black taxi" drivers are white, and over 90 percent of Uber drivers are minorities. The ones I talk to at the moment are all white.

I ask them to tell me what they feel about Nigel Farage.

"He's a good man, a good man!" they say. "We're all for Nigel Farage."

"He's a hero!" another driver chimes in.

They want out of the EU, they tell me, and they love Nigel Farage for fighting their fight. "I'm a working person and I know nothing," one of them, who gets quite emotional, tells me, "but I can see it!"

I leave the area and get to talk to an Uber driver who, like the black taxi drivers, hates Sadiq Aman Khan, London's mayor. "We go to the same mosque," the man, a Pakistani, tells me, "but since he became mayor, I don't talk to him. He betrayed us, he charges us more taxes." The man, who grew up in East London, tells me that life is hard. Too many young Muslim men are involved in drugs, there are too many shootings, and too much crime, in Muslim neighborhoods, yet Sadiq does nothing to help.

What do you think of Nigel Farage?

"He's a racist."

Even if he is, and I didn't see a proof for it yet, he's not the only one.

There are racists and human rights abusers on the part of British society that pretends to love all (with the exception of the Jews, of course) and dignify all.

Amnesty International folks are one such example.

Walking Nude at the National Theatre

Amnesty International, usually referred to in one word, Amnesty, is the NGO I encountered when I first reached England a few months ago, at their bookstore in Newcastle.

Amnesty, founded in London, with headquarters in London, is a mighty human rights NGO known worldwide. The people who run Amnesty are, supposedly, the nicest and finest humans on earth. And if there's anything inhuman happening anywhere on Planet Earth, Amnesty will find it, condemn it, chase the offenders, capture them, try them, and execute them on the highest posts of shame and derision. Amnesty, regarded as one of the most progressive, democratic, and liberal bodies ever invented, is, like any other NGO, a collection of self-appointed laymen and laywomen who view themselves as the sole arbiters of truth and justice. They serve as the policeman, prosecutor, and judge, all under the same roof, and nobody is entitled to question them.

Until today.

Today, unexpectedly, Amnesty got caught with its pants down, and the picture is ugly. The king, would you believe, is totally naked. Full Monty.

Here is the story, as published by the *Guardian*.

Headlined, "Amnesty International has a 'toxic' working environment, with widespread bullying, public humiliation, discrimination and other abuses of power, a report has found," the *Guardian*'s article recounts, "Staff reported multiple accounts of discrimination on the basis of race and gender and [sic] which women, staff of colour and LGBTQI employees were targeted or treated unfairly."

Well, enough about Amnesty. I'm not in this land for the purpose of checking them out. I am here because, among other things, I want to see English theater. In England.

So, let me go to the theater.

I have seen some, but I need to see more.

What show should I pick? Well, let me see *School of Rock*. It's not a new show, but it's new to me because I haven't seen it. It's £91.50 a ticket, and it plays at the Gillian Lynne Theatre.

When looking for shows, I notice that there are not many new shows in London, and much of what's offered on the London stages consists of recycled, tried-and-true shows, like this one, which was adapted from a film. Is London suffering from a shortage of talent and creative minds lately?

Music for *School of Rock* is by Andrew Lloyd Webber, book by Julian Fellowes, and lyrics by Glenn Slater.

Andrew Lloyd Webber, the man behind the hit shows *Cats*, *The Phantom of the Opera*, *Evita*, and others, is one of the most recognizable men of British theater, and I'm looking forward to seeing this *School of Rock*.

The theater is packed, and I assume that this must be a good show. I'm excited!

Lights down. Curtain up. Lights up.

And my excitement is gone. Pretty quick.

This *School* is disappointing. At no point do I believe any of the characters, at no point do I feel an urge to join in with the singers, and at no point does my brain feel challenged to have any participation in the proceedings. The plot is too simple, the music never inspiring, and the acting is mediocre at best.

What the show does bring to the fore is a nod to the politically correct. The rock school on the stage is made of a bunch of children.

Some are black, but their parents are white. Of course, no matter how politically correct you are, or not, if the show is not inspiring, no black and white will erase the missing colors of it.

Since I love theater, especially the English theater, I go to see another show on the following day.

Where? Well, not in the West End, the commercial side of London theater, but in the National Theatre, one of the most respected theaters in England.

What I'm going to see is *Tartuffe*. Yeah, Tartuffe. Not the one by RSC, the Pakistani Tartuffe that I saw in Stratford-upon-Avon. No, no. This *Tartuffe* is not Pakistani, Afghani or Syrian – it's English.

Tartuffe is still in previews, with no reviews yet, and the only one writing about it is the National Theatre itself. What does the NT say about its own production? It calls it "A ferocious new version of Molière's comic masterpiece," and warns the public that "this production contains mild language and some nudity."

I love that!

The "new version" of Molière's play was written by John Donnelly, directed by Blanche McIntyre, and the title role is played by Denis O'Hare, an American actor.

So far, so good. Now we have to see the execution.

The first thing I see is the stage, and it looks gorgeous. Really. The set must have cost a pretty penny, no doubt, and it pleases the eye.

But when the actors open their mouths, all I want to do is run. What bad acting! At no point do any of the actors arouse any emotion in me, except for the feeling that Denis O'Hare would have done much better for himself had he stayed in the US.

As for comic timing, since this is supposed to be a comedy, only one minor actor shows a slight possibility that he might one day be able to pull it off; the rest are all DOA, especially Denis.

What's going on here, are the leaders of NT on some prescription drugs?

Ferocious? Don't kid me. *Nudity*? Don't lie to me so brazenly. What this show is, in case you're curious, is political correctness.

Denis is white. His son, as presented here, is black. By itself, there's nothing wrong with it, but it seems that this was done this way for the purpose of showing political correctness, just like in *School of Rock*. RSC's *Tartuffe*, come to think of it, could have cast a white actor as Tartuffe's son, to show how colorblind they are, but this wouldn't be regarded as politically correct, would it?

Tartuffe, Molière's genius, is a brilliant comedy, but I was not laughing at the NT nor at the RSC, two of England's theater power-houses. Maybe it's not politically correct to laugh anymore, and we have to change every classic comedy into a dreadful drama.

This is not the first play I see in NT that I can't stand. Here I also saw *I'm Not Running*, another lousy piece, and I'm reminded of it as I leave the theater.

The English theater has changed from the days I remember it, over two decades ago, when I liked every show that I saw. English theater used to be brilliant, artsy, gutsy, humorous, emotional, funny, entertaining – but now it's half-half: some shows are good, even excellent, while others are dreadful. Why is this happening? I don't know. Maybe the English theater is more interested in preaching than playing nowadays, and maybe it has been influenced by pretentious European theaters over the years and tries to imitate them.

Yeah, I personally know quite a number of people from those European theaters, pretentious people who think that because they are very critical of Israel, they're outstanding artists.

Yeah, yeah, yeah.

On my way back to the hotel, I get myself a bottle of orange juice, find me a bench under the starry night of London – it's awesome weather now – and I think. Beautiful thoughts.

Well, not exactly.

There is a façade of democracy, rather than real democracy, at work in this country. The higher classes, among them the big theater producers, aim to inject their ideologies into the brains of theatergoers at every opportune moment.

The majority of the people voted Leave, but most of parliament says No. The people go to theaters, wishing to see a great show, and are given sermons instead.

I think of the shows that I liked most during this journey: none was impregnated with political correctness, nor did any of them pretend to be more righteous than me. *The Comedy about a Bank Robbery* is an example, or the *Macbeth* that I saw here.

That said, the great English theater is far from dead.

The two greatest shows on earth are playing in London right now, real-life Absurdist dramas: Brexit and anti-Semitism.

If you don't like these two, but you're still looking for more excitement in life, go to your nearest Ladbrokes, Paddy Power, or Betfred, where you can bet all you have. These betting companies are all over this land, and next to them are pawnshops. Just in case.

My recommendation: drop by at the House of Commons and watch the greatest actor of our time, John Bercow.

Yes, I know: I'm addicted to the palace. I might get numbed there and swear never to return again, but the next day I want my palace back. One hour. Two hours. Three. Four. This palace is like drugs. It numbs me, it damages me, but I want more and more of it. When I get up in the morning, when I go to sleep at night, the palace is with me. Outside London, I had my eagle; in London, I have lords and MPs.

If my eagle were here with me in London, I'd probably not go to the palace. But it's not here, and the palace is.

Yes, I'll go there tomorrow. Maybe I'll find my charming anti-Semite there.

The Racists of the Foreign Service

Yes, I did what I said I would do: I went to the Palace of Westminster the next day.

And on the day after, and the day after that, and then again on the day after that, and then again. Day after day after day. Nonstop. An extreme case of addiction, you might call it.

The other day, when I was at the security check at the entrance to the palace, one of the guards said to me: "You come here every day. Why don't you get a passholder card and save yourself the security check? It looks like this is your new home."

My second home, my friend.

As the days go by, I become more and more acquainted with my next-door neighbors, as you may well have imagined, and some of them teach me a lot of things, especially about the history of this country. The first blood libel against Jews, the claim that Jews slaughter Christian kids for the purpose of using their blood as a food ingredient, started in England, they tell me.

Well, where else? This is the land of the *Canterbury Tales*, after all, where the blood libel was elevated to high literature.

History can be rough.

Besides studying history, which is a great thing by itself, I also enjoy their company. They are interesting people, especially those from the House of Lords. Most of them are appointed for life, never running in any election, and they are the wise and the successful of this country. They are usually older, have achieved much, and at this stage of their lives, they can offer their experience and wisdom to the rest of us.

The "lords" is a great concept, let me tell you. In many other societies, when you get older, you retire, and what you've learned in a lifetime stays with you, benefiting no one. You advance in years, and all you do is shop, visit doctors, take trips to the zoo with your grandchildren – if you have any – retire in Switzerland, and spend a considerable amount of time arranging how exactly you would like to be cremated in Bradford. A total waste of time.

Enter the House of Lords.

You're a busy man. You have much to do, MPs ask for your opinion, company boards listen to you, citizens come to visit you, and your later years are the best for you and your society.

Genius.

Lord Stone of Blackheath told me about this the other day, but when I come here, I see how great this idea of the "lords" is in practice.

I enjoy my time with them – or, to be exact, most of them. Like in any society, there are exceptions to the rule, even in the House of Lords, which means that some of them I prefer not to have met. But most of them, the ones that I met and still meet, are a pleasure to talk to, to dine with, and, most often, to have a cup of tea with.

I have just met two very delightful lords, one Labour and the other a Tory. The first, Lord Baron Leslie Turnberg, a Labour peer, told me that there are between 750 and 800 active lords in the House, and that ninety-six of them are Jewish. Of course, it all depends on how you calculate.

Some lords admit that they are Jewish, he says, but others don't. Leslie himself is a proud Jew. Lord Stuart Polak, the Conservative, tells me that he was appointed to the House by former PM David Cameron.

Why did he appoint you? I asked him.

"He said to me," Lord Stuart recalled, "that when I'm in the House of Lords, I should continue my work 'to support Israel.' Those were his words."

They have interesting stories, my lords.

There's one downside to meeting lords: when asked political questions, they say nothing, especially in regard to sensitive issues, such as anti-Semitism in Britain. One day, I'll always remember it, a lord said to me: "You haven't heard anything interesting from me, right?"

Totally right. One after the other, I have the feeling, they lie to me when they deem my questions to be politically sensitive.

Yesterday, in a kind of a test, I turned off my recording equipment and asked the lord I was interviewing, a Jewish lord, to talk to me off the record. He did. And what he said off the record was exactly the opposite of what he told me on the record. What did he tell me off the record?

Well, here goes: anti-Semitism is ingrained in society, and in the highest levels of it; the Foreign Office is populated with anti-Israel, anti-Semitic officials; self-hating Jews lead anti-Semitic political organizations in Britain.

The last part, about the self-hating, is quite intriguing to me, and I want to chat about it with a local maven.

Maybe tomorrow.

Palestine Is a State of Mind

Tomorrow is here, and it's today, and I meet David Hirsh, an author and an academic who teaches sociology at Goldsmiths, University of London.

We meet on the steps just outside the Royal Academy of Arts, where cars are moving slowly next to us, people walking in an orderly manner just by us, and we are talking.

Correction: he is talking. What is he talking about? Yes, self-hating Jews.

"They mobilize their Jewish identity to give themselves more strength and more power. They stand up at Labour Party meetings and union meetings, and they begin by saying, 'We need to be courageous, we need to stand up and oppose the Zionist lobby, and we need to tell the truth.'"

Without those Jews, would we still have the problem of anti-Semitism as we have it today?

"No. Anti-Zionist Jews are amongst the vanguards and the leaders of the anti-Semitic movement."

In other words, without them we would not be where we are today.

"Sure."

Have you, my dear, been to the Royal Academy of Arts? If you have nothing better to do in your life, you should come here. It is a charming place for the kindred among us who will get excited by looking at big wood statues of naked men and small penises, presently on display.

David and I talk for some time, and he reminds me of my days in the university. Oh, those were some of my best times, when the world was wide open, and I could see the day when I would become the leader of either Saudi Arabia or China.

Yeah, I totally missed my calling.

Let me spend the rest of this day in a university, I say to myself. The question is, which one?

According to the QS World University Rankings, University College London (UCL) is in the top ten world universities, well above Yale, Columbia, Princeton, Cornell, and UC Berkeley.

I'm impressed. Let me go to UCL.

Uber takes me there in no time, and I meet Conor Rickford. Do you know Conor?

Well, I didn't know him a moment ago either, but now I do. Conor – let me introduce you – is managing European partnerships for UCL.

Nice, innit?

To break the ice, and to get to know him, I ask Conor to share with me his thoughts about anti-Semitism in Britain.

He does.

Yep. Anti-Semitism is the best ice breaker in the world! And this is what Conor tells me:

"I think the UK does have an issue with anti-Semitism, overall. I think it's easily caricatured as kind of an issue with the Labour Party. I actually think you'll hear less racial invective, maybe, around Jewish people, but you'll probably hear more conspiracy theories. Anybody who's into conspiracy theories, if you speak to them for thirty seconds, eventually you'll get on to Jewish people, no matter where it starts. It can start off talking with them about chemical trails in the sky, but eventually it'll always end with them talking about Jewish people."

That's a UCL man talking. Top of the line!

Do you think there's a big problem of anti-Semitism here in England?

"Yeah. It's caricatured as a kind of an issue that affects working-class people, who are going for this stuff, but I think it's actually more pervasive."

Is anti-Zionism racism, yes or no?

"I don't deal in yes or no, it's not a binary question."

Is it anti-Semitism to say that Jews don't have a right to a state?

"There's an anti-Semitic streak to that, if people think that there's no right to a Jewish state."

I didn't ask about a streak. Is it anti-Semitism or not?

"This is badgering now, this is hectoring."

Why is it that almost all the people I've asked so far told me that it's not anti-Semitic?

"Because of Palestine."

What do you mean?

"Palestine is a state of mind."

No one other than the people living on this island can use language so efficiently. "Palestine is a state of mind." It doesn't matter where Palestine is, where it's coming from, and where it's going to, or if it even exists. Nothing matters, because "Palestine" is bigger than reality.

I salute the man.

I decide to chat with students, just students. Dylan, a history major, is one of my favorites.

Dylan has a baby face, and if I didn't know that he's a student at UCL, I would think that he's a fourteen-year-old, but he's older than that.

There's a lot of discussion about anti-Semitism in the media; what do you think of it? I ask him, wondering to myself if this baby-face has got a clue as to what I'm talking about.

Well, he does.

"I dislike and distrust Jeremy Corbyn quite a bit," he says. "There's a lot of evidence to suggest that he hangs around with some very dodgy characters who certainly dislike Jews very much."

If somebody says that the Jews don't have a right to their own homeland, is that anti-Semitism?

"No, because I think that it's an extremely complex issue, and to label it 'racist' is too simplistic."

So young, so complex, so British, so English.

Somebody's got to pray for the people of this country. Who will it be? Maybe Her Majesty's Muslims.

Let me, the son of Jordan, grandson of the Prophet, join in prayer.

The Dive Bar Where Muslims Drink Guinness

Today is Friday, the Muslim holy day, and I go to join my Muslim cousins in prayer.

My Uber driver is Hindu, no Pakistani today, and he tells me that there are 33 million gods residing in the womb of a cow, and that is the reason it's forbidden to eat beef. In India today, he tells me, some people get killed because of suspicions that they have slaughtered a cow. Not so in London, God Bless the Queen.

Another Uber driver told me the other day that the figure was 3.3 million, considerably less than 33 million. Who is right? I don't know. I never had the chance to count the number of gods inside a cow's womb.

In any case, 33 or 3.3, we soon reach the Muslims, cow-eating humans, and the East London Mosque.

The East London Mosque, the largest mosque in the UK, according to the mosque's literature, is spacious enough for seven thousand people, all of whom seem to have shown up today, midday Friday, to pray.

I join them, worshipper number 7,001.

There's no security check here; this is not a synagogue, this is a mosque. There are no benches here to sit on; this is a mosque, not a church.

I enter the main hall and look for a free spot on the floor's carpet, where the worshippers sit, but there's no room here for even one more needle, not to mention a sizable man like me.

But worry not! With Allah's help, ushers direct people to other halls, and in moments I find myself one floor below the main hall.

The stream of people entering the mosque doesn't stop. Soon there will be more people here than in the whole of London, I think. I look at them, a never-ending ocean of people pouring in, a sight the Jews have not experienced since the biblical days of Mount Sinai. They are so happy to be here, which is amazing.

Upon entry, worshippers take off their shoes, since shoes are regarded as unclean. Some leave their shoes in shelves designed for this purpose at the entrance, others put them in plastic bags provided upon entry and carry their shoes with them.

As the service is about to start, an imam delivers a sermon, but, similarly to the House of Lords speeches, no one seems to be paying much attention. They have come here to talk to Allah, not to have another human talking to them.

The imam keeps talking, in a very heavy accent, and more people come in. Ushers tell the people who are already inside to squeeze more; this is not a hotel, this is a mosque.

Everybody complies. The service starts.

Everybody is up, standing like sardines inside the famous London Tube on rush hour, and all are ready for the spiritual ride.

Allahu Akbar, God is great, the muezzin chants, and all go down on their knees.

They bow and I bow; for them it's prayer, for me it's push-ups, but no one can tell the difference.

Once prayer time is over, all leave in a most orderly manner. Nobody is running away from the mosque, and everyone is patient.

Outside the mosque, there's a big sign in Arabic above the entrance doors: Allah (God). To the right of it there's another sign: "Main Entrance for Men."

Attached to the mosque is the London Muslim Centre. Here, women may enter as well, but they are asked to observe a dress code: "Please do not enter if you are wearing shorts or a skirt above the knee, nor if you are wearing a revealing top."

Many of the women passing by wear the hijab, some wear the niqab, and a store nearby is selling burkas to any woman wishing that no man see even one inch of her tempting flesh.

One day, maybe, I'll buy myself a burka and go to interview Boris Johnson. Can you imagine it? I certainly can.

Across the street from the mosque, I talk with some of the believers, most of whom were born abroad. They are happy to be in London, they say, and would never go back to their homelands. Being a Muslim in Britain is great, they tell me, and they appreciate the freedom they have here, something they didn't have back home. The only problem they have in this land is the increasing number of young people who traffic in drugs and bullets, a problem that other Muslims have confided to me in the past.

Ben, a bartender in a bar opposite the mosque, is a young, white English guy, an atheist, who likes the Muslims. "We actually have good relations" with the Muslims, he says. During Ramadan, he tells me, when Muslims are forbidden to smoke during the day, worshippers come by in the evening and sit on a bench he provides for them outside the bar to have their first cigarette of the day. In addition, some Muslims "will have half a Guinness every now and then." Alcohol is forbidden to Muslims, but Guinness is too good to pass up, I guess.

Who frequents his bar? Local Muslims and a few "rich, banker-type people," from the City, London's financial area nearby. Ben likes the Muslims, but he doesn't like the bankers, because they are "aggressive and rude." Luckily for him, not too many rich bankers frequent the bar. This bar is a "dive bar," he explains to me, meaning a bar for the "less classy" people.

East London, Ben says, used to be Jewish, and the mosque used to be a synagogue. On the back side of the mosque, he informs me, there is "Hebrew writing on the wall."

I'll check it later.

Ben, like some other young Brits I met, is consumed by Jews. Don't ask me why. "I'm reading a very good book at the moment, called *Out of the Ghetto*, which is by a guy called Joe Jacobs. He was an East End Jewish Communist, whose parents were Russian and Polish Jews who lived in this area, and he was very active in the Communist Party. Have you ever heard of the Battle of Cable Street? Cable Street is fifteen minutes from here; there's a very beautiful mural over there."

Yeah. I'm right near the place where the papa and mama of Jeremy Corbyn fell in love, at least according to Red Pete.

Anti-Semitism in the Labour Party is still consuming the British media, often on the front pages, but Ben is not impressed. "I think," he tells me, "that, in reality, they are trying to conflate anti-Semitism and anti-Zionism." But this is totally wrong.

Why so?

"Israel is a settler colonial project, a European settler colonial state."

Ben, a pure English soul, explains to me what Israel's all about: a vassal state dominated by the moneyed elite of Britain. Israel, says Ben, is working for the City. If that's not enough, he adds that Israel, a state that he calls "a running dog for imperialism," is ruled by a Jewish European elite that practices racism not only against Palestinians but also against "Mizrahi" Jews, meaning Jews whose ancestry is not European, and Ethiopian Jews "who are being treated like shit." He knows it all, he argues, because "I went to Palestine. It's apartheid, man."

I walk to the back of the mosque.

Engraved on stone, it reads: "Fieldgate Street Great Synagogue Communal Centre. This foundation stone was laid by Mr Nathan Zlotnicki, president of the synagogue, July 12 1959." Another stone, in Hebrew, reads: "Holy Community Shaar Yaakov Synagogue, 1899."

Across the street from these foundation stones, I see Omar, a man who sells "halal kosher burgers," believe it or not. The first in Britain, he says.

Time for another Uber driver, to take me back to my hotel.

This one tells me that he likes Jews, and he explains why. "The Jews have a lot of money, but they lead a humble life."

Good to know.

The driver drops me at my hotel, and I go to the smoking area to have a cigarette or two.

Next to me is a twenty-year-old guy by the name of Fadil, born and raised in Morocco, whose job is "boxing in a cage." What's boxing in a cage? I ask him. "MMA, mixed martial arts."

He misses his home food, he tells me, but here in the UK, he makes money. He asks me who I am. I tell him that I'm a Jordanian journalist.

Nobody here, he tells me, understands the Middle East.

What do you mean?

"Look at the Palestinians here. They stay in this hotel, I've seen them. This is an expensive hotel. How come they have money to stay here? In the English media they say that the Palestinians are all poor. It's all lies and delusions!"

Do you fast on Ramadan? I ask him, just to ascertain who this young man really is.

"Definitely. I'm a Muslim!"

For this Fadil, I can tell, Palestine is not a state of mind.

Once Fadil leaves, I'm the sole smoker in the area.

I light up the second cigarette, and I think of London, and how every passing day I get attached to it more and more. There's magic in this city, a magnet that draws me deeper and deeper into it and never lets me go. London offers a wonderful mix of peoples and styles, of buildings and souls, of art and finance, of sound and image, of past and future, of palaces and kiosks, of really bad food that's lusciously packaged, and of long-dead men and horses that never really died.

A glorious city.

I'm not leaving, not yet. Oh, no!

Brexit, Schmexit

For some time now, the British media has been reporting that a number of Labour MPs are planning to leave their party, but no specific date has been supplied. Well, I think I know when this will take place: in a matter of hours. How do I know? Tobias and Florian, meaning yours truly, has just received two separate messages, from Karie and Ayse respectively, that JC will not be able to meet, unfortunately.

The man is hiding.

Now, I think, we should definitely give him the title rabbi. Maybe even chief rabbi of British Jews.

Lovely!

I'll have to find another way to meet this chief rabbi, I guess. "If all doors are closed," Sheikh Ahmad Yassin used to say, "Allah opens a gate."

Inshallah.

According to the *Times*, in an article just published, "more people think Corbyn is himself anti-semitic (34%) or don't know (32%) than those who believe he is not."

But hold your horses, my dear. This is not the reason that certain MPs want to split from the party, though I have no doubt that at least some of them will include anti-Semitism as at least one of the reasons for their split from Labour. There is another reason, much dearer to MPs, that will make them entertain the idea of deserting their political tent: fear of being deselected by their local party, which means that they won't be able to run in the next election under the same banner.

There are also real issues on the line, to be fair.

The most visible political issue dragging Labour members in opposite directions nowadays is the People's Vote, which many in Labour would like to see happening but Jeremy Corbyn does not, at least not yet.

In any case, no public announcement of any MP leaving anywhere has been made yet, and I'm going to entertain myself somewhere else.

Welcome to the Speakers' Corner, Hyde Park.

The Speakers' Corner is, first and foremost, an idea. The idea is that every man or woman who wishes to shout like the average MP in the Commons shall be allowed to stand up, on a chair or a small ladder they bring with them, and deliver a lecture to the people at large.

In reality, London's Speakers' Corner is not exactly a corner but a wide area in Hyde Park. Usually, as far as I understand, it takes place in the part of the park closest to Marble Arch, and that's where it is being held today.

I'm here because I want to hear what's on the mind of the people of this country, the common man and woman. What do they have in their hearts that makes them feel the need to unload on their fellow citizens in beautiful Hyde Park? Will it be Brexit? Will it be the cost of living? Will it be the homeless issue? Will it be the congestion tax on cars entering central London? Will it be anti-Semitism? Will it be the EU? Will it be about boring theater? Will it be about JC and Me?

Well, surprise, surprise. None of the above. The people of this city, the ones who have bothered to come here, don't care about Brexit, EU, Theresa and you. Nope. That's not what's on their minds. What they care about, and the people who stop by to hear them, is something else altogether.

Would you like to know what? Jesus and Mohammed and Israel. You got that right.

Here's a man standing on his ladder with the words "Jesus is alive" all over his trousers. He holds the Quran in his hands, and he preaches against it. Did Mohammed make mistakes? It says in the Quran that he did! But Jesus, you can read in the New Testament, never made mistakes.

So, who is the truth? Jesus alone is truth. Jesus is the answer, Jesus is the cure, Jesus is truth, and Jesus is God.

Across from him is another guy, dressed in traditional Islamic garb, and he holds the Quran as well. Everything in life is about God and His Messenger, Prophet Mohammed. If Jesus was a God, he asks, how could it be that he died? God is almighty, right? Right. Almighty don't die. Moses was a Muslim. For sure. All prophets were.

The third speaker today doesn't believe in Jesus, doesn't care about Mohammed, but is very worried about the state of affairs of all humanity. He's a communist, and he feels the need to engage in war against the evil people and institutions the world over. Who are they? The capitalists. Who are the capitalists? He counts them: Britain, the USA, and Israel. They want to kill you, he tells the passersby in Hyde Park.

Forget Brexit and Schmexit. Welcome Jesus, Marx, and Mohammed.

I leave the place, a bit perplexed, and walk over to Edgware Road, right nearby.

Oh, Edgware Road, what would I have done without thee? Blessed be thou forever and ever, on earth and in heaven, in seas and on dry lands. Oh, Edgware Road, my soul and spirit thy bittersweet Arabic coffee craves. Will you irrigate thy thirsty Jew today?

Within minutes of walk in the Arab land of London, I see an interesting restaurant calling my name high and loud. *Come to me*, it calls, in big red color. I step toward it to make my acquaintance, and I find the place to be what my soul desires: a restaurant and a *shisha* (narghile) place, body and soul, answering to the name of Al Balad.

I sit down at a table outside on the sidewalk, and the owner immediately approaches me. "What would you like," he asks, "food or *shisha*?"

What's better? I ask him.

"We serve the best food in the world. Homemade, I guarantee," he answers, proudly and happily.

Okay, then, give me the menu.

He orders a waiter to bring me the menu, and I browse the news meantime. So, what's new?

The Sun writes: "Nigel Farage's new Brexit Party has signed up 100,000 members – just a week after it was formally registered."

The waiter arrives.

Good. *Halas* politics for today.

What's delicious in here? I ask the waiter.

He's happy to share with me: grilled chicken liver in outrageously delicious pomegranate juice, just-made falafel balls with the freshest of hummus, lamb kebab made from the best lambs ever, fresh tabbouleh, hot pita bread, tahini, labneh, olive oil from olives grown in heaven – and this is just the beginning.

I order them all.

I look at the people passing by. London, let me tell you, is the most diverse city in the world. You don't believe me? Come here and see for yourself. This is Arab land, as you can tell by the people passing by and the stores all around here, yet white people feel totally safe walking here as well.

Diversity at its best!

The food arrives.

What a taste! Come here, all you Hyde Park Speakers, and taste heaven!

This Al Balad, how lucky I am, has the best Middle Eastern food in the whole of the UK. This restaurant should get ten Michelin stars. I swear. No man or woman on this island can make better Middle Eastern food than the people of Al Balad.

I eat, eat, and eat. And drink, drink, and drink. When in Paradise, you don't stop.

The time passes, one hour after another.

When the belly can take no more, it's time for smoke and sleep.

Hours later, my Apple Watch wakes me up with the newest of news: MP Luciana Berger, calling the Labour Party "institutionally anti-Semitic," announces that she's quitting Labour, together with six other MPs, to form The Independent Group.

Interestingly, she's using the same language that Rachel Riley has been using, when she talked with me quite some time ago about the Labour Party: "institutionally anti-Semitic."

The political common denominator that all these seven MPs share, the *Guardian* writes, is that "all of the rebel MPs have backed a second referendum, which is not yet Labour policy."

The Independent Group is not a party, at least not yet, but a grouping of seven MPs in the House of Commons. Of course, only the blind and the deaf will believe that this group does not dream of forming a new party, but as of now they present themselves as the pure lambs of British politics, the ones – and the only ones – who care not about a seat but about a principle.

Are they such pure lambs as they present themselves?

When I talk to some people, off the record, about Luciana's reasoning for leaving Labour, they question her real motivation. During her first few years as an MP, she did not, so they say, raise the issue of anti-Semitism. If it affects her so much today, why was she silent yesterday? they ask.

As the hours progress, members of the new group call upon MPs from both main parties to join them, and they ask the public at large for donations.

As time passes, another Labour MP quits the party and joins the group, and in a few hours three Conservative MPs quit their party to join the group.

Since all of them want a second referendum, and since the main argument against Brexit is that it's detrimental to the economy, I schlepp myself to the City, the abode of financiers and Ben's colonialists, to find out if they agree with the prophets of doom and gloom.

My Uber driver drops me off at the London Stock Exchange, one of the oldest stock exchanges in the world, and I can't believe my eyes: the place is an eyesore; it looks deserted, it's dirty and quite poorly put together. I ask passersby if this is indeed the famed London Stock Exchange, and they say that yes, it is. I try to enter the building, but there's no entry. A guard, a lone guard, tells me that I am on the back side of the building, and that if I want to go in, I should go to the front.

I go to the front.

It's not dirty, nor ugly, yet it is quite unimpressive. The entrance to the average supermarket in London looks more attractive, but perhaps the rich of London are humble like the Jews and don't want to flaunt their wealth.

Could be.

Humble or not, the guards don't let me into the building. Well, what can I do? I will talk to the people outside.

Easier said than done. These people, creatures covered with clothes that cost hundreds – or thousands – of pounds are not exactly into talking to foreigners who approach them with recording devices. What's more, time is money, lots of money, and there's no real reason they should spend their time on me. Yes, I'm cute, no doubt, but money is money.

Luckily, there are some people who like to be immortalized in a book, and they are willing to engage in conversation with me.

Hugh is one of them.

Hugh makes his living in the financial world, and as far as I can tell, he's doing well for himself, thank you for asking. He is, as Ben and friends would say, a capitalist.

How will life be if Brexit goes through? I wonder.

He doesn't. "It's an exciting time," he says. "There's a lot of change, and I don't think we'll fully understand the change for a year or two, but there are a lot of opportunities. The markets are stable, the markets are very efficient, and I think we're well prepared for change." In other words, the prophets of doom and gloom had better study finance and financial markets before making their dire predictions.

I wonder what these people, folks who have it all, financially speaking, think of anti-Semitism, an issue that the House of Commons will devote three hours tomorrow to discuss and debate.

Yes, I just found out. The House, my house.

Hugh, dressed in a nice suit and no tie, knows finance, but he has no opinion about the anti-Semitism issue. Yes, he's read about it, he knows it exists, but he has no opinion. What he also knows is that "we're all Europeans," and Brexit or no Brexit, everybody will trade with everybody, and we'll all be rich.

Good.

Nolan, dressed in a lovely scarf and a long coat, holds practically the same opinion. When asked how Brexit, if it goes through, will affect the economy, he answers: "We may have a short-term recession, I don't know, but long-term, England will survive, and London will do well, without doubt. The City is bulletproof; you can put a bomb underneath it and it will bounce back."

Nolan knows finance well, and other things too, but he has no opinion about anti-Semitism in the country. Yeah, of course he's read about it and heard about it, but that's it; he has no opinion.

Alex, another money maker, has not a single worry about the future after Brexit. "We are very good at what we do, and I'm very positive," he says, summing up his feelings about the economy in the shortest of lines. As for anti-Semitism, he has another succinct line to explain it all: "This country has a disgusting problem with anti-Semitism." I suspect that this Alex is Jewish, but I can't prove it.

Steps away is St. Paul's Cathedral, and that's where I go. St. Paul's is gorgeous, but you can't just walk in there, unless there is an official service. If you want to pray at any other time, or just visit God at His house, you have to pay £20 first. God is a capitalist.

Jesus, the founder of Christianity, wouldn't like this one bit, and anybody who ever read the New Testament would know it. When Jesus saw the Temple courts in Jerusalem, we read in Mathew, he knocked over the tables of money changers. "And He said unto them, It is written, My house shall be called the house of prayer; but ye have made it a den of thieves."

Along the ages, anti-Semites have relied on this New Testament story as a proof that Jew and money were bound to one another from the beginning of time, and always will be.

But who's married to money here? The people of St. Paul's. Jesus is alive, said the man of Hyde Park.

Imagine, just imagine, if Jesus came over here now, to this St. Paul's, and the church people asked him to fork out £20. Oh, boy, what a scene we would have here!

Of course, had Jesus come here and made a scene, the anti-Semites of this country would find a way to blame the Jews.

Stay where you are, my dear Jesus. We don't need a troublemaking Jew in the UK these days. There's enough anti-Semitism here as is.

I will go, I promise thee, Jesus, to the House of Commons to witness their special session on anti-Semitism, and I'll report it to the people. My word, Jesus. I'll do it.

The Most Powerful People in the Most Powerful House Are Talking about Me

Lady Valerie Cocks, a fine lady who lives across the street from my hotel, has arranged for me to be the chief whip's guest, which means that I'll be seated at the chief whip's seats in the Commons Chamber when members discuss the Jews and whatnot. These seats are at the same level as the MPs', allowing me to see them up close and look them straight in the eye. Great!

Here's Luciana Berger, heavily pregnant, surrounded by two MPs on each side. She's clutching a bunch of papers in one hand and a cellphone in the other, typing on the cellphone one minute and writing on the papers the next, nonstop. During her first years in the Commons, a London Jew was telling me today (as I've already heard before), Luciana couldn't care less about anti-Semitism, but now this is her main issue.

The chamber is more than half empty, with fewer Tories than Labour, but this does not hinder the speakers from being quite emotional. The celeb of the moment is Luciana, with various MPs congratulating her on her bravery. Is she brave? Well, she's a politician, they are politicians, and it's all politics.

The MPs talk, one after another. Shadow International Trade Secretary Barry Gardiner, obviously of Labour, asks: "How can it be that we are struggling so badly to eradicate anti-Semitism from our own membership?" Addressing the Jewish community in general, he says: "I want on behalf of my party to publicly apologize to the Jewish community, that we have let you down." Speaking about MP Luciana Berger, he says: "I regret deeply that she has left our party. I regret most of all the anti-Semitic abuse which made her feel it was necessary to do so."

Here is Labour MP Margaret Hodge, whom I was supposed to interview a few weeks ago. She was very happy to be interviewed by a "German journalist" and asked for my name, to put in her diary. When she realized who I am, a Jew like her, she immediately cancelled the interview.

Well, I listen to her now. "I never, ever thought my Jewish identity would be central to my political work," she says.

I should use this line on her, with just one minor change: "I never, ever thought my Jewish identity would be central to my journalistic work."

Margaret is an interesting person. For God knows how long, her official constituency website featured one single article on its homepage, titled "Latest News. Gaza: There is no justification for shooting unarmed civilians." In the article, she accused Israel of "shooting unarmed civilians" and called for "an independent inquiry into the deaths." She went on and on, also accusing US president Donald Trump of making a "reckless and ill-judged decision" to move the American embassy from Tel Aviv to Jerusalem.

She is entitled to her views, but why is it that Israel is the only issue a British MP features on her homepage? Better yet, what do Jerusalem and Gaza have to do with her constituents to start with?

Margaret is not stupid. Now that Luciana Berger quit Labour, flashing the anti-Semitism card and riding the heroine journey, Margaret publicly joins Luciana's defenders, standing by her side every step of the way. And she fools everybody. So much so that when I met a leading Jewish official the other day, he excitedly told me how great he felt about Margaret. I told him to calm down, and

I showed him her website. He was shocked. "I'll call her today," he told me, his excitement totally gone. Promptly thereafter, Margaret took her website down.

Latest News

Gaza: There is no justification for shooting unarmed civilians

Many of my constituents have written to me about the Palestinians murdered and wounded in the most recent protests in Gaza.

The use of live ammunition by the Israel Defence Forces must always be a measure of last resort. There is no justification for shooting unarmed civilians behind the border of Israel, inside Gaza. The Israeli Government's response to legitimate protest by Palestinians was completely wrong. I welcome the condemnation of this action by world leaders and I join others in the call for an independent inquiry into the deaths.

The decision of the President of the United States to move his country's embassy from Tel Aviv to Jerusalem has poured fuel on the already raging fire of conflict between the countries of the Middle East. Donald Trump's reckless and ill-judged decision also flies in the face of decades of historical convention that ensured respect was given to the claims on Jerusalem of both Israelis and Palestinians. America's foolish gesture, coupled with Netanyahu's totally outrageous and aggressive actions, has created yet more obstacles to a peaceful resolution of the conflict.

Such is politics, where truth is only an occasional guest.

Interestingly, a Tory MP speaking now succeeds in being more honest here than his counterparts in Labour. He says that he won't blame anti-Semitism in the UK on "Corbynism" in the Labour Party, as there's more of it outside Labour as well. Anti-Semitism, he reminds us, exists not only in Britain. He tells us of passing by a Jewish school in Brussels, and how strange an image it was because the school was surrounded by armored personnel vehicles, put there to protect the kids from potential killers.

As MPs are talking, I notice quite a number of Labour MPs coming to Luciana. They tap her on the shoulder, whisper a word or two into her ear, or sit down for a moment for a quick chat. She is, at least today, the queen of the House.

Jeremy Corbyn is not here, but his spirit hovers all over the chamber. They allude to him, almost all of them, mostly without mentioning his name. He is the elephant in the room, the Satan in the hall, the cancer in the nation.

Where is Jeremy?

Luciana gets up to speak, reading from her papers. She tells the story of anti-Semitism in Labour, she talks about Red Pete without mentioning his name, and she reads aloud some of the hate mail that she has received.

Her speech is followed by other speeches, hour follows hour, and the House of Commons keeps on talking about anti-Semitism. Speaker John Bercow is presiding, but today he's not acting.

I watch all this and I feel very, very strange.

Yes, I have found much anti-Semitism in this land and have dedicated many pages to it, but I still don't fully believe it; I don't believe myself. I know it's there, but there's this part of me that constantly refuses to admit it. This cannot be true, I keep saying to myself.

And now I sit here, and I listen.

These most powerful people, occupying this highest hall of law of this powerful country, are dedicating their time to the virulent anti-Semitism in their midst.

It is real.

These people, these Brits, are talking about me, speaking to me. Yes, it is real.

It's tragic.

The people of this land hate me. I didn't make it up. They really do.

I leave the House.

The Taming of the Jew

No matter what the House of Commons – or the British media in general – says about anti-Semitism, you can always count on big-shot Jews to surprise you with their unique interpretations.

Get acquainted with the Right Honorable Baron Levy, aka Lord Levy, formerly the chief fundraiser of the Labour Party, a member of the board of the International Peace Institute, founder of Magnet Records, and former personal envoy and special advisor on the Middle East to Prime Minister Tony Blair – among other titles.

I go to this famous and rich Jew to hear what he has to say about the anti-Semitism row in his party and country.

I arrive timely at his private office, a lovely place on Marylebone Mews, but he's a bit late, and his sweet secretary offers me as many candies as I can dream of. After some time, when all the candy's gone, the lord shows up.

We sit in an adjacent room, ready to chat.

Does the Labour Party have an anti-Semitic problem? I ask the lord of lords.

"Well, firstly, I've been a member of the Labour Party for many years. I've been in the House of Lords on the Labour benches for twenty-two years. My basic entry into the political scene for Labour was with Tony Blair, and for many years I was at Prime Minister Blair's, as it was then, side, acted as his personal envoy in my office in the Foreign and Commonwealth Office. During that time, certainly

I found Blair a true friend of the Jewish community. He would come to every Jewish event. I joke he has more yarmulkes than I've got, because every time he would have a yarmulke and wear it, and he would never give it back. So, I'm sure somewhere he's got a collection, and I never found anything at all within the party under Blair remotely anti-Semitic."

Does the Labour Party now, not historically, but at the moment, have an anti-Semitic problem, yes or no?

This is a binary question, requiring a yes or no response.

But this baron, being a baron, answers my question by delivering a speech.

"You're asking a very difficult question. Does it have an anti-Semitic problem? If there are people within the Labour Party who are anti-Semitic, therefore the party, de facto, has a problem, and therefore it is essential that the party absolutely makes sure anyone who is anti-Semitic, who comes out with anti-Semitic comments, who comes out with anything on social media that is anti-Semitic, needs to be driven out of the Labour Party. There is no place in the Labour Party, or any other political party, for anti-Semitism or anyone who has anti-Semitic views."

In other words: there are a few bad apples in Labour, but other than that, everything's cool. I don't give up on the man, and I try a different angle.

According to the media, as far as I can tell, the Labour Party now has a huge anti-Semitic problem. And my question to you is: Does Labour have this problem or does it not?

"I've already answered you."

Yeah.

"If there're anti-Semites within the Labour Party, it has a problem. It's a very simple answer."

So, it does have a problem.

"If there are anti-Semites in the Labour Party – "

Are there?

"You've seen yourself there have been anti-Semitic comments from people who are in the Labour Party, and therefore there are problems. It is essential the party rids themselves of these problems, and therefore rids themselves of these people."

Within three months, maximum, he shares his belief with me, all the bad apples within Labour will be out.

In other words: Labour's great.

Time to move from party to country.

I spoke to some members of the Jewish community, I tell him, and they told me about nice Jewish kids having their yarmulkes snatched off their heads; they also told me about being pelted with eggs and about fires set to restaurants – in Manchester, in Golders Green. Does he have anything to say about that?

Well, that's all news to him.

"We live in a tolerant society," he tells me, a bit upset, "but have there been pockets of [anti-Semitic acts]? Absolutely, yes. So, taking a yarmulke off a child's head, that can happen. It can happen anywhere, but is it happening every minute, every hour of the day? I don't think so, no, and we monitor every anti-Semitic incident through an organization. So, I just ask you to perhaps think very carefully –"

I do.

"– in terms of what has been said to you, how it's been said to you, what the incidents specifically are, and how you actually analyze what those incidents are. We have police, we have security in this country. We're living in a democracy."

He neurotically enunciates every word as he talks to me, and he seems upset at me for asking him the questions I do.

"I live here in London. I haven't heard of any instance in Golders Green. My rabbi's family is from Stamford Hill; I haven't heard any incidents there. Now, are they happening? Perhaps they are, and perhaps, I don't know. I'm not absolutely saying that I know everything that is going on."

Yeah.

And what does he think about Jeremy Corbyn? Is JC an anti-Semite?

"I do believe that he has views on Israel that certainly need a very good education course, because I think his views on Israel are disproportionate, and they are not facing the reality of where Israel stands in the world today with all its problems."

In a word: no.

Labour is great. Corbyn needs an education. And as for anti-Semitism? Well, there are some idiots here and there, but who doesn't have idiots?

Red Pete, I'm sure, would appreciate this Jewish lord.

As for me, what can I say? Marylebone Mews looked quite lovelier before the baron showed up.

Lord Levy, as I see him, is a perfect example of present-day British Jews: extremely well tamed. The non-Jews, the real lords of the land, have tamed their Jews just perfectly. Here comes the day, I dread the moment, when Brits and tourists flock to see *The Taming of the Jew* on one of the bigger London stages, applauding its jesters with zest.

I won't be among them.

JC and Me, the Sequel

I have to find that man, that Jeremy Corbyn.

As soon as possible.

Well, I'll have to move my fat ass if I want to find him. Let's move.

First stop: the cafeteria in Portcullis House, a parliament office building across the street from the palace. With the aid of a pass-holder, a person possessing an entry card into the inner sanctum of the powerful, I enter the Portcullis House building and go to the cafeteria, where politicians and their helpers often wander.

I sit down and check the human landscape. Anybody I know here?

Wait a second! Is that man over there not him?

Yes, my eyes don't lie to me. It's him. The elephant, Satan, and saint. The rabbi. The belly dancer.

Truthfully, I didn't expect to succeed on my first try, and I'm not mentally ready. How should I handle this? I ask myself. How would my eagle do it, if it were here?

Walk over to him, I hear my eagle yelling from far, far away, probably Scotland's Highlands. Yes, of course! So simple! I walk over to him.

What's the story, Jeremy? I ask him. We were supposed to meet and then your ladies cancelled.

"Call the office and make a new appointment."

Are you playing games with me, Jeremy? I won't call your ladies again. They say one thing and they do the other. It's between us, you and me. Do you want to meet me or not? I like you, I'm a German who likes you, and I thought that you like me too.

"What do you want? I don't have my diary with me. I don't know my schedule for – "

You are your own boss. You make your own schedule. Don't you?

"Come to my office next week on Tuesday. Any time. You don't have to call the ladies. I'll tell them to expect you."

Where's your office?

"Norman Shaw South."

Far away on the mountains of Scotland, I can hear my eagle jumping for joy. Do you know, my eagle, where Norman Shaw South is?

My eagle doesn't answer; I'll have to find it on my own.

With my mission accomplished, and faster than I could even imagine, I leave the place.

Not far from me is the Church House, where the Church of England is holding its General Synod, and I take time to visit the learned men and women of the Church. In Scotland, I made my acquaintance with the Church of Scotland, so it's time I get acquainted with the English.

At the entrance, I pick up the *Church of England Newspaper*, a paper I never knew existed. There is one insert inside the paper, an envelope on which is written, "Breaking: Devastating Cuts for Palestinians. Healing: You can support Palestinians with medicines and life-saving health services." The only suffering people on earth, as every child of the Church knows, are Palestinians. Full stop. End.

Norman Shaw South. I have to find the place.

Wash This Blood off from My Guilty Hand

Have you been to Buckingham Palace?

Take a look at the gates to the palace, the black and golden gates. That's royalty, innit? Now look at the palace itself, a massive piece of real estate; what do you think?

The gates are locked, and the palace is closed to the public, but this doesn't stop the masses of people from pouring into this area. The number of people coming to see the unseeable is staggering, and they are totally fascinated by the locked estate in front of them.

I look at the exterior of this palace, and I wonder: Who, for heaven's sake, really needs this place?

Well, everybody around me, I guess, and all those who came yesterday and those who will come tomorrow. The monarchy is one big, huge, gigantic show, and everybody wants to watch it.

There were the days when kings and queens were the lords of this country, no Tories or Labour, and they ruled not only this country but many others as well.

I want to get a feel for those days, and since I'm into theater, I make up my mind to see *Richard II*, produced by none other than one of the most esteemed of English theaters, namely the Globe Theatre, Shakespeare's Globe Theatre. If anybody knows kings or queens, and if anybody knows English theater, I've been told time and again, it's the Globe people.

Uber takes me there.

Welcome to the world of the Globe Theatre. What do I see?

Shakespeare, I think, wouldn't recognize any of the characters of his play had he come here today. This production of *Richard II* is performed by a special cast. The lead role is played by a woman – a black woman – and the whole cast is made of "women of color." Yeah. Why? An elegant, young white English lady sitting next to me explains it thusly: "For generations women, especially women of color, have been denied the right to play important roles. Tonight they will. I think it's a wonderful idea."

Good.

The play starts.

The stage is poorly lit, mostly by candles, and you can never see quite clearly the expressions on the faces of the royals onstage, at least not from where I'm sitting. Most of the audience is seated on cushioned benches that have no back, for the three-hour duration of this performance. The actresses scream their lines, which at times makes me feel as if I were in a mental hospital, not in an English theater that pretends to be a palace. The set does not resemble a palace, any palace, English or not.

The "women of color" go on screaming, louder and louder. Why are they screaming? Is somebody hurting them? The woman who plays the lead role, King Richard II, seems to be an actress, albeit a mediocre one at best, but the others strike me more as bookkeepers than as actors. The costumes, which were most likely designed by a supermarket cashier, are yet another motive that evades my brain.

During intermission, I ask the elegant lady next to me for her thoughts. "I really like it! It's wonderful!" she says. Then she gets up, to have a little fresh air, but never returns.

That's English politeness for you. It was so wonderful that she had to leave.

The second half is a bit better, but far from what one would expect from a prestigious theater such as the Globe.

The people in charge of this theater believe, so it seems, that having a cast of "women of color" is the ultimate in anti-racism. I think that the opposite is true. By spending their time looking for "colored" women to cast their show, what they were actually doing is singling out a certain type of people as different from themselves. I would certainly never want any director to cast me in a show just because I'm Jewish. Being Jewish is between me and me, and nobody is to designate me as the "other." Personally, as a stage director at the Jewish Theater of New York, I've never cast anyone because of his or her race or ethnicity.

In any case, *Richard II* is butchered here, not in some prison as in the actual text, but on this Globe stage by incapable actors, director, and designers.

The good thing is that, with time, *Richard II* finally comes to an end, but not before Henry Bolingbroke, King Henry IV, utters the following words:

> I'll make a voyage to the Holy Land,
> To wash this blood off from my guilty hand:
> March sadly after; grace my mournings here;
> In weeping after this untimely bier.

Holy Land. Israel again.

No, these words of *Richard II* have nothing to do with anti-Semitism, but everything to do with the history of it. Yesterday and today are connected in body and interconnected in soul. The fascination of the gentile with the Jew, and the hatred thereof, started in ancient Israel and goes all the way through today's Israel, from the Jew of yesterday to the Jew of today. Both 1290 and 2019 are dates on the English calendar when the hatred tore apart the carpet that covered it. Yet, in their own eyes, the people sitting next to me view themselves as the most anti-racist on the planet. Are they?

Some days ago, I went to the magnificent and majestic Westminster Abbey, to attend a service. As I walked in, I was handed a page with the hymns and prayers for the service.

Here's what was written on the page:

> For mine eyes have seen thy salvation,
> Which thou hast prepared before the face of all people,
> To be a light to lighten the Gentiles,
> And to be a glory of thy people Israel.

The glory of thy people Israel.
Israel. Jews.
Interconnected.

These Are the English

On the next day, childish me, I go to the Globe again. Am I a masochist? Usually not, but perhaps London is changing my character.

What am I planning to see? Well, Christopher Marlowe's *Edward II*.

Edward II is playing at the very same theater as yesterday. This time, though, men and women are playing on the stage, some whites, others "people of color." Unlike in *Richard II*, the casting of blacks and whites in this production does not appear to be motivated by a need to be politically correct, but rather by talent or availability.

Oh, boy, what a difference between the two productions!

The lighting, by candles only, is for a reason, Globe's people tell me. They want to present shows the way they believe shows were presented in Shakespeare's time. Interesting. The set, which I think is the theater's permanent set, is beautiful.

This time, believe it or not, the candles don't bother me at all. Why? Well, when the acting is good, candlelit theater is actually great. In fact, everything works well with this presentation – and I think I know why. This production is not aimed to show how progressive the producers or artists are, nor does it have any obvious political aim. What the actors want to do here is one thing: to play. And it shows. There's a continuous drama on the stage, bringing Marlowe's words on the page to a full theatrical life on the stage.

What a pleasure to watch.

Edward II, King of England, is a man in love with another man. He betrays his wife and will as easily betray anyone else. The nobles of his court are much like him: they betray his trust, plan to depose him, kill him, and one of them is about to snatch the queen for himself. As the play moves along, while one is betraying the other, the English monarchy shines through, and I can better comprehend the roots of this country, the roots of these people, and why they still have the monarchy. The monarchy, as seen here, is this country's most powerful literature, most intimate pride, England's soul, Her Majesty's theater.

I now see Buckingham Palace in a totally different light. It was good to go there yesterday.

Tomorrow is Tuesday, the day I'm supposed to meet Jeremy Corbyn. Will the Labour leader open for me the doors to his office, as he said he would, or will he hide from me, as he did before?

We shall see.

JC and Me, Part Three

When morning arrives, I realize that I have no clue how to get to Norman Shaw South. Yes, I found out where it is, but there's one little problem: in order to get to Norman Shaw, south or not, I need first to pass through an entrance of another building, but that other building is not open to the public. The only way to get in is by being invited – and accompanied – by a passholder, which means that I need an MP, a lord, or a staff member to let me through. How am I going to arrange this?

I ask around for favors, from this and that, him and her, and luckily I find a passholder to escort me in.

Life's good.

The passholder and I go through the first building and then cross to Norman Shaw South. Perfect.

The passholder, a lady who can't stand Jeremy Corbyn, tells me that she doesn't want to see him and says goodbye near the entrance to the Norman Shaw building.

I'm on my own.

I go up the stairs, looking for Jeremy. Unfortunately, I can't find any sign that would indicate where in this building the man's office is.

I ask a maintenance man passing by if he could, please, direct me to Jeremy's office. Yes, he says, and immediately dispatches a security man in my direction.

This is not going well, damn it. The security man wants to know how in Jesus' name did I get to roam the place with no one accompanying me. We chat for a while and I try to charm him, but he still demands that I not roam the place on my own. Okay, I tell him. I'll get somebody from Jeremy's office to fetch me.

It's the last thing I want to do, but I have no choice. There are too many guns in this place, too many cops, and I don't want to be their target.

Certainly not today.

I call Jeremy's office and am passed on to Ayse, the diary manager who cancelled my earlier appointment with Jeremy.

It will be impossible to meet today, she tells me, because today is a very important day in the House of Commons. The prime minister, Theresa May, is about to give a very important statement, and Jeremy is in the Commons to deliver the opposition's response.

Everybody who's anybody is in the chamber, and there's no point in my sitting here. Well, I say to her, perhaps Jeremy and I could meet later on in the day.

Ayse thinks about it, argues with me, but finally agrees: I'll talk to Jeremy, she says, and he'll decide. But that will take a few hours, she adds.

No problem.

I quickly go to the House of Commons, accompanied by a staff member I know.

It's good to know people here, let me tell you. No door is locked if you know the right people.

Prime Minister Theresa May is not speaking yet, and the House is momentarily busy with "Oral Question to the Secretary of State," as I read in the official schedule.

MP Lloyd Russell-Moyle, the Labour MP who weeks ago tried to walk out of the chamber with the mace in his hands, is asking this question of the minister: "What recent diplomatic steps has he taken towards helping to secure a lasting peace between Israel and Palestine?"

What? The Israel-Palestine story is decades old. What makes the learned gentleman ask the honorable minister such a question at this time and date?

Good question. The answer? Simple: Palestine is a state of mind.

Time moves on, and the chamber is filling up, and before anybody knows it, the place is packed. This is, as you can see in the air, an important day.

Last evening, Jeremy Corbyn agreed, for the first time, to back a second referendum, the famed People's Vote, or "public's vote," after being warned that more MPs would either rebel against him through a vote in the Commons or even leave Labour altogether and join The Independent Group, also known as TIG, whose main platform is a call for a People's Vote. Allowing a second referendum, so the logic goes, will mean that Labour MPs who support such a referendum will have no reason to quit Labour and join the TIG.

Theresa May, who also faces a rebellion in her party, is about to give a "statement" on the issue of "Leaving the European Union" in just a few minutes. Will she cave in to her rebels the way Jeremy Corbyn caved in to his?

We'll soon – very soon – see.

And here she is. Theresa May is in, yes, and she starts speaking, giving her statement, all nine pages of it. What does she say? Well, the crux of her statement is seven words long: "A short, limited extension to Article 50." In other words, she's willing to delay UK's divorce from the EU, which was originally scheduled for March 29, 2019.

Like Jeremy Corbyn, Theresa May is caving in to rebels.

Or, perhaps, she's just playing politics. And, perhaps, Jeremy Corbyn was also just playing politics, trying to outsmart those who plot against him.

Theresa May goes on, and Jeremy Corbyn will soon respond. That's the way it works: the leader of the governing party speaks, and then the leader of the opposition responds.

Once she's done speaking, Jeremy Corbyn gets up to answer in the name of the opposition. Like the prime minister, he, too, reads from prepared pages. Nothing here is authentic; it's all scripted.

What does he say? He says that "Labour has a credible plan" for Brexit, but his words cause an outburst of loud laughter in the chamber.

More and more MPs talk, and here's a Scottish MP, Ian Blackford, a man who doesn't even pretend to be polite, and he says: "The prime minister is not fit for office!"

They can be cruel here, let me tell you.

And here goes Mr. Speaker, John Bercow. This man is having fun, enjoying every second. P-R-I-M-E M-I-N-I-S-T-E-R!!! he roars.

After about an hour at the chamber, I have had enough and leave.

When in the gallery downstairs, I call Ayse, to hear what's new. She's very nice to me and says that she would like to come and meet me in person.

Sounds good, doesn't it?

In twenty minutes or so, she arrives. Where are you from? I ask her. Turkey, she says. As far as I remember, in today's Turkey, journalists don't fare well, but I say nothing. So, what did Jeremy say? I ask her.

Can't have a meeting today, she answers, and suggests that I send her an email, so that she has something in writing, and she'll shoot me an email with a new date.

I do it on the spot, writing her an email and reading it out to her. She likes it.

I touch "send" on my iPhone. Big, huge, catastrophic mistake.

This never happened to me before, but I guess there's a first time for everything. By mistake, because I was too fast, I didn't pay attention from which email address I was emailing Ayse. I sent it, stupid me, from the email address of the Jewish Theater of New York. I, a man who's supposed to be a fat German gentile, blew my cover in less than a second.

I'll be surprised if I ever get an appointment with JC. As far as I can see it, this story is over.

I hear a laughter, and it sounds like the eagle's laughter. But I can't see any eagle around here. Strange.

Goodbye, London

I go out to the terrace, a place where friendly MPs go to smoke and drink. I light up, sip a Diet Coke, and relax, on this sunny day in London. What a beautiful, blue sky, what gorgeous architecture around me, and what a quiet River Thames.

As I sit here relaxing, images run up in my head, each of them competing with the other for a proper place in my memory cells, at times clinging one to the other.

Slowly, the last couple of days turn into a mix of sounds and images in my head. The court of Edward II with the courts of Theresa and Jeremy mix into one; the House of Commons becomes Shakespeare's Globe Theatre and vice versa. How similar they all are! Betrayals, plots, rebellions.

The power of politics and the politics of power vie for supremacy inside my head, as I'm about to leave the palace and this city.

At the end of *Edward II*, Edward III places the severed head of a noble named Mortimer next to his dead father, but somehow, in my mind at this particular moment, it takes place inside this building.

Oh, I need a bottle of Scottish whisky and a pack of Havana cigars.

But instead of the Scot and the Cuban, looks who is showing up at the terrace: Ivan Lewis. Remember him? He's the first MP I interviewed in the UK. How time flies! That was last year in Manchester.

When we met in Manchester, Ivan refused to label Jeremy Corbyn an anti-Semite. Will he now? Is Jeremy Corbyn an anti-Semite? I ask Ivan.

"Yes."

You didn't say it last time. Something changed in you?

"Yes."

What changed?

"Clarity," Ivan tells me; now that he's been out of Labour for a while, he has more clarity. "Moral clarity, yes."

Something changed in me as well, I tell Ivan. When we first met, I thought that the issue was Jeremy Corbyn's anti-Semitism, but now, after having interviewed many British people, I have come to the conclusion that the issue is not Jeremy Corbyn, but the people. It's the people who are anti-Semites, and it doesn't matter what Jeremy Corbyn is or is not.

"That's deeply concerning, that you found that on the streets of the United Kingdom. It's deeply concerning."

He's right.

I roam a bit more in the palace, a place that has become so familiar to me, and I know that I'll miss this place and its people.

I arrived in London six weeks ago, and I know that it's time to move on. Where shall I go next? Is there any place to go to after London? Will anything compare to the vibrancy, energy, and intrigue that London offers?

No.

But I've got to go.

I bid farewell to the palace and jump into an Uber. And in less than ninety minutes, he drops me off in Canterbury.

Why Canterbury? I've never been to Canterbury, but I love the *Canterbury Tales* – and that's why I asked my Uber driver to take me to Canterbury.

So simple.

It takes me less than twenty-five seconds to miss London, terribly so. But London is behind me now, with all its Brexit fights, anti-Semitism rows, Theresa and Jeremy. Oh, yeah, I just got an email from Ayse, notifying me that Jeremy won't meet me.

Adios, London. Goodbye, love. Hello, Canterbury!

They Cut the Top of His Skull and Scooped Things out of His Brain

Geoffrey Chaucer, they say, was the greatest poet of the Middle English period. Geoffrey is known best for his jewel of a book called the *Canterbury Tales*, one of the finest books ever written in the English language. The stories in the *Canterbury Tales* are framed around a group of pilgrims who are set on a journey from Southwark to Canterbury, where they will visit the shrine of Saint Thomas Becket, a place known to cure all ills, those of body and those of soul. To make the journey joyful and ever more productive, they agree between themselves that each will tell a tale, and that the one who tells the best tale will earn a free dinner. One of the tales is told by a prioress, a tale about Jews and kids which, interestingly enough, is quite similar to today's progressive Brits' stories about Zionists and kids. Titled the *Prioress's Tale*, it tells of a Christian kid who passes through a Jewish neighborhood every day when he goes to school, ever and always singing the Marian hymn "Alma Redemptoris Mater." One day, the Jews catch him and cut his throat, something that Jews obviously like to do to non-Jewish kids all through history.

Miraculously, the boy continues to sing the hymn, even though his throat has been cut and he's dead. As justice would demand, all Jews in the area are captured by lovely Christians and hanged.

How, I ask myself, is the *Canterbury Tales* presented in today's Canterbury?

Canterbury, in the county of Kent, is not London. It is a small city in the southeast of England, a home to many poor people, and also to many students. Tourism is important to the city's economic survival, and the *Canterbury Tales*, at least to book-loving tourists, is quite helpful.

Not far from where I stay is a pub that calls itself Canterbury Tales, and at the city's center there is a company that offers Canterbury Tales tours, where they reportedly enact the tales.

I go there, curious to see how they will enact the *Prioress's Tale*.

When the tour into the *Canterbury Tales* starts, we are greeted by an actor, a live actor, but then we proceed through different rooms and the tales are told through visuals and sounds that employ no live humans.

Fortunately, a talented actress, dressed in the captivating fashion of centuries ago, suddenly appears. She talks to us about the city's ancient hero, Saint Thomas Becket, without whom there would be no *Canterbury Tales*.

"Our story begins when Thomas Becket was a really good friend of Henry II. They were such good friends that the king decided to make Thomas the new archbishop of Canterbury, thinking that he could have more control over the church. What he didn't realize, though, was that Thomas Becket would take his new job incredibly seriously." The disagreements between the archbishop of Canterbury and the king of England became so disturbing that Thomas fled the country for six years, returning only after the king invited him to come back. But the old disagreements started all over again, and "one night it got so bad that the king stormed into his castle and shouted at the top of his lungs, 'Who will rid me of this turbulent priest?'"

Four knights heard these words and fast made their way to the Canterbury Cathedral. Once they were inside, they tried to seize the archbishop and bring him to the king, but soon realized that they could not seize him against his will. They didn't give up. They pulled their swords, "cutting the top of his skull and then scooping things out of the brain just to make sure that Thomas Becket is dead."

Three years later, the actress tells us, Thomas Becket was made Saint Thomas Becket, and many miracles have since been attributed to him.

Being that this is England, there's also a pub here called Thomas Becket.

By the end of the tour, only a few of the tales have been reenacted, and the *Prioress's Tale* was not among them. I talk to one of the guides and ask him what he thinks of the *Prioress's Tale* and if he can tell me what it is all about, since I heard that it's an interesting tale. Poor guy, he stutters and stutters, ever afraid to say the wrong word. There was a kid, he tells me finally, who used to go to his school passing through a ghetto, and he got killed in that ghetto. Ghetto? Who lived in what ghetto? I ask him. This he wouldn't say. He doesn't remember, he doesn't know.

When I'm done talking to him, a manager approaches me and asks that I not mention the guide's name.

I honor the request.

Later on, I meet Ryan, a medieval literature lecturer at the University of Kent who teaches the *Canterbury Tales* to young students. I ask him how the students react to the *Prioress's Tale* in class, and he tells me that they are horrified when first encountering the text. How do they express this horror? I ask him. Strangely, he has no answer to this; he can't find the words in English that will express this horror.

These are my English people, polite and fearful.

Thomas Becket's remains, so goes the story, rest in eternal peace inside the Canterbury Cathedral, arguably the most important cathedral of the Anglican Church.

I go there.

Entrance fee: £12.50. Here God charges less than in London.

At the entrance, there are a series of tablets hanging on the wall in memory of various soldiers and officers.

"To the glory of God," reads one of them, "and in memory of" – here comes a list of members of the armed forces – "who fell in action off the Falkland Islands 8th December 1914."

I walk over to the section in the cathedral called "Martyrdom," where, according to church officials, Thomas Becket was slaughtered. A tablet hangs on a wall here, on which it is written: "In this place hallowed by the martyrdom of Thomas Becket

29 December 1170 Pope John Paul II and Robert Runcie Archbishop of Canterbury knelt together in prayer 29 May 1982."

A cross, made of four swords, hangs on the wall. It's a strong visual, causing the visitor to imagine the last moments of Thomas Becket's life.

I walk down to the crypt, aka St. Gabriel's Chapel, in honor of a painting hanging on the north wall that depicts the exact moment when "Archangel Gabriel announces the birth of John the Baptist" in Jerusalem. Nearby is a special place for prayer requests, where visitors can leave Post-it Notes with requests to pray for their loved ones. "Your prayers," it reads, "will be placed on the Altar tomorrow at the 0800 Holy Communion Service."

I read one of the hand-written notes: "Please pray for my mother and my father." That's it. No names, and no other details.

Note: There is no cat and no rat in this crypt. We're in Canterbury, not Dublin.

Back in London, Peter Willsman is in the news again. According to the *Daily Mail*, Red Pete threatened "to 'do in' [a] fellow key activist," who happened to be Jewish, in yet another anti-Semitism feud. That's not the only news coming out of London, of course. The TIG, says the *Guardian*, is starting the process of becoming a party, a move that will cause some people to accuse the group of ulterior motives. The art world is also in the news. The National Theatre, writes the *Times*, is "holding a trans-only casting session next month."

And then there's news about refugees. Migrants, meaning refugees, writes the *Times*, "tried to stow away in the funnel of a cross-channel ferry," adding that "sailings from Calais were delayed overnight as hundreds of officers tried to clear the ferry and port after the migrants broke through security barriers. About 50 reached the ferry as she was about to dock. A total of 63 people were arrested."

I'm intrigued by this story, and fortunately I'm not far from the ferry and the refugees. Canterbury is less than twenty miles from Dover. Calais, France, is across the English Channel from Dover.

Let me drive to Dover, and from there take a ferry to Calais.

Beware of Refugees Throwing Stones

P&O Ferries offers a ninety-minute ferry ride service between Dover and Calais. Sounds perfect to my ears.

On I go.

I take a taxi to the port in Dover, where I am to board a bus provided by P&O that will, hopefully, take me to the ferry.

Well, not so fast.

Before anyone can board the bus, they have to go through security checks. To be more precise, three security checks. Then, thank goodness, we board the bus.

"We," by the way, is a total of fewer than ten passengers. How come so few? I don't know. Maybe no Brit wishes to go to France, or, perhaps, every Brit with a pound is already there.

The bus moves, not too fast, and then it stops. A policeman boards the bus, examines the people, and checks their documents. With that done, we are told to get off the bus for passport control. When this is done as well, we board the same bus again.

The security process here is very similar to security checks practiced by Israel at checkpoints between Israeli and Palestinian cities, which are often described by various human rights organizations as contradicting human rights.

I should have brought Red Pete with me.

In any case, after one more security check – screening of body and goods – I finally board the *Pride of Canterbury* ferry. Yeah, that's the name of this ferry; every ferry has a different name.

I don't know why ships get to have individual names, and buses don't. Even commercial airplanes don't. Why? Who knows?

As I board, I watch trucks entering the belly of the ferry, many trucks, huge trucks, all full of goodies going from Britain to France. I'm not sure what the Brits are exporting, but in all statistical likelihood it's fish and chips. There are also a few passenger cars boarding the ferry, a few of whose drivers now join us.

Tourism is dead, a security woman tells me. I wonder why.

I go up on the deck and look at England, staring at the white cliffs of Dover, the cliffs at England's border. As England gets smaller and smaller, images of the country become bigger and bigger. In my mind's eye, images of ancient wars and long-dead horses appear, with swords, kings, queens, and one archbishop. These images intermingle with images of people and palaces, Uber drivers and lords, MPs and farmers I've met in the previous months. England, Scotland, and the two parts of Ireland appear to me in frames, each next to the other, and within each of them, images and stories unfold.

The further I get from the UK, the more Britain turns in my mind into a museum, a museum of palaces and food banks. What a magnificent, sad, gigantic, and tiny museum.

Oh, Museum of Britain: Why do you hate me? I never had the chance to ask you this question, but now I do. Have I ever wronged you? Has any other Jew wronged you? Will you, my dear Britain, not be happy unless and until the last Jew has left you?

Slowly, Britain disappears, hiding in the distance. Welcome to France.

Calais.

After disembarking from the *Pride of Canterbury*, I leave the port and proceed to the taxi stand. No Uber here. Two taxis wait for passengers at the taxi pickup spot. The first cabbie says that I should take the other taxi because that cabbie speaks English. So, I go to the other taxi. This cabbie looks me in the eye, very upset, and says, "Why should I speak English with you? I'm in France, and here we speak French! I don't like English people!" He stares at me, this English man, and drives off so fast, it's as if he's running from a war zone.

I smile. Now I am an Englishman. Can you believe it?

I look around me.

There are fences all over in the port area, miles of them. Sometimes there are four of them in parallel, giving the impression that this is one huge maximum-security prison. It reminds me of

Israel's Separation Barrier, which European do-gooders use as proof that Israel is a racist state.

They should come here, right here in their midst. They don't have to travel far to the Middle East. Ms. Campbell of Scotland, the one with the Egyptian king, should come here as well. It would be nice to see what all of them will have to say.

Fat chance. They won't come here. But I have.

The fences and barriers were paid for by the British government, I'm told by a man passing by, and the Brits are also paying millions of pounds per year in security costs in and around this port.

Why are they doing this?

Well, there are thousands of refugees – twenty-six thousand last year, according to media reports that I read on the ferry – who try to cross from France into Britain every year, but Britain doesn't want them.

Why are refugees so keen on going to Britain? Because the UK is more generous to refugees than France, the man tells me, but I think that for some unexplainable reason, the refugees prefer British cooking.

I walk to a taxi that's unloading passengers, and once the passengers are out, I board it. I don't talk too much to the cabbie, so he won't run away from this Englishman, yours truly.

While riding in the taxi, I look up. Guess what I see? My eagle, my good eagle. It flies above for a short while, letting me know that everything will be alright in France, and then it flies back to where it came from, I'm not sure where.

It is at this very moment that the taxi reaches Calais City Center.

In Calais, I thought, based on what I have been told, I would see thousands of refugees sleeping on the streets – but this is not what I see. Where are the refugees? I ask people walking by. There aren't many refugees in Calais, they say; the refugees used to be here, but no more. Those of them who are still around, one man tells me, are next to the port. Another one says: the refugees were kicked out of Calais and they're hiding in the villages nearby. And yet another says they are in a place known as the Iranian Jungle, not far from the port.

Let's go to the Iranian Jungle. I like the name.

I call a taxi. The cabbie, how fortunate I am, doesn't hate English people. Take me to the Iranian Jungle, I ask him.

He does.

Welcome to the Iranian Jungle. The refugees are here; yes, indeed.

But there are no Iranians here. Perhaps at one point in the past, they were here, and maybe the smugglers are Iranians, but there are no Iranian refugees now. Not a single Iranian that I can spot. The Iranians are somewhere else, maybe in Iran, but not here. Here are Africans. Some of them are inside small tents, others sit or walk aimlessly next to the tents. They don't have much to do, except sleep in the tents, walk around them, or eat food that, I assume, is brought to them by people who support them.

As the taxi passes close by, I ask the driver to slow down a bit. He does. What a mistake on my part! A bunch of refugees jump at the car, hitting it, as their friends in the back start throwing stones at us, small and large, and rocks as well. As far as they are concerned, it will be better if we're dead. Killing the driver and me would, perhaps, give meaning to their lives on the French earth.

Luckily, the heavy gifts miss their target.

The driver picks up speed, before blood is spilled for nothing.

I met many refugees in Germany, mostly from Arab countries, and never encountered this aggressive behavior.

What is this?

They are Sudanese and Eritreans, the driver tells me, and they are the worst of the refugees. In Germany, I remember, a Turkish woman once told me that the Afghani refugees were the worst, but this driver obviously disagrees.

Calais residents, he shares with me, now carry their hunting guns with them because it's so dangerous.

Whatever the refugees' reason for wishing to be in Britain, their violence won't help them fulfill that wish. Their behavior, which the people of Calais experience on a daily basis, defies logic.

These refugees, or migrants, are asking people to have mercy on them, but most people are not motivated to help those who communicate with stones.

This is a war zone. In the city of Calais. No wonder tourists go elsewhere.

The cabbie drops me off at Calais City Center, and I move on to do the most logical thing I can: eat. I go to a restaurant, the first my eyes see, and I order food. Whatever. I don't pay attention. The restaurant seems to be pretty basic; nothing fancy here, and most likely every dish is as good, or as bad, as the other.

The clock moves and the food arrives: duck pâté, codfish, bread, and coffee – and French fries, which I didn't even order.

Oh, God, how good this food is! Every bite paradise, the pâté and the cod and the bread. Even the fries, which for the last few months I couldn't stand, are heavenly here.

And the coffee is delicious!

I haven't eaten such good food in quite some time.

It hits me, when I swallow the last crumb, that I am in France! Yes, France! This restaurant is in France. I'm in Calais, France. This is not Britain. The food is not British, and the cooks are not Brits. France here. France, a land whose people know food. Oh, they know!

Do they also know how to bake? I ask myself, and fast proceed to order an apple pie.

Have you heard of apple pies? Millions of them are being made and sold daily in Britain and in the USA, and rarely do any of them taste any good.

Well, not so in Calais.

Fly out, my dear, out of London and New York, and come here, to Calais, to take a look at this apple pie. Look closely, because you'll never see the likes of it where you come from.

Yes, yes. Look. What do you see? Apples. Apples, apples, and apples. Big chunks of apples joined together by caramel, I think, and a thin, really thin, layer of dough underneath. That's it.

How does it taste? It tastes like apples, the best of apples, and my body jumps out of happiness. Honey to my lips, food for my spirit, and a party for my stomach.

It is in this very restaurant that I meet a British TV journalist. Today, he says, he visited the Iranian Jungle, just like me, but with one tiny difference: he has been working with various people, who are familiar with the refugees, for the past month arranging for him to visit the Jungle. In other words, he didn't see the real life of these people but the life that has been arranged for him to see.

His story will definitely be different than mine.

His type of journalism, I'm afraid to say, is as good as the average British apple pie. He's not the only one doing this kind of journalism, I suspect.

Well, this is not my problem.

In an hour or so, I'll be leaving France, sailing back to Her Majesty's land. Guess where I'm going.

To Wales. Why Wales?

Truthfully, I know nothing about Wales, but the other day, an Englishwoman told me that the Welsh are rough people, primitive and nationalistic.

And that got me.

Rough, primitive, and nationalist is a good mix for a juicy story about lovely, poisonous villains – the exact mix for the next Oscar movie. I can visualize the characters: primitive Welsh, with long hair coming out of their armpits, engaged in rough love on top of brutal cliffs with members of a rival tribe of Welsh nationalists, who are armed with demonic weapons, and both chase away intellectual English nationals into the bottom of the ocean.

Isn't that great?

Adios, Calais. Hello, Cardiff!

Hapus, yn Neis ac yn Gynnes

I can't find words to express my excitement when my feet, for the first time ever, touch the ground of Wales.

Yes, I've arrived in Wales, via the train.

What's a Welsh person? I ask a young lady upon my arrival. "Happy, nice, and warm," she answers smilingly. "This is what people say about us."

Oops.

I can't find words to express my deep disappointment. Happy, nice, and warm. What a shame.

How did I fall so low to have reached this cursed Wales and its cursed happy, nice, and warm people? How have I sinned to deserve this harsh fate?

But that's life. One day you win, the next you don't.

I'm in Cardiff, the capital of Wales, and I'll try to make the best of it.

I choose the Indigo Hotel, a brand I'm a bit familiar with since my stay at the Indigo in Dundee, Scotland.

Oh, how time runs so fast! Wasn't it just yesterday that I was in Scotland? Well, no. Time is flying, my dear, faster than any Airbus.

A taxi, driven by a Sudanese, stops next to me.

No, this is not Calais here, and this Sudanese man is not about to throw stones at me.

I get into the taxi. The driver, let me tell you, is actually a very nice guy. Yes, yes, I swear.

The wild white man with an enormous share of hair under his armpit who I thought would be greeting me upon my arrival has been replaced by a dark-skinned Sudanese Muslim.

Welcome to Cardiff.

I look out the window, along the ride to Indigo, and I see women with niqab on Cardiff's streets. Forget cliffs. Forget rough lovemaking.

Niqabs.

My hotel, my horrible fate, is at the Dominions Arcade, a place where people come to shop, not to chase English nationals into the bottom of any ocean.

To the right of Indigo's entrance on Queens Street is a Thomas Cook branch, featuring this ad in its window: "Brexit Price Guarantee. Book now to secure the price of your Thomas Cook holiday." Next to it is a store by the name of iRepair, where they sell, fix, and unlock mobile phones. No buyer is in the shop now, and the person manning the shop is busy listening to the Quran, which is playing loudly for prospective Welsh shoppers. To the right of iRepair is an HMV store, where they sell DVDs and other goodies. Who's buying DVD these days?

I stroll a bit.

Cardiff City Center, I fast find out, is one big shopping center, with one shopping mall after another. Some central streets, in fact, are strictly pedestrian zones, no cars, and people can safely move from one shopping mall to the next without fear of being run over by a speeding car.

Yeah.

What is a man to do for pleasure in Cardiff when his romantic dreams of great stories have vanished in the cruel air of reality?

He smokes. Expensive British cigarettes, with horrific pictures of mutilated body parts on the cigarette box.

There are villains in the EU, let me tell you, owners of screwed up minds who have nothing better to do than force smokers to own such photos.

As far as I can guess, they don't live in Wales.

Not far from me is the New Theatre, where RSC's production of Shakespeare's flaming and doomed love story, *Romeo and Juliet*, is now playing.

This love story, between the children of the leaders of two feuding families, the Montagues and the Capulets, is one of Shakespeare's finest, a classic of literature's doomed love stories. How will RSC, one of England's finest theaters, present this show?

I go to the New Theatre. I hope that this production will be better than their *Tartuffe* I saw a while back in Stratford-upon-Avon.

Lights down, and R&J starts rolling.

Just as in *Tartuffe*, this *Romeo and Juliet* is politically correct. The Montagues and the Capulets on this stage are both houses of mixed races and ethnicities, and the lovers come from no rival communities. The feud between them is never explained, and there are no visible differences between them, be they ethnic, religious, tribal, or cultural. They are just the same. Politically correct and equal. Both families seem to be members of the same family, all living in love and equality, and no reason is evident for any animosity between them.

At Shakespeare's time, feuding families existed, and each had its own set of servants – so the play made sense, much sense, and one could immediately sense the extreme danger of the young couple falling in love.

Not here.

A favorite film adaptation of *Romeo and Juliet* from the last century is the fabulous *West Side Story*, where the feuding sides were a white gang versus a Puerto Rican gang. That's a drama. What a drama! What a romance! What a love!

Nothing of it here. Nada. Zilch. Zero. A total waste of time.

Yes, the theater scene has changed in Britain. What will it be in ten years hence? I ask myself. Maybe, though no one can tell, it depends on Brexit. The more integrated the UK is with the EU, probably the more European it will be, whatever that will mean in the years ahead. Otherwise, it will possibly return to its old days.

I leave the theater and go to my hotel.

The clock moves, fast and faster. At about two o'clock in the winter morning, I go out to smoke. It's rainy, cold, and very windy, but this doesn't stop people from enjoying the outdoors. Right here, on this very street where I now stand, I watch a continuous parade of young people, teenagers and students, all drunk and loud.

Take a look at them, my dear. They are dressed as if it were the middle of August, and some of them shamelessly urinate in the middle of the street, as if Cardiff were one huge lavatory. But look, here's a funny thing: a street sweeper drives by, and when the driver notices a young man urinating, he stops the car and shines his front bright lights on the offending youth. Only the young urinator, totally drunk, doesn't even notice.

What's going on with these young people? Will they find their way home? Will they fall asleep on the street?

There's a UK charitable organization, I find out the next day, that helps the young drunk, especially on Friday and Saturday nights. It dispatches volunteers, dressed in uniforms that identify them as Street Pastors, to busy spots in town, and when the "pastors" spot a youth in trouble, they rush to help him or her. The pastors carry bottles of water (water helps to sober up the drunk), flip-flops as well (for young drunk girls who take off their high-heeled shoes, walking barefoot on the street), and first aid. The name of the organization, I'm told, is the Message Trust, or the Message, and they have a "Wales hub team" in Dinas Powys, which is next to Cardiff.

I take an Uber to Dinas Powys, to see who those people are, and I meet the hub's leader, Gary Smith.

What's the Message Trust? I ask Gary.

"In 2018, the Message Trust was voted to be the best charity in the UK to work for, by the *Sunday Times*. We have about 150 staff across the UK. We work with the hardest to reach young people across the UK, and the urban areas of social deprivation is our expertise. We do that in a number of ways. We've got five bands of different musical styles that go into schools, and they do lessons in religious education, and also in personal and social education, on things like sex, self-image, bullying, and things like that. So that's one area."

Is the Message a religious institution?

"Yes."

Christian?

"Christian. We're very proud of that."

What denomination, Protestant?

"Protestant, but we work right across the spectrum of all churches."

Are you what they call in America "evangelicals"?

"I'm an evangelical, yes."

Is the organization evangelical?

"Yes, yes it would be. But we would…I think being defined as an evangelical in the UK is probably different to how they would define it in America. So, it's not a political statement, it's actually a statement about believing that the Bible is the authority – "

What do you mean?

"Very often in America you could interchange the words *evangelical* and *Republican* as being the same thing, and evangelicals are much more likely to vote for a Republican."

And here?

"The evangelicals in the UK would vote across the political spectrum."

Would the average UK evangelical be pro-choice or pro-life?

"Pro-life."

Gary's office is sparsely decorated, with two big paper maps on the left wall, and some basic furniture.

On his simple-looking desk is a computer, a Mac.

The Mac is off, but look, my dear, at the vinyl sticker of a Banksy graffiti on top of the Mac, an image that reveals a strong identification with the Palestinian people: "Rage, Flower Thrower."

Banksy, a world-famous artist whose real name is known to only a few, is believed to have been born in Yate, England, and is known to identify with Palestinians, many of whom admire him.

One of his most renowned works, "Rage, Flower Thrower," shows a masked rioter about to throw flowers, and is supposedly meant to depict a Palestinian fighter, a man whose language is flowers and not stones or bombs.

To those who cannot read his political message via art, Banksy will happily convey it via word. An example is his comments about the Balfour Declaration.

On November 2, 1917, the UK's Foreign Secretary Arthur Balfour wrote a letter to Lord Rothschild, a letter known since as the Balfour Declaration, declaring that "His Majesty's government view with favour the establishment in Palestine of a national home for the Jewish people." This declaration soon became the foundation for the State of Israel. One hundred years later, in 2017, Banksy made public his feelings about it, as published by the *Guardian*.

Explaining the establishment of his Walled Off Hotel in Bethlehem, meant to put Israel to shame for its Separation Wall, he said to the *Guardian*: "It's exactly 100 years since Britain took control of Palestine and started rearranging the furniture – with chaotic results. I don't know why, but it felt like a good time to reflect on what happens when the United Kingdom makes a huge political decision without fully comprehending the consequences." In other words, the declaration should have never been made, and Israel should have never been born.

This Banksy should build a Fenced Off Hotel in Calais. Will he? Fat chance.

Gary, obviously, likes this Banksy.

I didn't expect to be drawn into anything Palestinian today, but that's life. I flow with reality.

Do the evangelicals in the UK tend to be pro-Israel, like many of the evangelicals in the USA? I ask the man.

"No," he says. "Our general view as evangelicals is much more about what we understand our relationship with God to be, as it's expressed in the Bible, as opposed to how we position ourselves politically on issues."

Personally, are you pro-Israel or pro-Palestine?

"You are trying to get me to answer a question that I wouldn't answer – "

Why not?

"You see, I don't think, in my reading the scripture, that when Jesus said that you should love your enemies, that he meant that you should kill them."

Do you think Israel is killing its enemies?

"No. I think both parties kill one another and, therefore, I cannot support a response to violence that suggests that more violence will actually help that."

Oh, that's nice.

Only the man doesn't stop talking. "It's not as simple as that. We would have to acknowledge, for instance, that there are more Christians living in Palestine than are living within Israel."

This seems to be an attempt to criticize Israel, as it implies that the majority of Christians in the area are in the bullseye of Israel's bullets, but whatever the intent, he's simply wrong. And I tell him that.

According to a study published a few years ago by Bernard Sabella, author of *A Life Worth Living: The Story of a Palestinian Catholic*, and formerly associate professor at Bethlehem University, there were at the time 50,000 Palestinian Christians in the West Bank and Gaza Strip, and 125,000 in Israel. Now the number of Christians in the West Bank and Gaza is even smaller.

Gary is not convinced.

I move on. During the past five months that I've been in the UK, I say to Gary, anti-Semitism was and still is all over the place, a fact that is quite unexpected in a democratic society.

Well, he doesn't think so. "Some people would argue that if you spoke out against Israel, the political country, you are being anti-Semitic. It's very difficult to actually have a critique of anything that Israel does without being accused of being anti-Semitic."

The kind of anti-Semitism playing out in Britain these days has nothing to do with Israel but with hook-nosed Jews who control the world with their money… You are aware of this, right?

"Yeah, absolutely."

It has nothing to do with criticizing Israel, does it?

"No, but I am aware of people who've criticized Israel and have been accused of being anti-Semitic. I am aware of that."

That's a classic response I get from leftist atheists, those who are avid supporters of Palestinians, when the issue of anti-Semitism comes up.

I look at Gary and say to him: The anti-Semitism here, what I personally experienced for the past five months, and what I have seen and read during this time, has nothing to do with criticism of Israel. If this kind of anti-Semitism existed in the United States, especially in a mainstream party like Labour, there would have been hundreds of pastors, especially evangelical, who would rise and speak loudly and publicly against it.

"Yes."

Is there any reason that pastors in the UK, as far as I know, do not raise their voice against such –

"I don't think anybody would care."

Are you trying to tell me that UK pastors don't raise their voices on any issue, be it abortion or whatever, because nobody would care?

"No."

I get it. Pastors wouldn't talk against anti-Semitism in Britain because nobody cares what pastors think anyway. Pastors will talk against abortions, and other sins against Christianity in Britain, because everybody does care.

You gotta have a hole in your brain for this to make sense to you.

I have no doubt that Gary is doing a great service to his community by saving young people from a bitter future. Even the Street Pastors – which started elsewhere in the UK and was not initiated by the organization of which he is part– is a great concept and is needed in cities like Cardiff.

But I wonder why a man like him, whose job it is to be in the public's eye and preach to the people, cannot find the time and the hour to publicly condemn anti-Semitism in this land.

I leave the man and go to a bar. It makes me feel like an old-style European – one hour with the pastor, five hours in the bar – but that's life in Cardiff, at least for me at this point in my life.

And look who I meet in the bar: beautiful, vivacious, skinny Francesca, who eats nothing but explains everything to me about anything I ever wondered about.

Tell me, I ask the non-eating skinny beauty, how does it work with the likes of you, beauties who wear nothing in the freezing nights of Britain's streets?

"That's easy," she says. "It's called 'pre-lash.'"

What's pre-lash?

"Before I go out, I drink a bottle and a half of wine, or a small bottle of vodka, and then I can be with my bikini on the street, any weather."

And you're not cold?

"No. We call it 'beer blanket.'"

Genius!

I'll try it next time I feel like skiing naked in the midst of a snow-storm in the Swiss Alps.

But this is not the time for skiing, at least not in Cardiff. In Cardiff, and in the rest of Wales, this is rugby time.

Rugby. Have you heard of rugby? I have, and that's all I know about the game. But this afternoon, believe it or not, there's a game between Wales and Scotland, and everybody in Wales is either in Scotland or in a bar watching the game with their buddies, and drinking even more alcohol than usual.

Rugby, they tell me, is the Welsh national sport. Good.

Time passes, as it always does in a bar, and in due time, I move to another bar, a bigger bar. I'm bar hopping today.

More time passes, as it should in a bar, and the rugby game starts. I watch the game on a giant screen in this dirty-looking bar.

It takes me the whole of two seconds to fully understand rugby. Would you like me to teach you? Well, I'll gladly oblige. Rugby, you see, is about two teams of young males who possess a strong urge to lay their whole bodies on top of other males. That's it. Of course, to make it look less violent and less gay-ish, Rugby International, or some other fancy organization, long ago decreed that there must be a ball near the males who are lying one on top of the other and that each male must attempt to drag the ball from the other males.

I think that I would prefer women's rugby.

Don't dream, a fellow pub drinker tells me. "The women in wom-en's rugby look like men." Okay. I'll stick with the men.

Guess who wins the game, the men's game? Yeah, the happy, nice, and warm people.

I walk to my hotel. But before I go in, I sit down on a bench in front of the Indigo for a little smoke, when a mother and her teenage daughter stop near me.

"Do you support our rugby team?" the ladies ask.

I don't know rugby.

"You are a Welshman and you don't know rugby?" the mother asks, totally shocked.

I'm not Welsh, I'm a tourist. But I like the Welsh people. You are very nice people!

The young daughter pats me on my shoulders in thanks, as her mother drops a hot kiss on my face.

Wow! This German has never experienced anything remotely similar anywhere on the streets of Germany, not even on the drunk Bavaria streets.

I start liking these people, even though they are not cruel villains.

What's there not to like? They are warm, personal, nice, and kissing. What else can a man like me ask? What else can any man ask?

I hope I'll get more kisses here!

Let the world know: I am ready to be kissed!!

Wales is a small place on earth, at least in terms of people. Altogether there are about three million people in Wales, a far cry from the population in England, estimated to be over fifty-five million. And they love their language. Government and private businesses are bilingual, meaning that, for example, road signs or private signs are in both languages, English and Welsh.

Look at the store on the other side of the street from where I sit: *fferyllfa pharmacy, harddwch beauty.* Welsh first, English second.

Can you pronounce *harddwch*? Don't feel bad; I can't either.

How many people speak Welsh in Cardiff? Well, it's debatable. I ask around, and the answers I get are not the same. Some say 1 percent, others say 10 percent, and still others say 4 percent. "Up in the north, and in the west, most people speak Welsh, but not in Cardiff," one of the street experts tells me.

Like in Ireland and in Scotland, Big Brother England crushed these people's most important tool, their tongue, but in our era of political correctness, the "native" whites demand their heritage back.

What will they do with it? Who's going to speak Welsh to them? Well, the same ones who will speak Gaelic to the Irish and the Scots.

Fferyllfa. Harddwch. How do you pronounce these words?

According to Google Translate, this is how you say "happy, nice, and warm" in Welsh: *Hapus, yn neis ac yn gynnes.*

Yes, no doubt.

On to the Valleys of Drugs and Prostitution

Many in Cardiff tell me that I should go to the South Wales Valleys, a place where I will find the "real" Welsh. In the old days, before the late prime minister (1979–1990) Margaret Thatcher started a policy of closing the UK's coalmines, miners lived happily ever after in the valleys. But then they did not; mines were shut down for good, and everybody turned poor. The valleys, the mavens tell me, are now deprived areas, where grown-ups roam aimlessly, there are prostitutes galore, and the young sell drugs.

Not nice.

And so, I again rent a car, this time a Mercedes, and off I go to Rhondda Valleys, which encompasses many villages and a couple of towns in South Wales.

Will the young try to sell me drugs? If so, what kind of drugs? Are the prostitutes self-employed, or do pimps accompany them to the act?

Well, let's see.

I reach a small town by the name of Porth, at the foot of the Rhondda Valleys, and stop near a café called the Shed. "Sheds," I read in their online newsletter, "are places where people go to make new friends, learn new skills and have fun."

Time now is 3:00 p.m. I get out of my German and go to the Shed. I want to make new friends, Welsh folks who will give me drugs and take me to their beds.

Well, dream on, my dear.

There's one man in the café, an older man, and he tells me sorry, but he's closing now. Why? "There's no footfall after three o'clock." Footfall. What's footfall? "Customers." Three o'clock is too late for the people of Porth, I guess, because the day is over at two.

Luckily, Pots Vintage Tearoom and Pantry across the street is not closed. I walk in.

This is also a café, a small café, and I order coffee.

I look at the people around me, Welsh, "real" Welsh, and I start talking to them.

Will you sing for me, I ask the people at the table next to me – creatures I have never seen before – the Welsh anthem?

God, if I approached people in a California café asking them to sing for me an anthem, or whatever song, I would be arrested on the spot for sexual, mental, physical, religious, and psychological harassment. But guess what? These people are not Californians; they are Welsh.

And they sing their anthem for me.

"Hen Wlad Fy Nhadau" (Old Land of My Fathers).

It starts like this:

> Mae hen wlad fy nhadau yn annwyl i mi,
> Gwlad beirdd a chantorion, enwogion o fri;
> Ei gwrol ryfelwyr, gwladgarwyr tra mâd,
> Tros ryddid gollasant eu gwaed.

Beautiful, isn't it?

The anthem's original name, they tell me, was *Glan Rhondda*, meaning Banks of the Rhondda. And they are damn proud of it!

I ask them if they would also sing for me "God Save the Queen," the British national anthem. No, they say. They don't like the English. Period.

I ask again, and again, and finally they point to one of the workers at the café, an English lady. She's English, they say, but not us.

The English lady, a bit shy, says she's no singer, sorry. I tell her that it doesn't matter, not really. She's convinced.

Standing straight, and saluting the unseen queen, she sings "God Save the Queen" so tenderly and lovingly that everybody around is touched, some shedding a tear or two.

When she's done, the Welsh applaud heartily.

This is such a beautiful moment that I'll probably never forget it. So human, so touching, so warm.

If you're curious: most of the people here, like the majority of Welsh, voted Leave. They want out of the EU.

A young lady at the café, who studies drama and acting at a local university, wants Britain to remain. She says that the people who voted Leave were cheated.

Yes, a woman tells her, we were cheated, but so what? If there were another referendum tomorrow, I would vote Leave again!

Here, just like in the rest of the UK, most people don't discuss Brexit, because they're so fed up with it. Yes, the media is full of Brexit, and I myself keep asking people about it, but most people who are not journalists don't want to hear about it anymore.

In any case, back in London the House of Commons is about to vote on Theresa May's Brexit deal, which she claims is much better than the deal she presented to them last time. I can't see the big difference, but I'm not an MP yet and my vote doesn't count. We'll see what the House votes later.

Where are the drugs and the prostitutes? I ask the people. Oh, they are not here. They are miles away, in North Wales. Okay, my Mercedes is capable of getting there.

The Welsh Love My Belly and They Pat It

Last night, or evening it was, British MPs voted down Theresa May's deal, 391 to 242. This is the prime minister's second major defeat in the House.

That was in London, and I'm in Wales, driving around the valleys, across this and that village, seeing how people live.

I've been told that the valleys are the abode of paupers, the neighborhood of the sick. There you will see, I was told, the homes of the impoverished, where the poor barely hold on to dear life.

I look at the houses. If this is poor, may the Lord make me poor as well.

I look at the people, and they look quite normal to me. Nobody around me is selling drugs, and everybody around me seems quite content with their lives.

I pass a group of local teenagers, none of whom is a whore, and ask them if they will stay in the valleys once they grow older. "As long as there's a McDonald's next to me," one of them answers, "I'll stay here."

McDonald's. I don't like McDonald's. I prefer sticky toffee puddings.

I remember when I first encountered it in Scotland, thinking that Macca came up with it – he called it "Dundee Sticky Pudding" – not knowing that this extra-sweet dessert is available almost everywhere in Queen Elizabeth II's territories.

Sticky toffee pudding.

What's a typical Englishman for you? I ask a young man I chance to meet.

The Welsh are talkative, extremely friendly people, the friendliest of the island people, but this doesn't mean that they love everybody.

Here's the first image of the English that pops out from the mouth of this Welsh: "Bald head, nose up, bossy, and holds a beer in his hand."

Speaking of England, the *Oxford Student* reports today that "yesterday the Lord Mayor of Oxford and the Mayor of Ramallah signed the Twinning Agreement between Oxford and Ramallah, Palestine. The signing is the culmination of a 15-year friendship between the two cities, led by the Oxford-Ramallah Friendship Association and the Oxford City Council."

Good to know.

According to my iPhone, my location at present is "North Atlantic Ocean," and the weather is cloudy and quite warm: 83 degrees Fahrenheit.

Yeah. North Atlantic Ocean. The wonders of technology.

Maybe my eagle is in the Atlantic Ocean, but not me. I am, dear iPhone, in South Wales. With people, not in the middle of an ocean. And it's not 83 degrees; you're dreaming. It's cold here. The only thing warm here is the people.

Yes, they are.

And I meet many of them.

Almost every Welsh person I meet, when I'm not inside my car, touches me, literally, within minutes after we start talking to one another. Some even pat me on my big belly. Yes, I swear. These people touch, pat, and kiss.

I love it.

I park my car at the Heritage Park Hotel in Trehafod, Rhondda, South Wales, and call it a day.

I close my eyes, fall asleep, and I have the most wonderful dream: the ladies of Wales pat my belly, kiss my cheeks, and my eagle is flying above, inside my hotel room, happy like a baby with a candy.

Yes, that's what happens when you are in a place where you feel that the people don't hate you, or the Jew in you, and almost everybody touches you, or kisses you, or pats your belly.

Thanks, eagle, for being so happy for me.

By the way, I wanted to ask you something, my dear eagle: Why did you laugh when I made that stupid mistake and exposed my identity to Ayse? It was you, right?

Yes, says the eagle; it was me.

Why did you laugh?

Well, says my eagle, because you still refuse to get it: Corbyn is just the symptom, he is not the cause of anti-Semitism. I fly all over the UK and I know, I see the anti-Semites all over! Less of them in Wales, by the way. They say that there are no eagles in the UK – but I am here. For you.

Thank you so much, my eagle!

The eagle flies.

English Men Hide Their Right Hands

The next morning, I see a group of people in my hotel, all dressed their nicest, and with a daffodil on their jackets or dresses. Daffodil, they tell me, is the national flower of Wales, and they wear it today because they are attending an official event: the funeral of a man, a war hero, who passed away in bed late at night. "He went to sleep, and he didn't get up."

I walk out of the hotel, taking a puff.

A local man passes by me. Where can I find nice, good people? I ask him. "Go to the Lion Pub in Treorchy," he says.

I go there, and I meet Gary, a lively man sitting next to a glass of beer.

Gary, what do you think of the English people?

"Not a lot."

Why don't you like them?

"Nobody likes them."

The young of Treorchy, he tells me, have nothing to do, no work and no education, and they spend their time on alcohol and drugs. Whose fault is it? The English. The English rule mercilessly from London, and they don't care about the children of Wales.

He reminds me of the people in the pub in Dundee. They said similar things, blaming England for all their ills.

The English have taken the mines away, Gary says, and gave nothing in return. "This valley alone had forty-two mines, with thousands of people working in them. They have taken them all away. They think they still got the Empire going on."

Damn the English.

Luckily, there is rugby in the world, something to make the Welsh happy and busy.

Gary, once started, won't stop.

The lords in the House of Lords, he tells me, get £300 a day, but here people have nothing. "They don't give a shit what happens to us." He doesn't like MPs either. Members of Parliament, he informs me, lead a different life than the rest of the people. They "have smoking rooms. You go to Parliament, on Westminster Bridge, you don't see them having a fag on the balcony, because they got smoking rooms."

What do you think of Theresa May?

"She is a twat."

And then I meet Mark.

If you are not intelligent, there's nothing for you here, Mark tells me. There are IT companies in Cardiff and Newport, and some locals work there, but IT is not for everybody. In the old days, he says, you could work with your hands, you could be a miner, but those days are over.

Is there a big drug problem here?

There is, but it's not major. The people here, he explains to me, know how to solve social problems.

How?

"If you can't solve with your fist, don't take a knife."

Hmm, not bad.

What do you think of the English?

"I don't necessarily hate them. I don't trust them."

Listen, Mark: You are by the ocean, and two people are about to drown, a ninety-nine-year-old Welshman and a nine-year-old English boy. You can save only one, which one would that be?

"The Welsh. That's my blood."

Paint for me an Englishman.

"An Englishman smiles at you, with one hand behind his back, and you don't know what's in his hand."

What's the difference between a twenty-year-old Welsh girl and a twenty-year-old English girl?

"A twenty-year-old Welsh girl will love you forever and give you children. A twenty-year-old English girl will marry you, then divorce you, marry somebody else, and bye-bye to the house. Trust me, I was married to an English girl, and that's exactly what happened to me."

How was life here when the mines were operating? I wonder.

I go to the Rhondda Heritage Park, where they operate something like a museum, with tour guides who used to work in the mines.

How much money did a miner earn per week? I ask one of the former miners, a man who dearly misses his days at the mines.

"Between £130 to £175 per week," he says.

In other words, they were paid next to nothing. Why do these people miss the days of the mines? Beats me.

Later in the evening, when back in the hotel, I meet James, the grandson of the war hero, and I tell him that I'm sad to hear about his loss. He pats me on my shoulders and my back, saying thank you. He tells me how proud he is to be the grandson of such a man and how sad he is that he won't be able to see him anymore. I say to him that the spirit of his grandfather will forever be with him. Hearing this, he embraces me, hugging me tight, thanking me again and again and again.

Wales.

Her Majesty's Mercenary

The people who have smoking rooms are very busy this week in London. Here's the latest from BBC: "MPs have voted by 412 to 202 for Prime Minister Theresa May to ask the EU for a delay to Brexit."

The saga continues.

As for anti-Semitism, nobody knows anything anymore. For months, the "anti-Semitism row" featured on a continuous basis in the media, and suddenly it disappeared, and so did all the anti-Semites of Britain. Haven't you heard the story? A gigantic fish jumped out of the sea into the island, scooped up all the anti-Semites, swallowed them one by one, and then vomited them all into the depths of the sea. Yeah.

This is, at least, my impression when reading the British media. It's all Brexit, and nothing else. I light up a cigarette, outside, and think about the people of the UK, the four nations.

The Irish, passionate island people, are willing to die for every inch of their land but can't decide where their land starts and where it ends. They remind me of the Israelis, who have a similar problem. They should marry one another, the Irish and the Israelis, I think; it will be so much fun to watch. The Scots, this island's habitual complainers, will never forgive the English for making them drop the kilt. They should marry the Palestinians, and together they could breed as many complainers as possible, leading a life of perpetual tragedies, which is exactly what they want.

The English, the mightiest of the four nations on this island, are the biggest actors on the planet, though not necessarily onstage, and you can count on them to fool you. They are doing well, thank you, and don't have to marry anyone. They will find a way to make children from the trees; don't you worry about them.

The Welsh? Well, they are the friendliest, warmest of the bunch, and the best kissers to boot. Yeah!

But the Welsh, I'm told, are not the only ones to reside in Wales. There's another tribe in Wales, a Nepalese tribe, the Gurkha, and their symbol is not daffodils but swords. And some of them, I heard, can be found not far from here, in the town of Brecon.

Well, to Brecon I drive.

First off, of course, I go to the Gurkha Corner Restaurant, because without food you can't understand people.

The Gurkha Corner Restaurant is a small eatery, and the décor is as simple as possible, but what you get here, you won't get in any other restaurant around: the Gurkha story.

As part of the menu, and also online, the owners of this restaurant tell the diners:

> The Gurkhas are world famous soldiers, highly prized in the British Army and known for their bravery and courage. They come from the mountainous country of Nepal which nestles in the Himalayas, bordering Tibet in the north and India on its southern foothills.
>
> Gurkha units are closely associated with the khukuri, a forward-curving Nepalese knife. Former Chief of Staff of the Indian Army, Field Marshal Sam Manekshaw, once famously said about Gurkhas: "If a man says he is not afraid of dying, he is either lying or is a Gurkha."

The Welsh seem to like the Gurkhas quite a lot. Here's *Wales Online*:

> There are now some 70 serving Gurkhas in Brecon, who train and support future British Army leaders, but you're just as likely to see or meet a Gurkha who has retired, or one of their family, in the area.
>
> Gurkhas, all originally from the hills and towns of Nepal, were made honorary citizens of the town in 1985.
>
> It was a mark of the well-founded pride in soldiers who are characterised by toughness and bravery, from a brigade which has worked for the British Crown for over 200 years.

Why would any Nepalese join the British Army? I don't know, and this is not explained at this restaurant.

The food soon arrives, and though I can't pronounce the name of the dishes, they taste quite similar to Indian food in UK restaurants.

I look around me and notice that the diners are all white.

Are the waiters and the cooks Gurkhas? If the food is any witness, they are anything but.

Who, then, are the Gurkhas? It would be great if I could meet a Gurkha or two, I say to myself, but how does one get to meet a Gurkha?

The kind mayor of Brecon, the Honorable Manny Trailor, comes to my rescue and introduces me to Major (Res.) Guptaman Gurung.

That's a nice name; why don't I have a name like that?

Guptaman and I chat over a cup of coffee and a Pepsi Max at the mayor's hotel, Brecon Castle. Yes, the mayor is also a hotelier.

Everything, you should know, is possible in Wales. Yeah.

We sip, coffee and cola, which makes the two of us a perfect match.

Guptaman tells me his story.

He was born in Nepal and decided to join "the British Gurkha Brigade when I was eighteen years old." He retired from the British Army eight years ago, after serving the queen's army for thirty-two years.

You are Nepalese, right?

"Yes."

Tell me something: Why would a young Nepalese man join a foreign army?

"It's a tradition, from our fathers and our forefathers. The first career choice for us is joining the army, either the Indian Army or the British army. This history goes back to 1814."

Is there a Nepalese Army?

"Oh, yes."

If the Gurkhas like to join an army so much, why don't they – and you – join the Nepalese Army?

"Well, you get to travel. The salary is good, you know."

Better than the Nepalese Army?

"Far better. And when you finish the army, you get to travel all over, because of the British passport. For tribes like us, the first choice is to join the British army. If we are unsuccessful, then the second choice would be the Indian Army. But not the

Nepalese Army. The Nepalese Army is made of soldiers of Aryan origin, but we are of Mongol origin."

I'm not sure what's the difference, but it seems that it's a major one.

I ask my man: You have to swear allegiance, loyalty to Britain, to the queen. Why would anyone from Nepal do this?

"It's a career, a choice, and once you join an army, it makes no difference if you take an oath to protect the king or queen of a different country."

It doesn't make a difference because it's a good job?

"It is a good job."

How much did you get paid when you first joined the British army?

"In the old days, our terms and conditions were different. But since 2007 we get the same as the rest of the British army."

How much did you get paid when you first joined?

"When I joined, in 1979, we were in Hong Kong, and I was paid 420 Hong Kong dollars per month."

How much is the Hong Kong dollar?

"One pound is about ten Hong Kong dollars."

Forty-two pounds a month. That's next to nothing. And, still, the man left his country, swore allegiance to a British monarch, and could have died in action. For money. For about ten pounds a week.

Only the Brits, God save their souls, could convince people to die for ten pounds.

Among other places, Guptaman served in Afghanistan, where some of his friends died. For ten pounds.

Amazing.

Now you are on pension. How much do they pay you per month?

"I get £1,200 every month, after taxes."

Are you a British citizen?

"Yes."

When did you get your British citizenship?

"After my service. We can apply for citizenship only after we finish the army, with a minimum four-year service. After we finish the service, the British government has a duty to return us back to Nepal. Then it's entirely up to us what we want to do."

So, you were in Nepal, then asked for British citizenship, got it, and came back to Britain.

"Yes."

What do you feel inside you: Are you British or Nepalese?

"With my Nepalese passport, I can travel to Nepal. If I want to go to Europe, I need a visa, and it costs money, and it takes time. With a British passport, it's easy to travel."

Okay, got it. But what do you feel more, British or Nepalese?

"Nepalese."

You served the queen thirty-two years, you swore allegiance to this country, and yet you feel that you are Nepalese, not British.

"Yes."

Imagine: There's a war between Britain and Nepal, a war to the bitter end; which side would you join?

"Very difficult to choose."

Which side?

"Maybe I'll join the British, because I live in Britain now."

This means that you'll fight on the British side, and you will kill Nepalese.

Hearing this, and visualizing himself killing Nepalese people, he doesn't like it one bit.

"I will join the Nepalese Army," he says.

Blood, it seems, is thicker and heavier than an oath.

And the reddest of blood is rugby.

Today, hear me out, Wales beat Ireland to win the Six Nations Championship. Guess what's going on in Wales now? The Welsh are singing at the tops of their lungs, and if you walk by them, don't be surprised if they shower you with kisses. They want to spread the love; don't be overwhelmed. Accept it. It's good to be loved.

As for me, I move north, looking to meet the drug dealers, the prostitutes, and the pimps. Will they kiss me too?

Eleven Million Sheep

Welcome to Cemmaes, Wales.

Stormy weather, wrongly predicted in many places where I journeyed until now, catches up with me today. Today, the British forecasters got it right, mazel tov. Their average of right predictions, as far as I can tell, is 1:100. Lucky them, they get paid no matter what.

It's raining cats and dogs, and the winds threaten to fly my Mercedes back to Germany, with me inside it. But I persist. I'm stubborn like the English Brexit negotiators, and thickheaded like their European Brexit counterparts. Together with my German slave, the Mercedes, I fight nature and stick it out in Wales.

Yeah!

Well, the truth is, the most conspicuous trait the European Brexit negotiators exhibit nowadays is crude cruelty, combined with a sheer pleasure at humiliating the other side, the Brits. The humiliating conditions they impose on the Brits, over and over, will not be forgotten by the Brits when this is all over. Today the Europeans are laughing, joyful at the sight of the beaten Theresa May, but one day they will regret it, when it will be too late to change anything. With their ruthless actions today, they are planting the seeds for the next war inside Europe. The bad blood between the EU and the UK today could mushroom into hatred in the next generations and, if history is any guide, the next step is war.

An hour passes, or was it two, and I stop next to a small hotel, pub, and restaurant called Penrhos Arms Hotel.

This place is not an inn, a local tells me. Had it been an inn, the owner would have been obliged to greet you with bread and water.

What?

That's a law from the old days, he says, when people rode horses around Cammaes, and this law has not changed.

Bread and water. No butter, no milk, and no Diet Coke. Somebody needs to change the law to reflect our modern day!

Cammaes is a small place, with about 250 residents, and the combo hotel-pub-restaurant is an idea that intrigues me. I like it.

I check in.

What a far cry from my London abode! But I really like it.

Time to tend to my belly.

I'm not the only one around. The small pub is packed. The diners and drinkers are Welsh, and I can tell it in less than one minute of chatting with them: they touch me. Some of the waiters are English, and I can tell that in the same span of time: they don't touch me.

Oh, England, must you be cold?

There's another way to know who is Welsh around here: listen to them speak. They speak Welsh here. Yes, Welsh. Welsh, let me tell you, is a living language.

And they eat Welsh food. The food at Penrhos Arms, as in the other places I've been to in Wales, is actually good, much better than in England. I don't know why; it's just a fact.

At a table next to me is a young man, an actor, and he has two items on his table: a script and a beer. He drinks his beer at the same time that he tries to memorize lines from the script. How do these two items work together? Well, as you surely know by now, everything is possible in Wales.

This actor, by the way, also likes movies, not only plays. His favorite is *Star Wars*, and that's because of the film's character of Palpatine. He loves Palpatine. He is also interested in politics, especially international politics, and he fully supports the Palestinians. Why? "'Palestine' rhymes with 'Palpatine.'"

That's it.

People like him, my friend, you can find only in Penrhos. Isn't Penrhos wonderful?

Slowly I get to know more and more people here, and on Sunday morning, like any good Christian, I decide to join them in church. What church? Well, the one across the street from Penrhos, which is part of the Church of Wales.

As I enter, the deacon, a short lady with a great voice, reads from the book of Luke:

"Jerusalem, Jerusalem, the city that kills the prophets and stones those who are sent to it."

Good.

It reminds me of my visit to the Help Centre church in Newcastle.

"…he pleads with God against Israel, saying, 'Lord, they have killed Your prophets and torn down Your altars.'"

How many people are in attendance? Well, many fewer than I expected. Seven. Average age, seventy. Earlier today, I'm told, there was one more, but that was a farmer who was looking for a lost sheep.

When the service is over, I chat with the deacon. Normally, she tells me, there are more people in attendance, but a couple that usually attends was sick today.

May we talk about worldly issues? I wonder.

Yes, we may.

How about Brexit?

Speaking for herself, not the Church of Wales, the deacon tells me, she voted Remain. She doesn't understand, she shares with me, why anybody would vote differently.

She likes to talk about Brexit, but I ask her something else: What about, I ask her, the anti-Semitism in the Labour Party? Does she, as a woman of faith, have any opinion about it?

Oops. Sorry. That was the wrong question to ask. Why? Well, she doesn't have the time to talk anymore. She's late for a meeting. The church is calling. Many worshippers are waiting.

I move on, with my German car.

What a nice ride! Wherever I look, it's sheep that I see.

"In Wales we have eleven million sheep," Max, a lovely old man, tells me.

I spend the rest of the day visiting sheep, this farm and that farm, and I fall in love with them. Here's a herd, coming down from a hill up the road, but when they see me, they freeze. Literally. No, my sheep, I'm not going to slaughter you! I swear! Not me!

I love sheep. I love them alive.

I don't know what the sheep think about Brexit, or about Labour, but they are much sweeter, say, than John Bercow. "Theresa May's government has been plunged into constitutional chaos after the Speaker blocked the Prime Minister from asking MPs to vote on her Brexit deal for a third time unless it had fundamentally changed," writes the *Guardian*. "In a ruling that left ministers shaking with anger, the Speaker said that he was relying on 'very strong' convention dating back to 1604 to stop Mrs May tabling another vote on the same deal," writes the *Times*.

O-R-D-E-R!!

I drive on, moving up north, but then my Mercedes malfunctions. When I get out of my car late afternoon the next day, after hours of driving, the doors won't lock. This car is only a few months old, a lamb, and already misbehaving.

Maybe, just maybe, my Mercedes is upset that we've left Cemmaes. In Wales, don't you know, everything is possible.

In the UK, as I soon learn, not everything is.

Small-Town UK

What happens, for example, if you refer to a trans person by his or her original gender? In the UK, it turns out, it is a major offense.

Yes.

Under the headline, "Journalist faces police for 'misgendering' trans woman," the *Times* writes: "A Catholic journalist accused of misgendering a woman's trans daughter has said that police want to question her." The journalist is not making it up. The Surrey police, as quoted by the paper, is corroborating the story, saying that "a thorough investigation is being carried out to establish whether any criminal offences have taken place."

Misgendering.

I myself, of whatever gender you would like to refer to me as, have arrived in Bangor. Bangor, way up north.

I sit on a bench watching the rising water flowing into the Menai Strait. In six hours, a local by the name of John tells me, the tide will be at its highest, and then the water will recede. The change from low tide to high, and vice versa, occurs every six hours, John says; and if John says, John knows. John, let it be known, is an authority on anything water: oceans, rivers, ships, he knows them all.

John used to be a "captain on oil tankers," he tells me, as he invites me to come see his house. Today, at seventy-seven, he commands no ships, but he is still surrounded by water. His house is on the banks of the Menai Strait, because once a sailor, always a sailor, and the sea is forever his neighbor.

What a beautiful house! It looks like a beach house from the pages of a travel agency, a dream house.

John, a man who loves life, knows how to live well. The stunning views of the water and land peeking from every corner of his house are not enough for him. On the bottom level of his house, in the open area facing the sea, he installed a whirlpool, yes, and that's where he bathes when he feels the need to ponder the secretive nature of water. Often, he takes his camera with him, so that he can snap pictures of whatever shows up below or above the surface of the water while he's having a wet time in his whirlpool. Usually, what he catches on his camera is creatures of the sea, but one day he got really lucky: a beautiful dame swam right next to him. What did he do? No, he didn't try to date her. His wife would have killed him. Instead, he clicked his camera. How happy this has made him! He shows me the photo, proud fisherman that he is, of the lady in the bikini.

Of course, it is possible that the lady is a trans, not the kind of lady that John dreams of, but I don't say that to John. I can't tell how he would react, and I don't want this old man to end up in a British jail.

No, no.

Across the water, clearly seen from John's house, is the island of Anglesey, practically the end of Wales to the north. John calls Anglesey "island," as if Wales is not, as if Britain is not. Over there is the island; where we are is "mainland."

When Londoners say "mainland," they mean Europe. When Bangorners say "mainland," they mean Wales.

John loves Wales and doesn't seem to care much about Anglesey, the spot on the map where Britain ends, where Europe ends; he cares about Bangor. That's it. Here he was born. And here he will die.

Yes, he loves his city, but he used to love it much more when he was younger. Bangor has a population of about eighteen thousand, out of which over ten thousand are students. The students of Bangor University, John tells me, overrun the place. "If you walk from the pier to the station, which is about a mile, I don't think that you'll find more than four or five families living in the properties. When I was a child, everyone knew everyone here. No one locked the door."

Not anymore. Bangor University grew in size over the years, and today Bangor is a university city, not a community. When he was a kid, he used to go in and out of the houses around here, because in those days Bangor was one big family, but now he doesn't know the people living in those houses.

The TV is on in John's living room upstairs, where his wife is waiting for him to come up for tea and cake.

We go upstairs, where two big slices of fruit cake are waiting to be eaten, and the tea is ready.

Do you follow the news? I ask him.

"Yes."

What do you think of the anti-Semitism in the Labour Party?

"I went to sea as a youngster, and I went all over the world. And I'm not a racist in the slightest. I couldn't care less where you come from. But! We used to have names for everyone from this country, you'd call them some funny name, and some other countries some other funny names, and they would call us funny names. It was fun! Now, I am frightened. Someone the other day mentioned that someone was colored, and there was a huge big fuss about it. I'm afraid that's going too far. And although this isn't making me racist, I say: Good God, I'm frightened. What words are you allowed to use?"

The man didn't answer my question. So, I ask again: What do you think of the anti-Semitism in the Labour Party?

"I don't think it's as bad as they say."

Does Zionism equal racism?

"You are getting deep into things."

I ask again: Does Zionism equal racism?

"You are above my head now."

What do you think?

"Racism is getting on my nerves because I'm frightened to say things, in case I offend someone."

Yesterday's captain in the roaring seas is today a little kid in a democratic country, afraid to talk.

Do you like Theresa May?

"I think she deserves a medal."

Why?

"Well, how does she put up with it all? She can't win, no matter what she does. If she goes and the other fellow, what's his name, Jeremy Corbyn, gets in, he can't win either. She deserves a medal for her stamina."

She deserves a medal for her stamina. No politician or journalist I've met along the way has come up with such a line, which is as valid a judgment as any, but this sailor, who probably doesn't even know what Zionism is, did.

What do you think of Brexit?

He bursts out laughing.

"I voted to remain, but the sooner they get out and sort it the better!"

John explains Brexit to me, the tourist from Mars. "They had a vote. They asked people, who didn't have a clue, to vote. And nearly half voted one way and nearly half voted the other way. Why ask someone like me?"

That's democracy, isn't it?

"It might be fair, but it's stupid. You are asking a crowd of people who haven't got a clue to vote!"

In every British election, the people, the same people, are asked to choose between Labour and the Tories. What do people know about that?

"They don't."

Why, then, should there be any election?

"True. I agree with you. You may as well, every four or five years, toss a coin. Head or tail."

The best way to decide on the issue of Brexit, John tells me, is by a toss of a coin. Heads, Brexit; tails, no Brexit.

Life can be so simple!

I depart from John's house and get ready to move on. Where to? Anglesey. The end of Wales, the end of the good world. Enterprise, my car rental of choice, has given me another car, and off I go. The question is: Where in Anglesey should I go?

Amlwch. Yes, Amlwch. I don't know how to pronounce Amlwch, have no clue if the word has any meaning, so I drive there.

It takes time, not much, and then I am in Amlwch. Where should I go here?

As I drive, I see an old church, nothing glorious, but the tall trees in its backyard capture my attention. Many crows fly above and around the trees, and if you look up, you will see the nests on the treetops. But wait: look closer! Look at that crow on my left, the loudest of crows here. You see it? Do you recognize it? Yes, yes, yes! That's the crow from Edinburgh, Scotland, the one that I followed all the way to Edinburgh Castle. Yes, that's the one!

I think this crow wants me to stay near it. Don't you think so?

There's a hotel across the street from the church, called the Dinorben Arms Hotel. I think I should stay in that hotel.

Yeah. Definitely.

I check in.

Before going to my room, I light up on the sidewalk outside the hotel and, how sweet, people stop by to chat with me. These are the friendliest people I've ever met. They tell me all kinds of interesting things. For example: the mother tongue of most people here, 63 percent of them, is Welsh.

Amlwch.

Can you say Amlwch?

Takes a little practice, I know.

Here's Nirys and James, two Amlwch locals.

Are you a couple?

"No. We are 'friends of benefit.'"

What's that?

James: "We sleep with each other."

Nirys: "He's my partner, but we don't live together."

Good to know.

What's special about Amlwch?

Nirys: "Amlwch is nice. Everybody here knows everybody, and all help each other in times of need. It's a strong community."

Does everybody also sleep with each other here?

Nirys: "No."

James: "Yes."

These are not Amlwch's best days. Once upon a time, many, many, many years ago, the people of Amlwch were miners. A huge copper mine, a short ride from here, was the main employer. In fact, they tell me, I should take my car and see the old mine. "You'll feel like you're walking on Mars," they say.

Everybody lost their jobs, but then some factories opened in the area, and it was good to live in Amlwch again. But now, these days, very few employers are around.

The Brexit saga plays out loud in London, where every day brings another story of yet another politician trying to force Theresa May out of office, or another arrogant EU leader preaching and humiliating London, but in Amlwch nobody talks about Brexit. They have more pressing problems than Brexit. In Amlwch, Nirys tells me, you can't open a bank account.

Why?

"There used to be four banks in Amlwch, but for the past six years there are none. There used to be souvenir stores on High Street, not anymore. The German plastic factory in town, Rehau, will probably close soon, and about one hundred people will lose their jobs. There were plans to build a nuclear power station here, to replace the old one, but this is not going to happen. That's Amlwch. If you want to have dinner, the only places are the Dinorben Arms Hotel or an Indian restaurant. That's it. In other towns, the terminally ill get the possibility of traveling, to ease their condition, financed by the council, but not in Amlwch. In other towns, the authorities care for the disabled, but not in Amlwch. In Amlwch we take care of each other, and if someone is in need, including the terminally ill, we fundraise for them."

Is Amlwch so poor?

"The Anglesey Council is corrupt. The councillors don't give money to Amlwch. We pay the same taxes as everybody else, but the money doesn't come back here. In Amlwch, you can park your car anywhere you want; we don't have traffic wardens. That's the way it is. But I love Amlwch."

Why?

"It's home."

What's the denomination of the church across the street? I ask a local man.

"Church of Wales."

Still operational?

"Yes, all the time."

Really?

"Yes, yes. Many funerals are held there. More funerals than weddings."

How many funerals?

"Sometimes, three or four a week."

How many weddings?

"In the last two years, I think, I went to two weddings in the church."

It doesn't take long to fall in love with the people of Amlwch.

Unlike London, nothing is majestic here. I drive around, and I can immediately tell that no kings live here. No princesses. No dukes. No earls. No lords. Just people.

They are Welsh, and British too.

It is London and Amlwch together that make a UK. Big town and small town, big-town UK and small-town UK. But it is Amlwch that offers the clearest and sharpest lens through which the UK comes most nakedly in focus. Britain, at its soul, is about hierarchy; the high pedigree and the low, the Westminster Abbey and the church at Amlwch. No coronation takes place at the Amlwch church, just people coming to say goodbye to the dead. Amlwch is no Oxford either, and no Malaysian prime minister stops here. Here are people, friends of benefit, who try to make a living, and their voice is hardly heard.

Many Brits refer to themselves as "island people." They are not. If you want to see island people, come here, come to Amlwch.

I drive to Parys Mountain, where the copper mine once was. What a sight!

Here the earth opened its mouth, at one point in history, and the chasm in the belly of this earth is amazing. It's one huge pit, with tunnel openings still visible, and the gravel changes color every few feet. Here people worked, toiled, sweated, made friendships, and made a living – in the dark crevices of the earth's belly.

The people of Amlwch, at least some of them, are the great-grandchildren of the miners that once worked here. People born to hard work, to sip the bitter drinks, and to form the warmest of friendships. They are not monarchs; they are the slaves of the monarchy. Brexit? They would rather have a bank to deposit the meager amounts they possess, with Brexit or without it.

The chasm in Parys Mountain is a vivid image of the chasm in London. And like the chasm here, the chasm in London will last for generations, no matter how the Brexit story ends. What is being revealed throughout the process of Brexit will not disappear in the years to come. These are the moments of truth for Britain, and the dark hours are certain to follow. The split in British society is huge, forcing the two sides into parallel worlds that won't meet for generations to come, but it's not Brexit that caused the internal hate and animosity; Brexit only revealed it.

Amlwch is quiet, except for the sound of crows on top of the trees in the church's front yard.

The crows, too, are friends of benefit. And when evening comes, and darkness descends on Amlwch, silence takes over.

The town is quiet.

Not so London, a place on earth that has never befriended silence.

In London, Theresa May's government is standing on its last legs, or so it seems. Labour is not faring well either. The House of Commons is in one huge disarray. March 29, Brexit Day, will pass without Brexit. The EU has just agreed to extend Brexit Day for a couple of weeks, to April 12, giving Theresa May a little breathing space. But so far, the MPs don't want to deliver Brexit, at least not yet. The people want, but the politicians don't. Like Amlwch and London, so are the MPs and the people. A huge divide stands between them: the high pedigree and the low.

It's sad to watch a society so divided, so bitter, but luckily I'm in Amlwch, one big family at the end of the United Kingdom. The high pedigree of the UK should come here to roost, to be among the friends of benefit, and other lovely creatures, to witness a kinder way of life.

Fat chance.

Next to the old copper mine, there is this plaque:

> On the 2nd March 1768 a great mass of copper ore close to the surface was discovered at Parys Mountain. Roland Puw, a local miner who was present at the discovery, was rewarded with a bottle of brandy and a rent-free cottage for life.

Someone made tons of money, and Roland got a brandy.

Ain't that Britain?

"As the mountain's heart of metal ore was gradually removed," I keep on reading, "the nearby town of Amlwch grew into one of Wales' largest towns and the world's leading exporter of copper."

How the fortunes of a town can change.

I drive to Amlwch Port, the physical end of this country, looking for the whores, the pimps, and the drug dealers.

I can't find them. Have I missed them somewhere on the way? Maybe.

Instead of young whores, I meet Mike, a man born in Newcastle-upon-Tyne, but living in Amlwch for the past forty-three years. We chat, since in Amlwch everybody is chatting with everybody, and between this subject matter and another, Brexit comes up. An optimist by nature, Mike admits that the Brexit story is a "dog's breakfast," meaning total confusion, but that's okay. How did his country get itself into such a big mess? Some Brits, he answers me, still believe that "we are ruling the roost," that Britain is still an empire, and no mess is big enough for them, while others have this hope that in the end "something will come out of the wash," and everything will turn up roses. The Brits, he explains to me, are a bastard nation, a mix of Vikings, Anglo-Saxons, Celtics, and whatever else, and they have experienced many crises, such as foreign invasions, but they always "muddle through."

None of what Mike says will explain why misgendering could potentially constitute a criminal offense in this country, but not everything in life must be explained.

I drive to the church, to the crows, and say goodbye to the Edinburgh crow. I think, though I'm not sure, that my eagle sent this crow to me, to protect me from the famous Welsh dragons.

Yeah, there are dragons here. Just look at the flag of Wales; it's a dragon. Thank you, my eagle!

I move on.

Where to? To Holyhead, the port city by the Irish Sea facing Dublin, where I started my journey half a year ago. In fact, if I miss seeing tons of Palestinian flags, I can take the Stena Line ferry, and I'll be in Ireland in just over three hours.

It is in Holyhead, with a population of fewer than twelve thousand people, that I meet Patricia, a charming lady sixty years of age, and she tells me that Holyhead is an amazing place. We meet in Holyhead's town center, one of the gloomiest town centers I've ever seen. Very few stores are open: the betting house of Betfred, a third-hand used clothing store, a supermarket, a couple of pubs, and little else. "It's gone downhill a little bit," Patricia admits. "It's not as happy a place as it used to be. This town, when I was a little girl, was always full of people, always full of cars. All the shops were all open, all different shops that you could think of, but now it's just declined."

Why?

"People can't afford to pay the rates on the shops they rent. It's all too high for them to pay."

What happened? In the past people could afford to pay, why not now?

"Because of the Council. The Council just put up the rates, and the people can't afford to rent the shops. There was a big aluminum factory here, but that shut down. A lot of people have left, because there's no work to be had. We've got a big port in Holyhead, where the ferries go to Ireland; it is owned by Stena, who bought a lot of land in Holyhead."

Stena, a passerby joining us chips in, is doing nothing for Holyhead. They make huge sums of money in Holyhead, but they don't invest in the city. Shame on them.

Just like the people of Amlwch I met earlier, Patricia complains bitterly about Council members, her Council members. They are all thieves, she says. They make deals with big companies and pocket the money; they steal from the people. When a Council member died some time ago, "the whole city was celebrating. We call them 'mafia.' They are all mafia."

But she loves Holyhead and wouldn't live anywhere else.

Is there anything special about Holyhead?

Yes, there is.

What is it?

"The Holyhead people. When anything happens to anybody in Holyhead, they all rally around and help each other."

How many people do you personally know in Holyhead?

"I know everybody in Holyhead. Yeah, yeah."

That said, the people of Holyhead today are not like the people of Holyhead that she grew up with, Patricia tells me. "There used to be, you know, really good characters in Holyhead."

But no more?

"No. When I was a little girl there were a lot of characters. There used to be a lady called Winter Bottom; she used to own a sweet shop. There used to be my grandmother, she used to own a café."

What do you mean by "characters"?

"They had quirky personalities. And you could go and knock on their door and ask for a bottle of milk or a cup of sugar. You know, things like that."

Are there no more characters like them nowadays?

"Not anymore. I think that generations change. I always say: children today don't have what I had when I was a child. When I was a child there were no computers, no mobile phones. We went out and made our own fun. We would go to the beach during the day, with sugar sandwiches and a bottle of water, and spend all day long together, not in front of technology. The children today, they haven't got that anymore. Everything changed. It was much better in the old days. Oh, definitely!"

Tell me, Patricia, what do you think of Brexit?

"I voted to Leave."

Do you still want to leave?

"Yeah."

Do you think Britain will leave?

"I think so. I hope so."

Do you like Theresa May?

"No. None of them is any good for this country."

How about Jeremy Corbyn?

"Oh, no. Evil!"

Why is he evil?

"He supports ISIS, he supports the IRA. I think he's just an evil man. I really do."

ISIS stands for Islamic State of Iraq and Syria.

Are you religious?

"I'm a Catholic, but not a good Catholic…"

But you believe? I ask her.

"I do."

You pray from time to time?

"I do."

Dean, a Holyhead resident I meet later, is much younger than Patricia, and he voted Remain.

What do you think of the anti-Semitism in the Labour Party? I ask him.

Well, he's not sure how to answer this question. He votes Labour, yes, but he doesn't know what in the world I'm asking him. The reason? He's never heard the word *anti-Semitism* before.

I like Her Majesty's small towns.

Will the House of Commons Order Eternal Sunshine?

According to British media, about one million people are marching today in London, demanding a second vote, a People's Vote. Their main argument, as you already know, is that those who voted Leave have by now regretted it.

One million. Who counted them? Not me. But I'm willing to bet that, if the number is correct, then at least 999,997 of them are Remainers, mixed in with Europeans living in London. How do I know? Based on the people that I met, not one Leaver wants a second referendum. If anything, some Leavers told me that if their initial vote is not honored, they would not vote again, because they would have lost trust in the system. It's a self-destructing argument, because if there's a second vote and the Leavers don't vote, they will lose. But I understand the emotions behind this argument.

It is not a military secret in the UK that the Remainers are the ones who push for a second vote, but very few in the mainstream media will admit it. They, and the 999,997 marchers, try to give the impression that they speak in the name of the common men and women. They don't. They are snobs who will never count anyone who is not of their pedigree. They care not a bit about the little people, about the working class, about the poor. They are, as far as my eyes can see, the snobbish grandchildren of the Vikings, and they'll invade anything they find, land or truth.

I think of the cat and the rat in Dublin's Christ Church Cathedral, and of this country's society at large. And I see the similarities. The lofty, high pedigree people, purebred London cats, running to swallow the ugly rats, the little people, the people who can't afford to live in London, whose opinion doesn't matter anyway.

Interestingly, the number of one million is coming from the march's organizers. Are they experts on crowd estimates? No. But there are such experts. Keith Still, of Manchester Metropolitan University, for instance. Keith told the magazine *Wired* that, "based on the visuals from the helicopter image, it's between 312,000 and 400,000 people."

Later on, speaking at the European Parliament, European Council President Donald Tusk implores his listeners not to betray the "one million people who marched for a people's vote, or the increasing majority of people who want to remain in the EU."

One million. Increasing majorities. This man says whatever his lips will allow. Factual, not factual, who cares?

I watch this man on British TV, parading around with other EU big men, and they smile broadly at the expense of Theresa May, looking down at her, as if she were an ugly rat in an old church.

I'm not British and, therefore, I am on neither side of the Brexit divide, and either way the coin flips is perfectly fine with me. Yet, as an outsider it's exciting to be in Britain these days and watch the reserved, polite, friendly, warm, good – or whatever else they think of themselves – people in their full nakedness, Full Monty. If you want to catch a glimpse of who these people are, of who the Brits are, history offers you a small window, a teeny-tiny time period, to have a peek. The time is now, the window is Brexit. What will you see? For one, you'll see the monarchy. The monarchy in Britain, notwithstanding its beautiful royals, has no ruling power, but this doesn't mean that Britain is not a monarchy; it is. The upper class rules here supreme, and the working class is at the mercy of the "mafia."

I drive to the South Stack Lighthouse, a ten-minute ride from Holyhead's town center. What a gorgeous view! I'm awestruck by the beauty of the place, a magnificently bewitching landscape of rocks and sea. If there's Paradise, it must look like this.

The land ends here.

Oh, I'll miss Britain!

I'll miss these island people. I'll miss the Irish, the Scots, the English, and the Welsh. I'll miss Mike of Dublin, Marwan of Liverpool, Red Pete of Oxford, George of Inverness, the Nessie Monster, the pizza deliveryman of Newcastle, Rachel Riley of London, James of Amlwch, Jamal of Sheffield, Alex of Shrewsbury, Nigel Farage of London, Gary of Treorchy, the skinny girls of Leeds, Ms. Campbell of Edinburgh, the Uber drivers, the bird watchers of Grantown-on-Spey, the MPs, the lords, the lord mayors, the people at the food banks, even Jeremy Corbyn and the harem of women surrounding him, not to mention the cat and the rat of Dublin – to name but a few.

My journey is coming to its end, and Brexit is still hanging in the air. Will it ever happen?

Back in London, according to the *Times,* senior members of Theresa May's government have been plotting to oust her, but the coup failed because the senior vultures couldn't agree which one of them will inherit her seat. The House of Commons, with the help of rebel Tory MPs, "took the unprecedented step of voting to seize control of the parliamentary timetable," the BBC reports, thus enabling individual MPs to table various motions in the Commons, in the hope that one of their ideas will win a parliamentary majority. Called "indicative votes," these votes are meant to find out what the majority of MPs want, but they are non-binding. Still, this is the first time in the Brexit history that MPs will come up with their own ideas, instead of just rejecting the government's.

Will this process succeed? Do the MPs actually know what they want?

The *Guardian* quotes John Rentoul, chief political commentator of *The Independent*, who has an excellent answer to this question: "If people are allowed to put down motions proposing milk, honey and eternal sunshine, yes they might get more votes than WA & PD."

WA & PD stand for Withdrawal Agreement and Political Declaration. In simpler words: Brexit.

Should I go to London to witness firsthand this historic moment at the Commons?

Standing in front of the sea and thinking of London, I think of John of Gaunt's lines in Shakespeare's *Richard II*:

> This land of such dear souls, this dear dear land,
> Dear for her reputation through the world,
> Is now leased out – I die pronouncing it –
> Like to a tenement or a pelting farm.
> England, bound in with the triumphant sea,
> Whose rocky shore beats back the envious siege
> Of watery Neptune, is now bound in with shame,
> With inky blots and rotten parchment bonds.
> That England that was wont to conquer others
> Hath made a shameful conquest of itself.

Shame. Shameful.

I drop my rental car, a big, black van, and board the train to London.

I'm looking forward.

The Blonde Bombshell Flaunted Her Curves

What a sharp change in landscape – from a rocky shore and a triumphant sea in North Wales to a parcel of land with a million cameras in England.

What a difference.

I'm in London.

Everywhere you go in London, there's a camera right above your head ready to record your every move.

London, Britain's capital.

In addition to cameras, London has papers too, quite a number of them, and they all fight for our attention. Here is the *Daily Telegraph's* headline: "Tories tell May to set her exit day today."

They want her head. They are thirsty for her blood. And these are her friends, some of whom she put in power, making them ministers. This is their thank-you.

There are other papers in town, for example the *Daily Star*. This paper is more concerned about Rachel Riley, the TV persona I interviewed quite some weeks ago in my hotel room.

"COUNTDOWN'S Rachel Riley sizzled in a tight-fitting dress for today's show," the *Daily Star* writes, adding: "The blonde bombshell flaunted her curves in the clingy material as she did the numbers and letters."

Yeah, yeah.

My Apple Watch is sending me a message right now. What's the message? Fresh news from *Business Insider*. Here goes: "Theresa May says she will resign as Prime Minister if MPs back her Brexit deal."

She will do everything to get her Brexit deal, including offering her head on the Brexit shrine.

I look at the Palace of Westminster from my hotel room – yes, I'm back at the same hotel – and can't but admire its beauty, but the thought of the bloodbath taking place inside stops me from admiring it.

The next day, I go to the palace.

It's addictive. I've told you, haven't I?

The House of Commons will today have two major votes. One, called EU Exit Day Amendment, will take off the books the date of March 29, the original Brexit day, so that the UK will legally still stay in the EU. The second vote, or a series of votes, will be on eight different motions introduced by members of the Commons, the indicative votes.

Tensions are high. "I could tear this place down and bulldoze it into the river," says MP Steve Baker, a flaming Tory Brexiteer, according to some sources. But the most ruthless comment of this sitting belongs to Labour MP Angela Eagle. Referring to Theresa May, she sums up the recent news about the PM thus: "Back me, then sack me." I look at her; she seems very proud of herself for coming up with this line.

No mercy here.

The House is soon full, packed, and even Theresa May – wearing shiny red shoes – is in attendance. The vote to delay Brexit Day passes 441 to 105.

The ayes have it, Speaker Bercow says, tremendously enjoying himself.

Rest in peace, March 29.

As for the indicative votes, all eight motions are rejected.

Tomorrow's *Guardian* print version is now available. Its front-page headline, running across the page, reads: "Parliament finally has its say: No. No. No. No. No. No. No. No."

To the point.

Will this be the end of the Brexit story in the House?

Remainers want another day of indicative votes, Leavers say that's enough. John Bercow, who a couple of days ago announced that he won't allow Theresa May to table a meaningful vote again unless it's different from the last one, says that another day of indicative votes is totally fine with him. Funny John is not very funny today. He raises his voice, mocks MPs he doesn't like, and makes all kinds of strange faces and sounds that at times make me think he's some sort of an animal. I'm not the only one to think that. A London society lady tells me: "Bercow is a little worm, a little shmuck."

Naturally, I don't care about little shmucks. What I am interested in is Theresa May. Who is that lady? What is she made of?

Lord Harry Woolf, the man that Lord Andrew Stone spoke very highly of when we met at the Royal Gallery, is right next to me now. He's the former Lord Chief Justice of England and Wales, and he is my kind of man for today. A chief justice, I say to myself, is a person well equipped to judge character. Could he, an extremely well-dressed man, describe Theresa May for me in a short sentence of no more than one line? Yes, this man can. "May," he tells me, "is stubborn and tough." That's a short sentence! And then, smilingly, he adds: "Ladies can be stubborn…"

In some places on our planet, San Francisco for example, if you speak like this about women, you'll be arrested, you'll lose your job, your house will be confiscated by a court order, and your bank account will be seized by the authorities. Lucky Harry, we are in London, a gender-backward city.

As known throughout the world, yours truly believes in equal opportunity, which will explain why I decide to meet a female MP next, and one from the TIG.

Say a big hello to MP Joan Ryan, member of The Independent Group (TIG).

The eleven MPs of TIG, by the way, are moving on to create their own party, the *Times* reports, to be called Change UK.

Joan, a sixty-three-year-old impeccably dressed blonde, is a warm lady who looks a lot younger than her age.

We sit down in a nice lounge at the Lords, with a cup of coffee and a slice of cake. To be exact: she doesn't have a cake, only I do. A lemon cake.

You (TIG/ChangeUK) are all Remainers, if I understand correctly, I say to her.

"Yeah. We support the People's Vote, to put it back to the people."

The Remainers say that those who voted Leave were cheated by politicians, and if given another chance, the People's Vote, they would change their vote. The fact is, not one Leaver I've met said thank you for having another chance; what they usually said was eff you.

"I know that a lot of people who voted Leave still want to defend their decision, but equally there's an awful lot of people, and I meet them, particularly women between thirty and fifty, who say: 'What have we done? This isn't going to be good for our children's future.' A lot of people who voted Leave don't want to admit that they did something wrong. They only can admit it when it's pitched in a certain way."

I have no clue what she's talking about, but I'm willing to listen.

"I think that the ones who want to remain tend to be more progressive, a bit more center left maybe. If you think about the people who voted to leave, I think that the upper class has let them down. Especially the progressive upper class. We should have taken on the arguments a long time ago that immigration isn't to blame for the way our economy has not served certain groups of people well. It's not immigration that's responsible for the inequalities or the lack of decent housing or the lack of secured jobs or low wages. The complaints people have about their standards of living and their housing and their jobs are all absolutely valid, but the idea that they're caused by immigration is nonsense."

Let me translate this for you into American-English: the Remainers are intelligent, ideological people, while the Leavers are empty-headed deplorables who need to be spanked.

I ask her: Why can't we say that Remainers and Leavers are two groups of people who are motivated by different ideologies? Perhaps globalists versus nationalists.

Nope. She isn't having it. "It's too simplistic to say something like that," she tells me.

She, like many high-pedigree Brits, doesn't understand the Leavers. Just like the "million" marchers in London. She is the pure-bred cat, and the Leavers are rats. It's "too simplistic" to assume that their view is as valid as hers.

Suddenly, I hear a loud voice. It's my eagle, and its face is sour and pained.

No, dear eagle, don't give me that sour face of yours. I don't mean to say, here or anywhere else on these pages, that any human being is a cat or a rat. I'm not a Nazi, and I don't dehumanize people. It's just a metaphor, a parable. That's all.

The eagle, now smiling, flies away, and I walk over to the Commons and settle into their nice terrace by the Thames, from which I can look at my room on the other side of the river and, how great, have a cigarette as well.

It's time to talk to a male MP, wouldn't you say?

Who would that be?

Two tables ahead of me, I see MP Michael Fabricant, a Tory. He certainly looks interesting: a big, not particularly well fitting blond wig on his head, a pink tie, and a pink-blue scarf to match.

How do you predict Brexit will go? I ask the blond pink.

"I think it's impossible to predict at the moment."

What's your gut feeling?

"The issue is that we have a Remainer Parliament. So out of the 650 members of parliament, between four and five hundred don't want to Brexit. The Scottish Nationalists are open and honest about it, and they put down a resolution yesterday, which failed, as they all did yesterday, saying, 'Revoke Article 50. Stay in the European Union.' And I'll say to the SNP: At least you're honest!"

Did you vote for Theresa May's Brexit deal?

"I didn't, no. I voted against it twice, but I won't vote against it this time, because I think this is the only way we're ever gonna get any form of Brexit."

Will you vote for it?

"Yes, if it comes up."

The papers here say that it will.

"Well, they don't know, do they? They're guessing."

They are just guessing?

"They are newspaper journalists!"

Obviously, the blond pink doesn't think very highly of journalists.

The abode of the Speaker is a few feet away from us, which reminds me of the man.

Do you think that John Bercow is impartial? I ask him, changing the subject.

"I think what has happened is that, for a number of reasons, which I haven't got the time or the energy to go into, over the years he has alienated the Conservative Party. And because he's done that, he now feels he's got to keep in with the opposition parties. In the past, once a Speaker was elected, they were lofty individuals. You wouldn't dream of getting rid of a Speaker, and they would be very neutral, and all the rest of it. This one knows that if the Conservatives got the chance, they would get rid of him. So, he stays in with Labour, which forces him at times to do things which are, maybe, less than partial."

In other words, he cares about his seat more than he cares about the country.

"No, I'm not gonna say that. Actually, no, I'm not saying that. That's the sort of *Daily Mirror* type comment. No, I am not saying that he cares more about his seat than his country. It's got nothing to do with the country."

He cares about his seat. That's basically what you're saying –

"I'm not saying anything. You're saying it."

No wonder you became a politician!

"I was a broadcaster, so I know when people try to put words into other people's mouths. It's such a crude thing to do. You might do it in Europe, but it's so bloody obvious to a British person that you don't fall for it. Maybe Germans are pretty naïve. I don't know."

This man is the ultimate politician. If he led the Tories, the Brexit story probably would have had a totally different ending.

The Cat and the Rat, the Sequel

I stick around on the terrace, light up and think of my time in these British Isles, six months now. I take a puff, and then another one, and as I try to sum up this period of time, five words come out of my mouth: The cat and the rat. From my first day to this very day, it's all one game of cats and rats. The high classes versus the low classes; that's a cat and a rat. The globalist elite versus the common nationalists; that's a cat and a rat. The non-Jews versus the Jews; that's a cat and a rat. The politically correct theater makers and their audiences; that's a cat and a rat. The House of Commons versus the people; that's a cat and a rat. Everybody was playing this game, a cruel game – a chase to the finish, to the throne and fame or poverty and the grave.

I had it all on the first day of my journey, Tom and Jerry, only I didn't know.

In the House, on March 29, the day that was supposed to be Brexit Day, Theresa brings back her deal for a vote, with one change: the WA without the PD, whatever this means – long story.

It fails by 58 votes, as 286 MPs vote for it and 344 against it.

Parliament Square and adjoining streets fast fill up with Leave demonstrators, the rats. In the square itself, the March to Leave folks, protesters who have marched 270 miles from Sunderland to London, will soon arrive, and Nigel Farage, the figurehead of the Brexit movement, the biggest rat, will speak to them and their thousands of supporters. The image of Nigel comes up on a big screen in the square, and the crowd roars in applause.

An activist of the Leave Means Leave campaign, the organizer of this demonstration, comes up to the stage. "What do you want?" he yells, as loud as can be. "Brexit!" the crowd replies, as loud. "When do you want it?" he asks. "Now!" the thousands roar.

A helicopter is flying above us. Not always, though; sometimes it just sits above our heads, and we can hardly hear anything.

Speaker after speaker come up to the stage. "Don't despair," says one. "Brexit is not going away because we are not going away!" Another one says: "We don't have a million people here. Neither did they."

The demonstrators carry many a placard. Some homemade, such as this one: "HOUSE of B * * * * * * S and COWARDS. Leave now!" Or this: "Help. I am a slave to the EU. My vote is meaningless. Democracy is dead." Other placards are printed, such as, "HELL HATH NO FURY LIKE 17.4 MILLION VOTERS SCORNED!" Or this: "WE ARE THE 52%. DELIVER BREXIT."

These people, mostly English, are not very European, if I may say so. In many other European countries, demonstrations often turn violent – cars are set on fire, banks are stoned, rocks fly by – but not here. England is not enamored with revolutions. As Belinda told me in Losehill, speaking of the English: "We are a fairly calm race." The English talk, write poems and dramas, argue, and then they all go to eat fish and chips. And have a beer or three.

They talk here, but no violence.

When the names of Corbyn and Bercow are mentioned, they boo.

That's it.

And then, of course, Nigel Farage assumes the stage. "Being in Westminster," he says, "we are in enemy territory!"

The palace is where the cats are, and a few mice; the rats are here, in the square.

Here are the people who voted to leave; over on the other side are the uber-people who refuse to endorse the rats' verdict.

The crowd goes crazy. "Nigel, Nigel, Nigel!" they scream.

They love him, the chief rat.

The people here, most of whom seem to prefer a divorce from the EU without any deal, are not necessarily right-wingers. Not all the speakers on this stage – and this is important to understand – are right-wingers either. The people here, and in the other demonstrations around here, simply don't want to be part of the EU. Period.

I stand by the statue of Winston Churchill in the square, facing both the demonstrators and the Palace of Westminster, and see a nation divided: cats and rats running toward an organ that could kill them both.

I take a little peek at Churchill and think of Room 114 at the Londonderry Arms Hotel. And suddenly I can hear Nora, singing for me once more:

> How can you buy all the stars in the skies?
> How can you buy two blue Irish eyes?
> How can you purchase a fond mother's sighs?
> How can you buy Killarney?

When I wake up from my little Irish dream, Nigel has gone.

But before the people go as well, they sing a patriotic song, whose lyrics were written about a century ago by Sir Cecil Spring Rice.

> I vow to thee, my country, all earthly things above,
> Entire and whole and perfect, the service of my love;
> The love that asks no question, the love that stands the test,
> That lays upon the altar the dearest and the best...

And then they sing one more patriotic song, "Rule, Britannia," based on a poem written about three centuries ago by James Thomson.

> Rule, Britannia!
> Britannia, rule the waves
> Britons never, never, never shall be slaves.
> Rule, Britannia!
> Britannia, rule the waves.
> Britons never, never, never shall be slaves...

Farewell, London. Goodbye, Britain!

It's hard to say goodbye, but I think it's time.

Hey, people, look up! Open your eyes wide! What do you see? Yes, that's my eagle. Hello, sweet eagle! Have you come to say goodbye? So sweet of you! Where are you going next, my eagle? I have a suggestion. Wanna hear? If you have nothing better to do, fly to Dublin and get yourself inside the crypt of the Christ Church Cathedral. You'll see a very interesting pair in there, Tom and Jerry, a cat and a rat. But don't eat them, please!

My eagle smiles. Yes, eagles smile. At least mine.

I am leaving Britain, and I will never come back, my eagle says to me.

Why?

There are too many anti-Semites here, says my eagle, two teardrops falling from its eyes onto my face as it flies fast into the far heavens.

Epilogue

Having no wings, I take a bit longer to move out.

To wean myself slowly out of this polite pan known as the United Kingdom, I got myself out of my hotel in Westminster Bridge. It's too close to my second home, the Palace of Westminster. I moved to the Marble Arch London Hotel, to be with my cousins, the Arabs of the land. I have a small room, with a refrigerator and a window that I can open. Yeah! The hotel room serves as my living room, and Al Balad serves as my dining room. Paradise on earth. To complete the circle of pleasures, I bought a Saudi coffee. Yes. You should try it. It's not black coffee, but brown. Very interesting coffee!

I'll stick around for a few more weeks, I say to myself, in case something special develops that will require my attention. If nothing major happens, I agree between me and myself, I won't write anything.

The weeks pass, and here's a short list of what's happening:

Uber has passed the Congestion Tax charge to the passengers; Brexit Day is now scheduled for Halloween; Jeremy Corbyn admitted, in a one-on-one conversation with MP Margaret Hodge, secretly recorded by her and given to the press, that evidence of anti-Semitism within Labour's ranks was "mislaid, ignored or not used"; the UK unemployment rate is at its lowest in forty-four years, less than 4 percent; just out: half of England is owned by less than 1 percent of its people; Theresa May is still the prime minister, but Omar Al-Bashir was toppled; Liverpool FC beats Barcelona 4-0, guaranteeing its place at the Champions League final; weather forecast: sunny today, mostly cloudy tomorrow, risk of thundery showers by the end of the week.

Well, I guess it's time to go.

I put on my kilt, my lovely Scottish kilt, and make my way out of the UK.

Promptly following my departure, the British mess goes on: PM Theresa May resigns, not before accusing Labour of being a political party that "welcomes everybody except, it seems, Jews"; Nigel Farage's Brexit Party becomes the biggest winner in the UK election for the European Parliament, capturing close to 32 percent of the vote; the Equality and Human Rights Commission (EHRC) opens an investigation into charges of anti-Semitism in Labour; Labour suspends NEC member Red Pete, after his conversation with me becomes public; Liverpool FC wins the Champions League; more than half of TIG/Change UK's MPs quit the party; Boris Johnson, the "letter boxes" author, moves to 10 Downing Street, promising to leave the EU on Halloween, "do or die," and practically taking the wind out of Nigel Farage's sails; Mr. O-R-D-E-R, John Bercow, says he will step down on that same day; and the authorities in Northern Ireland announce – more than six months after the fact – that they will take legal action against the Hitler-loving pubgoers in Bogside Inn.

In between, the Jewish Dame Louise Ellman, facing deselection, quits Labour. Lord Stone of Blackheath, the Jew of the bag with twenty-seven different currencies, is suspended from Labour. Unlike the other Jew, MP Ivan Lewis, Lord Stone didn't touch any woman's leg. Oh, no, Lord Stone is no leg man. Lord Stone is accused of stroking one woman's arm, and grabbing another woman's arm, among some other similar offenses. Oy vey.

Before John stands down, the House of Commons succeeds in finally passing a resolution: new election in December; and the EU grants the UK another extension, three more months.

Halloween passes quietly, and Boris Johnson, if you care to know, is still alive.

Yeah.

Shortly before the election, and obviously following Dame Ellman's resignation from Labour, the UK's chief rabbi publishes an article in the *Times*, insinuating that JC is not fit for high office. In response, JC "apologizes" for the anti-Semitism in Labour. As quoted in the *Times*, he says: "Our party and me do not accept antisemitism in any form...obviously I'm very sorry for everything that has happened." Three days later, the Times issues a report that makes JC look like a classic liar: "Yesterday a video emerged of Mr Corbyn greeting an Islamic preacher convicted of using the 'blood libel' that Jews kill children for their blood." The land that started the blood libel, methinks, isn't ready to give it up.

And this same land is not ready to give up the pubs either. Newly released figures show that there are 39,135 pubs in the UK, 320 more than last year, which is not exactly what the pubgoers of Hilltown believed to be the case. What the people of this land do want to give up, no surprise, is their membership in the EU. Prime Minister Boris Johnson, who ran an election campaign for the Tories under the slogan Get Brexit Done, is the big winner of the election, held on the twelfth of December: 365 seats in the House of Commons, giving him quite a comfortable majority to pass Brexit. Ivan Lewis, Luciana Berger, and Dame Louise Ellman won't be in the next parliament; but the pro-Gaza Jewish MP, Margaret Hodge, is in. Joan Ryan is out, but Michael Fabricant is in. Change UK is no longer, and Labour is reduced to 203 seats. The actual breakdown between Conservatives and Labour: 13,966,565 votes for the Tories and 10,295,607 for Labour. Jeremy Corbyn, who is blamed by party members for not taking a clear stand on Brexit during the election campaign, announces that he will step down. Jo Swinson, the leader of the Liberal Democrats who ran a campaign that promised to cancel Brexit, loses her own seat in the Commons.

Those Brits who wanted a People's Vote, I guess, got their wish.

Only it didn't turn out the way they planned it.

Following the election, Boris Johnson's EU withdrawal bill passes the House of Commons by 358 to 234, a majority of 124. The old days of high drama in the Commons are over, at least for now, but – don't tell anybody I said it – I miss John Bercow.

What's next for the UK?

Nobody really knows. In fact, nobody knows what's next for any country anywhere. Just as Britain starts to wean itself out of the EU, a mysterious coronavirus spreads a disease known as COVID-19 all over the world, infecting millions upon millions and causing untold numbers of deaths all over Planet Earth. Boris Johnson gets infected, and Donald Trump as well, governments order citizens to put masks on their faces, and theaters across borders close their doors.

We, all of us, are left home alone.

Not the safest of places these days, mind you, if you happen to live in countries that champion progressive politics. Scotland, for example. Scotland's Cabinet Secretary for Justice Humza Haroon Yousaf, the man with the beard and the nice accent who tried manipulating me when we met, is working hard these very days on a new public order bill that would make it a criminal offense to "stir up hatred" even in one's own dwelling. This means that if you, in your lovely living room, say something against, let's say, Buddhists, Muslims, Indians, lesbians, or transgender people, you could end up spending years in prison.

Perhaps this is not as progressive as the Spanish Inquisition, but we're getting there.

And lest anyone forget about the anti-Semites of Britain during the hard days of the epidemic, the EHRC issues its long-awaited report about anti-Semitism in Labour as the year 2020 nears to a close. Its report, according to the BBC, asserts that "Labour acted unlawfully over anti-Semitism." Later on the same day, Jeremy Corbyn is ordered suspended from Labour, and "he has also had the whip removed from the parliamentary Labour party," the *Guardian* reports.

Yet life moves on, as it must.

Rumor has it, originated by yours truly, that once humanity rids itself of this virus, the National Theatre and Shakespeare's Globe will mount a coproduction of *Full Monty* with a trans-of-color cast, Monties fully exposed, to the delight of all UK cats. I plan to attend.

It is here, at this very point, that I bid all of you farewell. Until next time in London, at the trans Monties,

Tobias, King Tabbas Abdul Rahman ibn Mohammed II, Adrian, Ahmad, Florian, Tuvia

End

Acknowledgments

My thanks to the island people of Great Britain and Ireland for sharing with me their thoughts, fears, and obsessions. I am indebted to the English, Scotch, Irish, and Welsh citizens for teaching me the secrets of their being; and to the esteemed lords and MPs for guiding me through the maze of the Palace of Westminster's politics. Special thanks to Dame Valerie Cocks for accompanying me through the ironed gates of society; Jonathan Hoffman, for the initial editing of this book; Florian Krauss, for documenting it all on video; and Daniel Till, for recording every word.

Thanks and appreciation to the following establishments for providing their services at no charge: Jurys Inn Hotel, Belfast; Londonderry Arms Hotel, Ballymena; Beech Hill Country House Hotel, Derry-Londonderry; Hotel Indigo, Dundee; Grant Arms Hotel, Grantown-on-Spey; Gretna Hall Hotel, Gretna Green; Losehill House Hotel & Spa, Hope Valley.

Last but not least, my profound thanks to my dream mother-in-law, Isa Lowy, for spoiling me and caring for me always and forever.

About the Author

TUVIA TENENBOM, author of three best sellers in Germany and four in Israel, holds advanced degrees in both fine arts and science. He is a journalist, essayist, and dramatist, and the founder of the Jewish Theater of New York.

Tuvia's articles and essays have appeared in leading Western media including *Die Zeit* of Germany, *Corriere della Sera* of Italy, *Yedioth Ahronoth* of Israel, and the *Forward* of America. His previous books are *Hello, Refugees!*; *The Lies They Tell*; *Catch the Jew!*; *I Sleep in Hitler's Room*; and *Fett wie ein Turnschuh*.

Many of Tuvia's plays have been performed in New York and elsewhere. They include *Father of the Angels, The Blue Rope, The Last Virgin, One Hundred Gates, Diary of Adolf Eichmann, Love Letters to Adolf Hitler, Like Two Eagles, The Beggar of Borough Park, Love in Great Neck, The American Jew, The Suicide Bomber, Press #93 for Kosher Jewish Girls in Krakow, Kabbalah, Saida: A Tunisian Love Story,* and *Last Jew in Europe.*

.

Printed in Great Britain
by Amazon